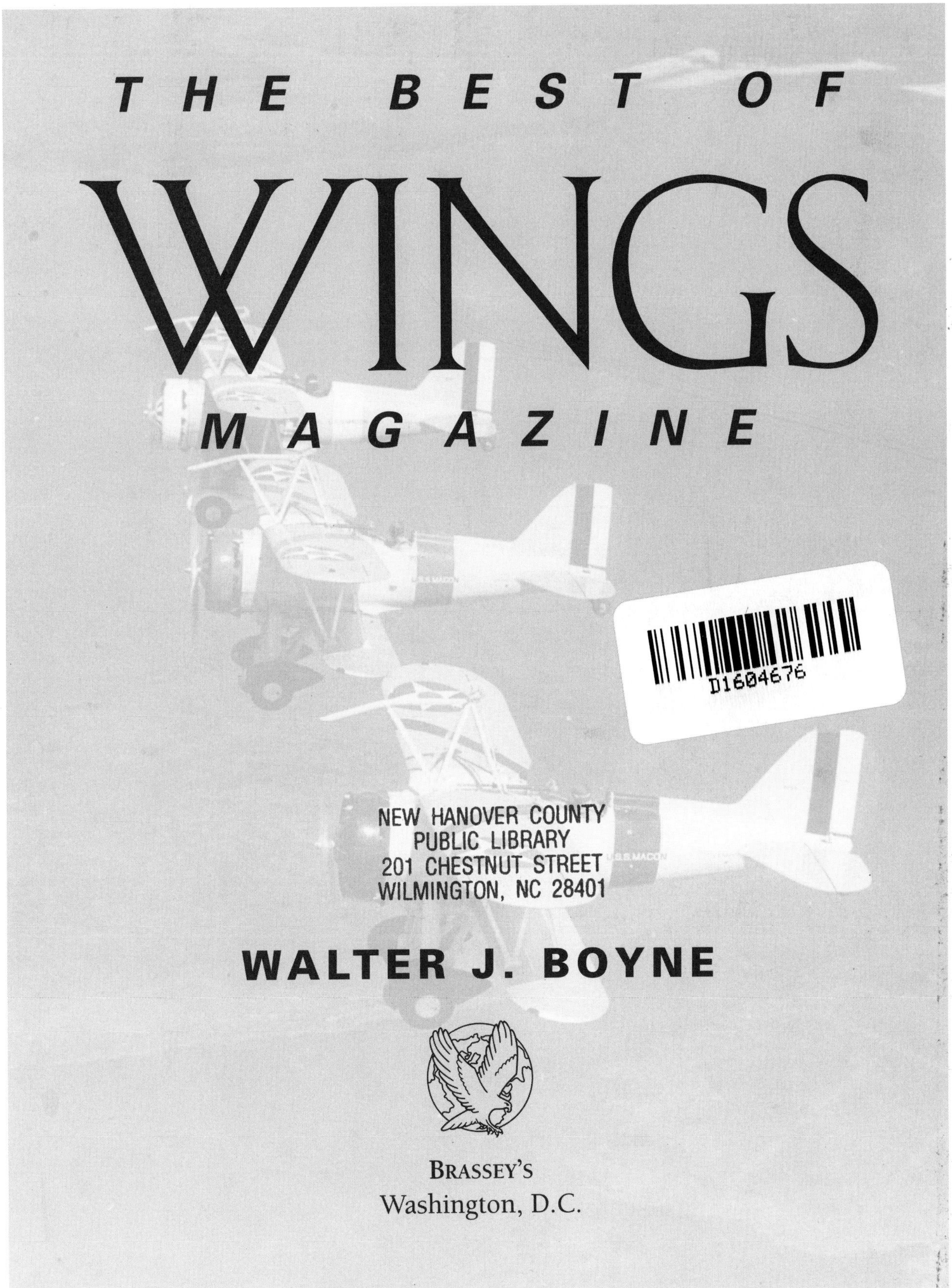

THE BEST OF WINGS MAGAZINE

WALTER J. BOYNE

BRASSEY'S
Washington, D.C.

ISBN 1-57488-368-2 (alk. paper)

Printed in the United States of America on acid-free paper that meets the American National Standards Institute Z39-48 Standard.

Brassey's, Inc.
22841 Quicksilver Drive
Dulles, Virginia 20166

First Edition

10 9 8 7 6 5 4 3 2 1

Contents

Preface

This book is intended as a tribute to the many people who have worked so hard over the years to create a vivid history of the wonderful first century of aviation. It is fitting to pay tribute to the men and women who toiled in the vineyard of aviation history. They received very little in the way of financial reward, but were happy with the substantial psychological and emotional rewards they received in pursuing a satisfying hobby.

No one will be surprised to know that two of the founders of aviation journalism in the United States were a bit eccentric. One was Victor Lougheed, brother to Alan and Malcolm Loughead (why he spelled his name differently is a mystery to all). Alan and Malcolm founded Lockheed Aircraft while pursuing unattainable aircraft design goals, and Victor published some excellent books on aviation. The other eccentric was Henry Woodhouse, who also published some excellent books, then ran into trouble with the law and eventually was incarcerated.

From this early start, aviation journalism and the writing of aviation history proceeded on two paths. On the one hand there were a very few excellent professional journals, including the predecessors of today's *Aviation Week and Space Technology.* These included *Aviation* and *Aviation Age* and were modeled to some degree on their English counterparts, *Flight* and *Aeroplane.* On the other hand there were a few model magazines (*Model Airplane News* being one of the best) and that wonderful hybrid, *Flying Aces,* which combined models with factual stories and ripping-yarn fiction. Down further on the quality scale, but still beloved, were the pulps, such as *Daredevil Aces, Sky Devils,* and many others.

In time some popular magazines emerged that were dedicated to contemporary events, and among these the best was *Popular Aviation,* which became today's *Flying* magazine. But there was very little reporting done on aviation history. It was really too soon for such an interest to develop, just as no general interest developed in classic cars until about the 1950s.

Some aviation-buff groups recognized the lack, and they formed the American Aviation Historical Society (AAHS) and the late, lamented Cross & Cockade (C&C) Society. Both groups produced excellent journals. The AAHS is still going strong, and while C&C expired, it has been replaced by the truly excellent Over the Front, the Journal of the League of World War I Aviation Historians. In a similar vein, Leo Opdycke has been a pioneer in the field, publishing *World War One Aeroplanes* and *Skyways* magazines.

In the 1960s there was one U.S. magazine, which will be nameless, that covered aviation history and for a time did a pretty fair job of it. For a variety of reasons, best also left obscure, it antagonized many authors and readers. Finally there appeared on the scene in 1971 two American aviation journals, *Wings* and *Airpower,* published by Joe Mizrahi. These at long last began publishing accurate stories on aviation history by reputable authors. The two were really just one magazine, but Joe used two names as a marketing ploy to give each issue as much shelf time on the newsstands as possible.

All of the magazines already named were supported by a relatively small band of historians and photographers who worked together to document American aviation history in stories and in film. I can only name a few of them here, but they included such premier pioneers as Rick Allen, Gerald Balzer, Fred Bamburger, Warren Bodie, Peter Bowers, Dusty Carter, Bob Cavanaugh, George Cooke, Jim Fahey, Brian Flanagan, Harry Gann, Peter Grosz, Peter Kilduff, Bill Larkins, Birch Matthews, Lonnie Raidor, Mauno Salo, Gene Sommerich, Gene Sumney, Gordy Williams, and many more. Please forgive me if I've omitted your name or a name important to you, but this is just an illustrative list, and each person named here would be quick to cite a dozen other figures more important than themselves.

There are many words that characterize this group, but the first that comes to mind is generosity. They quickly responded to requests from each other, trading photos and negatives with abandon, but they also graciously shared their photos and their knowledge with strangers. Among the other salient characteristics of this group and their peers, one could include integrity, scholarship, loyalty to their avocation, and yes, hedonism, for they reveled in the sheer pleasure of finding information on aircraft.

At about the time that Joe Mizrahi introduced his two magazines, there occurred an unusual phenomenon. There had already been a small market that was interested in factual articles that went into great detail on the history of aircraft, aviators, and aviation events, and this was satisfied in large part by the journals produced by the AAHS and C&C. Unfortunately for the general reader, the circulation of these two journals remained relatively low, never, even in combination, reaching the level of 5,000 copies. Mizrahi correctly perceived that there was a pent-up demand for such stories, especially if they were well illustrated with photos and drawings. Thus it was that *Wings* and *Airpower* made a notable impact when they debuted, and remain influential to this day, even when there are many excellent aviation journals on the market.

It must be noted that all during the period described above there had been really fine magazines focusing on aviation history being produced in the United Kingdom, including *Air Pictorial* and *Royal Air Force Flying Review,* which appeared in many subsequent reincarnations with different names. They were put out by very small staffs, but the articles were written and the photos supplied by such great names as William Green, Gordon Swanborough, and David Dorrell. In fact, in 1961 I sold my very first article, to *Royal Air Force Flying Review.* The title was "A Veteran's Last Flight," and it described the ferry flight of a Curtiss P-36 from Alabama to the United States Air Force Museum in Dayton. The P-36 may still be seen at that marvelous museum.

There have been many events in my life that I've considered great—graduating from flying school and winning my wings in the Air Force, getting married, greeting each child as it was born, and so on. But I have to admit that not many other things gave me the same intoxicating pleasure as the letter from *RAF Flying Review* saying that they were going to publish my article and were going to pay the substantial fee of $29 for it.

With such encouragement, it was only natural that I'd begin writing for Joe Mizrahi's two new magazines, and over the years Joe gave me a lot of leeway to pursue my interest in unusual aircraft. Furthermore, he allowed me to investigate not only the airplanes but the people behind them. This freedom was really delightful, for it enabled me to interview many interesting and outstanding people: test pilots such as Bill McAvoy and Sam Shannon, designers and engineers such as Don Berlin and Jack Real, entrepreneurs such as Willard Custer and Bill Besler, and towering personalities such as Charles Rocheville and Harold R. Harris.

Writing the stories was a joy, but the real pleasure came in the letters that came in from the buffs. They'd always have a nice word to say, but they would also always be able to point out a mistake—sometimes real, sometimes just in their minds. In time I realized that if one could write a perfect article, without a single error, it would be a sad thing, because it would deprive the ardent buff of one of the great pleasures in life—spotting a mistake.

In the 40 years that have followed that first article, I've written perhaps six or seven hundred more, along with 38 books. In that time the field has grown tremendously, with more magazines, and more and better writers. Today the standard of aviation journalism in America is equal to or better than any in the world, and that applies to the treatment of aviation history as well. Such prestigious magazines as the one I'm proud to say I founded, *Air & Space/Smithsonian,* along with *Flight Journal, Airways,* and *Aviation History,* have articles and photographs of a terrific quality. There are also many other magazines, some put out by associations, such as *Air Force Magazine, AOPA Pilot,* and EAA's fine *Sport Aviation.*

I should digress here and comment upon another phenomenon that parallels the great development of aviation history magazines, and that is the amazing growth of aviation art. One cannot directly relate *Wings* and *Airpower* to the growth of this phenomenon in American art, but the two magazines provided a venue both for early aviation artists, and more important, for the advertisement of their work. In recent years, *Aviation History* has been especially diligent in using reproductions of aviation art as a means of illustrating its stories.

For many years, aviation art was virtually nonexistent. Henry Farre had done wonderful things during World War I, and Charles Hubbell had created a name for himself in what was pejoratively termed "calendar art." But there was no market for aviation art as such. Then, simultaneously with the growth of aviation publications and reflecting the same general interest in the subject, aviation art began to flourish. In contrast to all past times, the public interested in such art was now quite educated, in large part due to the new aviation magazines, especially *Wings* and *Airpower.* The public demanded a high degree of accuracy, and the artists responded with very authentic renditions of aircraft, people, and events, such as the Doolittle Raid, the Flying Tigers, individual aces of all nations, and so on.

It is now a huge industry with new artists and new paintings appearing in great profusion. It is unfortunate that aviation artists, like aviation writers, have not yet received their due in either prestige or financial reward, but this is coming. If you'd like a quick overview of the current state of aviation art, you can do no better than to read the wonderful book by my friend and colleague Philip Handleman, *Aviation: A History Through Art.* Through words and pictures it offers true insight into a fast-growing element of American culture.

Oddly enough, future aviation historians face both an opportunity and a problem. The opportunity lies in the proliferation of media by which information can be both obtained and provided. This includes everything from dedicated television channels, such as Discovery Communications' Wings channel, to CD-roms, websites, the internet itself, and in the future perhaps even historical telepathy between affiliated buffs!

The problem lies with the subject matter. Where in decades past there were literally dozens of new aircraft appearing annually around the world, new aircraft now appear much more infrequently. Because modern aircraft are more efficient and last longer, there are fewer model changes in either military or commercial status. The reverse is true of general aviation, of course, where the blessed Experimental Aircraft Association has spawned an unending series of new arrivals. Thus it may be that future aviation historians will have to concentrate on general aviation aircraft rather than those staples of the past, military and commercial types. That may be satisfying, but I have to confess that I still prefer to write and read about the terrific products of World War I, the Fokkers and the Sopwith Camels, and the beauties of World War II, from sleek bombers like the A-20 to "mystery airplanes" like the Fisher XP-75. And in between is the glorious Golden Age of Flight, where you find such sterling examples of aviation courage and aspiration as the L.W.F. Owl and the mighty Martin B-10. There will be great airplanes in the future, for sure, but never as many and in such wonderful variety as in the past. Some of these past models you'll find in the following pages. I hope you enjoy your flight through aviation's history.

ACKNOWLEDGMENTS

Thanks must first of all be given to Joseph Mizrahi, publisher of *Wings* and *Airpower* magazines and a long-time friend. Aviation writers, photographers, and aviation buffs owe Joe a debt of gratitude for pioneering and persevering with *Wings* and *Airpower* in a very tough marketplace. By doing so, he made it possible for so many authors and photographers to gain experience and to tell their stories. Joe was gracious in allowing us to use the stories to create this book. Thank you, Joe, you are a gentleman who created two fine products; many are in your debt, particularly myself.

I would like to give special thanks to the following people who helped with the articles and also with this book. I could write a half a dozen paragraphs extolling each of the following, who were so very helpful and so generous not only to me, but to many other authors. The span of the stories in this book reaches back about a quarter of a century, so it is not surprising that some of the following have passed on in the interval. To all of them, both the living and the dead, I give my most profound thanks. Take a moment to read through this list, for I'm sure you'll see many familiar names:

> Richard Abel, Richard S. Allen, Hal Andrews, Mrs. Charles Arens, Jack Barbery, Hermann Barkey, Don Berlin, Frances Biese, Robert Blake, Wolfe Blitzer, Vaughn Blumenthal, Seffy Bodansky, Warren Bodie, Ludwig Boelkow, Peter M. Bowers, Roy W. Brown, Jack Bruce, Fred Buckendorff, John J. Burns, Dusty Carter, Ed Coffey, Marcus Cooper, Bill Cunliffe, Harold R. Custer, Willard R. Custer, Harry Davidson, Charles DeBellevue, Fred Dickey, Robert F. Dorr, Pearlie Draughn, Ralph Draut, James Eastman, Menachem Eini, E. E. Elliot, Robert Esposito, C. M. Fancher, Keith Ferris, Royal Frey, Adolph Galland, Harry Gann, Gordy Graham, William Gregory, John Gugliemetti, Mrs. Archibald Hall, Cargill Hall, Charles Ward Hall, Jr., Harold R. Harris, Richard Helms, Beverly Hodges, Erich Hohagen, Walter House, Fred Johnsen, Benjamin Kelsey, Peggy Kimball, Jack Krings, Gregory Krohn, Bob Lawson, Gordon Le Bert, Larry Lee, Virginia Lewis, Harvey Lippincott, Ernst Maison, George C. Martin, Birch Matthews, Phillips Melville, Dave Menard, Jack Nelson, Tim Nenninger, Gerhard Neumann, Lon Nordeen, Glenn Odekirk, Robin Olds, Merle Olmsted, George Page, Jr., Jack Real, Steve Ritchie, J. A. Roche, Charles E. Rocheville, George Schairer, Russ Schleeh, Vic Seely, Rudolph Sinner, Dean Smith, E. Morris Smith, George Spangenburg, John Strickler, O. E. Tibbs, Guy Townsend, John Underwood, Waldemar Voight, Harold E. Watson, Jack Wecker, Edward C. Wells, Paul White, Vivian White, Holden Whittington, Charles Worman

and many others whom I should have remembered and to whom I apologize for being forgetful.

It was a pleasure to work with the staff at Brassey's, including Don McKeon, David Arthur, Jeanne Hickman, Kristen Gustafson, and others.

Finally I think it fitting to pay tribute to everyone who has contributed to the preservation of aviation history over the years, be they authors, photographers, collectors, restorers, museum workers, or just plain fans. To all of them, this book is respectfully dedicated.

Walter J. Boyne (wboyne@cqi.com)
Ashburn, Virginia

1 The Treasures of McCook Field

America's First Aero-Engineering and Testing Center, Part I

Airpower July, 1975

Through these doors passed some of the most brilliant pilots and engineers in the history of U.S. aviation. Many of them became world famous as record-setters or as industrialists. For a brief period of time, McCook Field shined as an example of how the federal government can work well: provide the funds to bright young people, and do not interfere with the results. Consequently, McCook Field enabled the U.S. Air Service to maintain itself on pitifully low budgets.

The machine shop at McCook Field looks primitive by today's standards, but at the time (1918) it was world-class. It was a direct precursor of the magnificent set of laboratories that now exist at Wright-Patterson Air Force Base.

The nearest modern equivalent of the development of aeronautics at McCook Field is the development of the computer industry. In both cases, relatively young people were placed in situations where they could use their imaginations freely in a brand-new field, and in both cases, the progress they made was incredible.

There were other similarities. Just as one has to have a knack and a feeling for computers to be successful with them, so it was with aviation. People on the "outside" could not understand the fascination with noisy, expensive machines that were susceptible to crashing. People on the inside could not understand how you could be interested in anything else. And perhaps the greatest similarity of all was the feeling among those involved that they were dealing with the nation's very top people in their field.

There was one big difference between the aviation industry and the computer industry, however, and that was the monetary return. Far from making money, most people in aviation lost their shirts, either directly through investments that did not pay off, or indirectly by working in an industry where pay was low, job security was marginal, and the hazards were great.

Aviation was born in the United States with the Wright Brothers' wonderful *Flyer* in 1903, but it promptly went to sleep for almost fourteen years before waking up to the clamor of World War I. True enough, there had been many experimenters and flyers during that interval, but the production and development of new aircraft was of a very low order. For example: by August of 1916 the U.S. Army had less than 40 airplanes, none combat worthy. In the next two years, almost 14,000 would be produced, many of first line quality.

The manufacture of these aircraft and their associated engines and spares was little short of

McCook was also the center of Air Service technical education, and the Air Service Engineering School turned out many a great military and civilian leader. The officer is Lieutenant Edwin E. Aldrin, assistant commandant of the school, and father of astronaut Buzz Aldrin. The test pilots at McCook were in every way the equivalent of modern astronauts in terms of prestige and daring.

a miracle, and although the American production effort is remembered more for its waste and scandals than for its achievements, the essential fact is that an entire industry sprang into being overnight like soldiers from the dragon's teeth. The principal products of 1918 were admittedly rehashes of Allied types, but another year would have seen an impressive array of American aircraft including the Glenn Martin Bomber, Le Pere LUSAC 11, LWF G-2, Thomas Morse MB-3, Loening M-8, Vought VE-8, Orenco D, and others.

Much of the credit for this mammoth transformation of aviation from an amateur cottage industry into a serious scientifically oriented design and production effort belongs to the Engineering Division at McCook Field. This unit, which has survived more reorganizations than Italy has had governments, still functions today within several departments of the enormous, prestigious Air Force Aeronautical Systems Division at Wright-Patterson Air Force Base, Ohio. In many respects it was the single most influential organization in the history of American aviation, for it not only provided a start for some of the most talented men in the industry, but it set standards which they have continued to live up to.

The Engineering Division (we'll use this name throughout, although it was often modified to reflect changes in scope and direction) produced some 34 aircraft of 23 different types, only a few of which became well known. These ranged from tiny gliders and trainers to bombers and pursuits. Some were merely adaptations of well known foreign types; some were solid efforts of inspired engineers; some were wild forays into the improbable, and a few formed the cutting edge of the ever advancing state of the art. In the later designs we'll see how closely form followed function, and although the resultant airplanes set a standard of ugliness not attained again until the French efforts of the mid 1930s, they performed their job well. Furthermore, in addition to their own designs, the Division worked closely with all domestic manufacturers, who sometimes produced Air Service designed aircraft on contract.

While the larger part of these articles will deal with the airplanes, in many respects they were actually less important than the other work of the Division, work which rapidly investigated the many disciplines involved in aircraft design and manufacture, determined criteria, and later saw to it that the infant industry somehow survived in the agonizing days of low and even no appropriations.

The Engineering Division was born midst a series of rapid fire changes of direction as the 1917 declaration of war began to take effect in Washington. Between April and September 1917, the responsibility for producing military aircraft rested successively with the Signal Corps Aviation Section, the Aircraft Production Board, the Aircraft Engineering Division, and, finally, the Equipment Division, which was the major element prior to the Engineering Division. These agencies were faced with the problem of *doing something*; Congress and the public demanded, as they invariably do at the 11th hour, the clouds of airplanes that American know-how and automobile industry technique must inevitably bring forth. Unfortunately, no one in the country knew anything about the mass manufacture of aircraft, only a very few were knowledgeable about aircraft design, test and materials, and official guidance was perforce limited to bureaucratic reshufflings.

Lieutenant Wendell H. "Brook" Brookley proudly shows off his Oilcan and Dumbbell trophies. These were the Test Section's "Medals of Dishonor," awarded for the biggest error in test-flying for the period.

The Engineering Division at McCook Field functioned in a variety of ways, both building its own aircraft and designing aircraft for others to build. This is an Engineering Division design, the GA-2, that Boeing reluctantly built. It was a heavily armed ground-attack aircraft with terrible flying qualities. *Warren Bodie*

Influenced by Brigadier General Billy Mitchell's request for heavily armed ground-attack aircraft, McCook designed the GA-X for Boeing to build—again under protest. It was a heavily armored and armed triplane powered by two Liberty engines. Ten production aircraft were built, and pilots were assigned to fly them as punishment. *Peter M. Bowers*

The GA-X was equipped with a 37 mm cannon in the nose turret. The pilot is the irrepressible Harold R. Harris, who told wonderfully funny stories about flying the GA-X, which he described as "the nosiest airplane in history."

Things began to jell, however, when Captain Virginius E. Clark, a man about whom far too little has been written, returned from service with the Bolling Commission in Europe. Promoted to the rank of Lieutenant Colonel, Clark had the task of adapting the Bristol Fighter to American production methods and the Liberty engine. He also took over command of the Plane Design Section, located in the same corrugated tin building which now houses the Vin Fiz, Winnie Mae and Bell X-1 for the National Air & Space Museum in Washington, D.C.

In the meantime, a public (and profit) spirited group of citizens from Dayton had done the necessary fiscal and political spadework to have an experimental factory and testing ground located in their hometown rather than at Langley Field, the original choice. A site north of the city was chosen and named McCook Field in honor of a fighting family which had suffered grievously in the Civil War. The new facility opened on December 4, 1917, a primitive collection of raw wooden buildings on a 254 acre tract, just one and one half miles from Dayton's city center. Besides the usual leveled sod area, the flying field featured a 1,000 foot long, 100 foot wide runway of macadam and cinders, at the end of which was affixed a large sign which proclaimed: "This field is small, so use it all"—still good advice even on a 15,000 foot runway. This modest complex would blossom as no airfield had ever blossomed before, for from these unpainted buildings and soggy fields would come an organization which would be influential in World War I, very nearly decisive (and this is not extravagant) in World War II, and of tremendous importance throughout all the subsequent years of formal peace.

With a good fortune that seldom seems to bless great enterprises, the Engineering Division would have able commanders, brilliant engineers, and loyal workers. Perhaps it was particularly fortunate in having Colonel Thurman Bane in command from late 1918 through 1923, for Bane established a scientific rather than military environment, one in which status depended upon contribution rather than rank. The result was evident in the "old school tie" feeling among the Division personnel, most of whom went on to private industry, bringing with them the basic fundamentals learned at McCook, plus an integrity and a spirit of team play that would pay dividends time and again.

Although responsible to Army headquarters in Washington, the Division was in fact almost autonomous by reason that they *were* the experts. After all, no one else knew as much as they did. And while it was true that they became experts day by day, making lots of mistakes and learning swiftly by them, in the process they established a business like, scientific organization which would literally cover the entire field of aviation from engineering to quality control, to test procedures, to procurement, to flight test, to material analysis, training, and in fact to wherever necessity led them.

The incredible progress the Division made is understandable in today's world only if you stop to think of some of the things they didn't have. They didn't have automated data, so that decisions could not be made several levels up; they didn't have copying machines, so everyone didn't have to get in on the act; they didn't have rapid communications, so things couldn't be directed from 1,000 miles away; and perhaps most important, they didn't have years of deadwood and overhead accumulated in the form of lateral, passive "managers" who can delay but not expedite.

What they did have was a group of patriotic, involved, intelligent energetic young men, who loved aviation and who wanted to win the war. And for 1917 and 1918 at least, they had more damn money than they knew what to do with.

From just a handful, the group expanded to a very busy force of 2,358 personnel, including 443 military, by the end of the war. A report of the Engineering Division operations for the Calendar Year 1920 is interesting for the wide variety of technologies used and inventions demonstrated. Excluding aircraft temporarily, the Engineering Division had designed, built and tested the following: a 750 horsepower 18 cylinder engine; in collaboration with General Electric, a turbo supercharger which would establish altitude records of 30,900 feet in a Le Pere and 25,341 feet in a Martin bomber; portable hangars; a take-off mat of canvas and hickory slats, the predecessor of World War II's PSP; two types of engine starter, the Foulk and the Bijur; a "dummy observer" or automatic instrument panel camera; a pressure cabin, which worked too well, as we shall see; a turn indicator; flame resistant, self sealing tanks; three different types of parachutes, two way radios; the "Radio Dog", a radio controlled automobile that could be remotely controlled from the ground or the air, and which was reportedly driven through downtown Dayton traffic; a radio direction finder; and much ordnance equipment, including bomb racks, sights, synchronizing gear and so on, *ad infinitum.* (The Kettering "Bug" guided missile is, of course, worthy of a story all to itself.)

Far beyond this impressive array of "gadgets," however was an even more important output of procedures, tests, standards and materials. These ranged from simple instructions on reporting to work on time to complex parameters for the soon to be standard static sand bag test, and from intricate formulas for dopes and glues to simple specifications for hardware store items.

In the less technically complex but potentially more corrosive atmosphere of aircraft procurement, the Division had to learn how to write fair contracts, secure competition, weed out the frauds and eccentrics, and ensure performance. The record here has often been castigated, for lots of money was wasted on cost-plus contracts, and most deliveries were not achieved in time to use in Europe. But it was a vulnerable area, where young, inexperienced men with lots of patriotism and money were exploited by a very few vultures. For the most part, both manufacturers and the government tried to do a good job.

Fortunately, the Engineering Division was endowed with many hard working, honorable men, some near genius, who were able to meet the challenge. Besides Bane and Clark, they included Jean A. Roché, Alfred Verville, Major J. G. Vincent of Liberty engine fame, Sam D. Heron, whose contributions to engine design have never been properly acknowledged, Frank Caldwell, Alexander

Klemin, who as a Sergeant probably had more informal authority than any other noncommissioned officer in history, Allan Loomis, a whiz at cooling systems, A. L. Nelson, who devised an excellent synchronizer, I. M. Laddon, designer of the PBY, who was able to transfer much from his automotive background; L. V. Kelber, B. C. Boulton, H. G. Marmon; Don Berlin, who designed the Curtiss Hawk 75 series; the list goes on and on. Complementing the engineers was a Flight Test section similarly endowed, as we shall see.

The Dayton group actively sought assistance from respected sources and worked extensively with M.I.T. The task which generated the most interest both within and without the Division was of course complete aircraft, and one of the principal jobs was to learn how to make airplanes from the ground up, and to adapt foreign aircraft to U.S. mass production methods. The initial choices included the Bristol Fighter, de Havilland DH-4 and DH-9, Caproni and Handley Page bombers, and a few others. Wherever possible, these aircraft were to be redesigned to accommodate the ever popular Liberty engine in its six, eight or twelve cylinder versions.

Clark had begun these efforts with the Bristol Fighter, but the assumption of his new duties interrupted the task, which was passed over to Curtiss for completion. The resultant shambles of the program is a story which has been told several times; in brief Curtiss simply never came to grips with the production problems associated with the change over from a conventional structure and a Rolls Royce engine to a plywood sided, Liberty engine version. Despite immense efforts and lots of dollars, the program was cancelled on July 19, 1918, ostensibly because of a series of crashes. The crashes were not all the fault of the aircraft, as the unsuitability of the design to the powerful Liberty and the total lack of what today would be called configuration control were the real problems.

While Curtiss had futilely been wrestling with their Bristol/Liberty problem, the Engineering Division had in a very workmanlike manner gone about building an airplane which it hoped would be better than either the DH-4 or Bristol. This is the little known USAC-1 (also referred to as U.S.A.C.-1—the periods will be left out for simplicity) a very clean design whose general arrangement had been suggested by Clark, who had diligently sought out the opinions of pilots in France as to what a good observation plane should be. Working with about twenty draftsmen engineers, most of whom had never had anything to do with an airplane, Jean Roché did the detail design, performance estimates and stress analysis.

The USAC-1 resembled a cleaned up Bristol fighter, with a plywood fuselage and a rather fancy empennage. Gross weight was estimated to be 3,639 pounds, but this was exceeded by about 10% as weight control was as much a problem then as now. Although the aircraft was adequate, performance was little better than the DH-4 or Bristol, and production was not warranted, but it did firmly establish an engineering discipline at the Division which permitted rapid development of other aircraft.

The Division had made a more direct approach with the Bristol Fighter, modifying two sample airplanes, the first with a 300 horsepower Hispano Suiza and the second with a Liberty eight of 290 horsepower. These aircraft have often been mislabeled, and it might pay to straighten out the confusion now.

The two previously mentioned aircraft were English built Bristol fighters and carried as such on McCook Field records, where they were known as Plane 30 and 37, respectively. In April, 1918, the Air Service decided to build four more Bristol types, the USB-1, USB-2, USB-3 and USB-4. The first two were to have girder style fuselages, while the last two were to have plywood veneer fuselages. Construction was suspended on the USB-1 and -2, and the -3 and -4 were subsequently renamed XB-1 and XB-2. The XB-1 would be fitted with a 300 horsepower

A celebratory picture showing Jimmy Doolittle discussing the GE turbo-supercharger with its inventor, Sanford Moss, in 1946. Without Moss's long effort, the turbo-superchargers that allowed U.S. B-17s and B-24s to live in the skies over Europe would never have come into existence. The Engineering Division backed the experiments for many years.

Hisso and have fixed Marlin guns, while the XB-2 would have the ill-fated Liberty eight and Brownings.

The XB-2 was never completed, probably due to the Liberty's obvious problems in test, and the XB-1 was refitted with Brownings and redesignated XB-1A, receiving the McCook Field Plane No. 90. Its first flight was on July 3, 1919, and 83 hours and 25 minutes were logged before it was condemned on November 4, 1920. On Feb. 23, 1921, it was subjected to a destructive static test which showed that neither the flying nor the outdoor weathering had significantly affected the integrity of the fuselage.

Roché, father of the famous Aeronca, and a feisty, far thinking genius whose ideas appear again and again—the current crop of "winglets" on proposed energy saving transport designs are strikingly similar to his proposals of twenty-five years ago—had figured importantly in the design and test of several different types of plywood fuselages. The idea itself was not new, but was appealing because of the ease of production. The Division had taken full advantage of information on foreign methods, studying both German and French techniques. While the Germans had used a hardwood for their ply material, Roché had sought out the services of American furniture and lumber experts in order to use a lighter wood. Together they developed many new varieties of plywood, including combinations of poplar, maple, basswood and spruce. With spruce or basswood as the core, and poplar or spruce as the faces, they achieved a strong lightweight veneer which could be used in sheets as large as 104 × 28 inches. Just as a modeler dampens balsa to cover a curved area, these sheets were sponge dampened with warm water, and then nailed and glued to a laminated bulkhead/longeron substructure. The binder itself was another special development, a waterproof blood glue that Kurt Tank would have been glad to have had on his World War II answer to the Mosquito, the TA-154.

The result of this effort was a rugged light weight structure which could have relatively deep curvature for streamlining and still retain its strength. Comparative tests were made on four basic veneer fuselage types—the Davies-Putnam, Widman, L.W.F. and Haskelite, with the last being found to be most suitable.

The XB-1A was intensively experimented with, receiving many engine, propeller, instrument and armament installations, and Dayton Wright subsequently built 40 for service use. At least nine XB-1As received McCook Field Plane Numbers—90, 150, 151, 171, 179, 180, 181, 182, and 205—and all were apparently transferred or surveyed by the end of 1923.

Some products of McCook Field's research, development, and encouragement line up at the Merchant's Exchange Trophy Race in St. Louis on October 5, 1923.

Hottest version was the Wright Model H high compression engine P-90 modification, which indicated 129.5 mph at sea level. The H model engine was much better liked than the vibrating low compression version, or the Packard.

One especially interesting experiment was the faired fuselage version of XB1-A, the P-205. A fabric and stringer fairing was applied from the nose radiator all the way to the tail skid, smoothing the bottom wing in rather neatly with the fuselage, and giving it a sort of Roland *Walfisch* appearance. Tests were run comparing the normal configuration with the faired type, and also studying the effect of removing the wing dihedral. The faired, zero dihedral version showed a mild performance increase—speed went up 3.2 mph and absolute service ceiling went up 800 feet. Not unexpectedly, however, the performance improvement was at the expense of flying quality, and J. A. Macready, Chief of the Flying Section, recommended against the modification. Maneuverability and stability both decreased (somewhat unusual), and the aircraft was much more difficult to land.

Simultaneously with the intensive XB-1A development, it was necessary to redesign the de Havilland DH-9 to accept the Liberty engine and U.S. production methods. The original DH-9 had been anything but a success with the newly formed Royal Air Force, for it was fitted with the Siddley Puma engine of 230 horsepower, and represented a design regression when compared to the Rolls Royce powered DH-4s.

The basic airframe, with its improved cockpit/fuel tank arrangement was excellent, however, and McCook Field had only to mate it to the Liberty 12 engine to have a formidable warplane, the USD-9.

The Engineering Division XB1-A was an attempt to create an improved version of the famous Bristol F2B two-seat fighter. It was a creditable effort, given the infancy of the American aviation industry.

One of the great tragedies of aviation was that the beautiful Verville Sperry R-3 racer was not given sufficient development time to turn it into a front-line fighter. Here it was in 1924, looking for all the world like the prototype of the Hawker Hurricane, with its cantilever low-wing and retractable landing gear. Had just a few thousand (not hundreds of thousands, just a few thousand) dollars been spent on it, it could have entered service in 1926 and led the world by a decade. *Peter M. Bowers*

The USD-9 provided a general background for the greater USD-9A effort, much as the DH-9 had done for the DH-9A. The principal outward appearance difference in the two American planes was in the empennage. The original USD-9 had a more rounded rudder, perhaps influenced by the USAC-1, and an overhung elevator. There were other minor differences; the plywood fuselage covering was carried slightly further back and the nose cowl underpanning was louvered on the USD-9A.

Amazingly, one of the most unique factors on the 9A from the American point of view was the completion of over 3,000 construction drawings for the airframe. It was intended for mass manufacture (Curtiss alone was supposed to build 4,000) and McCook Field did not intend to have another Curtiss/Bristol fiasco on its hands.

The USD 9A naturally followed the DH-9A design closely, but there were significant internal and detail differences, plus some very real improvements.

In construction, for example, the American product had twenty four ribs and twenty four false ribs in its lower wing panel while the DH-9A used only twenty ribs and thirty six false ribs. A visual comparison of the two panels clearly indicates that the American version was designed for mass production, with fewer pieces and joints, while its British counterpart was still a tribute to the cabinet maker.

The Engineering Division had modified the original airfoil to a combined RAF 14/15 type, to obtain a slightly deeper spar and greater strength. The effect on performance was negligible, but this and other details were sufficient to cause a rather cool correspondence to flow between RAF liaison officers and McCook Field. The files reveal that the British "constructive criticism" grated on Air Force nerves, but a formal cordiality was preserved.

The RAF however could not find fault with two major improvements in the cooling and synchronizing systems.

Designed by Allan Loomis, the USD-9A's cooling system was intended for application with any liquid cooled engine. Loomis designed the expansion tank as the radiator shell proper, surrounding the core. A separate retractable booster was mounted aft of the engine in the lower part of the fuselage. An injector was fitted in the connection between the main and booster radiators, and it maintained a constant volume and pressure of circulating water, minimizing loss due to hot spot steaming or cavitation. It was the most significant advance in radiator design until the advent of Prestone.

A similar advance was made in synchronization, where the old fashioned, somewhat difficult Constantinesco-Colley system was replaced by A.L. Nelson's system. The forward fixed Browning was mounted on metal framework on the right hand side of the fuselage, and had two sights—a ring directly on the gun, and an Aldis on the left side of a diminutive wind screen. The gun's firing was timed by a control mounted directly on the camshaft driving member of the Liberty engine. It was not the ultimate synchronizer, but it was reliable and adaptable to all aircraft.

The USD-9A was an eminently successful effort, capable of serving in reconnaissance, day or night bomber roles.

In the reconnaissance version, at a gross weight of 4,520 pounds, it had a top speed of 124 mph. Its Liberty powered British DH-9A counterpart weighed in at only 4,200 pounds, and had a top speed of only 120 mph. The difference is probably due to the better finish of the American product, where small details like the aileron control pulleys received fairings. If the Armistice had not intervened, the plane would not only have given a good account of itself in combat, but would have supplanted the DH-4s in their long period of peace time use.

Besides this simultaneous development of the XB1-A, USAC-1, USAC-2 (never completed) and the USD 9 and 9A, the Division was also giving unstintingly of itself to many other designers and manufacturers, making its influence felt on such outstanding planes as Captain LePere's LUSAC-11, the Orenco D, the delicate Pomilios and many others. An October 21, 1918 status report from Bane to Vincent listed no less than 46 current experimental projects ranging from the S.E. 5 to such rare items as these: Berckman Liberty 12, Clark 320 ABC, Hittle Liberty 12, Lawson Armored Battler, LePere C-21 Bugatti, Standard E-10 with two 300 hp Hissos, Victory Liberty 12, Sperry Liberty 12, and so on. Many did not progress beyond the design stage, but they all laid a certain measure of work on the Division. Perhaps even more demanding were the requests made by Dr. Christmas and J.V. Martin, whose personalities and products would have exasperated anyone. (See March *Airpower* 1975).

The Armistice brought disruption and dislocation to the Air Service, and particularly to the Engineering Division. The reduction in appropriations was bad, but even worse was the natural flow of talented men from the Division back to industry.

Alfred Verville, fortunately, was one of those who chose to stay for a while. This mild mannered genial genius is another one of the truly great personalities in American aviation history who has never received the degree of recognition he deserved. Verville began his career with Curtiss at Hammondsport, and was a design draftsman on a wide variety of airplanes. He spent 1915 with Thomas Morse, and 1916 and 1917 with his own firm, the General Aeroplane Company. He paused briefly with Fisher in 1917, then came to the Engineering Division in 1918.

Among his first duties there was the design, in collaboration with Clark, of the swift, handsome VCP-1, a taper wing biplane using the 300 horsepower Hispano, and capa-

One of the many geniuses to lend their brilliance to McCook Field was Virginius E. Clark, designer of the Clark Y airfoil and of the Duramold construction process used on the Hughes flying boat. Admittedly a little eccentric, Clark turned out one beautiful design after another.

Virginius Clark worked with another genius, Alfred Verville, to create the Verville VCP-1, a very sleek pursuit plane deriving somewhat from the SPAD experience. *Peter M. Bowers*

The Engineering Division XCO-1 (CO for Corps Observation) was designed by Isaac Laddon, who would later design the Consolidated PBY amphibian, among many other aircraft. Despite its cumbersome appearance, it had a 117 mph top speed.

The XCO-1 was manufactured by Gallaudet, giving the firm experience in metal construction. The unusual reverse gull-wing center section was intended to provide better visibility. *Peter M. Bowers*

ble of a 150 mph top speed. All Verville designs were clean, with smooth flowing lines, and the two VCP-1s which were built were no exception.

The 2,617 pound fighter was of all wood construction, with a monocoque fuselage built in two halves of yellow poplar veneer, layered in a manner similar to that used by LWF. The two halves were joined, covered by a layer of mercerized cotton and warm glue, and then glued and nailed to the supporting bulkheads and engine mount. The skin was only 5/32″ thick, extremely strong, and quite rigid.

The single bay tapered wings were joined by I struts, and featured ailerons built into the lower wings, which were estimated to be the least efficient. The Hispano was cooled by a most unusual deep core annular radiator which anticipated the Focke Wulfe FW-190 D-9's arrangement by some twenty five years. While theoretically extremely efficient, the radiator had an inherent structural weakness which forced a change to a more conventional type. A clever camera shutter type set of louvers controlled the cooling. There were numerous other innovations as well, including detachable rubber covered fuel tank, armored seat, shoulder harness, cantilever tail surfaces and very carefully filleted wing and empennage butt fairings.

Both airplanes were later modified, one becoming the Army Air Service's first racer, the VCP-R and the other the VCP-1A.

The VCP-R received the huge 660 horsepower Packard 1A-2025 engine and numerous detail changes, including a higher pilot's headrest and a new underslung square radiator. The latter was unfortunately undersized, forcing the modern looking biplane to drop out of the first lap of the

The Gallaudet DB-1B (DB for Day Bomber) was very advanced in appearance, but was never flown because of concerns about its weight and structural strength.

James Gordon Bennett Cup race in 1920. A larger radiator and a more handsomely streamlined engine cowling were hastily fitted, and Captain Corliss Mosely flew it to win the 1920 Pulitzer at 156.5 mph. Two years later, Mosely (who died in July, 1974), would fly the same plane in the 1922 Pulitzer. Now called the R-1, and obviously obsolescent in the company of the sleek new breed of Curtiss racers and its own sister ships, the Verville Sperry R-3s, the still good looking biplane finished sixth at 179 mph.

The story of the R-3s will have to wait until the next installment of this article, which will deal with Verville's later designs, as well as with the ugly series of armored aircraft, the Barling Bomber, and the final group of aircraft which the Division would design as the Air Service matured slowly into the Air Corps.

2 The Treasures of McCook Field

America's First Aero-Engineering and Testing Center, Part II

Wings August, 1975

McCook Field was truly the cradle of the American aviation industry, since so many top engineers either worked or tried to sell their products there. Military appropriations were laughably small, and the U.S. Air Service tried to spread the money around to keep as many contractors in business as possible.

In a similar way, McCook was a hothouse for growing great pilots. The test pilots at McCook Field were in every way the equivalent of the modern astronauts in terms of their skill, daring, and public appeal. It is safe to say that if time travel were possible, the great test pilots of the early 1920s, men like Jimmy Doolittle, Alexander Pearson, Ed Aldrin (Buzz's father), and Harold Harris, could have succeeded in the Apollo program, just as men like Neil Armstrong and Frank Borman could have succeeded at McCook.

The number of developments pioneered at McCook is remarkable; they include controllable- and reversible-pitch propellers, self-sealing fuel tanks, superchargers, instrument flying, reconnaissance cameras, and many other innovations. More than anything else, however, McCook Field pioneered a "can-do" spirit that can still be found in the American aviation industry.

In the first part of this article, we saw how a rare combination of men, money and a sense of national urgency created, almost overnight, the single most influential agency in the early years of American airpower—the Engineering Division of McCook Field. The airplanes produced there were but a part of the total story of inventions, ideas, procedures, and regulations which formed an interdisciplinary approach to aviation. Like almost every other aviation center, there was a fascination with sheer velocity, and some of the most handsome racers ever flown sprang from the mind and hand of Alfred Verville.

While Verville was always the man the Air Service turned to in its quest for speed, he was extremely versatile, accepting any challenge of design.

One of his off beat efforts was the redesign of a standard DH-4 into an ambulance plane. He was assigned the task on December 10, 1919, and the plane rolled out on April 10, 1920. Verville had modified the rear of the fuselage to take two standard Navy Stokes litters, providing easy handling, and maintaining structural integrity. The rear cockpit was designed to carry the doctor to the scene of the crash; and once a patient had been placed inside the airplane in the upper litter, a roller curtain was pulled shut to provide protection from the air blast, the doctor presumably catching a taxi home.

A more famous design was his Messenger, a tiny 20 foot wing span airplane that was almost universally beloved, and which performed as many different duties and experiments as many a more ambitious type. The original idea was to provide a "dispatch rider of the sky," an aerial liaison runner. Verville conceived a small, easy to manufacture biplane powered by the new 60 hp. three cylinder Lawrance radial engine, and in one version was capable of a startling 96.7 mph. Macready's April 27, 1921 test report of P-152 was almost eulogistic, praising the flying qualities, general feel, and ground handling characteristics. Virtually his only criticisms were of the engine, and these were an understanding analysis of the teething problems inherent in the new design. The Air Service ordered a total of 42 airplanes, including the prototype, and Lawrence Sperry was chosen to manufacture the production series.

Despite the Messenger's small size, it was especially suitable for the installation of Sperry's automatic controls, and several were fitted out as radio controlled aerial torpedoes. Curiously, the aerial torpedo had an engine which performed better than the standard version, and provided much better performance.

A trapeze hook-up arrangement was mounted on the upper wing, and the aircraft made both hook-ups and drop-offs from the Army airship TC-5. Still another version was fitted with skids and special jettisonable landing gear, while others were used to test various airfoil sections.

Brilliant, young, handsome and very publicity conscious, Sperry himself used a personal Messenger in this country, flying from his home in Long Island, and making well covered flights to downtown Washington, D.C. Ironically, he was to perish when his special Messenger crashed into the English channel. The plane floated, and was recovered, but Sperry apparently attempted to swim ashore and drowned. An accident investigation revealed that the Lawrance had thrown a rod—a not uncommon occurrence.

The TW-1 was not a pretty airplane by any standard, but it included a very advanced concept in its energy-absorbing cockpit design. A heavily padded, spring-filled area was designed to absorb the shock of the pilot being thrown forward in a crash, an all-too-common occurrence in those days. Powered by the ill-fated Liberty six cylinder, 230 horsepower engine, it had a top speed of 97 mph.

The Engineering Division XCO-6 was the last aircraft built at McCook Field, thanks to pressure applied by manufacturers, who resented the Army building its own airplanes at a time when there were so few being purchased. Designed by Jean A. Roché (who also designed the Aeronca light plane), the XCO-6 was an excellent aircraft that went through a long series of modifications for test purposes. Two were built.

A lesser known effort was the redesign Verville did of the VCP-1. He had been attracted to steel tube fuselage construction, and employed it in the VCP-2, which was otherwise similar to the -1. Two airplanes were built, and these were subsequently redesignated PW-1 in the new numbering system, one later being converted with Fokker style wings to the PW-1A. While the PW-1 was less attractive looking than the original VCP-1, and achieved only 146 mph on its 350 horsepower Packard engine, it did use a tunnel style radiator. This, with its tapered wings, provided a remarkable similarity to the later and more successful Curtiss PW-8s and Boeing PW-9s.

Verville renewed his relationship with Sperry in the design and construction of the very advanced Verville Sperry R-3 racers, one of the most "might-have-been" airplanes in history. Despite Air Service backing, and despite three being ordered, there was simply not enough time allotted to the development of the plane to bring it to its full potential. For reasons of budget, prestige and perhaps just personal interest, the R-3 was cursed by a program which alternated between extreme urgency and utter unconcern. It was ramrodded into the 1922 Pulitzer without the development period which would surely have turned it into a serious contender not only for speed records, but also for production contracts.

Verville had designed a clean cantilever low wing monoplane with retractable landing gear, and had apparently intended to use the very latest innovations which would appear on the Curtiss racers then being developed—a Curtiss D-12 engine, wing skin radiators and a metal propeller. Fate or politics dictated otherwise, and he was forced to settle for the vibration prone Wright H-3 of 380 horsepower, a wooden propeller and the Lamblin beer keg radiators.

The Engineering Division PW-1 of 1921 was quite advanced. Powered by a 350 horsepower Packard engine, it had a top speed of 146 mph. The influence of the earlier VCP-1 racer is evident. The Engineering Division tunnel radiator is shown here; it would soon show up on Boeing and then Curtiss pursuit designs. Only two PW-1s were procured. *Peter M. Bowers*

Here then was a totally new design, inspiring to look at, but filled with the invisible glitches that plague any ambitious program. Vibration was the first and most serious problem, and this was certainly no surprise, for the Wright engine had jarred engine mounts loose in a variety of airplanes. Less obvious was the harmony and trim of the controls, a combination which almost always has to be carefully tuned over a long test period. Instead the aircraft were thrown pell mell into the 1922 Pulitzer at Detroit, Michigan.

The competition was fierce, for not only were the well developed Curtiss racers present, but also Navy Wright "Mystery" racers, the Bee Line racers, so similar in configuration to the R-3s, the hopeless Loening R-4s, and the equally ungainly looking Thomas Morse MB-7.

Predictably, the R-3s did not do well. Lieutenant Gene Barksdale finished in fifth place at 181.2 mph, and Lieutenant F. B. Johnson was seventh. Lt. St. Clair Streett was forced to drop out in the fifth lap.

1923 was even worse; only one R-3 airplane was entered in the Pulitzer, but it was reengined with the much smoother Curtiss D-12 engine, and numerous minor modifications were made to improve the flying characteristics. Pre-race speeds peaked at over 230 miles per hour, but an out of balance prop took the plane out of contention in the first lap.

The racer was cleaned up extensively in 1924, with lots of tape going over seams and gaps, and a new 500 horsepower Curtiss engine installed. With these modifications, Lt. H. A. Mills won the race, albeit at a disappointing 215.7 mph.

Oddly enough, the most distinguishing feature of the airplane, the retractable landing gear, was perhaps its most reliable component, never causing any trouble.

While Verville had spearheaded the quest for speed, others at the Engineering Division were exploring the possibilities of armored aircraft. The trench strafing success and relative invulnerability of such aircraft as the German Junkers J-1 of 1917–18 had inspired the Division to create three different special types of heavily protected planes.

The first of these was the awe-inspiring G.A.X. of 1919. (See *Wings,* Oct. 1971). This triplane was powered by twin pusher Liberty engines and encumbered by its almost five ton gross weight and yards of frontal area. Designed by I. W. Laddon, who would go on to the ultimate pusher with the B-36 at Consolidated Vultee, the G.A.X. was an attempt to provide a flying pill box which could chop enemy troops to pieces. General Billy Mitchell later wanted to extend the concept so that the G.A.X. would not only strafe, but would fly to a point in enemy territory, land, mount the guns in a defensive perimeter, and hold the ground until the infantry arrived. This concept, mercifully, did not get too far.

That grand old gentleman, Brigadier General Harold R. Harris, USAF (Ret) test flew the G.A.X., and he confirmed the disastrous flying qualities that had been rumored. The plane was not only overweight and hard to handle, but the rigid structure and heavy armor plate turned the ordinary vibrations of the two Liberty engines into the percussion section of the Moscow Philharmonic, resulting in serious hearing problems for the pilots. Single engine performance was nil, and the vibration seemed to induce the Liberties to shed their exhaust stacks, which promptly flew into the pusher props.

The original production order for 20 G.A.1 aircraft from Boeing was reduced to 10, and these received reluctant use by Air Service. Jimmy Doolittle was alleged by an Air Service newsletter to be the premier GA-1 pilot, but whether this was an admiring note or a gentle jibe is unknown.

Boeing also produced the next in the armored series, the GA-2, and has always rather pointedly noted that this was not a Boeing design. Powered by the 700 horsepower Engineering Division W-1A-18 engine, the odd looking GA-2 had 1,600 pounds of armor plate, a complete duplication in spars, braces and cables, and the kind of flying qualities you might expect from such an approach. It was redundancy squared, with frontal area to match, and totally unsuccessful.

The third aircraft was the uniquely ugly Aeromarine PG-1, which was intended to be a destroyer of armored attack planes of the GA-1 and GA-2 type. Designed by the Engineering Division and farmed out to Aeromarine for construction, the PG-1 was distinguished by its armored nose section which contained the pilot, fuel tanks and engine, and for a 37 mm cannon which was mounted in the V of the Wright K-2 engine. Previous reports have indicated that Aeromarine was unable to complete the contract and that Boeing completed production, but the Seattle firm denies this, probably feeling that the notoriety of the GA-1 and GA-2 was enough for anyone. The PG-1 had a top speed of 124 mph, and static tests indicated that it was very strongly built. Unfortunately, its excessive vibration, poor handling and bad visibility made it a plane to forget. Nevertheless, it was maintained on flying status for over four years.

A quick comparison of the three attack airplanes is interesting for it reveals the stark general fuselage and empennage outlines common to all three, while showing the common Laddon influence.

This lack of concern for aesthetics was to become more pronounced in later Engineering Division designs, particularly in training airplanes. Despite the reduction in appropriations and manpower, the Division was still interested in exploring the possibilities of all of the fifteen distinct types of aircraft that had been determined to be necessary, and trainers were no exception.

The first of these, the elephantine TW-1, had a 41 foot wingspan and a 230 hp Liberty six engine. Two were built, and while undistinguished in appearance or performance, they did incorporate a very advanced conception of a "safety cockpit". The seat belts were made extra long and in the event of a crash would release the occupant slowly forward into a cushioned, spring filled coaming mounted above and forward of each dash. Ironically, the TW-1 was one of the few planes of the time that didn't crash, and the device was never put to actual test.

The second trainer, the XTA-3, was designed by Roché, but passed to Dayton Wright for production. Thirteen were built, and these formed the basis for the development of Reuben Fleet's long and remunerative series of trainers at Consolidated, which succeeded the Dayton Wright firm.

Concurrently with the TW-1 and TA-3, the Engineering Division was embroiled in one of the biggest adventures (debacles) of its career, for at the instigation of General Mitchell, a competition was held for a "super bomber." A design submitted by Walter Barling won, and the airplane was built by Witteman-Lewis. Barling's previous attempt at a giant bomber had been the Tarrant Tabor in England, also a six engine triplane with circular monocoque fuselage. (The Tabor had nosed over on its first attempted takeoff, killing both pilots).

Not surprisingly, the Barling had in addition to its three wings, six Liberties, four rudders, two horizontal stabilizers and many struts, no less than ten wheels, four of which were positioned to prevent a nose over.

The giant bomber was a failure, although it set several records. Its 95 mph top speed and 170 mile range with a full bomb load was simply inadequate. Harold R. Harris made the first flight in the Barling, as he did in so many others, and recalls one flight in which the plane seemed particularly logy, as if it were vastly overloaded. On landing, small gashes were made in the wing fabric, and literally tons of accumulated rain water gushed out. The plane was laid up while a huge new hangar was constructed, one that would probably be more valuable to the Division than the airplane.

(In fairness to Mr. Barling, it should be pointed out that he designed some very excellent light planes later in his career.)

Part of the problem with the Barling, and with every other plane of the period, was the universal requirement to use the Liberty engine. Fortunately the Engineering Division would have an opportunity to correct this situation, for it extended help to Charles Lawrance in the development of radial engines, beginning with a contract to build his nine cylinder radial "R-1". This engine passed a 50 hour running test in July, 1921, generating 147 hp at 1,600.

The Navy joined forces with the Engineering Division, ordering five "J-1's", which were similar, except for a longer stroke, permitting 200 hp to be developed. From this basic engine emerged the famous Wright J-4s, J-5s, and in a very real sense, *all* other radials by Wright and Pratt & Whitney. It's probably not stretching the truth too much to say that the Engineering Division's foresight in backing Lawrance laid the foundation for air supremacy in World War II, when Pratt & Whitney alone turned out almost *370,000* round engines.

However, the Liberty continued to burden the development of two-seat fighters and the unorthodox TP-1 of 1922 was no exception. Hardly a milestone aircraft, the TP-1 is noteworthy primarily for the collaborative efforts of two young men whose mark would long endure in the industry. The first of these was B.C. Boulton, an M.I.T. graduate who would stay with the Division until 1924, when he joined Loening. When Keystone took over Loening, Boulton became chief engineer in charge of amphibian projects. He then moved to Martin, where he was project engineer on the famous B-10 series (see *Airpower,* May, 1972) and where his relationship with the Engineering Division helped smooth the heated discussions encountered on that project. Later as Chief Engineer at Martin he was responsible for the design of the PBM-1. He became eventually Vice President of Engineering before moving on, first to Lockheed where he was in on the original experimental shop fabrication group, and then to Douglas.

The second keyman was Lawrence V. Kerber, an aeronautical engineer from the University of Michigan, who served seven years with the Division before returning to his alma mater as a Guggenheim professor. He joined Spartan Aircraft as President, and guided it through its most successful years and designs, including the immortal Executive.

Their joint product, the TP-1, was a close coupled, two seat biplane fighter with a very short 36 foot wing span. The upper wing had a rather shallow camber and a 54″ chord, while the lower wing was thick and had a

Lawrence V. Kerber and B. C. Boulton collaborated on the design of the Engineering Division TP-1 (TP for Two-place Pursuit) fighter design. Kerber went on to Spartan and then Lockheed, while Boulton passed through Loening, Keystone, and Martin before rejoining Kerber at Lockheed; Boulton later worked for Douglas. The TP-1 went through a long series of successful modifications. With the installation of a supercharger and new wings, the TP-1 permitted the famous John Macready to set an altitude record of 38,704 feet. *Peter M. Bowers*

Another view of Roché's XCO-6. The pleasing lines of the wings contrast with the rather starkly angled fuselage. *Peter M. Bowers*

The Engineering Division created the world's fastest de Havilland DH-4, powering it with a 600 horsepower Packard engine that allowed it to reach speeds of over 150 mph. *Peter M. Bowers*

mammoth 90″ chord. The difference in chord combined with the normal stagger of a biplane cellule, resulted in misshapen "N" struts, the aft member having to lean forward at about 10 degrees greater angle than the forward strut.

The plane's biggest innovation was the G.E. supercharger mounted on the front of its Liberty engine. Speed was a creditable 130 mph, but the supercharger did generate some unwanted overheating problems. As McCook Field Plane 263, the TP-1 would go through numerous modifications, experiments and at least three overhauls before being surveyed at San Antonio in October, 1927, after 54 months of service. The aft fuselage was lengthened, *ala* Tony Fokker's treatment of the prototype D-VII, and additional vertical surface was added, hinting at a directional stability problem.

The supercharger installation was changed, moving to the right hand side of the nose, and later the aircraft was fitted with a standard Liberty engine.

The second TP-1 (A.S. #23-1204) was modified to become the sole XCO-5. The lower wing chord was reduced to 78″, the supercharger deleted, and a car type radiator was installed. About one year later the nose was cleaned up with a chin style radiator, and new equal span 43 ft. wings installed. These had a normal chord arrangement, the upper being 78 inches and the lower 54. Mr. R. C. Lockwood, a civilian test pilot, flew the plane, and his 22 November 1924 report reveals a guardedly positive attitude. He describes most features of the plane—accessibility, maneuverability, control, effectiveness, etc, as "fair", and in an equally laconic manner characterizes visibility as "no good".

The plane got a third lease on life in 1926, when it was extensively rebuilt. New thick two bay wings, large in span, gap, chord and camber, were installed and the rudder was enlarged. It was used by Macready to establish one last record before he left the service to enter commercial aviation; he reached 38,704 feet on January 29th, 1926. The same plane carried Captain St. Clair Streett and famous balloonist/photographer Captain A. W. Stephens to 37,854 feet on October 10th, 1928, an unofficial record for planes

One of the most famous aircraft to be purchased by the Air Service was the Barling Bomber, designed by Walter Barling and built by the Witteman-Lewis firm. With three wings, six engines, and lots of drag, it had a top speed of 95 mph. It was flown by Harold R. Harris (who could and did fly anything) to several altitude/payload records. Unfortunately it had no utility as a bomber, for it could not carry a load of bombs very far or very high. *Peter M. Bowers*

The Air Service purchased the Fokker T-2 from Anthony Fokker in Holland, then modified it at McCook Field for its transcontinental flight. Piloted by Oakley Kelly and John A. Macready, the trip was made on May 2–3, 1923, in just 26 hours and 50 minutes. *Terry Gwynn-Jones*

carrying more than one person. Popular accounts of the period indicate the plane was intended for high altitude photographic work, but there seems to have been no follow-up with the XCO-5.

The XCO-5 was one of a series of fourteen different Corps Observation planes tested by the Division during the first half of the 1920s. The first of these was Laddon's CO-1, a high wing all metal monoplane powered again, as were they all, by a Liberty. It was a relatively clean, if awkward appearing airplane, with its 55′9″ wing given character by a nipped in section near the fuselage, which left the steel tube spars exposed. In fact, the airplane could easily have passed for a Stout design because of its corrugated sides and angular appearance. Top speed was 117 mph.

Laddon's ambition had exceeded the available metallurgical state of the art, and the XCO-1 was not developed, although three were built—two by the Division, and one by Gallaudet, who made minor changes which made the airplane much more attractive.

Roché designed the next aircraft in the series, the CO-2. The CO-2 used a single bay wing to reduce drag, and its fuselage was assembled with heat treated fittings rather than being welded. The aircraft was conventional in appearance with a clean nose entry and extendable side radiators, and its 137 mph top speed exceeded all but one of the Corps Observation series.

The CO-2 made a successful first flight, but crashed during speed runs, killing its pilot L. P. Moriarity and observer Stonebraker. In his unpublished autobiography, Roché notes that the accident investigation revealed no probable cause for the accident. Yet he refrains from doing what many lesser men have done, placing the blame on pilot error. He simply says that a technical fault was probably the cause. They just don't make engineers like that anymore.

The Engineering Division had a small flirtation with gliders, manned and unmanned, with both programs under Roché's direction. He designed small target gliders which could be mounted on the upper wing of a JN-4 or DH-4, patented them, and assigned the patent to the government. He made the first flight test, riding with pilot Jimmy Johnson. The glider released properly, and went into the preplanned climb and loop, which permitted the release plane to come back and make a firing pass, if desired. It was successively improved with electronic controls and recovery parachutes and was in many respects the ancestor of the host of radio controlled targets we have today.

Roché was allocated a very limited budget for the other project, a man carrying glider which had been inspired by the efforts going on in Germany, and which was intended from the start to explore the potential of a glider as a combat troop delivery vehicle.

Using a pair of surplus JN-4 upper wings and a very economical fuselage structure, Roché created the GL-2, a very efficient glider which bore a strong resemblance to the later Aeronca light plane. Several flights were made from McCook Field, using a shock cord launch system and, later, others were made over slopes south of Dayton. Two famous racing pilots, Lt. Alex Pearson and W. H. Brookley, made most of the flights. Some reports say that the glider was also towed into the air by automobiles, but this hasn't been confirmed.

Times, however, were changing, and private aircraft manufacturers were resentful of the Engineering Division continuing to design and build aircraft. Part of their argument was that the group was no longer manned or funded adequately to remain in the forefront of aviation development, but the unstated thrust of their argument was to ensure that money was not spent in a government agency which could be spent just as easily in private industry. The Division would retain its important role in setting standards, however, and nowhere was this better established than the "Handbook of Instructions For Airplane Designers" which became the bible of manufacturers, and which was updated as required by the Division.

So it was that the last Air Service designed and built aircraft came into being in 1923, when Roché designed the XCO-6. It was perhaps the most handsome and best performing of the entire Corps Observation series, being graced by a handsome high aspect ratio 48 ft. span wing, and a relatively slender, functional looking fuselage.

Lt. E. C. Batten conducted the official performance test on the first XCO-6 (P-360) on November 25, 1924. This airplane had an inverted, watercooled Liberty engine installed, which provided a top speed of 132.7 mph. Batten liked the airplane very well, except for the engine, which had a tendency to foul the plugs in a glide, making it impossible to resume a climb, and requiring a limping trip home to the field.

Less than a month later, on December 13, Batten and Macready took the plane up again, this time with a standard upright Liberty mounted in a very neat cowling with a chin radiator. Speed improved to 134 mph, at the same 4,607 pound gross weight, with no loss in flying qualities.

Later in its career, the XCO-6C, as it was then designated, received an aircooled inverted Liberty, and was flown with great success for several years. Roché still feels that this airplane would have gone into production had it not been for the change in policy, believing that the XCO-6C's performance was better than the contemporary Douglas and Curtiss observation planes.

The XCO-6C brings the Engineering Division's aircraft building activities to a close, but we should take one quick look at the men who made the whole story possible, the underpaid, underpublicized pilots—and in the best sense of the term, genuine heroes—who comprised the Flight Test Section.

The pilot who volunteered for the Flight Test Section was guaranteed to be a man who loved flying, for there was literally no other reason to choose that duty. The pay was low, advancement was slow, and the danger was ever-present. Yet men like Doolittle, Barksdale, Schroeder, Kelly, Macready, Batten, Lockwood, Harris gave unstintingly of themselves. This little group set records of every kind—altitude, speed, distance—you name it, in every sort of airplane. We'll examine these pioneers in a follow on article, but it might be interesting to relate just one anecdote about that formidable record setter, astute businessman and skillful pilot, 1/Lt. Harold R. Harris.

The hazards of high altitude flight had been pointed up during the routine patrols of World War I, which were often conducted at 18,000 to 20,000 feet and even higher, and there are many written reports of the hardships endured by those pilots. Oxygen was used, particularly by the Germans, but the physiology of high altitude flight was just beginning to be understood.

The apparent success of supercharger experiments made it abundantly clear that the altitude capability of aircraft was going to be increased significantly, and it was obviously imperative to combat the problem. The Engineering Division came up with what later was to prove to be the universal solution, the pressure cabin.

A USD-9A, P-80, had been groomed for the test by removal of the pilot and observer's seats and substitution of

The Engineering Division fostered the development of many firms by backing their designs with contracts. This is the Dayton Wright TW-3 side-by-side trainer. Twenty were built by Consolidated and became the basis for Consolidated's famous PT-3 design.

a cylindrical tank made up of riveted and brazed steel. A minimum number of controls were admitted to the tank via the packing glands, and a two foot diameter door, designed to be sealed by internal air pressure, provided entrance for the pilot.

This is the original Army Aeronautical Museum at Wright Field, opened after McCook had closed and all its departments had moved to Wright. It housed a de Havilland and the Fokker "Bird of Paradise," which made the first flight from the United States to Hawaii in 1927. Sad to say, when war came the building was needed for wartime purposes, and these classic airplanes, and much else, were unceremoniously junked.

Visibility was restricted to the minimal range afforded by five six inch glass portholes, while all instrumentation, save for a single altimeter, was mounted on a board in front of the forward porthole.

A normal pilot's seat was fitted in the tank, and above the pilot's head was a three-fourths inch globe valve to provide for manual adjustment of cabin altitude.

Pressure was provided by a prop driven supercharger, installed on the leading edge of the lower left wing, and ducting air to the cabin via a two inch pipe.

It was June 8, 1921 when Harris had the modified biplane rolled from its hangar, and the fact that he was flying at all was pure chance. Harris was then Chief of the Flight Test Section, and a civilian pilot, diminutive Art Smith, had been selected to make the first flight a short time previously. Smith was about five foot three, and when it came time to close the big metal door, he lacked the leverage and musculature necessary to swing it into place.

Harris had no problem until he leveled off at 3,000 feet and swung the door that had frustrated Smith into place. Then the supercharger, which had been designed 100% oversize to compensate for expected leakage, began to pack one atmosphere in on top of another. The

The Engineering Division XCO-5B in which J. A. Macready set the altitude record (38,709 feet) in 1926. *Peter M. Bowers*

Not every engineering effort at McCook Field was successful. Among its failures were two products by J. V. Martin: the Kitten "high-altitude interceptor," and the giant bomber, two Liberty engines mounted inside the fuselage. McCook Field engineers were forced to accept the airplanes for test, but never flew them. The Kitten was taken for a brief hopping flight, but not under Army auspices.

The very handsome LUSAO-11 was designed by French Captain Jeorges LePere, who also designed the much more successful LUSAC-11, a record-setting airplane. With twin Liberties, the triplane could do 112 mph. The only example of the LUSAC-11 can be found in the Air Force Museum.

altimeter outside the tank continued to read 3,000 feet above sea level, while the one inside pegged itself at 3,000 feet *below* sea level.

Harris made sure the exhaust valve was full open, and then looked vainly around the cockpit to see if there was anything he could break a porthole with, for the door was sealed with the mighty weight of a column of air infinity minus 3,000 feet high.

While not under any immediate danger, Harris was alarmed by the rise in temperature, and by his inability to control the situation. There was nothing harder in the cockpit than the soles of his tennis shoes, so he reluctantly decided that a slow glide back to McCook was the answer.

He managed to get the airplane on the ground, and once the supercharger prop stopped spinning, the relatively light leakage began to equalize the pressure. In a few minutes the door was swung open, and he could breathe the sweet Ohio air.

The project was a low priority one, and although safety modifications were made, including brakes on the supercharger propeller, a safety valve installed, and a ball peen hammer fitted inside the cockpit, there were apparently no further flights made. It's a pity, for the little USD-9A had anticipated by some 16 years the flight of the world famous Lockheed XC-35, which won the Collier Trophy for its pressure cabin achievements in 1937.

The whole experiment was typical of the Flight Test Section, and of the Engineering Division—a minimum of money and a maximum of brains and bravery, pitted against the most formidable current challenge. It was a good outfit then, and it still is today.

"Shorty" Schroeder circles over McCook Field after setting a two-man altitude record of 30,900 feet in LePere-designed LUSAC-11 aircraft on September 24, 1919. At McCook there was a big sign that read "THIS FIELD IS SMALL SO USE IT ALL." It was, and the pilots always tried to—but didn't always succeed.

A vitally important team: Veteran test pilot Lieutenant John A. Macready; Dr. Sanford Moss, father of the turbo-supercharger; Major George E. A. Hallet, an engine expert; and General Electric technician Adolph Berger stand beside the record-setting LePere aircraft. The author met both Macready and Hallet in their later years; they were still sharp and forthcoming.

3 The Great Owl

Building and Flying the First of America's Super-Bombers

Airpower November, 1973

As is fitting for a nation that spans the continent from sea to sea, the United States has always had a penchant for gigantic aircraft. Building bigger in the United States almost always meant building better, as the transcontinental railroads, the Chrysler Building, Boulder Dam, and a hundred other examples illustrate.

When it came to building bombers, it was only natural that the United States would want the biggest and the best. Unfortunately, the terms "biggest" and "best" rarely went together in airplanes.

The United States had gotten its feet wet in large aircraft design with the Glenn Martin Bomber, an aircraft whose appearance was comparable to the famous German Gotha of World War I, but whose performance exceeded it. Ten MB-1s (as it was designated by the Air Service) were built, followed by 20 MB-2s, which gained fame by participating in Billy Mitchell's famed aircraft-versus-battleship extravaganza off the Virginia coast in 1921. More important, they inspired enduring faith in the concept of the big bomber. Other giants appeared, including the weird Johns Multiplane, and later, the Barling Bomber. Of all of the giants, the L.W.F. Owl was not only the best-looking, it had the best performance.

This is perhaps the best angle from which to view the huge LWF Owl. A three-quarter rear view allows you to appreciate the cleanliness of boom and nacelle, and the complications of the wings and empennage. Top speed was 105 mph and landing speed was 56—you really didn't need flaps with all that wing area! *John Underwood*

Any tri-motor biplane is going to be impressive looking, but the Owl really stands out because of the very clean entry of the engine/nacelle design. Like all big airplanes, it needed plenty of wheels upon which to land, and in this case, six seemed just about right! *John Underwood*

The Wooden Owl

The Owl was essentially the last gasp but one from the famous LWF Engineering Company, another of the many hot-house aircraft firms spawned by World War I. LWF grew from the 1916 handshake of its founders, Joseph Lowe, Jr., Charles F. Willard, and Robert G. Fowler, to a huge industrial enterprise in 1918, manufacturing trainers and flying boats.

The original founders didn't stay with the company long enough to enjoy the prosperity—they were forced out in less than a year as a result of a series of financial operations. (This is a sad but prevalent story in the aircraft industry—time after time the inventors and aviators are forced out by the debit and credit experts, who subsequently capitalize on the original genius. There are numerous examples, among which the Taylor-Piper story is the classic.) Perhaps it did not matter much, for LWF was not to survive for long in the harshly competitive post-war world.

Willard was the engineering mainspring of the firm, and he had patented a method of constructing a strong streamlined monocoque fuselage (see construction details below). By some happy acronymic happenstance, the laminated wood fuselage method of construction was the most

There was never a public relations man who did not like to park the smallest possible airplane next to the biggest one, and here a tiny French Farman biplane sits next to the Owl. The National Air & Space Museum has a Farman in its collection—but no Owl. *John Underwood*

Charles F. Willard was the engineering genius behind the Owl, and he enjoyed a long and distinguished career in the industry. He patented the laminated wood fuselage, which by happy coincidence had the same initials as the owners of the firm, Lowe, Willard, and Fowler.

You can get a good idea of the size of the airplane by comparing it to the soldier reaching up to just touch the lower wing. Raoul Hoffman was the chief designer of the Owl.

distinguishing feature of the LWF designs, enabling the new managers of the firm to place a different meaning on the familiar and valuable LWF trademark.

The genuine conceptual elegance provided by Willard's typical slender fuselage was lost among the profusion of struts in the early airplanes. The initial production efforts, 23 trainers and 140-plus reconnaissance planes, had wide gap wings similar to contemporary Standard aircraft and performance totally undistinguished except for a remarkable glide ratio, which has been described to me by an ex-95th Pursuit Squadron pilot as "better than 20 to 1—you had to do a vertical sidestep to lose altitude in a thermal."

The bread-and-butter contract for the firm was for 300 Curtiss HS-2L flying boats, 90 of which were completed by the Armistice. Although this was a competitor's design, it did give the firm experience in the mass manufacture of large airframes and set up a train of thought which would eventually evolve into the Owl.

Two other LWF planes deserve passing mention here. One is the "F", an aircraft famous for being the very first to fly with the Liberty engine, on August 21, 1917. The other is the "G" series of rugged reconnaissance aircraft which easily outperformed the de Havilland DH-4, but suffered a sad, even tragic fate which is an epic story in itself.

As with a thousand other companies of every type, the glorious news of the Armistice brought mixed emotions to the New York based firm; the happiness that the bloodletting had stopped was flawed by the immediate crisis of contract cancellations. L.W.F. had in being a virtually new plant, a just-trained labor force, a fine engineering staff, and a good reputation. To hedge their bets in the uncertain peacetime economy, the company embarked on a four-pronged strategy. First, it intended to keep its hand in Government business, and was somewhat successful in this, building 35 Martin-designed NSB-1 bombers for the Army (see *Wings*, Oct. 72) and 70 Douglas-designed DT-2 torpedo planes for the Navy. Second, it kept as close an association as possible with the Post Office, undertaking some unprofitable modification contacts just to maintain visibility, for it was assumed that air-mail service would soon be a high volume industry. Third, L.W.F. went after the illusory civilian market with a very pretty little light monoplane—the Model L "Butterfly"—which was later destroyed in a crash. And fourth, it embarked on a truly ambitious triple-threat giant aeroplane project, the Model H "Owl."

The L.W.F. brochures describe the outstanding features of this machine as "the monocoque fuselage and nacelle, the intercommunicating gasoline system, and the fire extinguishing system". But in reality the salient feature was the interchangeable central pod, which permitted one design to serve as a mail plane, a passenger carrier, or a night bomber.

No passenger pod was ever completed, and the bomber pod was actually a rebuild of the original mailplane section, but we're getting ahead of the story.

LWF had called in Raoul Hoffman to be chief designer of the Model H, and one has to admire the range of his imagination. He started with two huge 105 foot span wings, using the classic U.S.A. No. 6 airfoil, and providing more than 2,300 square feet of wing area. They were a four-square proposition, with an 11-foot gap, 11-foot chord, no sweep, no stagger, and lots of lift. The wing span is sometimes quoted as being 106′8″; after the first crash, the ailerons were rebuilt with a larger balance area in order to improve lateral control. This proved to be unsatisfactory and further modifications resulted in a slight change in the wingspan.

Hoffman had the huge wings sandwich twin booms and long tapering nacelles, each of which sported a 400-horsepower Liberty engine. The plane weighed 12,400 pounds empty, almost twice the empty weight of the Martin GMB. With a full load, the gross weight climbed to a maximum of 21,726 pounds, and the LWF-made propellers, each of 9′6″ diameter, had to churn mightily to keep the aircraft airborne. Official military tests were flown at 16,400 pounds, and the Owl still needed all three engines to stay aloft. The odds of maintaining three Liberty engines operating throughout a flight were slightly less than even, so pilots maintained a constant watch for forced landing fields.

Performance Estimate of Giant L.W.F.

	As Loaded During Tests	With Full Military Load	Full Load Packard Engines
Weights	16,400	21,726	24,476
Maximum Speed	101.6	99.2	115
Minimum Speed	57	66.5	70
Service Ceiling	13,700	8,100	10,800
Absolute Ceiling	15,700	10,100	13,000
Speed at Absolute Ceiling	75	77.5	86
Rate of Climb (Sea Level)	750	490	690
Time to 6,500 ft.	11.5	22	13.2
Time to 10,000 ft. (minutes)	22	50	28

LWF had never been able to get the Post Office Department to commit itself, and the Owl was tendered to the Air Service in April 1920, on Order No. 520,031. On May 12, Second Lieutenant Ernest E. "Tiny" Harmon reported to the LWF plant at College Point where he formed some favorable early impressions. His report comments on the well placed and "clearly visible" instruments (all 14 of them) and called the master control and switchboard "novel, exceedingly well placed and accessible." The accessibility would come in handy on three occasions when a quick chop of the switch prevented a postcrash fire.

Harmon considered the rudder and aileron controls to have too much play, and these were tightened—with possibly serious consequences, as we shall see. Finally, he was pleased with the six-wheel landing arrangement, noting that the Martin Bombers were having some gear problems with their four-wheel setup.

The plane was trucked to Mitchell Field on Saturday, May 15, with the long booms rolling along on special wheels, towed by racy chain-drive trucks. Six days later, a crew of 15 mechanics and 5 riggers had the Owl set up and tuned for the test flight.

Captain George Patterson, Harmon's friend and one of the very select fraternity of Owl pilots, reported the initial flight as follows:

"The first flight was made Saturday, May 22nd, at 6:30 p.m. after considerable difficulty in getting the engines started. The airplane took off against a 20 mile wind in 130 yards in 9 4/5 seconds. The load carried consisted of 1,200 lbs. of shot in the nose, 200 gallons of gasoline, pilot, and one passenger. The airplane made one large circle around the Field, attaining an altitude of 1,300 feet, and then came down intending to fly level across the Field, but the right-hand engine over-

The complexity of the Owl made a good head-on shot difficult to obtain; there were just too many horizontal and vertical surfaces, too many struts, and too many engines and propellers cluttering up the view.

A tail-on shot works a little better, because of the angle on which the aircraft sits, tail low. You can see over the multi-surfaced empennage to view the rest of the aircraft.

Engineers understood drag and streamlining to a limited degree at the time the Owl was designed. But they did not quite grasp the fact that a great deal of streamlining (as with the long booms here) can be for naught if there is a major drag-inducing element like a biplane elevator.

heated and lost about 400 r.p.m. so that the pilot made one more circle and landed. Pilot reported the balance very good, but a trifle nose heavy with power off, and the lateral balance slightly off on the left-hand side. The aileron control on this flight was quite sluggish. The left-wing heaviness was corrected on subsequent flights by changing the alignment of the wings, and the aileron control made more responsive by raising the trailing edge of the aileron about 1 inch above the wings. This means that the lateral control of the airplane is similar to ships having dihedral angle. Prior to the flight when the engines were running full out on the ground, no vibration of the wings or tail surfaces was visible and the tail skid construction showed no signs of strain. This has also been true of subsequent flights."

A 14-minute second flight took place on May 24, during which a 2,600-feet altitude was attained. The third flight took place a few minutes later, and while full power could not be obtained due to carburetor problems, the aircraft achieved an indicated 102 mph airspeed. The minimum airspeed was also determined to be about 56 mph—the prudent foresight of a good test pilot, as the next flight was to prove.

The hairy nature of the Owl's power-limited condition asserted itself on the fourth flight, made on the evening of May 25th. Nine brave mechanics of the LWF Company crowded onboard as passengers, and shortly after breaking ground from the rather long takeoff run (maybe 700 feet), the center engine lost power. Harmon kept the plane airborne, staggering nose high at minimum speed and barely maintaining a 75-foot altitude. He hoped to make a circuit of the field, but the left engine began to fail and, as many another pilot has done, he chose to land at nearby Roosevelt Field, where the nine mechanics were glad to leap out and embrace Mother Earth.

Although water in the fuel was believed to be the problem, there were some changes made in the fuel system, with gasoline now being delivered directly to the gravity tanks and thence to the engines.

The fifth flight was a 7-minute test flight, followed by final adjustments to the fuel pump. Then came the Owl's finest hour, the "record hop." Grossing 16,400 pounds, the Owl took off and climbed directly to 6,000 feet in just 15 minutes. The engines were allowed to cool, and a second climb was made, this time to 11,000 feet in only 7 minutes. So rapid was the rise that the pilot suspected that he might have been caught in an ascending current. On the glide to the field, fuel starvation stopped one engine, and the other two quit during the taxi back.

While Harmon was still generally pleased with the trim and balance of the aircraft, he did note that the aileron control was very stiff, both mechanically and aerodynamically.

On May 30th, the Owl was again loaded to 16,400 pounds and took off in a no-wind condition after a 450-yard run. The plane seemed excessively nose heavy, and the pilot made one wide circuit, intending to return and land. On the turn to final, a turn-buckle on the control column broke, causing entire loss of aileron control. Asymmetric power was used to keep the wings level, but at touchdown the right wing dropped, sluing the Owl around 90° to the direction of flight.

The accident investigation revealed that the outer right-hand lower aileron horn had touched the ground first, bending inwards from the slight sideslip. The right-hand wheels touched next, rolling for about 35 yards before being sheared off. The left gear then failed, and the airplane went up on its nose to a 45° angle, smashing the right-hand boom. The Owl then bounced onto the forward portion of the left boom, twisting the engine completely off. Throughout the crunching and the crumpling, the center

The Owl was so large that it had to be assembled outside, using a series of wooden scaffolds and ladders. Rigging the huge wings must have been a mechanics' nightmare!

nacelle remained virtually unharmed, keeping the crew uninjured if mildly terrified.

The very scientific crash analysis noted that the tail, center nacelle, and upper wing remained intact, a tribute to their structural integrity. Only two deficiencies were pointed out, the first naturally being the weak link of the aileron turnbuckle, and the second the rather flimsy connection of the landing gear to the wingspar.

The crash was a severe blow to LWF, but there was some comfort to be drawn from the fact that the monocoque fuselage had more than proved its strength.

After rebuilding, testing was resumed on October 11,

Test pilot Ernest "Tiny" Harmon was flying the Owl on May 30, 1920, when a control failure caused a landing accident. The rugged structure of the Owl prevented any injuries, and the aircraft was rebuilt and flown again. This was unusual in those cash-short days when a crash usually meant a trip to the boneyard for a new aircraft.

Assembling and rigging the Owl was hazardous duty; a fall from one of the rigging pylons would have easily broken a leg or a back. The job could not be done in a high wind, either.

The author had the privilege of becoming friends with Colonel Phillips Melville, who flew the Owl. Melville, an accomplished artist, had learned to fly Capronis at Foggia and was considered one of the finest "big airplane" men in the Air Service. He recalled the Owl as being pleasant to fly, but underpowered.

The landing gear was wiped out and the gear and engines damaged in the May 30, 1920, crash, but the basic structure of the aircraft was not harmed. Investigation revealed that an aileron turnbuckle had failed, causing a loss of lateral control. Harmon tried using asymmetric power to steer the aircraft, but could not avoid dragging a wing.

1920, with Harmon and Patterson again acting as pilots. The first takeoff was almost as startling as the last landing had been, for the wings rocked violently from side to side "faster than it is possible to rock a pursuit with a stick." After an exhausting 15-minute flight during which both pilots continuously fought the controls, the big green bird was safely landed.

The quick fix was to delete 15 square feet from the just-enlarged aileron balance area. The next flight proved this to be a partial solution, with the rocking gone but the ailerons still exceptionally stiff.

Harmon noted that the plane took off easily with a run of about 175 yards at light weight and 450 yards fully loaded. In-flight characteristics were satisfactory with the exception of the aileron control, which he recommended be completely redesigned. The glide was flat, and it was difficult to get the tail down, with almost all landings being wheeled on. Visibility was considered poor in flight, but good in a glide. The aft position of the cockpit was applauded for its obvious safety during a crash, but Harmon believed it would be very difficult to fly the airplane directly over a target to drop a bomb.

At this point Lieutenant Melville entered the scene, receiving two short instructional flights which were to qualify him as Chief Owl Pilot for the next 2 years.

Pete Melville enjoyed flying the airplane, primarily because it was the biggest thing in the air, thus providing a certain amount of prestige. However, he was well aware that it was underpowered, and wished that a trio of the then up-and-coming Packard engines could have been installed.

Melville probably flew the plane for more distinguished visitors than anyone else, demonstrating it on one occasion for the Congress, and on another treating Major General Mason M. Patrick to some vertical—well 80°—banks.

Another pilot was not so fortunate, dumping the Owl into the Messic Marshes just short of Langley Field on June 3, 1921. Lieutenant Charles Cummings had intended to make a short test hop, and it turned out to be about 200 yards too short. A variety of overheating problems led to engine failure, leaving him with no altitude and few ideas, and resulting in the Owl's third forced landing and second major crash.

The Owl languished at Langley for 4 months before being shipped back to the LWF plant for a final refurbishment. A DH-ish radiator was fitted to the center engine, the landing gear was cleaned up to a four-wheel configuration, and the pilot's cockpit was repositioned forward. A Scarff ring mounting for twin Lewis guns was fitted to the new rear gunner's cockpit.

Colonel Melville points out that the real design deficiency of the airplane was the external bomb stowage. He feels that the fuselage could have been redesigned to accommodate the bombs internally, and at the same time provide a more commodious bombardier's position. True to his first love, Melville feels that an even more significant improvement could have been made if the center engine had been a pusher. Even without these modifications, the plane had an inherent capability that would have been exploited in a wartime situation. The Owl could have done a job—the time simply wasn't right.

A close-up of how the engine broke away cleanly from the monocoque nacelle in the May 30, 1920, crash.

You can almost read the mechanic's mind as he stands there, hands on hip, surveying the damage of the May 30, 1920, crash. He's thinking, "I just hope I don't have to have this thing ready to go for a mission tomorrow morning."

Hoffman's brainchild almost had a final fling, being entered in the 1922 Aerial Mail Trophy Race sponsored by the *Detroit News.* Harmon would have piloted the Owl, but it was scratched. Lieutenant Erik Nelson ran away with the race in his highly polished Martin Transport, while Melville finished second in a slightly modified GMB.

The ultimate indignity for the once proud Owl came as a result of one of those weird little bureaucratic sleights of hand. The press had shown considerable interest in the cost of both the Owl and the Barling Bomber, and as neither had been a notable success, the Air Service was reluctant to call attention to their final disposition. In the case of the Owl, it so happened that a batch of surplus DH-4 hulks were scheduled to be burned. The Owl's serial number, AS 64012, was quietly appended to the list, and amidst a shabby group of anonymous old de Havillands, the lovingly constructed laminated wood fuselage special went up in smoke.

Construction and Performance

The twin booms and central nacelles were constructed in the patented LWF method, a process which would not have been too foreign to modern users of fiberglass, and was similar to that developed by the Lougheed brothers. A basic male mold was constructed, and this was covered first with muslin, and then three layers of superb quality 1/16th-inch thick spruce. On each inner layer of spruce a layer of tape was spiral wound. The inner spruce laminations were spiraled in opposite directions, while the outer layer was run straight fore and aft. The three laminations of spruce and two layers of tape were steeped in hot glue, with the final outer shell being covered with linen, doped on, and heavily enameled. The entire built-up structure was only ¼" thick, very light, perfectly smooth, and immensely strong. Openings were cut where necessary, and the interior was reinforced with formers.

Each of the huge wings was built-up in three panels, using hollow box spars composed of birch sides and spruce top and bottom. The typical Pratt truss of the period employed a double bracing of No. 8 solid piano wire and 3/16-inch hard cable. All external wire fittings were applied directly to the spars and projected through the fabric covering.

After the Owl was rebuilt it looked like this, with a de Havilland DH-4 style radiator on the center engine. I am sad to say that I cannot identify the men lined up for the photo, but look closely at their clothes: you can see that they got their hands dirty working on the airplane.

The Owl was designed for series production, and a great deal of thought had gone into its layout. The ailerons could be interchanged on each side, and the "power egg" was completely self-contained. The Liberty was equipped with Splitdorf ignition, electric starters, and a compression release. A pyrene fire extinguishing system could be directed to any of the engines.

The empennage was unique, consisting of two double-cambered horizontal stabilizers with interconnecting elevators. At the end of each boom there was a fin and rudder assembly, and a third balanced rudder was installed midway between the two. Total rudder area was 78.9 square feet.

Charles Arens, who passed away a few years ago, was a mechanic/engineer with LWF who made many contributions to the design of the Owl. He conceived the very simple and effective engine controls, which consisted of straight lengths of rod contained within a tube. Bends were negotiated by means of a tightly wound spiral spring which was also contained with the tubing. A cable inside the spring provided for the pull effort. These devices were successful on the Owl and had a sufficiently wide application to enable Arens to become a successful industrialist.

The landing gear was originally somewhat complicated, having two wheels side by side directly under the center of the boom, with the other two spaced equally between. Later, a cleaner four-wheel installation was made.

All in all, the Owl was quite an airplane, easy to fly, and with relatively good performance. If its wing design had been even roughly as advanced as the fuselage, it would have been an aerodynamic marvel. But, even with the old fashioned airfoil, unreliable powerplants and miles of drag-inducing struts and wires, the stylish trimotor could have done the jobs for which it was designed. Unfortunately, not one of these requirements—air mail, passenger, or bombing—materialized.

LWF had one more design up its sleeve—the overweight, ugly, and hopelessly inefficient XT-3—a total failure which did not employ the traditional fuselage construction. When that experiment failed, the company quietly expired.

Another photo comparing the Farman and the Owl.

4 "P" FOR PURSUIT

The Army's Biplane Hawks, Part I

Airpower March, 1976

Unlike the giant bombers of the period, the tiny Curtiss biplane fighters were not only good-looking, they were fast and maneuverable. Their great advantage stemmed from the excellent Curtiss D-12 engines that powered them. Designed by Arthur Nutt, the V-1570 engine (as it was designated) would power a score of designs, including those of Curtiss's arch-rival, Boeing. Nutt was a young man in a hurry, having, at the age of 26, moved from apprentice status to chief motor engineer in just six years. He demonstrated his hustle with the D-12, which went from drawing to test bench in just 12 weeks. The slim, needle-nosed engines were initially water-cooled, but soon took advantage of the new glycol coolants, which permitted a smaller radiator to be fitted.

The Curtiss fighters illustrated the benefits to be gained by the air racing, which was essentially a research and development program spurred by national pride. The D-12 powered the Curtiss R-6, which won the 1922 Pulitzer, hitting speeds of over 230 mph. From that point on, D-12–powered fighters, by Curtiss and by Boeing, were in demand.

Need often brings great fighter planes to fruition in pairs, particularly in wartime, when missions are so diverse that no one plane can fill all the needed roles. The Royal Air Force's Sopwith Camel and S.E.5A of 1917–18 were matched in World War II by the Hurricane and Spitfire. These worthies fought another pair, the Messerschmitt Bf 109 and the Focke Wulfe FW-190, and were soon reinforced by the redoubtable Mustang and Thunderbolt combination.

One war later it was North American and Republic again, with the F-86 Saber and F-84 Thunderjet sharing the spotlight in Korea. In a similar manner, the McDonnell Douglas F-4 and Republic F-105 divided the missions in Viet Nam. The F-4 comes about as close to an all purpose fighter as any, but in Nam there were certain specialized operations for which the Thud was far better suited.

Today there is a trend away from the multi-purpose fighter, as evidenced by a whole new crop of warplanes: F-14, F-15, F-16 and F-18, all coming into their own.

But in the peacetimes of the past, when war was so unusual and formal an event that England could afford to adopt the notorious "Ten Year Rule" (see if it looks like a war within the next ten years—if not, don't modernize your forces) it wasn't always possible to buy two different types of fighters in quantity, for there simply wasn't enough

The Curtiss Hawk series of biplanes had a racing heritage reaching all the way back to the 1920 Pulitzer Race. Curtiss, and the U.S. Army and Navy, saw the practical value of racers in testing the direction in which fighter development should go. It was expensive by the standards of the time, but well worth it when there was very little money available for research. These three photographs compare the latest concepts of the time, with the Verville Sperry R-3 at the top, the Curtiss R-6 of 1922 in the middle, and the Curtiss Navy racer of 1923 at the bottom.

funding available. Service planners held competitions, for which hopeful manufacturers would in six months' or a year's time design, develop and produce a prototype for comparative trials. The winner would get the "big" order—as many as one hundred and ten or as few as twenty-five—while the losers might have to be satisfied if the prototype was purchased for test.

Even so, the brass was always mindful of the need to keep more than one source of supply available, and to keep development going on in as many lines as possible. Thus it was that on July 10, 1931, at a time when the Boeing P-12 was the Army Air Corps' darling, no less a person than Lt. Colonel Henry H. Arnold signed a letter to the Chief of the Air Corps, recommending that he and the Secretary of War approve a nine item contract which covered forty six P-6E aircraft at $12,211 each, as well as spares, manuals, photos, etc. for a total of $704,629.33. (Note—it was for 46 P-6Es, not 45 P-22s or 45 P-6Es as has been stated.)

Arnold noted that the Curtiss P-1C was a standard type and the P-6 was a variant only in refinements and in the installation of the Curtiss V-1570C engine. As there had been a price increase—previous P-1s had cost as little as $9,862 and earlier P-6s as little as $9,300—he explained that the new plane incorporated improvements brought out in the experimental XP-20 and XP-22 airplanes which had physically been melded into the new XP-6E.

And so was born an airplane which would live on in the minds of many for the next five decades as the most beautiful pursuit ever built, the Curtiss P-6E "Hawk." The Hawk's legend would be enhanced—one is tempted to say created—by the talon insignia of the 17th Pursuit Squadron. The caparisoned Snow Bird badge drawing raves at air shows and air races, would gladden model makers' hearts forever.

But in a very real sense, and cruel as it is, the P-6E was made a fraud and an impostor by the adulation created by its pretty shape. Far from being the deadly weapon its clean lines suggested, it was freely acknowledged to be second rate before it was purchased, and the contract for which Arnold recommended approval had two major purposes only—to give Curtiss some business and to maintain development of the liquid cooled engine.

Strong words, but true, and backed by the proceedings of a distinguished Board of Officers which met at Wright Field on June 12, 1931, per Personnel Orders No. 137. It was a board of leaders, consisting of Majors Carl Spaatz and

The peak of the Curtiss racing line was reached with the R3C-1 of 1925, in which Lieutenant Cy Bettis won the Pulitzer at 249.975 mph. Note the smoothly streamlined cowling and the neat fairing of the headrest into the rudder. Outstanding-quality workmanship!

Jimmy Doolittle flew the same airplane that Bettis had raced in the Pulitzer to compete in the 1925 Schneider Trophy Race. Fitted with floats it became the R3C-2, and Doolittle won handily, at 232.573 mph. The airplane is now on display at the National Air & Space Museum, and the author had the privilege of escorting Doolittle up to the R3C-2 to examine it for a television production. He climbed right up the ladder and into the airplane as if he had last flown it only yesterday!

Gerald E. Brower, Captains Hugh M. Elmendorf, Frank O'Driscol Hunter and John K. Cannon, and First Lieutenants John S. Griffith and Alfred A. Kessler Jr.—a veritable roll call of future generals' stars and Air Force base dedications.

The Board was quick and to the point, leading off with this statement:

"The members of the Board compared the flying characteristics of the P-22 with the P-20, P-12D and the P-6D (Tur-

bo Type Supercharger). The P-22 appeared slightly faster up to 15,000 feet altitude than the P-12 D, but was less maneuverable at all altitudes. In view of the improved performance of the P-22 airplane, and for economic reasons, the desirability of giving the Curtiss Company business and for the furtherance of the development of the liquid cooled engine in pursuit airplanes, it is recommended that forty-six (46) of the P-22 airplanes as outlined by the Procurement Board, be purchased. It is the opinion of this Board that the relative merits of the P-22 and the P-12E as exemplified by the Boeing Model 218 are as follows: The P-12 is lighter, more maneuverable, and has better vision than the present P-22. The P-22 is somewhat faster. It is believed that the P-12 airplane is more acceptable to the service at this time. It is further recommended that no further procurement of P-22 type airplanes other than above be made."

In the 1920s the upstart Boeing Company in Seattle began competing directly with Curtiss for the U.S. Army fighter business, and Curtiss responded by modifying its own designs to match Boeings. In this photo, the Boeing XPW-9 is at the left, the Curtiss XPW8-B at the right. (X stood for experimental, P for pursuit, and W for water-cooled—as opposed to air-cooled.) The Curtiss was the eighth aircraft in the series looked at by the Army, and the Boeing was the ninth. Curtiss had followed Boeing's lead by adopting a tunnel radiator, and tapered, unequal span wings.

And there it was—not as good as the P-12, but Curtiss needs the business.

Some of the Board's other recommendations turned out to be more important than the decision to buy the P-6E (nee P-22). It addressed itself to some changes in pursuit directives, calling for the development of fuel injection and higher cylinder mean effective pressures. It also recommended that a 360 degree full swiveling, steerable tail wheel be installed in place of a tail skid in the future, and called for the reduction in the size of aircraft serial numbers to be no more than two inches high. Amazingly, the tail-wheel recommendation was hotly contested, and a strongly worded minority report by Gerald Brower called for a simple fixed wheel installation.

The Board's opinion of the P-6E, which was fully vindicated in its subsequent service, was later corroborated by a long series of competitive tests undertaken at Wright Field by pilots detached from Mather and Rockwell Fields. These 20th Pursuit Group pilots agreed that the Boeing P-12Cs and Ds already in service were vastly superior to the Curtiss XP-20 and XP-22 prototypes. (As we'll soon see, these two basically similar airplanes were combined to become the XP-6E.)

The original XPW-8 had a two-bay wing and wing-skin radiators, as developed on the racers. The wing-skin radiators reduced drag but were difficult to maintain and would have been a huge liability in combat—their large area would make a big target for enemy bullets.

The patented Curtiss wing-skin radiators are very apparent here. They were excellent for racers, but difficult to maintain on operational aircraft, where even an ordinary nose-over like this could cause many leaks.

2nd Lieutenant Joseph G. Hopkins flew the XP-20 for thirty minutes and commented:

"This P-1 type airplane powered with a Hornet engine in no way compared favorably with the present P-12C. Visibility is decreased, and (it) seems less maneuverable with "mushy" controls at low air speeds. Vibration was great and gas consumption unusually high. Cockpit arrangement was satisfactory, although not desirable as in P-12 types. No comparison made while in flight with other types. Only work done was takeoff and landings. Maximum climb to 500 feet, simulated combat and acrobatics. This ship did not impress this officer as having a single advantage over the P-12C with the possible exception of surplus power."

2nd Lieutenant Lee Q. Wasser commented:

"X-P-20. This airplane has slight superiority over P-12-D in climb and speed. Is very heavy on control although it seems to outmaneuver P-12-D at 6,000 feet in combat. However, it is not deemed advisable to procure same as standard pursuit type as the Cyclone installation under the limited gas capacity is very impracticable; and the size and performance of this airplane does not warrant its consideration as a pursuit type."

"X-P-22. This airplane very good for one phase of Pursuit work: speed to attack and run. Not considered for high altitude work or not practical for combat. Very heavy on controls compared to Boeing Pursuit though it has an obvious advantage in speed. Very smooth and steady in dive. Believe if two types of Pursuit planes are procured—this type has possibilities for low altitude pursuit to hit and run."

A group of West Point cadets admire a Curtiss PW8-A, which used a thicker airfoil than the prototype. Like the German Albatros fighter of World War I, it carried the radiator in the center section of the upper wing. This subjected the pilot to occasional sprays of hot water, and the operation of the radiator shutters affected trim.

Numerous other comments by other pursuit pilots emphasized the theme that the Curtiss product would be unable to survive in combat with the Boeing.

But enough debunking. Despite the many reservations, the Curtiss P-6E turned out to make sense in a variety of ways. The Air Corps was demonstrably correct in keeping Curtiss in business, for its later airplanes, particularly the P-40, made an invaluable contribution to the Allied cause in World War II, one that would not have been possible if the Curtiss line and interest in liquid cooled engines had been allowed to lapse.

Another excellent reason for buying the Hawk was the very real hazard that some unforeseen problem would crop up in the Boeing fighters—as indeed it did. The P-12Es in particular were beset by a carbon monoxide problem that threatened their grounding, causing an Air Corps wide investigation. A rash of complaints from P-12 pilots of headaches, dizziness, nausea, loss of control and fainting resulted in an experiment which rapidly measured CO levels of pilots suffering these symptoms. Concentrations of the deadly carbon monoxide, a colorless, odorless, highly poisonous gas, of as high as 26% were found, and the fault was traced to exhaust gasses from the number one stack being introduced into the fuselage and cockpit via the machine gun cartridge chute. This problem was solved, but another might not have been, and the P-6E would suddenly have looked very good.

So despite all that might be said that the P-6E was only a mediocre pursuit plane, the fact that a dynamite paint job gave it a place in history shouldn't be held against it.

Comparisons may be odious, but one might logically compare the P-6E/P-12 twosome with the first pair mentioned in this article, the Camel and the S.E.5a. There was a greater performance difference in the latter, of course, but the P-6E and S.E.5a were better gun platforms and less demanding to fly, while the Camel and P-12 were more of a handful for a pilot, but were surpassingly maneuverable. The differences between the P-12 and the P-6E stem not so much from the individual design teams which created them as they do from the basic philosophies of the companies involved. Curtiss was the establishment, a large, perhaps overmanaged company that had made a fortune stretching basic designs far beyond normal life expectancy. Boeing was smaller, hungrier, more flexible, and much more vulnerable, for it did not have Curtiss' enormous capital backing.

The P-12, as a development of the 1928 model 83, was the more modern airplane. The tapered wings which had brought success to the Boeing PW-9 were dispensed with—a move which required courage—the fuselage was

Curtiss unabashedly stole the concept of the tunnel radiator from Boeing, and applied it to a whole series of fighters. Of interest on this PW-8A is the Curtiss-Reed propeller, a one-piece, fixed-pitch metal propeller.

Doolittle stands on the pontoon of a Schneider Cup Racer.

shortened, and most important, the chosen power plant was a Pratt & Whitney R-1340 radial. Boeing accepted the increase in frontal area for the lighter weight and greater reliability. P&W was an affiliated company, and it was also a relief to know that there would be no supply problems with the engine.

This was the way Curtiss liked to make airplanes—a dependable Curtiss airframe, a powerful Curtiss engine, and an efficient Curtiss-Reed propeller. In the 1920s the Curtiss company had begun a policy that would in the long run prove fatal. It always tried to stretch its basic aircraft designs as far as they would go, rather than spending research and development funds on all-new designs. During the Depression years, when price was everything, this proved to be an effective policy, but when the war came, Curtiss lacked the R and D necessary to stay competitive after the P-40.

The P-6E, on the other hand, was one of the last squeezes from the already tightly rolled-up tube of the PW-8 design. The familiar tapered wing, which engineer emeritus George A. Page slyly admits had its "inspiration" in Boeing's PW-9, was identical on the P-6E to all of the previous Hawks. The fuselage, aft of the firewall, was almost interchangeable with the earlier airplanes. This meant that the P-6E was going to be cheap to build, and Curtiss management always had and would maintain a predilection for low manufacturing costs.

Boeing's comparative adaptability was signaled by the change over on the P-12E from a steel tube and fabric fuselage to an all metal semimonocoque type. This was expensive, and letters from Captain Oliver P. Gothlin, Jr., the Air Corps Plant Representative at Boeing, explained late deliveries as a result of the time needed to make the jigs, tools and so on to build the monocoque fuselage. Boeing was forced to not only work overtime, but to actually go to a double shift operation, a condition absolutely unheard of in the depth of the Depression.

An example of the Curtiss skill in stretching basic designs was its line of Falcon attack planes. This Curtiss A-3 of the 90th Attack Squadron, 3rd Attack Group, is shown at Fort Crockett, Texas. The A-3 had all the structural characteristics of the Hawk line, it was just scaled up. Interestingly enough, Boeing did not compete with Curtiss in this area.

The P-12E experience, however, would pay off in the later P-26 monoplane, while the P-6E's cheap but traditional structure could contribute very little to the Curtiss' first monoplane fighter, the XP-31, which needed all the help it could get. (See *Airpower,* March, 1974)

How the Hawks Began

The Boeing/Curtiss rivalry began almost immediately after World War I, when Boeing astonished the East by underbidding others on a contract to build Thomas Morse MB-3A pursuits. Curtiss, surprised at having lost out when it was known to have the best manufacturing facilities of the time, turned its hand to racers, where it had a tremendous advantage in both airframes and engines. Chief Engineer W. I. Gilmore was available to keep airframes strong, light and clean, and the Hispano Suiza engine had provided inspiration for the Curtiss-Kirkham K-12 engine, which in turn would serve as the basis for a whole series of liquid cooled V-12 power plants.

The first of all of the Curtiss racers was the Model 18-T airplane, called the "Wasp", a heavy fuselaged, stalky winged two seater that nonetheless was one of the fastest airplanes around in the early 1920s. The portly three-winger set both speed and altitude records, and these are probably still valid for triplanes. The Wasp was intended as a fighter type, however, and raced only because that happened to be the best way to use it at the time.

The first specialized Curtiss racer was the very sleek "Texas Wildcat" which was entered with great optimism in the 1920 James Gordon Bennett Cup Race in France. Sporting a clean wooden monocoque fuselage, sliding canopy and a beautifully faired Curtiss C-12 engine, the Wildcat proved to be a leap beyond the state of the art into a bucket of worms. Too wild to fly from the unimproved French airfields, the Wildcat was rolled into a ball and oblivion by Curtiss test pilot Roland Rohlfs. (Its sister ship, the Cactus Kitten, had a more auspicious career.)

Curtiss quickly reverted to an exquisite orthodoxy, producing what must be considered the most successful and beautiful series of racers in history, not excluding even the famous lines of Supermarine or Macchi Castoldi seaplanes. From 1921 through 1926 the trim biplanes were the planes to beat in the Pulitzer and Schneider races. A short table, below, shows not only their growth in performance, but also how completely they dominated two of the most important racing events in the world.

Thus in five years, the top speed of the little racers had increased 72.2 mph, from 176.7 to 248.9. Horsepower had been increased from the R-1's 405 to the R3C-1's 619, but the speed gain accrued primarily from the refinement of design, which permitted higher speeds

Year	Model	Race	Finish Position	Pilot	Speed
1921	CR-1	Pulitzer	First	Acosta	176.7 mph
1922	R-6	Pulitzer	First	Maughan	205.8 mph
	R-6	Pulitzer	Second	Maitland	198.8 mph
	CR-2	Pulitzer	Third	Brow	193.2 mph
	CR-1	Pulitzer	Fourth	Williams	188.0 mph
1923	R2C-1	Pulitzer	First	Williams	243.6 mph
	R2C-1	Pulitzer	Second	Brow	241.8 mph
	CR-3	Schneider	First	Rittenhouse	177.4 mph
	CR-3	Schneider	Second	Irvine	173.5 mph
1924	R-6	Pulitzer	Second	Brow	214.7 mph
1925	R3C-1	Pulitzer	First	Bettis	248.9 mph
	R3C-1	Pulitzer	Second	Williams	241.7 mph
	R3C-2	Schneider	First	Doolittle	232.5 mph
1926	R3C-2	Schneider	Second	Schilt	231.3 mph

The Falcon, with its twin guns mounted on a classic Scarff ring, looking for all the world like a World War I observation plane. Note the ring sight for the pilot.

without any loss of the pleasant handling characteristics. The stage had been set for Curtiss' golden fighter formula, and the first expression of this was the XPW-8, which incorporated the best features of the racers into a husky pursuit airframe.

The XPW-8 featured the new—for Curtiss—welded steel tube fuselage, and the fragile wing radiators which contributed so much to the racers' speed and even more to maintenance officers' migraines.

Twenty-five PW-8s helped Curtiss into the fighter business, setting up one of the two main development streams in U.S. pursuit aviation. The other was of course Boeing, who would build 113 of its waspish PW-9 counterparts to the PW-8.

The third prototype of the new series became the XPW-8B when the XPW-8A was modified with a PW-9-like tapered wing and tunnel radiator. This airplane matched the Boeing fighter in performance as well as appearance, and it was the actual father of the Hawk line. Later, the PW (Pursuit/Watercooled) designation was dropped and the first 110 of the soon to be famous Hawks became known as the P-1.

A total of 145 P-1 Hawks were procured from 1925 to 1929; of these some 52 had been ordered as AT (Advanced Trainer) -4 and AT-5 in a budget juggling exercise which probably fooled no one but the press and the public.

The series was continually improved, although "improved" usually translated as increases in weight and complexity. Refinements included more equipment, better shocks, brakes, and so on, and top speed dropped from the 163 of the first P-1 down to 155 in the P-1F—a thoroughly normal trend.

The P-1 served as a test vehicle for five different

The first Hawk line ran from the P-1 to the P-1F. The designations were changed for variations in the design, e.g., new engine, the installation of a supercharger, and so on. They were, for all practical purposes, one aircraft type, as exemplified by this P-1 of the 17th Pursuit Squadron, 1st Pursuit Group.

The Curtiss XP-3A had a radial engine and a beautiful cowling. Originally a P-1, it became the XP-3, then XP-3A, and finally XP-21. Five P-3s were ordered, a small production quantity, but enough for Curtiss to meet a few paydays. The man holding the airplane on his shoulder seems quite nonchalant.

The Curtiss P-5 differed from the P-1 in that it had a cockpit heater, oxygen, longer wheel struts, and a larger propeller—all required because the Curtiss V-1150 engines were fitted with turbo-superchargers for high-altitude performance. The P-5 could achieve 173 mph at 25,000 feet. Only five were procured, primarily because turbo-superchargers did not yet have the metals necessary for reliable performance.

Some of the most attractive of the Curtiss biplanes were experimental aircraft, like this XP-10. There was a fad for gull-wing aircraft during this period, primarily because it promised good visibility. The XP-10 reverted to the use of wing-skin radiators, which were low-drag, but highly vulnerable to damage.

engines, superchargers, and cowlings and a variety of designations were applied—XP-2, P-2, XP-3, P-3A, XP-5, P-5, etc. (Relating the exact details of this evolution is beyond the scope of this article; but for those interested there is no better source than Peter M. Bowers' Profile No. 45, the Curtiss Army Hawks.)

In round numbers, Curtiss had through the P-5 sold some 160 Hawks to the U.S. Army, and certainly had not neglected either the Navy or the foreign market, whose combined total of sales over the years of all Hawk varieties would exceed 450.

Despite the myriad face lifts, the basic design was becoming tired and Curtiss tried to inject new life into it with new engines, better cooling and new designations.

Always conscious of their racing heritage, the U.S. Army decided to enter some special Hawks fitted with the new Curtiss V-1570 engine in the 1927 National Air Races.

Although the planes were designated XP-6 and XP-6A, the two racers were as different as Hawks could be. The XP-6 had earlier been both a P-1 and a P-2 before the new 600 horsepower V-12 Conqueror engine was installed. The XP-6A combined the radiator skinned wing panels of a PW-8 with a P-1A fuselage into which a Conqueror engine had been placed.

Hybrid though it was, the XP-6A won the Nationals at slightly over 201 mph. Its cousinship, the XP-6 was second at 189 mph, and the 12 mph difference was due almost entirely to the drag of the XP-6's radiator, which had to cool the 15 gallons of water in the standard radiator of the day; yet only a few insiders at Wright Field knew what important development in cooling loomed just over the horizon.

Performance was not the only thing impaired by the radiator: looks suffered as well. The XP-6 and production P-6s were fat and bulky appearing with the old P-1 fuselage faired to meld with the bigger V-1570 engine; eighteen P-6s were ordered, and the usual variations on a theme resulted in modifications which received A through D designations.

Certainly the most significant development of this series was the introduction of Prestone (ethylene glycol) as coolant instead of water. Prestone had both a higher boiling and a lower freezing point, and was a far more efficient heat conductor than plain water. Radiator capacities could thus be reduced by one third, with a corresponding reduction in frontal area, and elimination of the levers and shutters which had bedeviled water cooled engines for so long.

While various earlier P-6s were further tested with superchargers, three bladed propellers and so on, Curtiss, at last, proposed some rather fundamental changes in two aircraft, the YP-20 and XP-22.

The YP-20 had started life as a P-11, which was to have been a P-6 modified to take the unsuccessful Curtiss H-1640 engine. As it happened, the airplane was equipped with the Wright R-1820 Cyclone of 575 horsepower. This was not a winning combination, as Lt. Hopkins' earlier

The Curtiss YP-20 was actually a Curtiss P-11, but rather than using the usual Curtiss H-1640 engine, it was equipped with a Wright R-1820. Later it was converted back to a standard P-6 configuration by the installation of a Curtiss Conqueror engine. Still, with the cowling and the slick wheel pants, this is a good-looking airplane.

In a similar way, this Curtiss P-22 was actually a P-6A with a Prestone coolant radiator mounted neatly between the landing gear legs. It had a top speed of 202 mph, the fastest yet for an Army fighter, when it appeared in May, 1931.

statement indicates, and the YP-20 was not considered for production.

The XP-22 was the third P-6A revised with a very clean but complicated single strut hydraulic shock undercarriage, a closely cowled coffin-like nose, and altered tail surfaces. It offered more promise than the YP-20, but it was not quite the right mixture of components.

Therefore, the next step was for Curtiss to graft the new features of the XP-22 to the YP-20, and the result—at last—was the XP-6E.

There were other changes in designation in the process (YIP-22, e.g.), but these are of interest only to the purist, and the main thing is that the new airplane was considered worthwhile as a means to keep Curtiss in business.

The first production—built from the ground up—P-6E 32-233, was tested at Wright Field and gave immediate notice that it was a great cross country and impress-

The very last aircraft on the Curtiss P-6E contract was modified with a finely pointed nose, a turbo-supercharger, and a three-bladed propeller. It represented both the peak of Army Hawk development and the second-fastest of the line, for it was capable of 223 mph. It was then retrofitted with a geared Curtiss engine that did not have a turbo-supercharger and became the YP-23 shown here. Many believe it to be the most attractive of all the Hawks.

The Curtiss XP-6A is shown here on September 9, 1927 (with its tail neatly balanced on a bale of hay!). This was essentially a P-1 fitted with XPW-8A wings. The wing-skin radiators once again delivered low drag and high speed (193 mph) but they were not practical—and Curtiss knew it by now.

The pilot's head in the cockpit gives a good idea of the relative size of the XP-6A. This was a sleek aircraft, more a racer than a fighter.

your-girl machine. It did not give the impression that it had revolutionized the world of fighters.

The next forty-four production machines were assigned to the famous 1st Pursuit Group at Selfridge Field, Michigan, an assignment that was to ensure its immortality.

The 17th Pursuit Squadron was commanded by a granite visaged, famous Hawk pilot, Captain Ross G. Hoyt. Hoyt, now a retired Brigadier General, recalls the P-6E with a mixture of affection and exasperation, for the pleasure derived from flying the airplane and showing off its fancy snow bird colors at air shows and races was mitigated by the extensive maintenance problems caused by the new Prestone cooled V-1570 engines. The Conquerors would often quit in a dive, or when placed in a negative G flight mode, and Curtiss was requested to solve the problem, fast. The troubles were overcome, but the hassle had not enhanced the P-6E in the eyes of its pilots. Worse, the airplane's operational career was to be so short that it had scarcely become fit for duty before it was being phased out.

Hoyt's friend, Harry A. Johnson, Major General, USAF (Retired) was commander of the 94th during part of its time with the P-6E, and he is less charitable in his comments. The 94th had a bad introduction to the airplane, losing seven in the first six months of operation. Six were lost in three separate mid-air collisions; by a major miracle none of the pilots were killed.

However much the P-6E was ultimately liked as an airplane, it was discounted as a fighter, for its pilots were continually waxed by anybody in roughly contemporary equipment. It was no match for the Boeing P-12s, and the

Like the P-1 series, the P-6 series saw a number of modifications. This XP-6D received a side-mounted turbo-supercharger. This was in the days before Dzus fasteners, and horseshoe style clips were used to hold the cowling in place. *John Underwood*

A side view of the XP-23 shows the turbo-supercharger installation that lifted its speed to 223 mph. In this configuration, the XP-23 rivals the British Hawker Fury for "best-looking biplane" honors.

Navy liked nothing better than to jump it with one of their new Grummans.

The 33rd Pursuit Squadron of the 8th Pursuit Group at Langley operated the airplane for the longest time, from 1932 to 1935. By then its numbers had diminished so much that it was really not useful in a tactical unit, and it was parcelled out to other bases where it served primarily to keep the hand in of fighter pilots serving in staff assignments.

5 "P" FOR PURSUIT

The Army's Biplane Hawks, Part II

Wings April, 1976

As previously noted, in the 1920s the Curtiss biplane fighters were both inspired by and promoted by a series of racers that dominated the Pulitzer Trophy race and converted the Schneider Trophy race from a contest among manufacturers to a contest among nations. Both Italy and Great Britain responded to the performance of the Curtiss racers with inspired designs and magnificent engines, and in the process raised the cost of racing in the Schneider to levels prohibitive even for national governments to fund.

Boeing and Curtiss were locked in a bitter competition throughout the next decade, each seeking to provide the U.S. Army Air Corps with the standard fighter. The competition took an interesting course: Curtiss tended to stay with its basic formula, an aircraft that was adapted to serve as a trainer, and, slightly scaled up, as a two-seat observation or attack aircraft. Boeing was much more adventuresome and moved sooner to more modern designs featuring air-cooled engines and metal construction.

Further information on the genesis of Curtiss fighters can be found in the books and articles of Peter Bowers and in the late Tom Foxworth's superb The Speed Seekers *(Doubleday, 1981).*

The XP-6F was fitted with a turbo-supercharger and a canopy, and it became the fastest of the line, with a top speed of 225 mph at 18,000 feet. Unfortunately, above that altitude the engine overheated, so its true performance potential was never reached.

Despite the lack-luster career in operational units, the P-6E served as a test bed for several experimental modifications. The interest was centered purely on the modification, and not the airframe, for by 1932, no more P-6s—or for that matter, any other biplane—would enter production as an Army fighter.

The Curtiss Hawks were hardy, and often operated with skis. Maintenance under such conditions was miserable, however, and the operations very rarely lasted for a sustained period.

The top of the Army Hawk biplane line, the Curtiss P-6E, is shown here next to its arch rival, the Boeing P-12. The P-6E, while wildly popular with the public because of its striking paint scheme and general good looks, was a troubled aircraft with a high accident rate.

This is the classic P-6E color scheme, as seen in countless photographs of the period. This example was built up by Purdue University and now may be seen in the Air Force Museum at Wright-Patterson Air Force Base in Dayton, Ohio.

The P-6F was fitted with a V-1570 F engine which had a turbosupercharger incorporated on the right side. The installation was quite neat, not adding much drag, but it was heavy, the XP-6F weighing almost 400 pounds more than a standard P-6E. A small part of this was due to the sliding canopy which improved the looks of the airplane—not an easy task, for it was already almost too handsome. When the turbo functioned properly, the XP-6F could reach a sensational 225 mph at 15,000 feet. Below that altitude however, the additional weight kept the performance inferior to that of the P-6E.

The last of the P-6 line was the XP-6H, which in the involuted style of the series, was actually the first production P-6E, retrofitted with a new gun installation. Two .30 caliber machine guns were mounted in the upper wings, and two in the lower wings. It was a remarkably attractive installation, although what it gained in simplicity by deleting the requirement for a synchronizer, it lost in the need for an elaborate gun-charging system.

The new gun placement was a structural mistake, for the tired old wooden wings were already overburdened. The gross weight of the P-6E was almost six hundred pounds more than that of the P-1; not too bad in itself, but if you pulled 4 Gs in a pull-out, that 600 pounds grew to 2,400, and things would begin to give, with severest strains being imposed on the upper wing attachment fittings. On February 13, 1934, P-6E No. 32-236 lost its wings in a power dive from 9,000 to 5,000 feet, and other incidents resulted in a temporary grounding order until new fittings could be installed.

Like any aircraft, the P-6E's weight continued to creep up as additional equipment—communication gear, oxygen bottles, etc.—were added. The form-fitting belly tank added problems of its own, for not only did the auxiliary fuel up the weight, but it also had an adverse effect on the center of gravity, moving it so far aft that spin recovery became very difficult. In October, 1937, Wright Field recommended that all possible extra equipment be removed, or that the P-6E be restricted only to cross country flying with the auxiliary tank installed. No maneuvers which might result in a spin were authorized, and if an inadvertent spin occurred,

Curtiss also built big bombers like this XNBS-4. Big, angular, with lots of drag, it had a top speed of 100 mph and was not much of an improvement over the early Martin bombers.

With its biplane wing, biplane tail, and fixed gear, this later Curtiss B-2 was not exactly as stealthy a bomber as the Northrop Grumman B-2 would be. Designed by George Page and first flown in September, 1927, the B-2 was the best bomber of the era. It was so expensive, however, that only 12 production versions were purchased at a total price of just over $1 million.

This Condor is from the 11th Bomb Squadron at March Field, California.

The U.S. Navy also operated Curtiss Hawks. This is an F6C-3 on floats. The F6C-3 was the last Navy fighter to use a liquid-cooled engine, which was more troublesome to maintain onboard an aircraft carrier. *Peter M. Bowers*

pilots were cautioned to recover quickly and pull out gradually.

The directive was modified in December, 1937, in response to protests from the field that it would be impossible to fulfill mission requirements with the aircraft so restricted. Wright Field reluctantly restored P-6Es, without the auxiliary tank, to unrestricted status, but cautioned that it might be difficult, if not impossible, to recover from a spin.

In January, 1937, there were still 18 P-6Es still in service, 14 of them at the Air Corps Tactical Center at Maxwell Field, and all due for overhaul. The Commander at Maxwell recommended that in view of the inadequate performance, undesirable flight characteristics, excessive maintenance, fatigue failures and general obsolescence, no P-6Es should be reconditioned. It was the end of the road.

During June and July, 1939, most of the 18 P-6Es were transferred to the National Youth Administration and to civilian aviation schools for ground instruction purposes. The last P6-E on Air Corps inventory, number 32-261, went to the NYA at Drew Field at Tampa, Florida, with some 1,858 hours on the airframe; it had had an unprepossessing career, serving first at Selfridge, then Langley for four years, then shorter tours at Barksdale, Maxwell and Fairfield Air Depot. On September 14, 1939 it was sent to Drew Field where, presumably, it served in silence while mechanics learned aircraft maintenance.

In 1956, long after everyone had supposed that there were no more P-6Es extant, S.D. Johnson and E.W. Slade, of Marietta, Georgia discovered major portions of the aircraft. They had the good sense to store it prior to selling it to E.S. Perkins of Anniston, Alabama, who, incidentally, also gave the Air Force Museum its P-36. The sale was conditional on Perkins donating the airplane to the Air Force Museum, which he, a long time booster of the Museum, was happy to do.

It was accepted by the Air Force on June 29, 1960, and was sent to the Department of Aviation Technology, Purdue University, where two and one half years of intensive effort resulted in the thing of beauty on display today in Dayton. It was delivered to the Air Force Museum in July, 1963, resplendent in the markings of Captain Hoyt's famous 32-240.

Boeing and Curtiss competed for Navy contracts just as they did for Army contracts. This F6C-4 was powered by the reliable Pratt & Whitney R-1340 (the same engine used in the T-6 trainer) and had a top speed of 153 mph. *Peter M. Bowers*

Construction Details

The standard Hawk wing which had served so many airplanes, air forces, nations and Curtiss so well, was graceful to look at, easy to build, and absolutely conventional. The entire structure was wooden, with built up box spars and latticed ribs. The leading edge was stiffened by a thin dural sheet extending back to the front spar, and the covering was, of course, fabric.

The all metal ailerons, inset into the upper wings only, were operated by a push rod running from an arm on the control stick shaft to a bell crank in the lower wing panel.

The Navy called the F11C-2 "The Goshawk." It was similar to the Army P-6E, except for the installation of a radial engine. Performance features included a 202 mph top speed, fast for a Navy fighter of the day. The Top Hat insignia was famous. *Peter M. Bowers*

The Navy always managed to make their aircraft more colorful and snazzier looking than their Army counterparts. They also did their bit toward confusing the nomenclature. This was originally a Curtiss F11C-2; it was re-designated BFC-2 when the plane's dive-bombing ability became evident. A Curtiss of this type so impressed Ernst Udet that he persuaded the Luftwaffe to look into dive-bombing as a tactic. *Peter M. Bowers*

The fuselage was made up of chrome-molybdenum steel tubing, with welded joints, and built in three sections. These were riveted together just aft of the pilot's cockpit and again aft of the tail wheel. A detachable engine mount secured the power plant to the fuselage; four taper pins and one bolt providing easy removal.

This Curtiss F7C-1 was designed by Rex Beisel, the same man who designed the famous Chance Vought F4U Corsair. The F7C-1 design was started in 1926, the F4U design only a dozen years later, but what a world of difference in the aircraft! *Peter M. Bowers*

The tubular structure gave some problems, however, and as late as 1937 aircraft were being flown on one time flights—*No Acrobatics*—to depots, to have complete inspections for cracks in all tubular structures, welded joints and the wing and empennage attachment fittings. Moreover, new replacement fittings for the struts were issued to attempt to keep the airplane safe during its short remaining active life span.

The empennage was all metal, fabric covered and braced, as were the wings, by stainless steel streamlined wires. The stabilizer was adjustable from the cockpit from 2½ degrees nose up, through 2 degrees nose down.

Curiously, the undercarriage represented the most advanced and sophisticated element of the design. The clean single strut main gear was about the best you could do in terms of drag reduction, barring gear retraction. Landing shocks were cushioned by the 8:50 × 10 inch Goodrich tires and the rather complicated oleo struts.

The oleo struts had undergone an intensive testing program at Wright Field, and for a long time it appeared as if they simply were not going to pass the rigorous drop tests. It turned out that the oil level and length of stroke of the oleos were critically important. If the level was too low, the metering pin wouldn't work, resulting in the loss of shock absorption. If it was too high, the volume of air above the chamber was reduced too much—resulting in a loss of shock absorption.

The tests forecast later maintenance problems in the field, for the shocks were a bear to work on, and the aircraft had to be raised so that there was no weight on the gear, and then carefully serviced.

The tail wheel, which had been so hotly contested early in the P-6E's career, was the most modern yet built. Operated via the rudder pedals, the tail wheel could be steered through a total of 60 degrees (30 left and right)

Designed originally as just a smaller fighter, for reasons of economy the Curtiss F9C Sparrowhawk was soon adapted for use on aerial aircraft carriers, the dirigibles *Akron* and *Macon*. It was an excellent concept, for it expanded the scouting range of the dirigibles. Unfortunately, fate was cruel, and both the *Akron* and the *Macon* were lost, the latter carrying all but one of the F9C-2s with it. The sole survivor was restored at the National Air & Space Museum's Garber Facility. *Peter M. Bowers*

and a release mechanism permitted a full 360 degree swivel.

The Curtiss V-1570-23 "Conqueror" provided some 600 horsepower; it was enclosed in a tight fitting metal cowl that added as much to the airplane's look as the "coffin nose" hood did to the contemporary Cord 812 automobile. The small eight gallon capacity radiator kept the nose slim and trim, but the engine had reached the end of its development line in a manner entirely consistent with the airframe. Both airframe and engine had been winners when they were young; both served in a long series of developments, and both had been overtaken by progress.

When the portly Grumman fighters, with their retractable landing gear, began winning contracts, Curtiss reacted as it always did: stretch an old airframe by adding on a new piece of equipment—in this case, retractable landing gear. The XF11C-3 was handsome enough, and became the XBF2C-1 when the dive-bombing role was added. Unfortunately, Curtiss also modernized the structure, making the wings of metal rather than spruce, and the airplane had severe vibration problems that forced its withdrawal from service. *Peter M. Bowers*

Curtiss had more luck selling the F11C abroad as the Hawk III; 137 were sold. This example may be seen in the Royal Thai Air Force Museum in Bangkok, along with some other rare aircraft.

The P-6E could be armed with either two .30 caliber machine guns, or one .30 and one .50 caliber, and a G-1 gun camera could be installed. Standard A-3 bomb racks could be installed when the auxiliary fuel tank was not in place. Given the condition of the P-6E's wing fittings, it was not exactly suited for dive bombing.

Performance

The P-6E was fast for its time, with an official 193 mph being logged on an Army flight test of May 19, 1932. Speed fell off with altitude, naturally, and at 20,000 feet, the top was 167 mph. An index to the plane's relative efficiency was the 132 mph spread between the sea level top speed and the stall speed of 61 mph. Initial rate of climb was a sprightly 2,460 feet per minute; this dropped to 100 fpm at the service ceiling of 23,900. Absolute ceiling at the flight test weight of 3,436 pounds was 24,900. At 10,000 feet, the Hawk could cruise for almost three hours at 166 mph, on the full 100 gallons provided by the main and auxiliary tanks.

Epilogue

The Curtiss P-6E Hawk was an artistic triumph even if it lacked some of the qualities which would have made it a champion fighter aircraft. Perhaps the most important point is that very few people besides the fighter pilots concerned knew this, and the P-6E was able to fulfill an important role in glamorizing air power at a time when the Army Air Corps needed all the help it could get. And that may have been quite enough in itself.

A stock-finish Curtiss P-6E in flight.

6 HUFF-DALAND

A Little-Known Aviation Pioneer, Part I

Wings December, 1977

The latter part of the 20th century saw a number of acquisitions and mergers in the aviation field. These included Lockheed's acquisition of General Dynamics and its subsequent merger with Martin Marietta to become Lockheed Martin. In addition, Northrop and Grumman joined forces, and Boeing acquired both McDonnell Douglas and North American Rockwell. Many of us mourn the passing of the great names, but it is simply a fact of life in the industry, and it has been going on for many years.

Huff-Daland, for example, was reorganized as Keystone in 1927. Keystone was taken over by Curtiss Wright in 1931. Travel Air, formed by Walter Beech, Clyde Cessna, and Lloyd Stearman in 1925, had to be taken over by Curtiss Wright in 1930 because of the Depression. The same process went on all over the world.

Despite these changes, the aviation industry had a hidden continuity in the form of the engineers who moved from one company to the next, taking their ideas with them. One stellar example was James McDonnell, who was one of Huff-Daland's engineers when the company was starting up. He worked with many other companies, including Ford and Martin, before forming his own firm in 1939. "Mr. Mac," as he was affectionately known, passed away before his own firm was absorbed by Boeing, but he would have understood the situation.

The full story of Huff-Daland has never been told, not only because its aircraft were usually unattractive, or because none of them set any earth shattering records, but primarily because the company's name was changed to Keystone just as it reached the zenith of its short lived influence.

Huff-Daland actually made a number of very important contributions to aviation, as we shall see. The company is also noteworthy because it provides a capsule view of a little known segment of American aviation history. It emerged at a time when, just after the first World War, numerous bands of gutsy young men started aircraft companies in the face of huge war surplus stocks, lack of government orders, and a dearth of genuine civil requirement for planes. Most of these firms—Elias, Eberhardt, Cox Kelmin, Orenco, to name just a few—endured only briefly and then disappeared.

Huff-Daland survived, and after an initial series of mistakes, went to McCook Field to learn how to build military airplanes and then merchandise what it had learned in civil, military and foreign markets. The original Huff-Daland designs, once they had passed through the purifying fires of McCook Field evaluation, served as the basis for an important series of planes which evolved into the Keystone bombers that were for many years almost the entire U.S. bombing force. In addition, the progressive management of Huff-Daland experimented with crop dusting, and in the process of creating the outstanding Huff-Daland crop dusters, established the agricultural flying industry. Finally, the management of the crop dusting firm, Huff-Daland Dusters, subsequently founded Delta Air Lines, which can trace its ancestry directly back to the little plant in Ogdensburg, New York, where it all started.

Thomas Henri Huff was 37 years old in 1920, when he founded the company which bore his name. A graduate of the Massachusetts Institute of Technology, and an instructor of aeronautical engineering there, Huff had a meteoric early career that included responsible management positions in a number of aircraft companies. He was an engineer for Sturtevant, whose curiously angular biplanes had a brief vogue with both the U.S. Signal Corps and Navy before the firm turned to subcontracting. He was Chief Engineer at the Standard Aircraft Corporation when the Standard SJ was a true competitor of the Curtiss Jenny. He left Standard to become a designer for the Naval Aircraft Factory, and thus had the benefit of experience both with McCook Field and its naval near-equivalent. Huff was a brilliant man . . . though apparently somewhat difficult to deal with . . . after he left the firm he founded in 1927, he went on to work for Fokker and Martin before becoming a consulting engineer.

His partner, Elliot Daland, was four years younger but similarly well educated, with post-graduate work at both Harvard and M.I.T. He worked under Huff at Standard, and had a brief stint with Curtiss in 1920. In his later years, his interest turned to vertical lift aircraft, and he worked with Burke Wilford of the Pennsylvania Syndicate, and

After trying some really hopeless designs, Huff-Daland began to listen to suggestions from McCook Field and presented the TA-2. The inspiration provided by the German Fokker D VII is evident; the D VII, even in 1922, was regarded as the standard in fighter construction.

then with helicopter pioneer, Piasecki. A cheerful man, undaunted by an almost total lack of vision which required him to wear glasses resembling jeweler's lenses, Daland remained active in aviation throughout his life.

In 1920, the two men apparently started business as the "Ogdensburg Aeroway Corporation", according to contemporary newspaper accounts. Delaware incorporation papers permitted a change of name to Huff, Daland & Company, and they selected a plant site at Ogdensburg, N.Y., in the northern corner of the state, across the St. Lawrence River from Canada. Ogdensburg had a large pool of skilled labor, and the initial 35 man work force consisted almost entirely of craftsmen who had learned their trade building boats.

Huff and Daland were very ambitious, and laid down an initial series of four aircraft, characterized by unusual structural techniques and light hearted, almost "goofy" names. The first of these aircraft proposed by the firm in 1920 was the HD-1 "Early Bird" a twin engine aircraft designed for "joy riding or short hauls." A casual inspection of this "bird" would indicate that most of the hauls would have been short, indeed, and that there would have been very little joy in the riding. Oddly enough, the plane not only performed well, but conducted some little known tests in aerial pick-up methods.

The HD-1 was planned in three models—the HD-1 with 60 horsepower Lawrance engines, the HD-1A with 80 hp Le Rhones, and the HD-1B with 100 horsepower Anzanis. After initial flight tests, the HD-1A was used to test the aerial pickup device created by Godfrey L. Cabot.

Cabot conceived of ferrying multi-engine aircraft overseas by having them pick up fuel from sea stations which were similar in concept to the air mail pick-ups used with such success by All American Aviation in the 1930s. Captain Claude Devitalis flew the first series of tests in April, 1921, but the Le Rhones were troublesome, and a forced landing in rough country forced a major rebuild. In the second version, the Anzanis were fitted, and pick-ups were made in July, 1921 from a device set on a scow in the Anacostia River at Washington D.C.

Lt. Harold R. Harris of McCook Field flew this second series of tests, thus initiating a long relationship with Huff, Daland and Company. The device still needed improvement, and in September 1921, a third series was flown, using the HD-4 "Bridget", of which more later. Lt. E.H. Barksdale was the pilot.

The HD-1 incorporated a number of curious engineering characteristics. Each wing had a different airfoil; the upper had a modified R.A.F. 4 propeller section, while the lower had a Glenn Martin M.2 curve. It's hard to believe that there were aerodynamic considerations worth the manufacturing difficulties involved in building the plane in this manner.

The HD-1 carried five people, including the pilot, at a reputed 90 mph, and with an all-up weight of 2,860 pounds. Some of this weight was almost certainly unnecessary, for the fuselage was built up of four very heavy longerons, connected to a stout three ply skin. One of the longerons on each side of the fortress-like fuselage ran above the cockpit area to form part of what must be called a cabane, for want of a better term.

During this very early 1920–22 period, the most distinctive aspect of Huff-Daland aircraft was the use of the much advertised "flying struts" in lieu of flying or landing wires. These were girder-like sections which ran inboard from the lower fuselage longeron to the upper outer N struts. These contributed not only to the HD-1 "Early Bird's" lack of aesthetic appeal, but also to its fragile, willowy appearance that was reflected by its undulating structural movements in flight.

A later design, the AT-1, was a dead-ringer for the Fokker D VII and shows how well the Huff-Daland firm took advice from Harold R. Harris, a McCook Field test pilot. Ten AT-1s were purchased, an order that kept Huff-Daland in business.

The Huff-Daland Petrel was a civil derivative of the AT-1 that had been tested and sold to the Air Service. It was the first American aircraft to receive a Canadian air worthiness certificate. The Petrel did well under all weather conditions and operated off floats and skis; occasionally it was even used with dog teams, as shown here.

The second aircraft, built at about the same time as the HD-1, was the HD-4 "Bridget", a trainer with tandem seating. It appears to be a single engine version of the Early Bird, and employed some advanced features. Leak proof tanks were mounted above the center wing section, and the engine mount was hinged for easy servicing. On its third flight, the occasion of the Cabot pick-up device trials, the ugly "flying struts" were replaced by conventional wire bracing in an attempt to stiffen the structure.

The third aircraft was the HD-7 "Dizzy Dog", a three seat sport flying boat. I have found no hard evidence that this aircraft was ever completed. The fourth of the initial series was the HD-8 "Plover", intended for advanced training, and perhaps the best of the first attempts.

It is remarkable that a new firm could launch so many projects at once, and it is a tribute to the energy and intelligence of both Huff and Daland. There is much more material still to be gathered on these two men and their company. People who knew the firm say it was unique for its time in combining an intellectual elitism at the top with a warm sense of camaraderie throughout the plant. There are stories about the weekly Friday night parties which indicate that life was not all flying struts and contracts.

One of the most important persons in the company was Charles Talbot Porter, who began as treasurer and, after 1922, became Chief Engineer. Porter, a hearty, likeable man, is almost certainly responsible for breaking away from the original Huff-Daland designs, and turning to McCook Field for guidance. Of the many services furnished to American aviation by the men of McCook Field (see *Airpower* July, 1975 & *Wings* Aug. 1975) none is more important than the *Handbook of Instruction to Aircraft Designers,* which provided prospective contractors with information on required load capabilities, material specifications, design criteria, equipment specifications, test standards, and so on. Huff-Daland came to McCook knowing almost nothing; it left a major competitor in the aviation industry.

McCook Field ordered three planes from Huff-Daland as TA-2s, two for flight test and one for static test. These were essentially the HD-4 Bridget designed for the 140 horsepower Lawrance radial rather than the 100 horsepower Anzani. As the Lawrance was not available, a 140 horsepower A.B.C. Wasp was installed instead.

The first TA-2 received McCook Field P number 162, and Lieutenant Harris conducted the flight tests, making the first on March 24, 1921. He liked the way the TA-2 taxied, took-off and landed, but felt that lateral control was poor. The A.B.C. engine vibrated as it always did, but Harris commented that "the most noticeable feature of this aircraft is the extreme flexibility of all its parts. This is very undesirable on account of the effect on the pilot while inspecting previous to flight. In maneuvering, top loads gave the impression that the wing was very loose."

The static tests by famed engineer C.N. Monteith bore out Harris' observations. There were many structural failures, including those of the spars and the diagonal "flying struts", which did not properly distribute the loads.

Someone evidently felt that either the design or the company had merit, however, and in January 1922 a $15,000 contract was let to redesign the aircraft with entirely new wings.

In the meantime, Huff-Daland had offered the HD-9A, an improvement over the original TA-2 concept. The HD-9A featured very unusual thick wings, irregular struts, elephant ear ailerons, and the ten cylinder Anzani engine. It was the start of Huff-Daland's drift to Fokker D-VII type construction, and very probably reflects the increasing importance of Charles T. Porter's influence on design.

Also in 1922, the original HD-8 "Plover" was again offered as the HD-8A "Petrel", a name that would be used for years by Huff-Daland. This aircraft was basically a three place version of the HD-9A, using a Curtiss OX-5 engine of 90 horsepower, neatly cowled, and located behind a "Hunnish" looking radiator. From the front you would swear you were looking at a Fokker D-VII, but from the top or side you could see many differences.

The two rebuilt TA-2s which returned from McCook Field from Ogdensburg were even more similar to the famous German fighter. Gone were the flimsy looking "flying struts"; instead there were two very dissimilar but still business-like airplanes.

The original P-166 was now P-238 (Air Service 64218), and the A.B.C. Wasp had been replaced by an OX-5. The fuselage was vastly refined, and a balanced rudder was fitted. Only the odd, strangely repulsive fuselage longeron-to wing-juncture remained to identify it as the original TA-2.

The thick wings were considerably reduced in size, upper wing span now being 29 feet, and total wing area was reduced by almost 30%, to 228 square feet, using Gottingen 387 section airfoil.

Despite the drastic drop in horsepower from 140 in the ABC to 90 in the OX-5, performance remained almost the same. Top speed at sea level was 81.8 mph, and absolute ceiling was 10,200 feet. The original TA-2 had been slightly faster, at 85.6 mph, and had a slightly higher ceiling.

Wing construction now consisted of spruce spars and wooden ribs, with internal drag bracing. Unlike the Fokker wing, there was no plywood outer skin, just a conventional fabric covering. The fuselage structure was made lighter by extensive routing and back in Ogdensburg, the lessons being learned at McCook had the plant leaders already looking into the use of welded steel tube construction.

The flying qualities of the modified TA-2 were considered to be far superior to those of the Curtiss JN-6H, but there were still two major drawbacks to the design. The first was the abysmal visibility, particularly from the front seat. The second was the extreme difficulty in getting in or out of the cockpits. Abandoning the airplane in an emergency would have been almost impossible.

The second TA-2, P-242, was fitted with the nine cylinder 140 horsepower Lawrance radial. Performance jumped dramatically, with a 114.1 mph top speed and a 17,450 foot ceiling.

Some of the increased speed came from the clipped wings, which now spanned only 26 ft. 1 in. from tip to tip. A sharp taper cut the wing area to only 176.54 square feet. The general shape of the wings was very similar to that of the Boeing PW-9 fighter. Art Smith tested the plane on September 21, 1922, and found it to be very maneuverable. It was difficult to spin, and excellent to roll. Landing, however, was a bit of a problem, for it was hard to get the tail down, and the plane had a tendency to ground loop. Visibility, as in the other TA-2, was very poor.

No orders were forthcoming, however, and once again Porter went back to the drawing boards. The firm now called Huff, Daland & Company, Inc., was undaunted, and laid out another series of new aircraft based on the McCook Field experience, and all of them even closer in design to the inspirational Fokker D-VII.

The new aircraft featured fuselages constructed of welded steel tubing, and H-D press releases always noted that "while alignment problems during manufacture presented unusual difficulties, they were more than compensated for by the rugged structure obtained, which does away with the necessity of realignment due to hard usage or climatic changes." No bracing wires were used in the fuselage.

The firm was able to market this third generation of aircraft with considerable skill. The Navy ordered nine units, of three separate types. These were three Wright Hisso powered HN-1s (A-6349 to 6351), three Lawrance powered HN-2s (A-6701 to 6703) and three Wright powered HO-1s (A-6560 to 6562).

The Air Service was even more enthusiastic, ordering seventeen trainers between 1923 and 1925. The Lawrance powered TA-5 was actually a throwback, being an improved TA-2 with tandem seats, but the others were all of the new D-VII influenced type. There were five TW-5s (23-1211 to 1215), a single TW5-C version which reverted to the Navy, and 10 AT-1s which were improved and redesignated TW-5s (25-235 to 244). A single AT-2, the

The Fokker D VII motif proved successful, and the Petrel IV featured two cockpits and a Wright-Hisso engine. The simple straightforward construction of the Huff-Daland aircraft made repairs relatively easy.

With the cowling removed, access to the Petrel IV's radiator and engine was very easy. An engineer will note that the engine has a slight down-thrust.

"Dog Ship", also received intensive testing, but was on loan from Huff-Daland.

These aircraft, with the exception of the TA-6, were all remarkably similar in dimensions, construction and performance. As a typical example, a discussion of the TW-5/AT-1 will be sufficient coverage for anyone except an absolute Huff-Daland fanatic.

The wings of the TW-5 were similar in outline to the D-VII, except for a pronounced taper in planform. The U.S. 35 airfoil provided ample lift from a total of 214 square inches of wing area. The upper wing spanned 29 feet 4 inches, while the lower one was 23 feet 10 inches long. Ailerons were of the balanced, elephant ear type, and were mounted on the upper wing only.

The fuselage built of chrome molybdenum steel tubing had conventional tandem seating and a conventional cabane, and there were no longer any problems of visibility or access.

Lieutenant Macready and Mr. Lockwood—two famous names at McCook—tested the aircraft on November 17, 1924, and found that at 2,212 pounds it had a remarkably good performance with the 190 horsepower Wright E engine. At sea level, and with the full 1800 rpms necessary to generate the rated horsepower, the TW-5 clocked a creditable 115.6 mph. Service ceiling was 14,750 feet, and estimated full throttle endurance was 3 hours and 45 minutes.

Macready thought that the airplane flew very well, being very maneuverable around the roll axis, and acceptable otherwise. The only "downcheck" was an excessive nose heaviness with power off.

In short, Huff-Daland was delivering serviceable, well built aircraft of adequate performance, and the twenty seven articles ordered by the two services formed a respectable manufacturing base.

Two other Huff-Dalands of the period should be mentioned here. The TA-6 was an attempt to marry the TA-2 fuselage with TW-5 type wings, using a Lawrance J-1 engine of 205 horsepower. Despite a performance comparable to the TW-5 (115.2 mph top speed at sea level and 18,600 foot service ceiling) the wood fuselage construction was passé and the project was dropped.

The other aircraft, the AT-2, was officially known as the "Huff-Daland Convertible Training Airplane (Dog Ship)", and was intended to serve as an advanced trainer for pursuit or observation. Tests conducted on September 12, 1925 indicated that the Ogdensburg factory may have been over optimistic, for the machine gun installations were unsatisfactory. The front gun was difficult to service, and when the observer moved about to use the flexible rear Lewis, the control of the aircraft was appreciably affected. A chronic Huff-Daland flaw, excessive vibration, was also commented on. Like the TA-6, the AT-2 was quietly dropped, although it was ballyhooed as the "Panther" for a while.

There were certain other distinguishing characteristics about this series of Navy and Air Service types. Floats were interchangeable with the landing gear on the Navy aircraft. The new Huff-Daland undercarriage eliminated the cross axle, and featured rubber cord shock absorbers mounted at the upper end of the long main landing gear members. Whenever additional load carrying capacity was required, as on the HN-2 and HO-1, which sometimes operated on floats, Huff-Daland would revert to non-tapered wings to gain a little more wing area.

7 HUFF-DALAND

A Little-Known Aviation Pioneer, Part II

Airpower January, 1978

The Huff-Daland company represents many things, including the benefits of the infamous military-industrial complex. Huff-Daland would not have survived in business if it had not learned what was required of military aircraft by forming a close relationship with the famous test pilot Harold R. Harris. And had Huff-Daland not survived, the world would have been a poorer place, for the type of airplane it developed served as one of the first built-for-purpose agricultural aircraft. It was on the success of this aircraft that what is now known as Delta Air Lines was built. To learn more about the company's history, the book to read is Delta, The History of an Airline, *by W. David Lewis and Wesley Phillips Newton (U. of Georgia Press, 1979).*

Huff-Daland designs became the basis for the highly successful Keystone bombers that made up the largest part of the Air Corps bomber fleet in the late 1920s and early 1930s. The Keystones were a familiar sight at air shows around the country, but they became obsolete and were eventually scrapped. None survive, but the marvelous United States Air Force Museum is converting the remains of a wreck into a restored aircraft that will be exhibited at the museum's magnificent Dayton facility.

By 1925 Huff-Daland had established itself as a bonafide builder of aircraft. Contracts were beginning to come in on a regular basis, and it was at this time, that the firm's rather disturbing penchant for unusual names begins to trouble the historian, for the civilian equivalents of service types began to receive sea-bird names, and these were then sometimes carried over to the military versions. Names like Petrel and Pelican were used over and over, so that there are late model Keystone Pelicans, Petrel IVs and Petrel 5s, and so on.

The Petrel IV, which appeared almost simultaneously with the TW-5, was essentially the same airplane with a slightly wider fuselage to accommodate two passengers in the front cockpit. Dimensions and performance were otherwise the same as the AT-1/TW-5.

The Petrel IV generated a great deal of foreign interest and Huff-Daland got a publicity break when the respected Fairchild Aerial Surveys of Canada, Ltd, chose a Petrel 5 for aerial photography and forest survey work. The Petrel 5 was a slightly larger airplane, with a 33 foot span and an all up weight of 2,715 pounds in the float version. It was the first American aircraft to receive a Canadian air worthiness certificate.

Fairchild operated the Petrel on skis in severe weather conditions over the Gaspé Peninsula in Quebec. In that area, temperatures often reached 30 degrees below zero, and seven foot accumulation of snow on the ground was not unusual, but the Petrel flew regularly, without incident.

The Petrel 5 was also used in crop dusting experiments with great success, and as we shall see, formed the basis for what became the first successful commercial crop dusting firm in the world. It also inspired the much larger Petrel 31, which was built to carry a full 1,000 pound load of the toxic, calcium arsenate dust.

The Petrel 31 was a scaled up Petrel 5, with a 50 foot wingspan, a fully loaded weight of 5,250 pounds, and a

The Huff-Daland Company made history with the introduction of the Petrel 5, the first truly successful commercial crop duster. ("Cropduster" is regarded as a pejorative term by today's agricultural pilots, but at the time that's what they were called.) Delta Air Lines can directly trace its ancestry to this airplane.

As Huff-Daland Dusters, Incorporated, expanded, Huff-Daland went on to build a series of bigger dusters. The company even began operations in Peru, where the seasons are just the opposite of those in the United States.

400 horsepower Liberty engine. It was called the Puffer, so there was a "Huff'n Puffer", no less.

The success in scaling up the Petrel 5 had two direct effects upon the company; first it seemed to convince it that size was the name of the design game, and the scaling up process was subsequently taken past the point of diminishing returns. Second, it opened up the whole new field of agricultural, and ultimately, airline operations.

Bigger airplanes required a bigger plant, and the firm bought a first rate, modern factory from the Harriman Shipbuilding Company in Bristol, Pennsylvania. The new facility had over 40,000 square feet of area, including a single open bay that was over 1,000 feet long.

The move to the new plant was a good time to update the company name, as well, and in July, 1925, it became Huff-Daland Airplanes, Inc.

Management had every reason to be pleased with itself, for it was competing successfully in a tough market with many larger companies. It had manufactured 80 aircraft of 25 different types, and had a respectable civil line to offer. Ultimately, six aircraft would go to Peru, eight to the Argentine Navy, one to Mexico, and one to Brazil. This was in addition to the dusters which transferred from the U.S. to Peru as a part of Huff-Daland Dusters, Inc.

Work on the first of the new and even bigger Huff-Dalands, the XLB-1 Pegasus, had started at Ogdensburg, a 66 foot 6 inch span aircraft which was basically a Petrel 5 with an overworked pituitary.

The XLB-1 had a single huge Packard 2A-2540 power plant of 800 intended horsepower, driving an enormous 11 foot diameter fixed-pitch, wooden propeller. The Huff-Daland company was already acutely conscious of the value of publicity and reports of the big bomber had been in the press weeks before its roll out. In its first actual public appearance, the XLB-1 covered itself with honor, winning the Detroit News Air Transport Trophy Race at the New York Air Races in October, 1925. Lieutenant E.E. Harmon beat twelve other Army, Navy and Marine pilots by herding the big Pegasus around the 120 mile course at an average speed of 119.91 mph.

The XLB-1 weighed 5,323 pounds empty, and carried a remarkable useful load of 5,909 pounds; this sort of efficiency was very rare at the time, and could be attributed to the cleanliness of the single engine design.

Tests of the XLB-1 were promising enough for the Army to order an additional service test quantity of nine LB-1s, thus setting the course for Huff-Daland's and later Keystone's success as supplier of Army bombers. The contract was for a total of $505,000, and also called for an even larger experimental aircraft.

The service test manual for the LB-1 stated that its mission was to be able to perform at high speed over a considerable distance, carrying a moderate load of bombs and machine guns. The LB-1 achieved these goals, for though it may have been ungainly in appearance its airframe and powerplant both offered theoretical advantages.

Unfortunately, the Packard engine, (the 2A-2540 in the LB-1s) was extremely unreliable, and the very features which were its claim to efficiency were the ones which spelled its ultimate failure and forced its abandonment. This did not mean the end of the line for the airframe, however.

The Pegasus had a number of firsts for American bombardment aircraft. It had two fixed .30 caliber machine guns mounted in the lower wing and fired by the pilot. The "bombers compartment" (the term bombardier hadn't been adopted yet) was located underneath the pilot's seat, and had relatively good vision through windows—until they became obscured with oil.

The most remarkable provision of this double-size Petrel, however, was the continued use of the single bay wing cellule. The upper wing consisted of a large, wide center section, with two tapered outer panels attached. The lower wing was formed by the two wing stubs and two tapered outer panels.

Construction was conventional, with two parallel box spruce spars, wooden ribs, built up spruce compression members and wire drag bracing. The entire wing was fabric covered, with a plywood reinforced leading edge. The two 175 gallon main fuel tanks and reserve tank were

Huff-Daland hankered after more military business, of course, and created the XLB-1 "Pegasus" by simply scaling up the Petrel by about 100 percent. The Pegasus had a wingspan of 66 feet, 6 inches, but used only a single bay of struts, most unusual for an aircraft of this size. The engine was the Packard 2A-2540, which had 800 horsepower—and lots of mechanical problems. Packard, which ultimately did a remarkable job producing the Rolls-Royce Merlin, never had much luck with engines of its own design.

located in the upper wing section and were gravity feed.

The fuselage was pure Huff-Daland, with chrome-moly steel tubing welded with box like rigidity. There was ample room for the pilot, radio operator, bomber and gunner, who operated two flexible Lewis guns on a ring mount. The armament inspection report indicated that the floor mounted machine gun was to be remotely controlled, but did not elaborate on how this was to be done.

The split landing gear had an oil and spring oleo shock absorber, as did the steerable tail skid.

From an historical viewpoint, the records of the testing of the XLB-1 and the LB-1 are perhaps even more important than the aircraft's story itself. One of McCook Field's greatest contributions was its *Handbook of Instructions for Aircraft Designers*, which, as noted in Pt 1 of this article, advised prospective manufacturers of what the Air Service expected in its airplanes. The Pegasus was exhaustively examined against this handbook, and hundreds of pages of reports were generated on every aspect of the airplane. Each section at McCook—Armament, Flying, Material, and so on—had to complete comprehensive ten and twelve page questionnaires which not only delved into minute detail, but also showed a great deal of thought in their preparation.

The various reports were accomplished by outstanding people who subsequently became famous. For the LB-1, for example, 1/Lt. (later Major General) F.O. Carrol wrote the report on the Service Test Manual; C.J. Cleary did the Material Section Inspection Report; Louis Meister did the Flying Section Report; George Polk and G.E. Lawrence did the Equipment Report; Don Berlin (who designed the P-40 a few years later) did the wind tunnel study—the list goes on and on.

The beauty of these reports is in their comprehensiveness, directness and succinctness. They are models of brevity; if one symbol will do, that's all there is. Simple "yes" and "no" answers abound.

Despite the fact that the LB-1 was generally well regarded, there were thousands of write ups, recommending changes and improvements for the production articles. Lieutenant (later Major General) V.E. Bertrandais, for example, offered no less than 93 comments on the aircraft, ranging from "wheel greasing unit not standard" to "landing light brackets not rigid as called for on Page 291, Handbook."

The point of all this is that these were not just fanatical nit pickers, but men of vision, determined to create an engineering discipline that would ensure the U.S. Army of first rate aircraft.

The most attractive thing about the Pegasus was its great load carrying capacity; its biggest drawback was that single engine bombers were already coming into disfavor, and the Packard was certainly not the engine to reverse this

Huff-Daland tried an even larger single engine design, the XHB-1 (HB for Heavy Bomber) "Cyclops," which had an 84 foot 7 inch wing span and was intended to have a single 1,200 horsepower 24 cylinder engine, which did not materialize. (Small wonder—it would take Allison years to develop 1,200 horsepower with their V-12.) When fitted with two smaller Packard 2A-1530 engines, it was redesignated XB-1. The smaller Packards were also unsatisfactory; they were unreliable and able to power the XB-1 at a top speed of only 110 mph.

trend. While there were great advantages to the single engine layout in terms of reduced drag, greater maneuverability and so on, the appeal of an aircraft that could maintain altitude even if one of its two engines failed was becoming increasingly important.

Unlike most designs, the production versions of the Pegasus did not suffer much loss of performance when compared to the prototype. In the November 27, 1926 performance test, flown by H. Johnson at a loaded weight of 10,346 pounds, the XLB-1 attained a top speed of 121 mph at sea level and a service ceiling of 14,725 feet. On July 6, 1927, Joe Hutchinson flew a service test LB-1 (26-379) at 12,414 pounds gross weight. He achieved 120 mph at sea level and a service ceiling of 11,150 feet. Landing speed had increased slightly to 61 mph, compared to the XLB-1's 55 mph.

Prejudice against the single engine bomber, with its restricted pilot's vision, no nose gunner, and oil-smeared "bomber" windows, plus the difficulties with the Packard engine forced Huff-Daland to create the XLB-3, which was the LB-1 airframe with two inverted Liberty engines at the conventional wing location. This version of the Liberty also gave trouble, and the aircraft was converted to the XLB-3A by installing two Pratt & Whitney R-1340 engines. This aircraft was the start of the famous twin engine Keystone bomber line, which was to remain in service for a decade, until 1935.

Corporate expansion was the name of the game as the Roaring Twenties drew to a close. The Loening Aeronautical Engineering Corporation had already merged with Huff-Daland, and a general reorganization of the firm occurred in December, 1926. Thomas Huff resigned, and was replaced by Edgar N. Gott as President and Chairman of the Board. The exact reasons for the change are unclear, for Huff had guided the firm to a successful position in the marketplace. Gott, a young tiger type executive, had formerly been president of Boeing and vice president of Fokker, and the management change probably represented politics as well as the altered financial position of the firm, resulting from an increase in capital to the then lofty sum of $1,000,000. The company name was formally changed to the Keystone Aircraft Corporation (no doubt reflecting the main plant's location in Pennsylvania) on March 8, 1927. However, the name change did not coincide with aircraft delivery schedules, so there were Huff-Daland as well as Keystone LB-5 bombers.

The firm was running out of options when it created a smaller aircraft, the Huff-Daland XLB-3. But once again the airplane was saddled with a poor choice of engines, an air-cooled version of the Liberty. When the company was reorganized as the Keystone Aircraft Company, its luck changed. The XLB-3 (LB for light bomber) shown here started a dynasty of Keystone bombers in the Army Air Corps that lasted until the advent of the Martin B-10. The last Keystone B-6A, pictured, was delivered in 1932, but they served for years after.

This is the story of Huff-Daland, however, and there are three other branches still to pursue. One is the final, scaled up Petrel, the huge XHB-1 Cyclops; the second is a brief review of the agricultural flying operations and the

Many a USAAF bomber commander in World War II cut his teeth on aircraft like the Keystone bomber and was glad to do so. It is an attractive aircraft in flight, but its performance (121 mph top speed, 363 mile range) was not much of an improvement over the German Gotha of World War I.

subsequent development of Delta Air Lines, certainly a story all by itself, and the third is a brief look at a later U.S. Navy evaluation of the Huff-Daland "Pelican".

The Cyclops project was gotten underway before the Pegasus was even complete. It was originally intended to put a gigantic 1,200 horsepower "X" type engine in the Cyclops, but the plant was not available and the unsatisfactory Packard 2A-2540 used in the LB-1s had to be substituted. The XHB-1 had an 84 foot 7 inch wing span, weighed 16,600 pounds, and was advertised as 60% larger than the Pegasus, although the figures do not come out that way.

Huff-Daland had commercial and trans-Atlantic plans for this aircraft, and publicized it heavily throughout its construction. It was called the "Mystery Ship", and there were vague promises of a 135 mph cruise speed between New York and London.

The XHB-1, whose major departure from the Pegasus, other than size, was the use of a two-bay, all metal wing structure, was tested and found wanting. The single Packard packed up, resulting in a forced landing only one half mile from the Dayton airport.

Once again the logical solution was a twin engine configuration, and thus the penultimate Huff-Daland bomber, the XB-1 was created. This "Super Cyclops" had two Packard 2A-1500 water cooled engines, each of 550 horsepower, and not much more reliable than the larger ones. When a ground fire forced rebuilding, the much more satisfactory Curtiss Conqueror engines were installed, creating the XB-1B. By this time, however, the Air Service was committed to a mixed force of Curtiss B-2s and smaller Keystone bombers, and the XB-1B was dropped.

But let's go back to a more enduring facet of the Huff-Daland story, the Huff-Daland Duster; for while Keystone would be able to market the basic Huff-Daland line for a few more years after becoming the Keystone Division of the Curtiss-Wright Corporation, no new salable ideas were produced and the company eventually expired.

It so happened that the success of the Petrel IV and 5 biplanes coincided with the work of the U.S. Department of Agriculture Delta Laboratory in Tallulah, Louisiana. There, under the direction of Dr. B. B. Coad, two years of experimentation using U.S. Army aircraft as dusters had proved the efficacy of crop dusting. Huff-Daland representatives had worked with Dr. Coad as early as 1923, and knew exactly the type of aircraft that was needed.

A new company, Huff-Daland Dusters, Inc., was formed, and 18 Huff-Dalands were procured to do the dusting. This was an enormous civil order for the time. A network of nine different airports was created, so that two aircraft could operate from each. Chief of Operations was none other than Harold R. Harris, released from the Air Service to direct the effort.

Crop dusting was an instant commercial success, and soon 60,000 southern acres were being protected. The service was sold to farmers at a price of $7.00 per acre for a series of five spray applications.

The Huff-Daland operation was extended to Peru, whose growing season coincided with the off-season in the U.S. and Harris went along to run things. From this he went to top executive jobs in a number of airlines, eventually becoming president of Northwest Airlines.

C.E. Woolman, who had guided the corporate operations of Huff-Daland Dusters, perceived the need in the South for an airline service. He founded Delta Air Service, from which the present Delta Air Lines stems.

Woolman died in 1966, and as a tribute to him the remaining parts of two of the original Huff-Daland dusters were rebuilt into a single restored aircraft which was presented to the National Air & Space Museum in 1968. It may be seen today at the Museum's Silver Hill facility, and is the last surviving Huff-Daland in the world.

One final word about Huff-Daland's Navy activities. The company had tried for years to sell its "Navy Five Purpose Training Plane" which was intended for use as a wheel or float equipped trainer, an observation plane, a submarine spotter or "for combating with either fixed or moveable aerial machine guns". Various models of the Petrel were touted over the years, until finally, the "Pelican" evolved. Powered with a Wright J-5 engine of 220 horsepower, it had a top speed of 120 mph as a landplane and 111 mph as a seaplane. In the final Huff-Daland version of this aircraft, a bombing compartment was located aft of the second cockpit. The observer would unhook a jury rigged boatswain's chair (honest!) and crawl aft to lie prone in the fuselage. A hole in the floor boards in the cockpit provided visibility for bomb dropping.

For some reason, after years of balanced surfaces, the Huff-Daland engineers deleted the fixed vertical fin, and while this change did not produce too noticeable an effect in the land plane version, it was vicious in the sea plane configuration.

As with previous multi-purpose types, no sales were made, although Keystone attempted to sell it for a few years more. The final door had been shut on Huff-Daland designs. It was time, for although they were fully competitive for a period, a new day of metal monoplane structures had already dawned, and neither Huff-Daland nor Keystone had the capacity to compete.

8 THE FLYING HALLMARKS

The Hall Aluminum Classics

Wings June, 1975

One of the most rewarding aspects of researching and writing about older aircraft is the wonderful people that you meet. In preparing these articles on the Hall Aluminum aircraft, it was my pleasure to meet and correspond with Charles Ward Hall, Jr., the son of the founder of the company, Charles Ward Hall, and with Mrs. Archibald Hall, his daughter-in-law.

The Halls were very proud of C.W. Hall, Sr.'s accomplishments, and more than willing to place them in perspective. The Hall Aluminum Aircraft Corporation is an example of America at its best. Charles Ward Hall was successful because he selected a niche market in aviation for the period: the manufacture of aircraft made primarily out of aluminum. He managed to succeed by staying small. The intricate designs of the Hall Aluminum planes were not always apparent upon inspection. For the most part, Hall Aluminum airplanes looked like conventional biplane flying boats and fighters. The difference was in their construction, particularly their circular main spars and beautifully designed aluminum fittings. It was the Hall practice to design each part to the exact strength that it would be required to meet in flight. These parts were often elegant in design and consequently expensive to build, but they were weight-saving, which was just the attribute that Hall was seeking. This approach worked well in a small company, just as Hall intended.

The name Charles Ward Hall doesn't mean quite the same thing to aviation that Ettore Bugatti's does to automobiles—but it should. Hall's products had the same uncompromising quality and thoroughly unorthodox engineering as Bugatti's, and they were a similar mixture of advanced and antique, radical and reactionary, ugly and beautiful, and even the large and the small.

Only in the golden years of aviation could a firm like Hall Aluminum have prospered so long, remained so small, done so much, and made so very little money.

Hall's engineering methods and his concepts of materials and designs were Ayn Randian in their scope, and in many respects are far more important than the 31 aircraft he was responsible for, although these ranged from a most unusual light plane to a huge four-engine patrol boat. More than any other man he convinced the U.S. Navy of the practicability of all aluminum construction, and he was at least 25 crucial years ahead of his time in his concern for weight control.

There are some curious contradictions in the appearance and even the sequence of Hall aircraft. While all are characterized by his innovative construction techniques, some look to be totally orthodox, even banal, while others were avant garde. The same is true of design detail on a particular aircraft; the beautiful PTBH-2, for example, had its clean cantilever wing followed through the air by a strut and sometimes wire-supported empennage.

None of this was accidental—no element of a Hall design ever was. Like Frank Lloyd Wright, he insisted that form follow function, and optimized efficiency was his credo. If an increment of aerodynamic gain was too expensive in terms of production effort, it was altered. He strived always for a harmonious balance, insisting that every element of the airplane make its fullest contribution, and also exact from aerodynamic forces any benefits of stress relief or transfer. He saw the airplanes as Tony Fokker saw them, "with the spray."

Being thrown out of business may be as good a way as any for entering aviation, and that's how Hall started. He had been a building contractor in New York, but his methods were too efficient for the unions to tolerate. It was physically impossible for Hall to watch things done in the traditional jurisdictional building code manner, when he could improve methods, cut time, and save money. But cutting times means cutting jobs, and there is no quicker way OUT of the building trades.

Hall had first been inoculated with the aviation bug by a ride with Ruth Law at Daytona Beach in 1909. This early interest was stimulated considerably when his son, Charles Ward Hall, Jr., joined the LaFayette Flying Corps. Hall, Sr., learned to fly in 1916; Dave McCollough was his instructor at the Rodman Wanamaker Flying School in Port Washington, Long Island, using a Curtiss MF flying boat. It was the start of a satisfying and profitable relationship with Curtiss products.

Flying interested Hall first as an adventure and, secondly, as an engineering challenge. It's hard to realize now,

The first "Hall Aluminum Flying Boat" was not really a very impressive airplane, but it was one heck of a sailboat! It was actually a sailboat hull fitted with a pivoting mast and equipped with a war-surplus Thomas Morse wing. This unusual craft was important because it got Charles Ward Hall thinking about flying boats made of aluminum at a time when they were invariably made of wood.

Besides being an inventor and engineer, Charles Ward Hall also liked to fly, and he flew this Hall "Monoped" for both business and pleasure. It used the typical Hall Aluminum construction techniques and was distinguished by its single main landing gear (to save weight and drag) aided by outriggers. In theory this landing gear was not unlike the later landing gear of the Boeing B-47. Hall lost his life in this machine when he crashed into a tree when attempting a landing in heavy fog on August 21, 1936.

but there were many aircraft designers in those early days—but damn few aero engineers. Grover Loening was the first, and those who followed him had focused their attention more on aerodynamics than on structure.

The first thing that Hall built with wings was a boat—not a flying boat, just a boat. He rigged a 20-foot sailboat hull with a special pivoting mast and a surplus Thomas Morse wing, complete with insignia. As he sailed it around Long Island Sound, a new idea formed in the back of his mind—an aluminum flying boat.

This matured into the first "Hall Aluminum," a tiny, trim plane built in 1922. The 25-foot span upper wing was made of wood, but the rest—tail booms, empennage, two-place hull and lower wing—was aluminum. The Loening-like fuselage had a three-cylinder 60-horsepower Wright "Gale" engine perched rather precariously on struts.

Not surprisingly, the plane was light. Fully loaded with two passengers and fuel (10 gallons), it grossed 950 pounds. Archibald McClay Hall, the No. 2 son, said that the airplane was extremely pleasant to fly and a great novelty on Long Island Sound.

Corrosion was then and is now the greatest enemy of aluminum, and Hall approached the problem with his usual simple, direct manner. The entire aircraft was lightly coated with grease; and after a flight, it was washed down and regreased. It was time consuming, but effective, and the plane remained airworthy for over 7 years.

The first experimental aircraft gave Hall sufficient experience and confidence to set up an engineering firm,

One of the Hall Aluminum company's greatest successes was the sale of patrol boats to the United States Coast Guard, which valued them for their excellent rough-water capabilities. This is the PH-2, one of 23 of the PH series purchased by the Coast Guard between 1930 and 1941. The two Wright Cyclone engines provided good short takeoff capabilities.

In the days before the skies over Washington D.C. became so crowded, flying boats were often tested at the Naval Air Station in Anacostia. This photo shows Fort McNair in the background.

Charles Ward Hall, Incorporated. The Navy was interested in his work and awarded a contract to build an aluminum wing for comparison with a standard wooden one from a Curtiss HS-2L flying boat.

Hall more than fulfilled the contract, creating a structure with equal strength but half the weight. There was no intention on the Navy's part to refit their aging HS-2L fleet, but it did point the way to the future. The Navy liked Hall's expert engineering service combined with a custom manufacturing capability, and thus it was to sustain him through the worst depression in history.

Curtiss had just furnished the Navy with its first squadron of fighters, the rather awkward-appearing TS-1. Powered by a 220-hp Lawrance radial, the little wooden biplane had a span of 25 feet and a loaded weight of 1,929 pounds. It probably wouldn't have lasted long on the Western Front, but it was an ideal vehicle for the new Navy fighter squadrons.

The Naval Aircraft Factory in Philadelphia also built additional TS-1s, and decided to have Hall build two of aluminum for both static test and flight comparisons. This, the "Curtiss-Hall F4C-1," was modified to the extent that there was no Bristol Fighter gap between fuselage and the lower wing, but in all other respects it followed the TS-1 design faithfully. The use of aluminum allowed refinement, and the heavy drag-inducing struts of the original model were considerably slimmed down.

But the biggest improvement was in gross weight, for the tiny F4C-1 weighed in at a shade under 1,700 pounds with full military load. Performance improved considerably, with top speed increased by 7 mph to 131 mph, and improvements in the rate of climb and ceiling.

Affectionately called "the Iron Duke" by Navy personnel, the all metal fighter was never intended for production, for the snorting Curtiss F6C and Boeing FB-1 were already on the horizon, but the F4C-1 did establish Hall's special relationship with the Navy, one which would endure both during the booming 20's and the dying 30's.

The regard of the senior service was expressed in 1929 when they awarded the new Hall Aluminum Aircraft Corporation two contracts for two totally different types of airplanes, the XFH-1 and XPH-1. At the time the firm was housed in the same Buffalo, New York, plant as Consolidated Aircraft, and these new airplanes would take shape under the envious eye of future business colleagues.

The projects were a tremendous personal stress, for Hall was almost totally responsible for all phases of the custom operation. His son has told me how the senior Hall would rove from the drafting room to the shop to the front offices, overseeing every operation. In addition, he was an astute businessman, personally negotiating contractual details with the Navy.

Archibald McClay Hall's pride for his father is evident, although he himself is a famous name in aviation, serving as the firm's Vice President, and later joining Consolidat-

The PH boats had a four-man crew—two pilots side-by-side, and a gunner fore and aft. The aircrafts' biggest improvements over previous Navy flying boats were their superior handling in water, thanks to an improved hull design, and, in later models, the enclosed cockpit.

The XPH-1 was operated with an open cockpit. The author has talked to Navy mechanics who worked on the Hall boats, and while they admired the clever structure and the use of weight-saving devices, they admitted that those same features made the airplane more complicated and difficult to service in the field. Particularly problematic was the manner in which control surfaces were attached by a long, complex piano-wire hinge.

ed as a special assistant to the President, Reuben Fleet; the younger Hall confided that "Father did everything. He would do the preliminary calculations to arrive at a tentative configuration, then sketch out the planform for the small engineering staff to begin work on. From then on, he'd monitor everything to make sure the design developed according to his conception."

In some respects the XPH-1 was the greater experimental challenge, for Hall was being asked to improve upon an aircraft whose lineage went directly back to the Curtiss F-5L and upon which a host of companies had employed their talent. The Naval Aircraft Factory had redesigned the F-5L extensively, creating a series of planes including the PN-7, -8, -9, -10, -11, and -12. (The PN-9 was the most famous of the lot being flown and sailed by Commander John Rodgers from San Francisco to Hawaii.)

The last of the line, the PN-12 had a 72-foot span and two Wright 575-horsepower engines, and the Navy considered it worthy of large scale production. Keystone was awarded a contract for 18 PK-1s, Douglas built 25 as PD-1s, and Martin built 30 PM-1s and 25 PM-2s, each firm introducing all the refinement of which it was capable.

Hall's task was to execute the same airplane in aluminum, and he applied himself with his usual vigor. He'd been nettled by some adverse Navy comments on workmanship on the F4C-1, and the conventional-appearing flying boat which grew in the Buffalo hangar had an unbelievable craftsmanship lavished upon it. Every detail was scrutinized for fit and finish, and the plane which materialized was considerably cleaner than any of its predecessors. Hall did his work well as the following table indicates:

	Martin PM-2	Hall PH-1	
Empty Weight	9,919	8,251	(16% decrease)
Gross Weight	16,969	15,447	(9% decrease)
Top Speed	116	134.5	(16% increase)
Service Ceiling	8,800	11,400	(30% increase)

Hall had worked closely with the National Advisory Committee on Aeronautics on the hull design, and created remarkable handling characteristics which would ultimately make it attractive to the Coast Guard. The hull displacement/resistance ratio was 6.3 to 1, compared to the usual 5 to 1.

The XPH-1 had 537-horsepower Wright engines, and a top speed of only 126 mph, but when the diminutive designer showed the Navy performance estimates for a production version, they agreed to what would be Hall's largest order ever, a full *nine* aircraft.

The production PH-1s had 620-hp Wright R-1820-86 engines with short-chord cowlings. Numerous design refinements were made, the most noticeable being increased canopy area, the addition of servo controls on the elevator, and relocation of the rear gunner's cockpit.

Extensive tests were run on the production PH-1 from October 19, to December 10, 1931, under a competent team led by Lieutenant Ralph A. Ofstie, who set records in the 1920s and was a brilliant combat leader as a Rear Admiral in 1944. Ofstie was very enthusiastic about the PH-1's excellent controllability on the water and its general performance, considering it to be a great advance over all previous patrol airplanes tested. The PH-1 could leap off from smooth water in just 25 seconds; in rough water, with irregular choppy waves four to five feet high, and a 16 knot wind, it was off in just 17.7 seconds, bouncing into the air below flying speed, but hanging in and flying without touching down again. Ofstie did recommend numerous refinements, the most important of which was some structural reinforcement in the forward nose section, and provision for access platforms for servicing the engines. It seemed clear from the evaluation, however, that if there had been more funds available, more PH-1s might have been ordered. As it turned out, only one Navy squadron, VP-8 used the PH-1, which served with honor from 1932 to 1937.

Landing the Hall flying boat was easy, and the hull was stout enough to take hard landings in rough seas.

"On the step." The Hall Aluminum flying boat got on the step and off the water quickly, even with heavy loads in heavy seas.

Unlike any other peacetime aircraft, the basic design was called back into production twice again. In June, 1936, the U.S. Coast Guard bought seven, designated PH-2, for air-sea rescue duty. Larger 750 hp Wright R-1820F-51 engines provided greater performance and improved cruise-control techniques permitted a needed range increase from the earlier version's 1,868 to 2,170 miles. Gun positions were deleted, and the cockpit was fully enclosed.

The Coast Guard liked the PH-2 well enough to order seven improved versions in 1939. These PH-3s had many small changes, resulting in a very handsome biplane. Drag was sufficiently reduced by the low-drag long-chord cowlings, finer nose entry, and other improvements to boost top speed to 159 mph. Range was extended to a very useful 2,300 miles with increased fuel tankage. The PH-3s served in World War II on anti-submarine patrol, just as their forerunners, the F-5Ls had served in World War I.

The other 1929 project was really the first original Hall design for the Navy. Time has a way of altering our memory, and Archibald Hall assured me that the XFH-1 fighter was the fastest thing in the sky. It really wasn't, but it was a unique design distinguished by a totally new construction philosophy.

Hall personally assessed each part, analyzing it both statically and dynamically to ensure that strength was *adequate* and weight was at a *minimum*. This is a risky philosophy for any but an assured engineer; most early aircraft were penalized by extremely conservative strength estimates, that resulted in heavier-than-necessary structures.

In the course of his subcontracting and consulting, Hall had designed a variety of flanged, closed (hollow bulbed) aluminum tubing shapes which he built for stock and used in the primary aircraft structure. He would combine two, three, four, or as many as eight of these tubes as load requirements dictated. Structure was continuous, but the member would have a varying number of tubes, based on predicted stresses. To complement these, bulkheads were built up of drawn sections, riveted, and reinforced with gussets.

In the XFH-1's wing structure, these multiple tubes were cambered in such a manner that the airload straightened—and effectively strengthened—the spar, thus the wing drooped slightly on the ground, but was absolutely straight under maximum flight loading.

The wing set-up had a number of other unique features. The ribs were set at an 88-degree angle to the spars, and the ailerons were mounted to the top wing (only) by continuous "piano" hinges. These reduced drag by sealing the aileron gap, but were a maintenance nightmare. An old friend of mine, Earl George, was a Navy metalsmith who worked on many of the Hall planes, and he still curses with exasperation when he recalls the knuckle-slicing effort involved in installing a Hall aileron. In general, however, Hall always kept an eye on production ease and many parts were made in small subassemblies which could be built-up on riveting machines.

The fighter had rather uncommon lines, mainly due to the 6-degree sweepback of the upper wing contrasting with the 4-degree sweep forward of the lower. This provided exceptional forward visibility, but an odd shadow. The flying wires were attached to a single point forward of the lower wing's leading edge, instead of being routed parallel with the wing spars.

The XFH-1 was delivered to Anacostia for testing from September 25, 1929 through February 3, 1930, and Ofstie was again one of the testers, proving indisputably his total objectivity in regard to Hall products. The poor little fighter simply didn't fare very well, from its delivery by freight on June 18th, where it had its tail skag broken off, to its final inadvertent bath when the engine failed.

The Navy had insisted on some immediate structural changes even before flight, and although the airplane ulti-

It speaks very well for the Hall that in 1939 the Coast Guard decided to procure another seven PH-3s, even when the Consolidated PBY was also available. The PH-3 was slightly cleaned up, with longer chord cowlings and a smoother cockpit design. They served during the war, flying antisubmarine patrol until March 1944.

The number of struts and wires looks pretty complicated to us today, but the Hall flying boats were remarkably clean compared to their biplane predecessors.

mately filled all of its performance guarantees, it's probable that Hall simply didn't have the feel for fighter planes that he did for larger aircraft.

The preliminary contractor pilot demonstration was unsatisfactory to the Navy, primarily because it felt that the maneuvers were too gentle and the dives too shallow, but also because the rib stitching carried away on several ribs, with the ribs bending. Hall added additional ribs and reduced spacing on rib stitching from 4 inches to 2 inches, but an irrevocably bad impression had been made.

The Navy started its performance tests on the 25th of September, and problems developed immediately. The rudder was overbalanced, and if the pilot's feet were removed from the rudder bar even for a few seconds, violent oscillations would develop, sufficient to destroy the airplane if not checked quickly. The *ad hoc* solution was to remove a significant portion of the rudder balance area.

A few days later in a 200 mph power dive, the rear spar of the upper wing buckled and partially froze the aileron control. The wing was removed and returned to Hall for remanufacture and strengthening. Tests were resumed in February, and during arresting gear tests the engine failed, and the plane dropped into the water with its wheels still on. It floated for forty minutes before being salvaged. The wheel jettisoning feature was considered to be undesirable, as the airplane was considered to be more likely to porpoise if it landed clean, and the wheels would serve to dissipate the forces of impact.

Ofstie and company were especially critical of the complexity of the structure required for the waterproof hull, which made maintenance very difficult. The hull

The Hall XFH-1 was purchased by the Navy to test all-aluminum construction in a watertight fuselage. The gear could be dropped in the event of a water landing. Performance was only mediocre, with a top speed of 153 mph.

This profile shows the XFH-1's unusual wing-sweep. The top wing was swept back and the bottom wing swept forward to give the pilot a better view.

proved itself in later tests, however, remaining afloat for over an hour and forty minutes, and surviving towing both by the nose and by the tail.

The airplane was just not a contender as a fighter, however, having neither the speed nor the maneuverability of contemporary aircraft. Top speed was 152.6 mph, despite the fact that the empty weight of 1,773 pounds was 300 to 500 pounds less than similar fighters. Even if performance had been much better, the problems associated with achieving and maintaining a watertight hull would have ruled against production. Yet while other American manufacturers were desperately seeking orders or quietly going out of business, the Navy signed still another experimental contract with Hall. On June 30, 1930 (suspiciously close to the end of the fiscal year, when a small unspent pot may have been discovered), Hall received an order for the largest American flying boat since the Curtiss NC-4.

This was the XP2H-1, a gigantic patrol plane of extremely handsome lines. The 112-foot span had an elegant trapezoidal planform, with the center section chord of 185 inches tapering gracefully to 85 inches at the tip. A Clark Y variant airfoil was used, and there was a colossal 2,608 square feet of area.

The Navy wanted the plane to investigate extremely long-range patrol operations, and the only configuration which would meet the demands was a biplane, although Hall recognized this as an essentially retrograde step at the time. Fuel was the name of the game, and each engine nacelle not only mounted two 600-hp Curtiss GV 1570 Conqueror engines in tandem, but also a 600-gallon tank. Another 3,400 gallons were carried in an elaborate series of tanks in the upper wing center section and the lower wing stubs.

Empty weight of the XP2H-1 was 20,417 pounds, while maximum gross takeoff weight was 44,000 pounds. The 64′6½″-long fuselage followed earlier Hall practice closely in outline, construction, and hull design.

The normal crew of six called for a pilot and copilot seated side by side in the enclosed cockpit. An open bow position, relic of the PH-1s, was available for the gunner bombardier, as well as for mooring operations. Navigation and radio equipment were located just aft of the pilots, and behind this were the "living quarters" for use on extra long flights. The flight mechanic was situated far to the rear, aft of the main spar, where he had a complex arrangement of engine instruments, fuel valves, and so on, while the rear gunner was located midway aft on the fuselage.

The Navy was very impressed with XP2H-1's sea and air handling qualities. Its 139.6 mph top speed exceeded the Navy Yard's wind tunnel estimate by 11 mph, and its engine-out performance was far better than expected. The specification called for a 1,500 foot ceiling capability with one engine out, but the big Hall boat could maintain 1,500 feet on just the two rear engines, and actually climb slowly on just the two front engines. With one power plant out, it could maintain 7,000 feet, a considerable achievement when you realize that these were fixed pitch propellers. (Curiously, the two forward propellers had a left hand rotation, while the two rear had right hand rotation.)

Once again, a Hall flying boat showed excellent takeoff characteristics, getting off from rough water (six foot seas) in just 21.5 seconds. The structure did not readily absorb rough sea handling, however, and the Board deemed it unsuitable. The plane had a flat approach, and touch down was usually quite positive, resulting in a

The huge XP2H-1 was probably the largest single-bay biplane ever built; with a 112-foot span, it weighed nearly 22 tons. Four Curtiss Conqueror engines were mounted, tandem fashion, in two streamlined nacelles.

In flight, the XP2H-1 was a very pretty aircraft. It was not unlike the British Short Singapore III in appearance, but with more graceful tapered wings.

The beaching gear for the XP2H-1 was very cleverly designed and easy to install. The famous test pilot Bill McAvoy tested the aircraft and was very impressed with its high top speed (139.6 mph) and its performance with an engine shut down. The big boat could actually climb with both rear engines shut down. This was a great achievement, for the fixed-pitch propellers could, of course, not be feathered.

The XP2H-1 would not have been a Hall Aluminum aircraft if it did not have great takeoff characteristics, for the company prided itself on that feature. It could take off, fully laden, from six-foot seas in just 21.5 seconds.

pounding which loosened the center section incidence wires and deranged interior tie rods in both nacelles; therefore, the flight home from rough water tests had to be conducted with full left rudder.

Operational equipment called for a radio, Mark XI bombsight, five flexible machine guns, and racks for 500 and 1,000 pound bombs. Even with this load, the airplane was extremely stable and the airplane could be flown under complete control with 2,000 pounds under one wing, and none under the other.

One unusual item of equipment for the time was a 1½ horsepower, air-cooled, single cylinder gasoline engine used to raise the 250 pound anchor.

All things considered, performance of the big bird was very good, with the top speed of almost 140 mph a tribute to its clean design.

Metalsmith George was present at the first flight of the behemoth, which almost ended in disaster. Test pilot William A. McAvoy (See *Airpower*, Sept. 1974) lifted the plane off, and it started the first one-eighth of a loop, something even Bob Hoover wouldn't have tried. McAvoy chopped the throttles, and the plane slammed down into the water, damaging the wingfloat and hull. The elevator had been incorrectly installed.

The only other major problem during test was with the lowest-bidder type radiators, which leaked excessively when the four big engines set them vibrating. New and expensive silver-soldered radiators were substituted in the very clean nacelle installation, and the difficulty was solved.

Hall achieved the Navy's design requirement, for the XP2H-1 (which resembled the British Short Singapore III) with a maximum range of 4,560 miles. A very sophisticated cruise control was used; as weight burned off, engines were shut down—first, number four, then number three, the final leg of a long mission being completed on two engines.

The XP2H-1 made only two big splashes—the first was when it flew nonstop from Norfolk, Virginia, to Coco Solo, Panama Canal Zone, in 1935. The second was a forced landing at sea, during which the plane broke up and sank.

Even as it was manufacturing the big Hall XP2H-1, the company was hard at work on a new design, the only pre-war Navy plane designed for three missions—Patrol, Torpedo, and Bombing. This was the XPTBH-2, a really beautiful aircraft, very advanced in design and structure. Featuring the standard tubular main spar, the XPTBH-2 had engines and floats mounted integrally in a very strong unit.

The twin floats made it possible for the XPTBH-2 to carry the standard naval torpedo. The elegant seaplane had a top speed of 184.5 mph while carrying two 1,000-pound bombs. But no real Navy requirement ever emerged and there were no production orders.

I asked Grover Loening what he thought about the XP2H-1, and he commented that though he had seen the plane only once, "there was obviously nothing to be learned from it—it was a dead end design."

The final Hall aircraft was the truly lovely XPTBH-2, the only prewar Navy plane designed for three missions—Patrol, Torpedo, and Bombing.

This three-way challenge seemed to inspire Hall, for there was an opportunity to apply all of his ideas, structural and aerodynamic, into one airplane.

The plane which emerged from the new Bristol, Pennsylvania, plant in April 1937 was surely one of the most beautiful in the world. As will be related shortly, Charles Ward Hall, Sr., was not there to see it.

The Navy had specified that the new multimission plane be capable of dropping the standard destroyer-type torpedo, which was almost twice the size of conventional aerial types. Hall perceived the best solution to this requirement would be a twin-float seaplane rather than the traditional flying boat.

Characteristically, he went to the structural core of the problem, the wing spar, and employed there once again his traditional aluminum tubing. This time, however, he chose a massive tube, 36 inches in diameter at the wing root, tapering to 9 inches at the tip, and made up of riveted 24 ST material. The spar was placed at the center of pressure in the wide chord wing and carried both flight and water loads. The floats were directly connected to it with a similar tubular arrangement. This immensely strong combination of Brooklyn Bridge type structures eliminated the need for cross-bracing the floats, permitting a free drop of the torpedo.

The interior of the 79′4″ span wing consisted of smaller tubing to create ribs and bracing. The aluminum skin of the leading edge was essentially nonload bearing, and the main portion of the wing was fabric covered, as were the metal-framed ailerons and trailing-edge split flaps, in a lifting surface designed to flex 19 inches at the tip.

The slender 55′4″-long aluminum semimonocoque fuselage had very little frontal area, and sported a Hall-designed revolving turret which housed a single .30-caliber machine gun. Below the gunner's turret there was space for the bombardier, who would sight through an optically flat window.

The pilot and copilot had plenty of visibility from the very austere cockpit. Instrumentation was very simple, with flight instruments in front of each pilot, and engine instruments centered.

The copilot served as a combination navigator, bombardier, and torpedo man, while the flight mechanic and radio operator doubled as gunners. Rear defense was comprised of two .30-caliber machine guns, mounted in dorsal and ventral openings, or one .50 and one .30.

The floats were the distillation of years of Hall experience, and while the relationship of the step, center of gravity, and center of buoyancy were identical to the PH-1, the cross section was much narrower. Extensive water-basin tests on models confirmed the design.

Molded in a streamlined unit with wing and float strut were the exquisitely cowled Pratt & Whitney XR 1830-60 radial engines of 800 hp. The engine mounts attached directly to the tubular main spar. (The XPTBH-1 was to have had Wright engines.) An early version of the three-bladed, three position Curtiss electric propeller was also installed.

McAvoy, long-time chief pilot for the NACA, was test pilot for the first flight. I have a copy of the film covering the first flight, and the day's excitement is communicated by the brisk activity of the launching crew, contrasting with the almost frozen expectancy of the onlookers. Everything went well on the initial hop except for a slight sluggishness in roll response. In a pragmatic approach that would have pleased the company's founder, a semicircular flat plate of aluminum was guy wired into place under the rudder for the second series of flights. This provided the necessary additional rear vertical surface to offset the side area of the floats, and control response improved immediately. The delighted Hall engineers then modified the plane with a wickedly elegant ventral surface that gave an inexplicable touch of class.

One curious feature of the plane's hydrodynamics stands out in the film. As it gathers speed, a rooster's tail forms about 100 feet behind each float. The tail grows as the plane accelerates, reaching a Gold Cup-like peak just prior to getting on step, then, of course, disappearing at lift-off. On touchdown, the spray kicks up immediately, then slowly moves up toward the rear of the floats as the plane decelerates.

Twin engine float planes were not exactly common even to the experienced test pilots at Anacostia and Norfolk, and they were delighted with its excellent taxiing and water handling in smooth water. In rough water the plane still behaved well, but needed considerably more power to turn, as the lower fin of the tail would submerge during a turn in heavy seas. No flaps were necessary for take off, as the plane would hop on the step almost instantly with almost no effort on the part of the pilots. Considerable back pressure was required when landing, however, especially when no bombs or torpedoes were carried, as there was a tendency for the tip of the floats to bury themselves otherwise. There was absolutely no tendency to porpoise either on take-off or landing, but the pilots were aware of a "flexing" which resulted from the two independent floats reacting in a different manner to water pressure.

The only down checks concerned the beaching gear, which although compact and light was difficult to attach in even a slightly rough sea, and the usual complaints to be expected about fuel tank venting, control linkages, and so on.

All in all, the XPTBH-2 was a success, meeting performance requirements on all three of its intended missions. At the maximum gross weight for patrol of 21,397 pounds, the XPTBH-2 had a top speed of 182 mph. At the 17,913-pounds gross for the torpedo mission, top speed rose to 186 mph, and service ceiling was improved to 20,400 feet, up 4,000 feet.

The Germans used the same formula as the XPTBH-2 in the very successful and quite handsome Heinkel He-115.

Archibald Hall felt that a change in Navy politics had been the real reason why the unusual plane did not receive a production order. The sole example of the XPTBH-2 came to a sad end, being destroyed at the Naval Torpedo Station, Newport, Rhode Island, during the 1938 hurricane.

Time and capital were running out on Hall Aluminum, and the company almost gratefully accepted an offer from Consolidated Aircraft in 1940. All of the assets, patents, etc., were assigned to Consolidated, and many Hall personnel joined the growing firm.

There is one other aircraft in the Hall Aluminum story, and it is one of the most interesting as well as the most tragic.

As noted, Charles Ward Hall conducted the day-today business of the firm, and he traveled extensively to meet with Government and business officials. Airline travel was rather primitive, so he designed a personal plane for himself with many custom features.

This plane, the "Monoped" can best be described as a rather porcine Rearwin Speedster. It derives its name from the unusual landing gear, a single central retractable Goodyear 22 × 10.4 wheel, supplemented by small outriggers located in a sesqui-wing lifting strut combination.

A Ranger six-cylinder model 390 engine of 120 hp swung a steel Hamilton Standard prop and gave a reported 130 mph top speed. Arch Hall recalled the airplane as being easy to fly, although he admitted to one embarrassing occasion when he failed to lower the gear.

Earl George also recalls this airplane, and says that the senior Hall used to joke about reading the newspaper while flying down to the Naval station. The cockpit of the little private transport was well instrumented and had a Lear radio. The control stick was suspended from an overhead mounting in the cockpit, thus reducing the number of control cable pulleys required. Hall lost his life in the Monoped on August 21, 1936, when the aircraft struck a tree in heavy fog at Hopewell, New Jersey. At the time of the crash, the plane had logged more than 530 hours.

No example of Hall's handiwork survives today, except in the extensive use that has been made of his ideas and his philosophy. Weight saving has become more important than ever before, and the legions of engineers who labor over the minute parts of modern aircraft, striving desperately to shave half an ounce here, an ounce there, would undoubtedly be glad to have him at their side.

9 The Tunison Scout

A Rare Bird

Wings August, 1978

The founder, publisher, and editor of Wings *and* Air Power *magazines, Joe Mizrahi, deserves a great deal of credit for publishing articles on historic aircraft. (*Wings *and* Air Power*, published in alternating months, were essentially the same magazine; two different names were used because that allowed each issue to stay on the newsstand for two months instead of just one.) When* Wings *and* Air Power *debuted, they had no real competition in the United States. There was another magazine with a similar format, but it had alienated many people because of the way it dealt with authors and with its sometimes careless handling of facts. So Joe's publications made a significant contribution to aviation journalism in the U.S.*

Joe really did not care for the "rare bird" kind of article that I liked to submit from time to time. They posed editorial and space problems, because the subjects were usually so arcane that there were only a few photographs and not enough material to fill more than a page or two. Still, he was kind enough to let me pursue my interest in unique, one-of-a-kind aircraft like the Tunison Scout.

The Tunison Scout was an odd combination of advanced engineering techniques, smooth lines, and a strangely obsolescent planform. Designed and built by M.C. Tunison on the West Coast, this low wing aircraft was built entirely of molded plywood, and featured some extremely unusual design features.

The heart of the aircraft was the hollow molded wing, which carried all its stresses in the skin, with only a minimum of interior bracing—four ribs on either side, and *no spar*.

Strength was built into the structure by varying the number of laminations of the Sitka spruce plywood. At the wing root, where a Gottingen 398 airfoil was used, 39 layers of the 1/16th inch thick veneer were built up into a two and 5/8″ thick section. At the tip, where the airfoil had transitioned into one similar to the Clark Y, there were five layers of material, naturally 5/16″ thick.

The strong plywood also provided a very smooth surface, which was covered with Fabrikoid, waxed and highly polished. Three molds were used to lay out the wing—one for each surface, and one for the leading edge. These were doweled together, and then given a heat and pressure treatment to form them into a solid one piece structure.

The four ribs were located to prevent flutter. One was at the 12 foot chord wing root, where the fuselage attached; two were over the landing gear housing, to transmit landing stresses to the upper wing, and the last was near the wing tip, which measured an enormous five foot six inches in length. The ailerons were cut on a bias, resulting in their having their maximum thickness at the tip, an unlikely way to obtain efficient control response.

The fuselage was bolted to the wing; it was a monocoque structure built with internal bulkheads. The prototype had three seats in the streamlined cabin, with the pilot

The Tunison Scout was built entirely of molded plywood and was exceedingly advanced for 1929. The wing had no spar at all; the stress was carried entirely by the wing skin. The 300 horsepower Wright-Hisso engine was supposed to enable a top speed of 190 mph. If it actually reached that speed, this was a sensational airplane for the day. What ever happened to it? *John W. Underwood*

The Scout's ailerons were oddly shaped, with an inverse taper. There was a hatch in the cabin roof for entry. The famous Jimmy Angel (he of Angel Falls) made the first flight on December 21, 1928, and was—as all test pilots were after first flights—extremely laudatory.
John W. Underwood

A modification of the Tunison involved the installation of a Miller engine (of racing car fame) and a cooling system that involved no less than seven Model T radiators.
John W. Underwood

sitting forward of the two passengers. Later versions were to have four seats, two abreast. A most unusual feature was that the seats were actually mounted in a hole cut in the upper surface of the wing, with the lower surface acting as a floor. On the first, and I believe, only Scout, the long cockpit canopy was bolted to the fuselage. Entrance was via a trap door in the roof. Production versions were to have a large door.

Perhaps the most notable element of streamlining were the ultra wide landing gear fairings, which were, like the rest of the plane, made of molded plywood, and resembled those used on the early Antoinnette, as well as the later Northrop Gamma. An elaborate shock cord mechanism and a patented roller spring mechanism soaked up shocks. Jimmy Angel made the first flight on December 21st, 1928, and gave all the expected laudatory comments, while a confident Tunison provided the press some optimistic performance figures. With a 300 horsepower Wright-Hispano engine, he claimed a top speed of 190 mph, 165 mph cruise and an 18,000 foot service ceiling. Wingspan was 36 feet, length 31 feet, wing area 270 square feet and gross weight 3,650 pounds.

The Scout's clean lines were somewhat marred by the antiquated vertical fin and rudder, and the low aspect ratio wing was a curious contrast to the high aspect ratio, 16 foot long horizontal stabilizer.

A group called Pacific Air Industries, Inc., took over the manufacturing rights for the Scout, and asserted that they were going to build the type in series, powered by engines ranging from 75 to 500 horsepower. In addition, they were to manufacture a line of Tunison engines across a wide horsepower range. What was the ultimate fate of the aircraft? What was it really like? Was it just a promotional scheme, as so many were, or was it a genuine effort that failed for yet to be disclosed reasons? Somebody out there must know—let's hear from you, for the Tunison Scout seems to have disappeared among history's obscure pages.

A head-on view shows how sleek this airplane was—compare it to Lindbergh's Ryan NYP of the same period.

10 Emsco Aircraft Corporation

An Aviation Pioneer Lost in the Pages of Time, Part I

Wings June, 1973

In many ways, Charles F. Rocheville anticipated the Experimental Aircraft Association by 30 years. He began designing "home-built" aircraft when he was very young and continued doing so for his whole life.

Rocheville represents a fascinating period in American aviation, when intuitive young men with a flair for design could create aircraft even though they lacked engineering degrees. It was also a period when such projects could be self-financed, although this usually meant that the young man's family had to do without a lot of things that it might otherwise have enjoyed.

I met with Charles Rocheville on two occasions and enjoyed both meetings immensely. He was advanced in age at the time, but his mind was crystal clear, and his interests had transcended aviation to include space flight. Interestingly enough, he also had an interest in the supernatural that extended back to the days when he flew for oil companies seeking potential drilling areas in the Middle East.

Rocheville made a great impression upon me, so much so that I modeled the character Hadley Roget in my trilogy of novels that began with Trophy for Eagles *on him. I think Rocheville would have been pleased with Hadley.*

If you had been a shrewd investor back in the palmy spring of 1929, what would you have thought of the investment prospects in an aircraft firm which offered:

(1) A spanking new million dollar plant, with the most modern facilities in the business.

(2) The talents of an expert designer and world famous pilot.

(3) Almost unlimited financial backing by a huge industrial empire.

(4) A complete line of beautiful planes, ranging from a Smilin' Jack-like two-seat sport plane, to a four engine F-32 equivalent?

Like me, you'd probably have anted-up your life savings to get in on the ground floor, only to have that floor sink swiftly and forever into the California landscape.

But if ever, *if ever*, a company should have succeeded, it was Emsco Aircraft Corporation, which had absolutely everything going for it but the luck of the draw.

Emsco

In a scandalously short corporate career which lasted, fleetingly, from its inception in 1929 to its *de facto* demise in the fall

There are many similarities in the approaches to aviation taken by Charles Rocheville and the founder of the Experimental Aircraft Association, Paul Poberezny. Both were fascinated with aircraft, both modified existing aircraft to suit their needs, and both designed new aircraft. This is young Charles Rocheville with his first modification, a Curtiss OX-5 engine installed in a surplus Thomas Morse SC-4.

This aircraft was originally a Fokker DVII and converted into a very handsome design by Rocheville. It had a Wright-Hispano engine, and was later used for variable camber experiments. The stub-wing arrangement is clever, providing an attachment point for both landing gear and wing strut. *John W. Underwood*

of 1931, Emsco was a veritable hot house of aircraft design. There were eleven separate Emsco types germinated during this period, nine of which actually bore fruit and were flown. Genealogically, the line should include at least twelve other distinct types which flowered in the fertile mind of the mainspring of the organization: veteran flyer, explorer, inventor, scientist and entrepreneur, Charles F. Rocheville. The stories of Rocheville and Emsco are interdependent, of course, but each is so varied that justice can be done only in separate articles. The next issue of *Airpower* will cover Rocheville's other aircraft, some of which have never before been described. A third story will deal with his flying adventures.

From this imaginative and varied design series, a total of sixteen aircraft were built under the Emsco trademark. (Several rather extensive modifications complicate the story.) Each of these aircraft made a significant contribution to a history which is checkered by an almost unbelievable run of bad luck, and relieved only by a few golden moments, when it seemed that Emsco might really join the roster of aviation giants.

The Background

The end of the third decade of the twentieth century was highlighted by a series of fantastic flights and by the birth of numerous optimistic aviation companies, each, if you believe the advertisements, offering the public a product which was unique for its performance and quality. Emsco briefly appeared among these, another, almost anonymous, milestone in the heritage of flight. Yet, today, even among aviation buffs, few are able to recognize the distinctive portly lines of the Downey, California firm's products.

The engineering spark plug of the firm was Charlie Rocheville, one of the dwindling number of pioneer flyers whose career can truly be called legendary. An early member of the Royal Canadian Flying Corps, Rocheville transferred to the U.S. Naval Air Service in 1917, and eventually rose to the rank of Lieutenant Commander. He was a member of Admiral Byrd's North Greenland Arctic Expedition, and then served with Admiral Donald B. MacMillan in exploring Labrador and Greenland. He flew short hulled, Liberty engined Loenings in the U.S. Navy's Aerial Survey of Southwest Alaska, and then, as a later exploration venture, conducted a photo-mapping expedition which covered the richest oil-bearing sections of Saudi Arabia. An important byproduct of the latter was his research into carbon-based dry lubricant materials which have been used on scores of space applications including lunar excursion modules.

Today Rocheville still has his eyes on the future, and his son Charles has a hard time dissuading him from launching new ventures. The senior Rocheville is a gentle, soft-spoken man, able for the first time in his life to take time from arduous business ventures and reflect on past accomplishments. His eyes flash as he looks at his early designs—a variable-camber wing SPAD, a graceful 90 ft. span tri-motor, a unique, double-hulled photo plane—and he can call out the individual characteristics that made them unique. He can become positively eloquent on the space age application of his still secret, even mysterious, dry lubricants, whose properties can't be explained or duplicated by the most advanced industrial laboratories, but are, nevertheless, employed in countless scientific vehicles. Taking notes becomes a problem; he gets so interesting the pencil just stops working. It was Rocheville's varied talents as engineer, designer, craftsman and pilot which permitted the fledgling company to field, in bewildering succession, the extensive series of aircraft that bore the Emsco name. Perhaps the most amazing thing is that the airplanes were not only handsome and efficient, but that they featured some very advanced design innovations, including the built-in capability of changing quickly from tri-motor to bi-motor, to single engine, as well as to change from wheels to floats. All of the aircraft were so smoothly sculptured that they were equally agreeable to the eye and to the air flowing over them. Much use was made of formers and stringers, even for the unusually large built up wheel pants. Workmanship and finish were outstanding, and bright contrasting colors complemented the smooth lines. (Charles E. Rocheville, the designer's son, ruefully recalls just how exacting his father was—rib stitches had to be perfect, and woe betide him if he made an error in hand-burling any metal finish.)

The financial backing of the operations was provided by E. M. Smith, a sort of Daddy Warbucks of the oil derrick industry. Thus the name "Emsco", from his initials. Smith apparently felt it was time to add an aircraft division to his formidable industrial aggregation which already manufactured asbestos, belting, rubber products, brake linings, forgings, oil derricks, fire bricks, engines, diesels, valves, and which controlled, in one manner or another, numerous financial institutions.

Smith was finance sheet and stock oriented, however, possessed of an ability to make money with paper, as well as with products, and this was to have an unfortunate effect on the company's future.

In the beginning, though, E. M. believed in doing it right, and with a happy eye for future property values, he moseyed down the street from his Downey, California (Pop. 8000) asbestos plant and bought 73 flat acres of the Hughan ranch. This real estate was then a true boondocks, and would so remain for many years, later becoming the home of Vultee and, finally, North American.

The firm was incorporated for a cool $1,000,000. This may not seem like much today when a hamburger stand franchise goes for $75K, but at a time when the Granville brothers or Jimmy Wedell would have been amazed to see even $5,000, it was a tidy sum.

A 60,000 square foot plant was designed to "build everything from the wheels up" and it was planned to start a complete aviation school for pilots and mechanics.

As the plant was being built, Smith acquired the assets and talents of the American Albatross Company, and the first three Emsco planes, according to the FAA records provided by Jack Barber, were actually completed at the firm's Long Beach facility. Rocheville doesn't recall this to be the case today, maintaining that only the very first plane was completed there, and the records may be the result of an administrative oversight.

In keeping with his method of doing things right, Smith announced the new venture in a brilliant series of advertisements in *Western Flying, Aero Digest, Aviation,* and *Oil Weekly,* emphasizing the solid industrial backing of the new aviation dynasty. Everything was on hand: designs, plant and finances, and Emsco stood eagerly on tip toes, awaiting fortune's kiss.

Almost all of Rocheville's designs would have made great free-flight or radio-controlled models, because they had a lot of wing area and a long fuselage to provide stability. This Albatross B-1 was owned and operated by Al Ebrite in 1929–1930. *John W. Underwood*

With a fancier paint job, the Albatross B-1 was named the *"Pride of Hollywood"* and was intended for endurance flights. It ultimately ended its days as a freighter in Mexico. Note the Maddux Ford Tri-Motor in the background. *John W. Underwood*

The Emscos, One by One

Rocheville's career with Emsco really starts with the products of his own companies (variously called "Midway", "Zenith" and "American Albatross"), for he designed and built three shapely aircraft in the 1927–1929 period which provided the foundation for the later firm. The very first was the superbly crafted 90 foot wingspan tri-motor, X-3662, at the time the largest airplane ever built on the West Coast, and one capable of lifting 2.47 times its own weight. Built with the delicate woodworking tracery that would characterize most of Rocheville's later designs, it was powered by Ryan marketed Siemens-Halske engines of 125 nominal horsepower, but actually capable of putting out 90. The smart money was betting that the three little engines would not get the 13,898 pound gross weight aircraft off the ground, but they did—and that's yet another facet of the Rocheville story. (Years later X-3662 became the "Schofield Albatross".)

The second and third planes were also called Albatross, and sometimes the Albatross B-1. Similar in construction to the first plane, these were smaller, with a 56 foot wing span. The B-1s were really rather plain aircraft, lacking the later Emscos' Mae Westian voluptuousness, but possessing the same healthy proportions of broad wings and long fuselage which made them such docile flying machines. (And would today make them superb radio-controlled scale model designs.)

The first B-1 was powered by a 250 hp Menasco Salmson. Registered X-6772, it would be used by Lee Schoen-

The Zenith Albatross was designed to set an endurance record and bears the hallmarks of Rocheville designs of the period: a beautiful finish and a strong but light structure. *John W. Underwood*

hair and Johnny Gugliemetti in endurance record attempts.

The second B-1, X-331E, was powered by a Pratt & Whitney Wasp and sold to Al Ebrite, who used it in charter work in Mexico, where it performed very well from short, rough, mining camp strips.

The purchase of Albatross by Emsco in early 1929 resulted in some confusing press coverage. For example, the April, 1929 issue of *Western Flying* shows a picture of the "Emsco Albatross B-2".

These three airplanes are a story in themselves, and will receive a complete treatment in a future issue.

The Emsco "Challenger"

The very first official Emsco, and the plane that was used in the clever Emsco trademark, was the B-2 "Challenger", which was licensed as X849E on May 17, 1929. Emsco internal records designated the plane as 8PCM, designed to carry two crew and six passengers. The name "Challenger" derived of course from the use of three Curtiss "Challenger" engines of 170 hp each, (c/n's 196, 207 and 208) even though the practice of naming the aircraft after the engine would inevitably result in confusion when engine changes were made.

The B-2 had a top speed of 130 mph, cruise of 100, and a service ceiling of 15,000 feet. It also had the advertised capability to take off with a full load with any two engines operating.

An engine transplant performed in January, 1930 converted the plane to a B-5, using two 300 hp Wright J-6 engines. A somewhat pointy rounded nose supplanted the central power plant. In this configuration it was naturally called the Emsco "Whirlwind" and was sold in an intracorporate deal to Emsco Derrick and Equipment Company, which used it on a 7,000 mile advertising junket. On July 13, 1933, it was sold to *Compania Nacional de Aviación, Incorporated,* for a bargain $3,500; it was operated in Guatemala and its subsequent disposition is unknown. Original factory price was in the $20,000 to $25,000 range.

The First B-3

The second Emsco was the B-3, X-832H which was substantially a single engine version of the B-2, with minor changes. Wing span was widely reported to be 57 feet, although Rocheville maintains that all of the series carried the standard 60 foot wing, the figure used in *Janes*. Thomas D. "Jack" Reid, an Emsco employee and long time friend of Rocheville, broke the world's endurance record with the aircraft at the National Air Races on August 21, 1929. Reid's take-off had been delayed by some administrative red tape, and the balding, smiling pilot had been up for many hours prior to getting a go-ahead. Sadly, and with the ill-fortune that somehow seemed to dog the firm, Reid had flown 38 hours and 40 minutes when the B-3 was observed to descend in a spiral. It struck a beech tree at Fairview Village, Ohio, destroying the plane and killing the apparently sleeping pilot.

The Cirrus

The third aircraft was perhaps the most photographed of the line. The pretty little Emsco "Cirrus" was a trim midwing two placer proudly labeled "Test Ship No. 2". A flight by John Gugliemetti from Downey to Oakland in 3 hours and 45 minutes was widely publicized for its amazing fuel economy. Burning only 4.8 gallons per hour, the trip cost $4.14 in a day when av. gas went for 23 cents a gallon. Gugliemetti today recalls the flight as having been a spontaneous thing, the outgrowth of his having a need to go to Oakland, and Rocheville having an airplane available.

The construction of the B-4, as the "Cirrus" was designated, was similar to that outlined below for the B-2. The trainer/sport plane weighed only 1,090 pounds empty and 1,650 pounds fully loaded. Wing span was 36 feet, length 21′10″ and height 7 feet. The 95 hp Cirrus Mark III provided a top speed of 135 mph and a cruise of 100 mph. Landing speed was quoted variously as 50 and 55 mph, but the landing was made easy by the six foot tread of the divided axle gear, which had Aerol shock absorbers.

There is a mystery about the B-4 type, of which a total of six were built. The manufacturer requested that the license of the prototype, X 369H, be cancelled on July 18, 1930. Its disposition is unknown, but it may have been used later in the variable camber experiments of Rocheville and his brother Harry.

The second B-4, X 846N, is described as a low wing, externally braced monoplane, and is also supposed to have been scrapped prior to November, 1930. Little else is known about the plane, except that it may have been rebuilt for use by Rocheville in the Deeble Double Action engine experiment, which again, is a story in itself.

The third B-4, X 869, started life as a standard "Cirrus", but was converted to a B-7 on February 28, 1930 and approved for NC 869 license under ATC 403 on February 21, 1931. This airplane had a 165 hp Wright R-540 engine. Wingspan was the same as the B-4, but length had increased to 23′9″ and height to 8′1″. Gross weight had climbed to 2,100 pounds, and max speed declined to 130.

The first B-7 was destroyed in an accident at Grand Central Air Terminal on March 22, 1931. A relatively inexperienced Emsco demonstration pilot, 22 year old Ailine

Miller, had just picked up veteran movie pilot Ivan de Villiers for a joy ride.

The plane was seen to rise sharply to about 400 feet, as if the pilot were showing off a bit, then stall and crash, breaking apart just aft of the rear cockpit. The entire forward portion was demolished, and the pilots died on the way to the hospital.

The three remaining "Mid Wing Sports", X 870N, X 871N and X 872N, have enigmatic FAA records, which indicate only that the license was applied for and that the aircraft were "scrapped prior to November 1930".

If one thing is sure, it's that there was some good reason for the factory not trying to sell them as B-4s, possibly relating to the granting of the ATC license for the B-7. Rocheville left the firm about this time, and FAA records are incomplete, but it's safe to assume that these aircraft were converted to X 909 Y, NC 969Y and NC 12247, of which more later.

The Second B-2

The ninth Emsco to be built was another B-2, which was approved for license NC 823N on January 4, 1930 under Group 2-171. The original three Curtiss Challenger engines (c/n 283, 284, 285) were replaced by a single 425 hp Wasp, changing it to a B-3. Later, on February 5, 1931, it became NC 823N again under ATC 400, as a model B-3A. Some records indicate a 57 foot wing span for this plane, but Rocheville stoutly maintains that it was a sixty footer, pointing out that they used only one set of jigs to build wings. The plane was sold on October 13, 1933 to Francisco Sarabia (who was fated to die in the last of the Gee Bees, the Q.E.D.) for use in Mexico, where it became lost to history.

The Flying Wing

Perhaps the most innovative of the Emsco line was the tenth aircraft, the "Flying Wing". Designed for a trans-Pacific flight by Rocheville and salesman Ted Lundgren, the plane featured a streamlined tandem, two-place, all-metal nacelle placed on top of the standard 60 foot span, 9 foot chord wing. Two slender metal booms supported a delicate single fin and rudder empennage, and were protected by metal tail bumpers.

This is the Emsco (for E. M. Smith Company) B-7. Mid-wing designs were relatively rare, and Emsco had more success with them than most. Ailine Miller crashed on takeoff in this airplane on March 23, 1931, at Glendale, California. *John W. Underwood*

Rocheville created a "blown wing" for this aircraft. Inlet ducts, just aft of the long chord cowling surrounding the Pratt & Whitney Wasp Jr. engine, carried air through the wings and out of slots set about ⅓ of the way forward from the trailing edge. The device created about a 35 mph increase in cruise speed, according to Rocheville, by reducing the turbulence.

Another unusual feature of the Model B-8 was a reverse tricycle gear. Two wheels with large balloon tires were set in a framework which would ultimately have been faired over in a manner similar to the Northrop *Gamma*, while a third wheel, slightly smaller, was mounted under the rear of the nacelle.

Rocheville says that the performance of the aircraft was excellent, literally leaping off the ground even when under heavy load, and flying well under all conditions. He discounts a notation in the FAA files that the trans-Pacific flight was abandoned due to a wing-flutter problem which occurred at half-fuel load. Instead, it was the financial drought that dried Emsco up when E. M. Smith began having some tax problems, and declined to fund the company further, causing the flights' cancellation.

The "Wing" differed from usual Rocheville practice in that it held the tanks for all but 75 of the 875 gallon fuel capacity.

X-55W, as it was registered, was a stylish airplane that might well have been successfully developed had there been sufficient time and money. It, like some of the others, was scrapped prior to November 28, 1930.

This brings to a close Part One of the Emsco story; Part Two (July) will cover the remaining Emsco aircraft, including the unlucky *"Morelos"*, struck by lightning and lost at sea; the most famous of the line, the *"City of Tacoma"*; the handsome B-3 which was to have been flown by Prince Ghica of Rumania; the "high wing", supposedly designed by Gerry Vultee from basic B-4 stock; the B-7C and B-7CH and two unfinished Emscos. In addition there'll be pilot recollections of the quality and flying characteristics of the planes, plus a detailed description of the pure craftsmanship which went into the planes' construction. As with this article, there will be a comprehensive photo coverage, with many never previously published candid shots.

11 Emsco Aircraft Corporation

An Aviation Pioneer Lost in the Pages of Time, Part II

Airpower July, 1973

You need skill to become a successful aircraft designer, but you need luck as well. Charles Rocheville had plenty of skill, but he was a little deficient in the luck department.

Much of Rocheville's skill in design can be seen in the beautiful lines of his aircraft, which are all quite elegant. His son Charles told me that his father was extremely demanding in regard to quality control and fit and finish and had no compunctions about ordering an aircraft to be repainted if he found the slightest flaw in the finish. He was also an advanced thinker, investigating boundary-layer control and other challenging engineering ideas long before they were studied at Langley Field.

Yet his choice of business partners and his timing were often bad; while he could create great airplanes, he rarely could create them at the right time and with the necessary financial backing. Had he been able to hold on for just a few more years, his firm, like others, would have been saved by World War II, and we might have seen some really interesting Rocheville combat aircraft.

One of the prettiest of the line was the Emsco B-3, the *"Morelos"* built for Mexican Colonel Pablo Sidar. The fit and finish of Emsco aircraft was superb. Charles Rocheville was a perfectionist and demanded that everything from structure to covering to the color scheme be perfect. The *"Morelos"* was lost on a flight from Mexico to Argentina, probably from a lightning strike. *John W. Underwood*

By mid-summer 1930, the firm had consumed its own substance, and while a few modified designs were still to be created, very few sales were to be made. It was time for Rocheville to think about leaving. Gerard F. Vultee and then T.V. Van Stone succeeded him in the Chief Engineer role, but it was apparent that Emsco was a spent force. Yet there were still flights to make, and unfortunately, accidents to be encountered.

Colonel Pablo Sidar and Charles Rocheville. Rocheville was an explorer in his own right—he served on the McMillan expeditions and did his own survey work for oil companies in the Middle East. The author interviewed Rocheville extensively in 1972 and was amazed at how little he had changed physically from this 1930 picture. *John W. Underwood*

The Unlucky *Morelos*

The eleventh aircraft to be built was an extremely beautiful Model B-3, sold to the Mexican Government as the "Emsco Wasp" and registered X-BACO. Christened *"Morelos"* after a revolutionary Mexican patriot, the plane was fitted with special fuselage tanks for a proposed record long distance flight attempt from Oaxaca, Mexico to Buenos

This Emsco B-3 was sold to the Mexican airline owned by Francisco Sarabia, who was killed in the crash of the Gee Bee Q.E.D. *"Conquistador del Cielo"* after a takeoff from the airport in Washington D.C. One interesting feature of the Emsco design was that they could be fitted with one, two, or three engines, as required by the customer. *John W. Underwood*

Perhaps the most famous of all the Emsco aircraft, the Emsco B-3 *"Clasina Madge"* (formerly the *"City of Tacoma"*) is shown ready for a dawn launch in Japan from a specially prepared wooden ramp. The idea of using a ramp to facilitate takeoff intrigued aviators through World War II, when a huge ramp was built at Wright Field to test its effect on takeoffs. Tests proved that there was no net gain in using a ramp. *John W. Underwood*

Aires. In what was becoming typical of Emsco luck, the *"Morelos"* was apparently struck by lightning and crashed into the sea off Puerto Limon, Costa Rica, killing pilots Lt. Col. Pablo Sidar and Captain Carlos Rovirosa.

Here is the *"Clasina Madge"* at the Glendale Airport in 1931. It was flown by Don Moyle and Cecil Allen. Allen would also lose his life in a Gee Bee, crashing on takeoff in the hybrid R-1/R-2 *"Spirit of Right"* in the 1935 Bendix Race. *John W. Underwood*

The *"City of Tacoma"*

The twelfth Emsco was undoubtedly the most famous of all, being the fourth of an ill fated "City of Tacoma" line, three Lockheed aircraft having previously borne the title. Registered NR 153W, this B-3 had a 1,005 gallon fuel capacity and was, of course, intended for the long range flights which Emsco devoutly hoped would at last capture the public's eye.

Its career was both fortunate and unfortunate. Purchased by the indefatigable lumber man John Buffelen on July 11, 1930 for a bargain price of $15,000, the plane was to be used for a Tokyo to Tacoma flight by Harold Bromley and Harold Gatty. The pair did fly some 2,500 miles in the attempt, but turned back, beaten by the weather.

The next year a brash but not bold pilot named Tom Ash changed the name of the plane to *"Pacific"* and announced that he would make the flight that Bromley had abandoned. After a great deal of activity and preparation, the ex-Army pilot made an abortive take-off run, ground looped, and stalked off with many unkind words about the airplane, declaring it unfit for a Pacific flight.

Then, in August, 1931, Don Moyle and Cecil Allen (who, like Sarabia, would fall prey to a Gee Bee, this one the hybrid 7-11 version) went to Japan to refurbish the plane for another attempt at crossing the Pacific. The Japanese government was understandably becoming concerned about the Emsco and the inability of American flyers to make it perform, and there was some pressure on the pair of flyers to abandon the attempt. They pressed on, however, installing a new stabilizer, elevator, fin, rudder,

Another view of the *"Clasina Madge"* in this photo undergoing maintenance at the Pomona Airport. Check out the names on the hangars behind it—Fairchild, Monoprep, Monocoach, Cadet Aircraft. Those were the golden days of aviation. *John W. Underwood*

cowling and supercharger, and rechristened the plane *"Clasina Madge"*, after Buffelen's daughter. (Rocheville, looking at a picture of the *"Clasina Madge"* in November, 1972, said, "that cowling wouldn't help a bit at the airspeed they were going to fly". Then, he mellowed a little and said "Oh well, I'm not going to criticize some one else trying to improve things".)

Using an inclined wooden ramp to help them get off with their enormous fuel load, they rolled down the firmly packed sand of Sabushiro Beach for a successful take-off, much to the relief of Japanese officialdom, embarking on an epic series of misadventures on September 8th, 1931. As assets, they had youth, hope, a good plane and lots of fuel; on the debit side, they had almost no practical experience in either navigation or instrument flying.

After a nightmarish flight through storms, winds and ice, the *"Clasina Madge"* made its first unscheduled stop on a minuscule deserted Aleutian island. The rocky little landing spot was, at first, a welcome haven to Moyle and Allen, but after five days of near starvation, they miraculously cranked up the trusty Pratt & Whitney and took off again. This time their unerring dead reckoning took them to a tiny Siberian mining town, where they were royally entertained. They filled up their tanks with Russian paint thinner (you read it correctly!), and flew on to Alaska, where they spent two weeks in Nome curing the Wasp of chronic indigestion. Flying first to Skagway, and then on to Tacoma, the pair finally completed their trip some 28 days after their take-off. Their part of the venture was capped off by landing at the wrong airport, thereby missing Buffelen's loyal welcoming committee.

But the cruelest blow of all fell when they learned that Clyde Pangborn and Hugh Herndon had just finished a successful nonstop trans-Pacific flight from Tokyo to Wenatchee, Washington.

This was not the end of NR-153's bad luck, however. Moyle bought the aircraft for $4,000 on March 1, 1932, having it modified to carry fish and cargo. He allegedly chose to carry some passengers also, and a violation was filed against him. Moyle fled, taking the plane to Mexico, where it was registered XB-AFV. It was left to weather at Torreon, and eventually scrapped for a lack of repairs, much to the chagrin of a Japanese delegation who came to the United States many years later, hoping to find *"Clasina Madge"* and restore her.

The Rumanian B-3

The thirteenth Emsco was NR 166W, a duplicate of the *"City of Tacoma"* except for a 1,120 gallon fuel capacity. Nobody tried harder to catch the public eye than Emsco personnel themselves, and Ted Lundgren and Roger Q. Williams planned to fly around the world via New York, Berlin and Tokyo. The attempt was abandoned due to weather conditions, and the plane was sold to the Rumanian government. It was intended that Prince Jean Ghica would use it for a world long distance record attempt from Bucharest to Durban, South Africa. The beautiful blue and orange craft was delivered to the Rumanians early in 1931, named *"Regele Carol II"* and registered CV-GOI. Unfortunately, Ghica was killed in a sports plane crash before the flight could take place, and the Emsco's subsequent career is unknown.

Roger Q. Williams, a feisty 82 and living in retirement in Fremont, California, still chuckles at the memory of the troubles he and Ted Lundgren had in their own beautiful blue and red Wasp powered Emsco B-3 NR-166W. After bad luck and bad weather had ruined their chances for a world flight, they decided to take a crack at the Transcontinental record. High above Oklahoma farm lands, the

The Emsco B-5 was a twin engine version of the tri-motor Emsco B-2. The wide-tread gear made the Emscos easy to land. *John W. Underwood*

The Emsco B-2 had Curtiss Challenger engines in its tri-motor form. This aircraft ultimately served with a Guatemalan airline. The engines on the B-2 could be replaced with two Wrights or a single Pratt & Whitney. *John W. Underwood*

cherry red of the manifold gave way to tiny tongues of flame as the collector ring began to melt away. The flames grew longer, beginning to lick at the fabric of the fuel laden Emsco, and Williams chose to force land in a tiny farm yard. He brought it off very well, and he and Lundgren were busy congratulating each other when a squad of state police arrived, busting them on bank robbery charges! Furthermore, it was impossible to convince the law that just because bank robbers had fled in a red and blue airplane, that this wasn't that particular airplane! After a long hassle someone finally recognized Roger, and the police reluctantly let them go. Meantime, the short stacks requested from Dallas had arrived, and the pair lost no time in getting the Emsco ready. The runway was actually a farmer's yard, all too short, with a fence and line of trees at the end of it. Roger and Ted trundled the portly Emsco so that its tail was placed on a ramp leading to the barn, and had rocks placed in front of the wheels, so that they could runup to full power before starting. With all 425 hp churning, Roger gave the signal and the

The Rumanian Prince Jean Ghica with the Emsco B-3 he purchased to make a long-distance flight from Bucharest to Durban, South Africa. Named the *"Regele Carol II,"* it was exported to Rumania. Unfortunately, Ghica was killed in the crash of another airplane, and the flight never took place. The ultimate disposition of this plane is unknown. *John W. Underwood*

A side view of the Emsco B-2 shows what a great deal of wing area it had, as well as the long moment arm of the tail. This photo was shot by Bill Larkins, passed along to Rick Allen, thence to Peter Bowers, and finally to me. *Peter M. Bowers*

farmhands, who weren't going to forget this week, watched the monoplane hop skip and just clear the trees. Williams made a low pass to wave goodbye, and nearly fell out of the seat laughing—the prop blast had festooned every pig, cow, chicken and farmhand below with loose bits of hay.

The neat little Emsco B-4, famous as "Test Ship No. 2," set a lot of records in its day. One record was for the number of variations that were built using its basic design. Top speed of 135 mph was obtained on an 85 horsepower Cirrus engine—I don't know of any other airplane that approached this performance with the Cirrus. Note the tail skid and the adjustable stabilizer. *Peter M. Bowers*

Another Emsco Mystery, Gerry Vultee's *"High Wing"*

The fourteenth Emsco, the Model B-10, is another mystery ship, one of which had some obvious surgery performed on it. It was originally registered X 909Y, and described as a mid-wing monoplane powered by a 165 hp Continental A-70 engine (c/n 121). Span was 36 feet, and length 24′2″. It was later described as a "remodelled Challenger engine job", Emsco High Wing, manufactured February, 1933, with Curtiss Challenger engine No. 209 and a Westinghouse Micarta propeller.

Gerry Vultee reportedly redesigned the airplane from a mid-wing to a parasol during his short tenure with Emsco, and photos reveal clearly where the fabric was removed and recovered in the "transplant" process.

However, Roger Williams says that, despite most reports to the contrary, Gerard Vultee did not have a hand in the "mystery high wing"; instead he and the Emsco staff had done a series of modifications on a mid wing in an attempt to improve spin characteristics, and the result was the rather attractive Model B-10.

Cecil A. Allen later bought the plane with only 15 hours on it, keeping it for about thirty months. He wasn't too enamored with the hybrid, as he tried to trade it to Fred Buckendorff (see below) for his B-7C. It passed through the hands of five more owners before being involved in an accident at Arlington, Oregon in December, 1940 by an unlicensed pilot. I was able to contact one of its owners, Mr. C.M. Fancher of Grand Junction Colorado. Mr. Fancher flew the plane strictly for sport, enjoying it very much. He regarded it as mildly "hot", having been cautioned against spinning it—probably good advice.

One variation on the B-4 theme was Harry Rocheville's variable camber airplane. Harry, Charles's brother, is shown here; he's indicating the way the wing's camber can be altered in flight. *John W. Underwood*

The B-7C Mid Wing Sport

The fifteenth Emsco was the B-7C, powered by a Continental A-7 engine of 165 horsepower, and registered NC 969Y, under ATC 424. The plane was basically an improved B-4, with different fuselage and empennage contours, and was probably designed by T.V. Van Stone, who took over after Vultee left the firm. The standard B-4 wing was retained, but the fuselage was larger and more commodious than the earlier model. Price was quoted as

This is the B-10 "mystery Emsco," a high wing aircraft that Gerard Vultee is said to have created from a B-4 structure in 1933. However, Roger Q. Williams, the famous long-distance flyer, told me that it was strictly an Emsco staff design. *John W. Underwood*

$5,950 at the factory, but the original owner scooped it up for $930.00 in the kind of lucky story that pilots daydream about.

Fred Buckendorff was indulging himself in that perennial past time of time-building, hopping from one Southern California airstrip to the next in his OX-5 Waco. Passing over Downey, he noticed an abandoned strip and what appeared to be a shut-down factory. On impulse he landed, and taxied up to inspect the premises. Peering in the window he was face to face with a somewhat be-draggled B-7C. The prop was off, the tires were flat, and the windshield was gone, but there was a real beauty to the plane that intrigued him. A little detective work revealed that Emsco had been overtaken by financial problems, but that Earl G. Heath was still acting as Secretary for the almost totally defunct firm. After two or three months of bargaining, Heath agreed to sell for $930.00, with $450 down and monthly payments of $40.00.

Buckendorff put the propeller on, changed the plugs, oil, etc., and did a visual inspection. Then he cranked up the inertia starter and the Continental turned over as if it had just been flown the day before. After a careful run-up, Buckendorff took off for a flight around the pattern. He landed, in love with a "beaut" of an airplane.

After some fifty hours flying time on the virtually unrigged Waco, the Emsco seemed like a Cadillac. He bought an Irving chute and proceeded to teach himself acrobatics, doing spins, loops, rolls, Immelmans, and so on. The plane had no eccentricities, and on one occasion, due to a little confusion between the occupants of the front and rear cockpit as to who was flying the airplane, actually landed itself.

Buckendorff worked in aircraft quality assurance for over thirty-two years, being employed first by the Air Force, and then by Vultee, Convair, General Dynamics and others. In his opinion, no other aircraft, civilian or military, measured up to the Emsco in terms of quality of materials or workmanship.

His story does have a sad end to it, however. The plane was "borrowed" without his knowledge and plowed into a Fleet, completely destroying the latter. When the Emsco was rebuilt, purportedly at the expense of the "borrower", a mechanic's lien was slapped on it for $1,000, and Buckendorff was forced to sell.

NC-969Y went on to serve seven other owners before being scrapped by Nagel Aircraft in 1946, a sad end to an airplane that apparently had no vices.

The B-7CH

The sixteenth and last Emsco to be completed was similar to the B-7C except for the use of the Challenger R-600 engine of 185 horsepower. Registered NC 12247, the plane had six owners prior to being sold to the Multnomah College Aviation School in Portland, Oregon on March 21, 1950. It was salvaged for parts and the registration cancelled on June 5, 1951.

Two Unfinished Emscos

The Emsco advertisements had proclaimed almost from the first that two more aircraft would be added to their expanding line. The first was variously described as a twin or tri-motor amphibian, but it is believed that this project did not progress much beyond the drawing board. The second was a very ambitious 112 foot wing span, 78 foot long, 32 passenger transport, to be powered by four Pratt & Whitney Wasp engines mounted in tandem on a stub wing, in the manner of the Douglas Dolphin or DO-X. While F.E. Samuels of *Aviation* reported seeing the completed aircraft, less covering, in 1930, Mr. Rocheville says that this could not have been so. The wing, fuselage, and nacelle structures had been completed, but not covered. Perhaps the most interesting feature was the use of corrugated metal for strength, covered by light metal for a smooth, stressed skin surface. This technique was used by several other planes, including the Martin B-10, but it originated with Rocheville.

The Final Rocheville Designs

Rocheville's engineering genius flourished despite the disappointments of Emsco, and he finished three other aircraft before embarking on his exploring/inventing career. The first was the previously mentioned low wing, NX 12270, which was specially built for the Deeble Double Action engine. The second was the variable camber winged B-4, and the third was a most unusual twin-hulled amphibian called the "Arctic Tern". Rocheville planned to use this aircraft in an aerial mapping of Alaska. It featured a Lockheed Sirius wing and a Vega tail, combined with two Edo floats. Rocheville flew the plane for about a month before it crashed as a result of a fuel feed failure.

Construction Details

Let's take a look at the construction techniques employed on the first of the line, the Emsco "Challenger", which were characteristic of all of the later planes.

First, it is important to note that Rocheville was and is a virtual fanatic on quality, both in workmanship or materials. Things have to be *right* or they get redone. He had a very pragmatic approach to design problems, making sure that he solved the things that mattered, and never being distracted by the irrelevant. He let materials and structures work for him, much in the manner of Charles Ward Hall, and he was extremely weight conscious. Rocheville faired and proportioned all exposed parts to get the best streamlining, so that his products all had a very sleek appearance.

The Challenger had its monoplane wing mounted directly on the six-passenger cabin, braced with parallel struts to the lower longerons. These struts were faired and had the same aerodynamic section as the wing itself, a modified Gottingen 398.

(In a later version of the aircraft, the B-5, these struts were joined by a fairing in a sort of stub-wing. In addition, small fins were added to the horizontal stabilizer.)

Wing construction was typical Rocheville, with box type spars with 1/8 inch three-ply side plates, spruce cap strips and spruce interior structure of Warren truss type. Five bays of drag bracing were used in each wing panel, with steel tube compression members mounted against a steel plate fitting at each spar, the drag wires being threaded through this fitting in such a way that the entire structure was rigidly tied together.

Ribs were of spruce in truss form, gussetted with plywood, their spacing varied according to the airflow expected to be encountered. Rocheville was very conscious of the importance of maintaining an airfoil, and studied both top and bottom surfaces of the wing during flight to ensure that there was no deformation. Duraluminum sheeting was used over the leading edge, top and bottom, to give a true curve as far back as the front spar. The wing tips were also faired by steel tubing, and the ailerons were well inset to avoid disturbing the airflow at the tip.

Charles Rocheville designed this extremely advanced aircraft for a proposed flight between Japan and the United States. The "Flying Wing," as it was inevitably called, had a very short takeoff run even when heavily loaded. It featured a blown wing, a far-out idea for the time. *John W. Underwood*

The twin boom aircraft featured a very long span. You can see the slots used for the blown-wing feature in this shot. Unfortunately, the aircraft had a flutter problem and the long-distance flight was shelved. *John W. Underwood*

The Emsco B-7C was the 15th aircraft of the line. It was powered by a Continental A-7 engine of 165 horsepower and was reputedly designed by T. V. Van Stone after Rocheville and Gerard Vultee had already left the firm. Originally priced at $5,950, it remained unsold for years and was finally picked up for $930 by Fred Buckendorff, who loved the aircraft and flew it for years. *Peter M. Bowers*

The fuselage and empennage structures were made of welded chrome molybdenum steel tubing, finished inside and out with Lionoil to prevent corrosion. The fuselage cross section was oval, with four longerons and heavy bulkheads, the latter braced with a K type truss. Sheet plywood formed the interior and exterior walls of the cabin, with heavy insulation in between for soundproofing.

The entire aircraft was then covered with the finest quality fabric, heavily finished with pigmented dope for a high gloss.

The original Challenger had a showstopper color scheme. Outboard nacelles were natural aluminum, with struts, wings and tail surfaces in gold. The fuselage and landing gear were finished in two tones of green, with black and gold striping.

Entry to the really spacious interior was by means of a patented "air stair" ladder on the door on the left side. A lavatory compartment was on the right as you entered, while a glance to the left revealed six wicker seats luxuriously upholstered with tapestry covered cushions.

The interior plywood sheeting was left in a varnished natural gum finish, and was relieved by two large windows. The "galley" consisted of a thermos flask mounted on the forward cabin wall, which also contained an altimeter, airspeed indicator and clock.

The spacious pilot's compartment provided ample room for the two-man crew, and visibility was outstanding through the large curved *glass* windows. Large pyralin windows below the windshield provided a view of the landing gear and engine mounted instruments. Instrumentation was as spartan as other 1929 aircraft, and the pilot had a neck-twisting cross check, as oil pressure, temperature and tachometers were mounted on the outboard engines directly. The center engine instruments were located on the front cockpit panel, along with compass, inclinometer, altimeter and airspeed. Throttles and "altitude adjustment levers" were centrally located, convenient to either pilot.

The undercarriage was of the divided type, each side consisting of one "Aerol" oleo strut attached to the apex of the steel tube landing gear structure. The large wheels were provided with Bendix brakes and streamlined by a huge wood and cloth built-up structure that added both speed and beauty.

Engine mountings were unusual both in their placement above the juncture of the landing gear and wing struts, and in that they were readily adaptable to changes in engine type.

Each of the engines had an eight gallon oil tank, while gasoline was normally carried in two wing tanks with a total of 130 gallons capacity. Optional tankage configurations were available, and used, in all subsequent aircraft.

The Emsco Cirrus, or B-4, had basically the same construction, adapted to the different configuration. Perhaps the only unusual feature was the method of wing mounting. The wings were set just above the line of thrust, and had a dihedral angle of three degrees. They were braced, top and bottom, with MacWhyte streamline wires to two tripod structures, the upper of which was enclosed entirely within the fuselage, while the lower extended, in Bellanca "Flash" style, beneath the bottom surface.

Conclusion

With all that Emsco had going for it, it is a shame that Fortune didn't smile just once. If Bromley and Gatty had succeeded in their flight, or even Sidar his, the plane might have caught the public fancy and become another Lockheed. Smith's financial problems could have been overcome by a simple sale; certainly Lockheed itself weathered enough financial difficulties, primarily because it had a famous product. But it was not to be, and the name and the planes disappeared into an undeserved oblivion. Charles F. Rocheville went on to new heights, however, and his story will appear in a future issue.

12 BOEING B-9 "DEATH ANGEL"

Airpower November, 1971

Here, the Model 215 is decked out in civil registration and Boeing colors. At that time Boeing-built aircraft were a light French Grey overall, with International Orange on the top surface of the upper wing and sometimes the lower wing. Fuselage and tail were initially trimmed with a dark green. Note the two-blade adjustable-pitch propeller and the lack of a fairing on the landing gear.

Surprisingly little has been written about the Boeing XB-9 "Death Angel," despite its obvious importance as the ancestor of both the 247 transport and the B-17 bomber. Its general layout and structure derived from the Boeing Model 200 Monomail. Two versions of the aircraft were developed, the Model 214 and Model 215, and these differed only in their engine installation. The Model 214 was equipped with two 600 horsepower Prestone-cooled Curtiss GIV-1510C engines, while the Model 215 had two Pratt & Whitney Hornets, also of 600 horsepower. Boeing financed both of the prototypes, and most of the company's assets were tied up in the program. The Air Corps was very much excited by the two aircraft, and Boeing received unofficial word that there would be large production orders for the B-9. Unfortunately for Boeing, those production orders would go to its arch rival, Martin, for

The clean lines of the airplane are apparent here. It is difficult today to understand just how radical this airplane appeared at the time, when the standard U.S. Army Air Corps bomber was the Keystone biplane. The Model 215 became the XB-9 when purchased by the Army, and acquired a different paint job. Buffs will note the neat little Monocoupe parked at the left.

It was, no doubt, an advertising man who set up this photo showing three Boeing P-12 fighters roaring across the field above the new (and faster!) B-9 bomber. The B-9 was a transitional aircraft, retaining some old-fashioned features such as the open cockpit. Cockpit entrance was from the outside only, and the bombardier and gunner had a hazardous task just to get in position. Structurally, the B-9 was a direct outgrowth of the preceding Boeing Monomail aircraft.

the sleeker and faster B-10. It was a fertile time at Boeing, when several advanced types were on the drawing board, including the Boeing P-26 and XP-29. Perhaps the greatest legacy of the B-9 was that it engendered enough confidence in Boeing that the company undertook even bigger projects, including the B-15 and B-17 bombers.

The early thirties were days of triumph and tragedy for the Boeing Aircraft Company. While their steady stream of pugnacious F4B and P-26 fighters provided a prospering line of work, the Seattle firm sought to broaden its efforts with two sensational new aircraft, both years head of anything then flying. Both planes met with instant initial acclaim, and both were heartbreakingly eclipsed for the big money contracts by competitors who came on just a little later and offered just a little more.

One was the famous 247 airliner, a 10 passenger, all metal, 180 mph. design whose first flight on February 8, 1933 figuratively swept all existing airline equipment from the skies. The 247 did garner orders for 70 aircraft—not an inconsiderable amount—but far less than the company had hoped for, before it was outclassed by the stable of speedy Douglas DC classics.

The other was the B-9, an angular, wicked-looking, twin engine, all metal, cantilever monoplane bomber, whose startling supremacy over the contemporary bailing wire Keystone biplanes revolutionized Air Corps thinking. Sadly for Boeing, the B-9 was to have a far less illustrious career than the 247, for within fifteen months of its appearance, Martin's sleeker, faster, more capable and much more salable B-10 would flash across the sky at Wright Field, and doom the Death Angel to service test obscurity.

Yet when the B-9 was taking shape, Air Corps planners could scarcely believe the extent of the advance being offered. Bomber aviation had been stagnant for years, seemingly tied forever to the thin winged, rigidly braced, fixed gear, twin engine biplane concept that did not vary, even in appearance, from World War I designs. In the ten years of peace there had been appallingly little increase in bomber performance or capability. The 1918 Martin GMB had a top speed of 105 mph, a ceiling of 12,500 feet, and a range of 390 miles with 1,040 pounds of bombs. In 1928, the Keystone LB-5 had a top speed of 107 mph, a ceiling of 8,000 feet, and a range of 435 miles with 2300 pounds of bombs. Hardly hellbent progress.

Suddenly Boeing was offering pursuit aircraft speed, a 2400 pound bomb load, and a tremendous potential for growth, all wrapped up in a low risk package they were prepared to finance themselves!

The Boeing Y1B-9 (Boeing Model 214) was one of a kind, fitted with Curtiss Conqueror GIV-1570 C (-29)'s engines of 600 horsepower. Even though the more streamlined liquid-cooled Curtiss engines should have cut down drag and increased performance, they did not, for top speed fell from the prototype's 188 mph to only 173 mph.

Boeing has always been a conservative company whose evolutionary design process ensures a familiar thread of appearance or structure to link one aircraft to the next. So as revolutionary as this first all metal, retractable gear bomber appeared to the world, it was really just another step along the road, one milestone past the *Monomail transport,* whose empennage, wing tip and elongated sweep of the fuselage were reflected in the B-9.

Had this not been true, Boeing would hardly have dared to bankroll the construction of *two* prototypes in hopes of a yet non-existent Army requirement. The planes, designated Models 214 and 215, differed only in the use of Curtiss Conqueror in line engines in the former, and Pratt & Whitney Hornets in the latter. Although there was no Army money available to assist Boeing in the effort (and this fact was repeatedly impressed upon the firm) there was a visceral interest on the part of flyers who wanted to insure the quantum leap from the Keystones to the B-9. The eager cooperation of the impoverished Air Corps makes an interesting story, for the success of not only the B-9, but also the B-17, stems from the translation of the original drawings to the operational aircraft via a fertile maturing process which began with the initial mock-up inspection and continued through the heavy bomber competition on into the extended service test. (The Martin B-10 went through an even longer period of cross fertilization, having started out in life as a fixed gear biplane—but that's another story!)

After viewing the original drawings, the Air Corps was delighted to send a group of five officers and two civilians to Seattle for a full scale mock-up inspection of the Model 215 on June 23, 1930. The group, headed by Major Willis

The Curtiss-powered version of the B-9 was unquestionably cleaner-looking, with its three-bladed props, used when the engine was upgraded to the supercharged 1570-F series engine. This experiment with liquid-cooled engines on a bomber was the last for more than 10 years. Not until World War II were similar experiments made, when in-line engines were applied to the B-17 on the Vega XB-38 and the gigantic, one-of-a-kind Douglas B-19A.

D. Hale, covered the radically clean 215 from front gun to tail wheel, making hundreds of suggestions for improvements or modifications to meet Air Corps needs—all the while stoutly proclaiming that there was no money available, and that Congress would have to decide in favor of the project before there would be.

The Board's most significant recommendation was switching the cockpit positions of the pilot and the bomber, as the bombardier was called in those less lethal days. The change in location provided the pilot a much better view to the rear, with less loss of forward vision, while having the incidental value of reducing the length of control cable run.

As at any mock-up inspection (and if you held 100 inspections of the same aircraft, the last would be exactly like the first) there was an unending stream of "human factors" recommendations. Then, as now, everyone was an expert in cockpit design and control layout, and there were more than fifty suggestions on instrument placement, control configuration, and so on. All engine instruments, for example, were required to be placed directly on the engine nacelles, to be indirectly lit, and to be well protected from oil and rain.

As their enthusiasm increased, so did the scope of their suggestions. Emergency, fold away dual controls were recommended to be fitted to the bomber's position, an idea that was repeated in the B-10. Major Hale recommended that the external bomb racks be modified so that a single battleship-busting 2,000 pound bomb could be carried as an alternate load. As a step further, he asked that Boeing consider widening the mid-section of the aircraft so that the bombs could be carried internally. Bob Minshall, chief designer for the B-9, threw up his hands in horror at this, for Boeing already had too much money invested in the project to begin redesign efforts. The suggestion was dropped, but the feature was picked up, along with many others, in the later B-10.

With the mock-up behind them, and encouraged by the complimentary remarks of the Army pilots, Boeing began work on the prototypes in earnest, and on April 13, 1931, the radial engine Model 215, decked out in Boeing colors and civilian registration, made its first flight. The Army tested the aircraft as the XB-901; when it was purchased it became the YB-9, and was given the serial number 32-301.

The long, lean look of the Death Angel concealed one of its drawbacks: a tendency for the aft fuselage to oscillate disconcertingly in flight. The B-9 would undoubtedly have been ordered in greater numbers had it not been faced with the competition of the Martin B-10, which brought everything to the table that the Death Angel did—plus a lot more. Boeing would later find itself in the same situation in the commercial field, when it introduced the B-9's civilian cousin, the Model 247 transport. When it appeared, it was revolutionary and beat all the competition. Then Douglas brought out the DC-1 and DC-2, which beat out the Model 247 commercially.

The sound of a Pratt & Whitney R-1830 engine became commonplace in just a few years, but at the time of this photo it was almost brand-new. The two 600 horsepower engines provide a top speed of 188 mph. Even with its wheels down, the Death Angel could do 172 mph—faster than most fighters of the day.

While still the XB-901, the "tissue paper bomber," as it was called by Wright Field engineers, because of the chronic wrinkling and flexing of its metal skin, it was pitted against the Ford XB-906 in a competition for heavy bombers.

The Ford, basically a standard 5-AT transport (See *Airpower* Sept. 1971) fitted with a single pilot cockpit, bomb racks and gun positions, fared surprisingly well in terms of performance, considering that it was a much older design, and had to drag a fancy spatted fixed gear along. The XB-901, whose R-1830-13 engines generated 575 horsepower each, recorded a speed of 163.0 mph at sea level, compared to the Ford's 144.6; yet as altitude went up the gap narrowed until, at 10,000 feet, the Ford was actually faster, 156.0 mph to 152.7 mph. The Seattle product had a 19,400 foot service ceiling, just 1,000 feet more than the tri-motor, and it had a slightly better rate of climb.

Ah, but when it came to flying qualities, there was absolutely no comparison. The Boeing was rated as excellent, while the XB-906 was criticized for high stick forces, miserable visibility, excessive attitude changes with changes in power settings, and extremely heavy vibrations at low power settings. Furthermore, the front gunner's position was considered absolutely useless, as the slip stream made the gun impossible to handle.

With this in mind, a Board of Officers, again headed by Major Hale, and including three future Generals (Captain Eugene Eubank, First Lieutenant Hugo P. Rush and First Lieutenant Ralph A. Snavely) issued a report which waxed rhapsodic about the XB-901. Everything about the plane was considered outstanding—structure, speed, armament, flying qualities—*everything*. It was clearly superior to anything previously tested, and was probably the best bomber in the world.

Although not figuring directly in the comparison, the Board had also inspected and tested the Douglas XB-7, an attractive monoplane with retractable gear, metal fuselage and fabric covered gull wing. While full data had not been obtained, the aircraft was obviously fast and capable. The Board felt, however, that the Boeing entrant was such a remarkable advance in bombardment aviation that it should be purchased in sufficient quantity to equip a squadron for service test.

When the results were announced, Ford put up a howl, claiming that all of the faults alleged by the Board could be easily remedied, and that they were entitled to receive an order so that an aircraft production capability would be maintained in the Detroit area.

Lt. Col. Hap Arnold was given the task of implementing the Board's recommendations, and he did so in a letter to the Chief of the Air Corps on August 6, 1931. To partially placate Ford, he suggested that the XB-906 be purchased, thus helping to pay at least part of the development expense.

Rather than buy a full squadron's worth of B-9s, however, he recommended that a Service Test Program be set up which would procure seven B-9s and seven XB-7s.

The decision stemmed purely from a lack of funds. Although he recognized the Boeing as a far more desirable aircraft, the B-9 was slated to cost $100,000 each for the first two, and $87,875 each for the next five. By contrast, the XB-7s cost only $30,400 each. Then, as now, money talked.

Hap changed the Board's recommendations in other, smaller ways. He overruled their desire to have a tunnel gun (shades of the Gotha) installed, saying that the narrow fuselage of the B-9 would permit the rear gunner an almost vertical downward field of fire. He also asked that the gas load be increased from 308 to 525 gallons; Boeing was happy to comply, as there was plenty of room in the deep, wide chord wings for auxiliary tanks.

Nevertheless, Boeing was mildly disappointed with the results, for the standard service test quantity of thirteen aircraft would have given them a far better chance to earn a return on the investment. Still, half a loaf, and all that, and the little Duwamish river plant began to hum with a sound which would characterize Seattle for the next forty years—rivet guns popping on big multi-engine aircraft. The contract, signed on August 21,

1931, was for a total of $696,324.00, for the two prototypes and five follow on Y1B-9 As, including spares, manuals and blueprints.

Wright Field was naturally anxious to get its hands on the hot new bomber, and the YB-9 was refurbished in Army colors and sent on ahead. Its sistership, now the Y1B-9, was completed in service finish, with first flight coming on November 5, 1931.

The testing at Wright Field revealed just how great an advance Boeing had achieved, for the sleek bomber could show its heels to everything but the very latest fighter products, while its shortcomings were relatively minor. Testing was sophisticated for its time, and quite exhaustive, particularly in the Wright Field labs, where static and fatigue components were completely examined.

Two of the many test pilot reports give an indication of the extent of the testing and the degree of Boeing's success. The first was written by Lt. Levi L. Berry on February 2, 1932, and details the performance of the Pratt & Whitney SG1R-1860 B powered YB-9, now fitted with a three bladed prop. At a gross weight of 13,351 pounds, and carrying two 1,000 pound bombs, the "Death Angel" could clock 188 mph at 6,000 feet, causing considerable embarrassment to local pursuit jocks; even with wheels down, the YB-9 reached 172.5 mph at a 1920 rpm power setting. Take off distance was less than 1,200 feet, and even without flaps, the broad thick wing made a comfortable 63 mph landing speed possible.

The B-9's long slender fuselage resulted in some innovations in crew placement. The gunner occupied the nose, followed by the bombardier, the pilot and the rear gunner. A radio operator could be carried, but this was considered an "overload" by Boeing.

Berry reports that the narrow pilot's cockpit was comfortable, and fairly easy to climb into. The bomber's position was considered to be hazardous to enter—a long fall was possible, and there was something disconcerting about the big propellers turning over at the elbow. His comments on the mechanical operation of the gear were understandably caustic—raising the gear required the combined efforts of two men struggling in the narrow cockpit, and they had to have at least one rest period before they could get an up and locked indication. Lowering the gear was not much better—on one occasion, over 2,300 feet was lost in the glide while the gear was coming down. As a result, production models had

Another standard public relations photo of the era showed a big aircraft towering over a smaller one. In this case, both airplanes are from Boeing, the Death Angel's wing protectively hanging over the Y1P-26 "Peashooter." When this photo was taken, Boeing held the lead over all other manufacturers in both fighters and bombers. But in the aviation business it is difficult to hold on to the lead for long. These aircraft are parked very near where the great Air Force Museum is now located in Dayton, Ohio.

The Boeing Y1P-26 flies in close formation with the YB-9, displaying the similarities and differences between the two. The YB-9 is technically more advanced, having a true cantilever wing and retractable landing gear. Note how the retracted wheels still protrude enough to ease the pain of a gear-up belly landing. Both aircraft bear the insignia of Wright Field, where all good airplanes went to be tested.

The Boeing Y1B-9A in the washable paint used in war games. This is May, 1933, and the B-9s simulated an attack on Cincinnati, Ohio—"obliterating" it, according to the judges ruling on the maneuvers. During this month, the Death Angels flew more than in any other month of their short careers, accumulating about 55 to 60 hours each. Normally they flew from four to 10 hours per month.

an electrically powered system, with a manual back-up.

On another test in December, 1932, Captain Victor Strahm conducted a series of flights to determine single engine capability. With a full load, level flight could be maintained on either engine at 4,200 feet, which is especially impressive when you remember that the props were not the full-feathering type. Considerable rudder force was required—it was impossible to hold a straight course with rudder only, the use of the Flettner balance being essential. With the right engine shut down, and the left at full power, a violent tail flutter was induced, requiring a power reduction, but not otherwise impairing the single engine capability.

By early 1932, the Y1B-9 with 600 horsepower Curtiss GIV-1570 C (-29's) engines was under test. The plane, serialed 32-302, weighed 8,618 pounds empty, some 356 pounds more than the YB-9. Differences in equipment and ballast reduced this to 240 pounds at the maximum gross weight, the Y1B-9 weighing 13,591 pounds to the YB-9's 13,351.

The YB-9, whose –11 series Hornet also put out 600 horsepower, had a significantly better performance than the Y1B-9 in every area. As the radial engine unquestionably had more drag, the difference must have been attributable to the propellers. The Hornet swung an 11′6″ prop with 30.5 degrees of pitch at the 42 inch station; the Conqueror engine had a 9′10″ prop with a 22.2 degree pitch at the same station.

With two bombs weighing a total of 2,050 pounds, the Y1B-9 attained 173.5 mph at 2445 rpm at 6,000 feet, and 156.0 mph at 2280 rpm at 15,000 feet. As previously noted, its round-engined sister ship clocked 188.0 mph at 6,000 feet at 2,020 rpm and 177 mph at 15,000 feet at 1,950 rpm. The YB-9 had a 3,400 foot advantage over the Y1B-9 at its service ceiling of 22,600 feet.

After further tests with a supercharged engine (GIV-1570 F) the Y1B-9 was converted to the production YB-9A standard by installation of Hornets on December 31, 1932.

Boeing delivered the last of the five service test

Data Sheet

Characteristic	YB-9**	Y1B-9	Y1B-9A
Wing Span	76′8¾″	76′8¾″	76′8¾″
Length	51′6″	51′6″	52′0″
Height	12′8″	12′8″	12′0″
Empty Weight	8,362	8,618	8,941
Gross Weight	13,351	13,591	14,320
Wing Area	954.1 sq ft	954.1 sq ft	954.1 sq ft
Service Ceiling	22,600′	19,200′	20,750′
Absolute Ceiling	22,400′	21,000′	22,500′
Range	495 miles/ 1997 lbs bombs	495 miles/ 1997 lbs bombs	540 miles/ 2260 lbs bombs
Maximum Speed*	188 mph	173.5 mph	188 mph
Engines	P&W SG1R—1860B Hornet (R-1830-11)	Curtiss GIV-1570C Conqueror (V-1570-29)	P&W R11860-11 Hornet
Wing Section	Modified Boeing 106	Modified Boeing 106	Modified Boeing 106

*At 6,000 feet, with two 1,000 lb bombs carried externally

**As updated from XB-901

Source: Official Performance Tests, U.S. Air Corps, supplemented by Ray Wagner's *American Combat Planes*

The Boeing B-9 was relatively expensive for the time; the first two service-test articles cost $100,000, and the next five were $87,875 each. The numbers seem absurd in today's market, when bombers bought in small quantities can run into the billions of dollars each. The wide, deep chord wing provided plenty of lift and allowed landing speeds as low as 63 mph. While the prototype had manually raised gear that was exhausting to operate, the service-test models had electrically operated gear.

Y1B-9As (Boeing Model 246) by March of 1933, and while their outward appearance to the prototypes was almost identical, there were numerous interior changes and refinements. The vertical fin and rudder had acquired a smoother new shape that would be seen again in the 247. The major differences were in details which improved ease of maintenance and service. For example, on the prototypes, it had been necessary to remove the exhaust system prior to removing the upper engine cowling. New oil coolers were installed, replacing the jury-rigged standard Air Force types that had been placed on the XB-901. The planes had originally been designed without a firewall (like the Heinkel 177) and had been equipped with Pratt and Whitney air intake oil coolers. When the Air Corps required Boeing to install a firewall on a hurry-up basis, the oil coolers were bolted to the outside of the cowling, an obvious afterthought.

The service test was long and exacting, and the individual aircraft rendered excellent service. The original model 215 stayed at Wright Field throughout its career, logging 161 flight hours before being surveyed on December 26, 1934. One landing accident, apparently relatively minor, is recorded on its flight record card.

The Model 214 also stayed at Wright Field, accumulating 151 hours before being dropped from the records in September, 1933.

The Y1B-9As had a more varied career. 32-303 was assigned to Wright Field initially, then transferred to Langley, where it racked up most of its 309 hours of flying time. May, 1933 was a big month for all of the service test B-9s, as they participated in the annual war games, leading an attack on May 8th which reportedly "obliterated Cincinnati" according to the judges; 303 logged 62 hours in this month, and its sisterships did about as well.

32-304 was also assigned to Wright initially, and then circulated between there and Langley while building up 278 hours of time. It was surveyed in April, 1935.

The third plane, 32-305, stayed at Langley throughout its service; flight record cards indicate a total of 276 hours time when it was surveyed on May 21, 1934.

High time B-9 was 32-306, which logged 371 flight hours between March, 1933 and March, 1935, when it was surveyed. All but 53 hours were flown from Langley.

The number five aircraft, 32-307, proved to be the only true Death Angel, crashing on June 25th, 1933 and killing all four crew members. The plane, marked 190 on the fuselage, took off from Logan Field, Baltimore at 2020

All Boeing aircraft have to be photographed with Mount Rainier in the background, and here is a beautifully painted Death Angel having its portrait made.

This was about as formidable as the U.S. Army Air Corps could get in the early 1930s—a flight of five B-9s in pretty good formation. They foreshadowed future formations of B-17s, in which aircraft would number in the hundreds.

hours, on a routine night training mission to Langley. 2/Lt. Lewis Horvath was the pilot and 2/Lt. H. W. Macklean the copilot; the two apparently encountered difficulties about 2200 hours, and attempted to crash land in the James River, about 1 mile from Rushmere Island. The B-9 struck the water nose first, broke in half, and sank, leaving only the tip of its tail exposed. A sad end to the last of the B-9s.

The introduction of the Martin B-10 ruled out any further development of the B-9, although the Air Corps and Boeing did discuss a B-9B model with cockpits covered by sliding canopies, and featuring other refinements. Nothing came of the talks, for the Martin not only performed better, but was far less expensive.

Thus even while the production contract was far smaller than Boeing had hoped for, this first all metal monoplane bomber did instill confidence in Boeing's ability to build big aircraft, inspiring them to carry on with the great new Models 294 and 299—the XB-15 and the B-17. This alone is surely enough to win a place in history for their almost forgotten, pioneering forerunner—the B-9—Boeing's benign Death Angel.

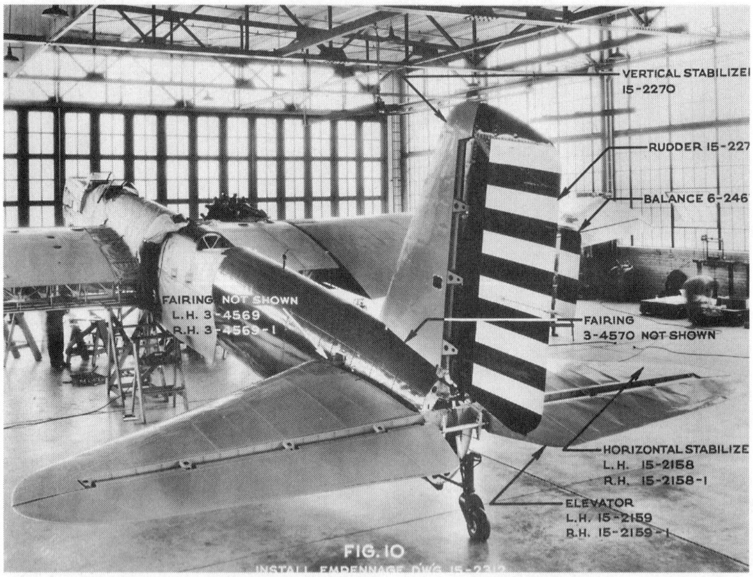

A Boeing photograph intended for use in manuals to show part numbers and placement. The wing structure can be seen at left; it is remarkably like that of the Boeing B-17. Note how paper is used to protect the finish. A stoutly built aircraft. *Author's collection, courtesy Vic Seely*

A Boeing company photograph shows the radical retracting landing gear, a real innovation for the time. The simplicity of the gear is in stark contrast to that of the later B-47 or B-52. *Author's collection, courtesy Vic Seely*

13 Martin B-10

The Bird That Took the Air Corps Out of the Stone Age

Airpower May, 1972

Discussions about classic airplanes, particularly older ones, almost always center around fighters. You can find ardent proponents of the Curtiss P-6E or Boeing P-12 or Hawker Fury, but you rarely find people who are enamored of the Vickers Wellesley or Dornier Do 23. Sadly, a very important aircraft is included in this category of overlooked types, and that is the Martin B-10. The B-10 was not exactly a revolutionary design; it was preceded by the Boeing B-9, which was also a twin-engine cantilever all-metal monoplane. Yet the B-10 managed to combine those features into a more attractive, stronger, and faster package, and in doing so, influence Air Corps thinking—and procurement practice—for the next decade.

The B-10 outperformed contemporary first line pursuit aircraft, and it was the first to have the Norden bombsight as standard. The accuracy of the Norden was so sensational (though not yet tested under wartime conditions) that bombers became the be-all and end-all of Air Corps planning. The end result was that the Martin B-10/B-12 series trained the generation of Air Corps officers that would lead the Army Air Forces in World War II. The B-10/B-12 also established an Air Corps precedent—a new emphasis on bombers, which led to the procurement of the B-17 and the creation of the policy of precision bombardment.

It was called the "Flying Whale" or the "Mystery Bomber," depending upon which newspaper account you read. Although well received by the press, this prototype of the Martin B-10, the XB-907, had such poor flying qualities that it was almost cancelled.

Incredibly, the Glenn L. Martin Company wanted to sell the Air Corps a biplane, and only reluctantly submitted a monoplane design.

A side view shows that, like the Boeing B-9, the original aircraft had open cockpits.

Any veteran late-late show watcher knows exactly how airplanes are designed. Two guys—one Fred McMurray and the other Andy Devine—are sitting around a hangar which houses a Stinson SR-5, a Travel Air A-4000 and what appears to be the tail section of the Capelis transport. Fred says, "I've got it," grabs an envelope from Andy's lunchbox, and rapidly sketches:

1. A Seversky P-35, or
2. a Boeing 247, or
3. the Phillips Aeroneer.

Andy, who will later prang into the field's resident high tension wire, bleats, "Aw Gee, Loop, that General Handley

Stafford won't buy no ship that ain't no biplane."

Sometimes real life is different than reel life, and so it was with the beautiful Martin B-10, a landmark design in American bomber aviation, the last surviving example of which is now awaiting restoration at the magnificent new Air Force Museum.

The B-10, unlike movie aircraft, was not conceived in a single blinding stroke of genius; rather it evolved from a sometimes heated two year brainstorming session between Wright Field's Materiel Division's engineers and the Martin staff.

This mutual development effort conflicts completely with the stereotyped concept of muddled military bureaucrats hampering brilliant but unorthodox designers, for in this instance, it was the Materiel Division which pleaded, begged, cajoled and eventually ordered Martin to adopt new techniques and concepts. Having been blessed with an unbelievable wealth of talent, including engineers like J. A. Rochê, I. M. Laddon, Colonel Carl Green, Dr. Younger, and others and pilots like McCready, Schroeder, Brookley, Harman, Harris, Eaker, and many more, the Materiel Division (and the Engineering Division which preceded it) had a long history of daring and successful innovation. Martin, on the other hand, was a well respected builder of rugged but rather orthodox military aircraft.

Martin's mock-up of the turret design, which was quite radical for the early 1930s. This was called a "Plastacelle" turret transparency. The vertical gun opening was rotated to the rear in normal flight, blocking the rush of air into the gunner's compartment.

The joint effort was worthwhile, for the developments of the original Martin 123 were important in many ways. The first really modern bomber procured in quantity for the U. S. Army Air Corps, the plane pioneered in scores of areas. When it was released for export, no less than seven Air Forces snapped at the chance to buy it. Perhaps historically most significant of all, it was the first American designed bomber to see combat.

Incredible as it may seem, Martin had responded to the design directive for a new bomber, MN 32-4, issued on December 16, 1929, with two separate proposals, one a rather unlovely monoplane, and the other a fixed gear, thin winged biplane. In the August 11, 1930 letter accompanying the submission, Martin strongly advocated building the biplane, because of "the advantages inherent in the smaller overall dimensions"—this at a time when Boeing had a mock up of their XB-901 Death Angel under review.

The letter kicked off an endless series of conferences, memos, visits and impassioned telephone calls which resulted in Martin very reluctantly submitting on August 20, 1930, another design for a twin engine monoplane bomber. Perhaps in defiance, or to show their conservatism, they retained a solid, ground-gripper fixed gear.

The initial series of meetings proved to be merely a prelude to a tempestuous two year marriage of conven-

The rear defense was weak, but typical of the period: a single .30 caliber Browning machine gun mounted in the gunner's cockpit, and another firing through a tunnel in the floor.

Wright Field practically had to beat the Martin Company about the head and shoulders, but gradually the design ideas that the Army wanted in the airplane were incorporated, one by one. In this version, the turret is installed, but the cockpit is still open. Note that the landing gear design makes it difficult to change the wheels.

When all the ideas finally came together, the B-10 was a beautiful airplane. This is the personal aircraft of Lieutenant Colonel (later Major General) Clarence L. Tinker. Tinker was killed on a raid on Wake Island in June, 1942; Tinker Air Force Base in Oklahoma City was named after him.

ience. When it ended, the Materiel Division was exhausted, but it had the airplane it wanted. Martin was delighted—it had world acclaim for a great airplane, a contract to build 48 more of them, and the Collier Trophy for 1932. However, it is only fair to note that the Materiel Division displayed no little pique on learning of Glenn Martin's words of acceptance for the Collier Trophy. These were, in essence, "I owe it all to my mother."

The Air Corps seemed almost to be laying for Martin's first request to make changes in their Model 123. The Baltimore engineers, wishing to decrease wing loading a trifle, had asked permission to increase wing area from 460 to 500 square feet. The Materiel Division assented but only providing that a new style of wing construction, which it had just devised, be used. The Wright Fielders had just completed building a 55 foot long wing section in which stresses were taken by corrugated metal sheets attached to ribs and spars, and covered with a smooth metal outer surface.

Somewhat diffidently Martin agreed, and a few weeks later invited the Dayton engineers to the plant to view their progress. Tempers flared when the government feather merchants allowed as how the wing itself was acceptable, but they had really wanted the wing and fuselage center sections to be built as an integral unit to save weight. To make matters worse, they had the gall to criticize Martin's traditional empennage, which closely resembled an assortment of barn doors wired together at right angles. It was suggested that a cantilever structure would be more acceptable, one with smooth lines and less overhang.

Perhaps these arguments would not have been so heated if there had not already transpired the little matter of the landing gear. The Air Corps insisted that the rollers be retractable, and offered Martin the results of its efforts in designing the gear used on the Fokker XO-27. Martin adapted the design, and despite advice to the contrary, created a two leg gear, not unlike that which appeared later on the DC-1.

While all these hassles were taking place, the Martin model department had been working overtime to incorporate the seemingly endless series of Air Corps changes into a scale wind tunnel model. The first one shipped to Dayton was returned as completely inaccurate. The second, begun on July 16, 1931, was accurate but revealed all too clearly that the design was almost hopelessly lacking in directional stability.

This photo was taken over San Antonio on January 24, 1940, long after the Martin's heyday. Note that the bomb bay doors are removed, and a panel on top of the engine is open. It is still a good-looking airplane, and within two years, its brothers in Dutch colors would be fighting the Japanese.

Dropping their slide rules for the modeler's knife, the Materiel Division engineers tried endless varieties of wing fillets before hitting on the idea of slightly turning up the trailing edge of the wing where it blended into the fuselage. Air flow over the stabilizer was smoothed and stability immediately improved.

Eventually all development efforts reach an end (in folklore at the point where the engineers are shot) and the first flight of the XB-907 took place at the Martin plant on

The left-hand side of the pilot's cockpit shows the throttle quadrant, trim tab, fuel selectors, and part of the instrument panel. Airplanes were becoming complex!

The right-hand side of the pilot's cockpit. The control wheel is massive, more suitable for a ship than an airplane.

The B-10s were deployed to the Philippine Islands and were still flyable when the Japanese attacked. This one is flying near Southern Luzon.

February 26, 1932. The plane made an impressive sight, with its modern bellied fuselage, capable of carrying 2,000 pounds of bombs internally, and its new NACA short chord cowlings encircling the 600 horsepower Wright Cyclone engines. The first flight was almost a disaster, however, as the engines vibrated so excessively that they had to be returned to the factory for rework and it was not until April 20, 1932, that Materiel Division pilots had a chance to fly the plane. Their comments were far from favorable. The XB-907 was longitudinally unstable, and even with no bomb load and half flaps, the landing speed was a sizzling 83 mph. Lightly loaded with bombs, the landing speed was 91 mph—44% faster than the next hottest thing around, Boeing's B-9, and a real psychological hazard.

Part of the problem lay in the Martin designed strut fairing which presented about four square feet of flat plate area when the gear was down. While it did streamline the bottom of the wing when retracted, it contributed greatly to the excessively long take-off runs and the high landing speeds. These problems were largely resolved when the Wright Field engineers finally reached for their wrenches and bolt cutters, discarding the fairing for good.

Security was not exactly fool proof in those days, and the press was full of speculation about the "flying whale" or "mystery bomber" being tested at Wright Field: Rumor was rife; the airplane was reputed to be faster than anything in the sky, and heavily armed, to boot. It made good copy, but in fact the XB-907 was perilously close to being cancelled on the basis of its poor flying qualities. The Boeing B-9 was well into its test program, and while it was more costly than the Martin, it was proving to be relatively trouble free.

The XB-907 was sent back to the Martin factory with a long list of recommended changes which the Materiel Division people thought might possibly salvage the project. These were the most basic suggestions:

1. Move engine nacelles forward on wing to eliminate interference encountered at high angles of attack.

2. Enlarge wing fillets, and marry them with the upturned trailing edge of the wings.

3. Cut off trailing edge of rudder to reduce control forces; increase area of "rudder vane" (servo) to aid in single engine operation.

4. Incorporate a single strut landing gear of the type designed by J. A. Rochê (Rochê was father of the Aeronaca).

5. Sweep wing back to increase stability.

6. Provide for emergency bomb door operation.

7. Provide jack pads so that wheels could be changed without hoisting entire aircraft by a crane.

8. Improve brakes.

Somewhat shaken by the ordeal, and alarmed by the Air Corps' disenchantment, the Martin Company made voluble assurances that they would correct the deficiencies, and also come up with a means to satisfy the expressed desire for a turret.

During August, 1932, the Baltimore firm installed yet a third set of engines on the XB-907, using R1820F's this time. A mock-up of the new turret was made and Martin eagerly incorporated suggestions of the Wright Field engineers who, by now, spent as much time at the plant as they did in Dayton.

What was now called the XB-907 was flown at the plant on October 4th, and at Wright Field on October 7th. Wingspan had been increased to 70′7″ from the prototype's 62′2″, and gross weight had climbed almost 2000 pounds.

It was immediately apparent to everyone that all the effort had been worthwhile, for the sleek looking plane with its snazzy turret was now stable, fast (207 mph) and had an acceptable 71 mph landing speed. The Martin and Materiel division engineers fell into each other's arms with loud cries of relief—at last they had a product!

The new bomber still had a few shortcomings, and it went back to the factory once again, primarily to have the Cleveland Pneumatic single oleo gear installed. Besides numerous detail refinements, a final major appearance change was made—stylish sliding canopies were installed over the pilot and rear gunner's compartments, creating what was probably the most comfortable bomber yet built.

It is a tribute to the Martin Com-

Ground crew greatly preferred the B-10 over the earlier Keystone biplane bombers, which were much more difficult to rig and to service.

A whole series of Martins were obtained by the Air Corps, including the YB-10, YB-10A, B-10B, YB-12, B-12, and YB-14. A different designation was allocated with changes in the engine or the equipment. This is a B-12. Note the wide, smooth fillet between the wing and the fuselage—this was the correct solution to the Martin's original control problems, as it smoothed out the air over the empennage.

B-10 bombers of the 49th and 96th Bombardment Squadron lined up looking spic and span and ready for action.

A YB-12 on floats was the Army's attempt to address itself to the Coastal Defense Mission. The aircraft performed well, but like all large float planes, there were difficulties in ground support equipment and servicing. The EDO company built the floats.

The retractable landing gear was a new feature, and wheels-up landings were not uncommon.

pany that it was willing to take the seemingly endless flow of suggestions from the Materiel Division and translate a fixed gear biplane into the XB-907. And that was truly only the beginning of the B-10 saga, which grew more impressive under the continuing influence of the company's engineers and sales staff. In the next six years, Martin incorporated improvement after improvement into the design, so that seven countries in four continents would eagerly buy it. Later on, and somewhat past their prime, the classic bombers would fight gallantly in four wars.

Yet when all is said, the greatest service rendered by the airplane was to its native United States, for it provided the just maturing Air Corps with a serviceable vehicle with which to develop the modern bomber tactics that would be crucial in World War II.

The 155 aircraft acquired by the Air Corps would ultimately serve in no fewer than 28 combat squadrons. Their initial debut was with famous first line outfits like the 1st, 9th, 11th and 96th Bombardment Squadrons. Then, with the inexorable process of age and obsolescence they worked their way through lesser squadrons, finally winding up in associate units in a variety of roles ranging from instrument trainer to tow target plane.

The original XB-10, 33-157, was retained at Wright Field for 60 hours of testing before being transferred to Langley. On October 9th, 1933, an incident occurred which would cast the long shadow of future maintenance problems over the airplane. On a routine hop, Lt. E. A. Hilary found that the landing gear would not extend; on advice from the ground he parachuted to safety, and the shiny new pride of the Air Corps, with only 132 hours total flying time, plunged into the Virginia earth.

The crew chief does not look too unhappy at this gear-up landing. The pilot certainly was, especially after the C.O. got through with him. *Author's collection, courtesy Fred C. Dickey, Jr.*

The enclosed turret was required because of the "colossal speeds of more than 200 mph that the gunner experienced."

Earlier this might have proved disastrous for the program, but Air Corps Contract AC 5665 had been executed on January 24, 1933, and had shown just how serious the Army was about the new bomber. The first option of the contract was for 14 service test YB-10s, which differed slightly in dimensions and detail from the prototype. (See table on page 98.) R-1820-25 Wright Cyclones of 675 horsepower were installed, but top speed had dropped below the highly touted 200 mph mark.

The contract also called for a single YB-10A, which had the -31 engine with a F-2F supercharger and a controllable pitch propeller. The fastest of all the Army Martins, it had an honest top speed of 236 mph at 25,000. This was truly outstanding performance for 1933, but superchargers had not yet reached a state of development which would permit their widespread use, and 33-154 was soon converted to B-12 configuration. It had accumulated only 260 hours of flying time before a final landing accident at Chicago, Illinois on February 7, 1939 spelled an end to its career. D. E. Ridings ground looped the airplane, which was then sent by freight car to Lowry Field as a non-flying instructional machine.

Contract 5565 also called for seven YB-12s and 25 YB-12As. The first YB-12s had Pratt & Whitney R-1690-11 Hornet engines of 775 horsepower, which brought the top speed back up to 212 mph. The twenty-five YB-12As had the same engines, but were configured for long overwater flights. Either a 250 gallon or a 580 gallon auxiliary tank could be installed, and extra oil tankage was provided. The YB-12As incorporated the extensive flotation type construction—sealed compartments in wing and stabilizer—which would be fitted to 127 of the aircraft.

The last aircraft on the initial contract was the YB-14, which sported huge 950 horsepower Pratt & Whitney R-1830-9 Twin Wasps. The plane was very fast (222 mph) but being one of a kind it was difficult to maintain, and was converted to standard YB-12 configuration in February, 1936. Like almost all of its sister ships it suffered a landing accident, and was surveyed, with only 458 hours total time, on May 22, 1939.

In the depression year of 1933, a 48 aircraft contract for almost $2,500,000 dollars was almost too good to be true, but the Air Corps was so delighted with the new bomber, that it determined to spend almost all of its 1934 procurement money on 88 B-10Bs. A further 15 were purchased on the same Air Corps contract AC-6861, using Fiscal Year 1935 funds.

The B-10Bs featured all the equipment and detail refinements developed during the service tests, and were powered with Wright R-1820-33 engines of 790 horsepower. They could attain 213 mph at 10,000 feet, and would form the backbone of U. S. bomber aviation for the next three years.

The Air Corps acquired three B-10s under somewhat unusual circumstances. Two (36-347 and 36-348) were assembled from spare and possibly salvaged parts by the Middletown Air Depot, at Olmstead, Pennsylvania. Number 347 flew 1,325 hours before being surveyed in July 1942; the record card for 348 is unfortunately unreadable.

The third extra Martin, somewhat unkindly and ingloriously named *Miss Latrine of 1930* by irreverent Yanks in 1942, was in reality the sole survivor of the gallant Martins of the Dutch East Indies Air Force—of this, more later.

The B-10s gave good service, some logging as much as 3,000 hours flying time before being salvaged, their many notable flights providing badly needed prestige to the Air Corps, assisting it in the perennial fight for funds.

The new YB-10s were scarcely run in when ten of them were selected for the famous Alaska flight, with Hap Arnold leading them on the 8900 mile round trip from Washington, D.C. The venture was an outstanding success, with over 20,000 square miles of Alaskan territory being

The YB-12 on floats was truly a handsome aircraft. It would be interesting to know how much flying time was accumulated in this configuration.

photographed, and with a great many maintenance lessons learned. Only one accident occurred—33-145, piloted by Lt. Larson, had fuel management problems and made an emergency landing in Cook's Bay. The plane sank in forty feet of water, but was immediately raised and put back into

The engine installation was very clean. Note that instruments are mounted directly on the engine, close enough for the pilot to read.

flying shape in a week. (Some years later, another Martin force landed in the James River—it floated for two days before being rescued.) Number 145 went on to accumulate 1947 hours before being surveyed in 1943, no longer a proud veteran of the Alaskan flight, but just so much sheet metal for the war efforts. It's not improbable that it and many other B-10s were reincarnated as B-17s or B-24s, via the salvager's melting pot.

The Air Corps flew the new Martins intensively, routinely achieving fifty hours per month utilization, and often reaching as high as 80 or 90. The B-10s made possible a whole new gamut of bomber techniques and tactics, and there were countless experiments with new radios, oxygen equipment, bomb sights, guns and so on. There was also a brief moment when it was considered for conversion to a multiseat fighter, a premature Airacuda.

The heavy flying schedule quickly showed that there were going to be major maintenance problems. First, last and always there were difficulties with the undercarriage. Almost every Air Corps Martin had at least one landing accident and many had several. Some occurred through pilot error, "the horn was blowing so loud I forgot to put the gear down" type of thing. Most, however, were due to mechanical faults. The gear was not stout enough to take

This was the "aft emergency pilot station," useful when the pilot wanted to rest a bit or was momentarily indisposed.

The crew models the latest in high-altitude gear, July 12, 1935. Oxygen was of the continuous-flow type, plugged into tubes in the mask. On the aircraft, note the new controllable-pitch propellers, which added greatly to the altitude capability.

the wear and tear of service life; over a period of time it gradually worked out of adjustment, or simply failed.

Control rigging was another worry, one that caused consternation among pilots early in the plane's career. Serious aileron flutter was encountered, often at very low air speeds. An immediate grounding order was issued, and telegrams flew back and forth from the field, for it was imperative that the expensive new bombers stay operational. Redesign and altered maintenance procedures eventually corrected the situation, but not before several pale faced pilots had nearly abandoned ship.

In 1937 wing spar cracks began to show up, and the fleet was again grounded for inspection and repair. Boiler plate patches were devised, and the problem cured—for this airplane, for this time.

Ugliest of the Martin's problems were the rumors that began to spread that the plane really did not have the capability to maintain flight on a single engine. A rash of accidents—three between October 1936 and June 1937 alone—seemed to confirm the rumor. General Westover ordered extensive tests to be carried out and Wright Field test pilots reportedly demonstrated not only single engine flight, but also single engine take-offs. The truth of the matter was that service pilots were not proficient enough in single engine operation, a malady which plagues civil aviation today. Air Corps' bulletins recommended thorough training in this area, and the use of lighter gross weights wherever possible.

Oddly enough, the maintenance problems may have been a blessing in disguise, for they helped convert a small group of Liberty engine men into a cadre of trained mechanics who would maintain the complex aircraft of World War II.

Despite these shortcomings, the swift two engine bomber was popular. All of the pilots I've interviewed who flew the plane agreed that it was a gentleman's aircraft, particularly for one which took them from bailing wire and fabric directly into the front rank of aviation. Col. Phillips Melville, (USAF, retired) who had participated in the mock-up inspection of the original XB-907, flew the B-12 when it arrived in Hawaii with the 5th Composite Group. He recalls it as a very nice airplane, comfortable, with a short take-off roll and a good turn of speed. After years of flying Capronis, Handley Pages, the LWF Owl, the earlier biplane

A Martin B-12 in flight, November 21, 1934. Just think how these fellows must feel. The rest of the country is locked in The Depression, millions are out of work, and they are getting paid to fly around in a wonderful aircraft!

An aircraft from the 31st Bombardment Squadron in an embarrassing position. Nose-ups were common—a little excess speed taxiing, then a little excess pressure on the brakes, and wham—over on the nose. Looks like the prop was caught, too, meaning an engine change was needed.

This YB-12 featured Pratt & Whitney R-1690-11 Hornet engines. The Martins were also equipped with the Norden bombsight, which gave them an unprecedented capability for bombing.

For some reason, the Martin publicity people chose to touch up this photograph, giving it a somewhat phony look. The photo does show how the insignia were placed on the upper side of the wings.

Martins, and of course the Keystones, the modern bomber from Baltimore had an almost Rolls Royce quality.

Yet the B-10s had been operational only for a relatively short time when both the B-17 and B-18 began to loom on the horizon. Martin had attempted to meet this competition with the Model 146, which was basically an expanded B-10 with a 75 foot wing span, Fowler flaps and a wider, heavier body. Much to Glenn Martin's chagrin, the B-18 bested the Model 146; he protested loud and long that the Air Corps really should buy the airplane, but to no avail. Tony Fokker expressed interest in the design, and an agreement was almost reached by which the Netherlands based firm would act as a European outlet. The plan did not materialize, although other Martins would soon play an important role for the Dutch.

The success of the B-18 and more particularly the promise of the B-17 induced the U. S. Army to yield to Martin's repeated request to release the B-10 for export. The market seemed almost limitless to Martin, for war was imminent in almost every quarter of the globe and good guys everywhere were rearming.

Russia, enigmatic then as now, bought the first model released in 1936, the Model 139-WR. Identical to the Air Corps B-10B except for use of the GR-1850-F 53 engines and two position Hamilton Standard propellers (and of course, minus sensitive equipment) the plane was purchased by the USSR's trading corporation Amtorg. Its subsequent fate is unknown, but it was probably used to study U. S. manufacturing methods. One by-product of the sale was that the SB-2s used in the Civil War in Spain were called "Martins" by correspondents, even though the Tupolev designed bomber owed nothing to the bird from Baltimore.

The Dutch purchased 13 Model 139 WH-1s in 1937. These were virtual duplicates of the 139WR. They doubled the order next year, buying 26, 139 WH-2s, which differed only in their use of the Curtiss constant speed propellers.

The heavy impact of these buys was felt both in the Dutch treasury and in the national pride, and there was much parliamentary debate on the subject. Yet the planes suited the plans of the East Indies defense staff so well that a further order for 78 aircraft was placed in 1938, fear of the increasingly tangible threat from Japan having overcome fiscal trepidation.

Delivered in two groups of 39, designated 139WH-3 and 139WH-3A respectively, the new Martins were to prove to be the most stubborn and the most effective aerial resistance the Japanese were to meet until well into 1942.

Powered by 900 horsepower Wright R-1820-G-102 engines, the last batch of Martins featured a long slender greenhouse which covered the entire crew. With a top speed of 250 mph and a 2,200 pound bomb load, these Martins easily constituted the strongest, most homogenous Allied force in the South Pacific at the time.

The Dutch were vigorous in their deployment, sending them into action on December 17th, as soon as Japanese targets were in range. Not content to sit back and defend their own possessions, they generously deployed

Over time the Martin became obsolete, and when spare parts became scarce, a broken-down aircraft often was relegated to some isolated area on the field before being scrapped. Sad to see, but part of an airplane's life cycle.

Martins with British Commonwealth squadrons in Malaya.

For almost eighty days the Martins slugged away at the invading Japanese, flying at first in squadrons, then in flights, and finally in brave solo sorties. The Dutch took a heavy toll of transports, sinking several, damaging others, and drowning an estimated 26,000 Japanese troops. The 139s also staged spectacular raids on the newly established Japanese airfields, destroying many airplanes on the ground, and giving the enemy a taste of the treatment he had been handing out so successfully for the past few months.

This photograph was identified as a Martin 139-WAA, which would indicate an Argentine aircraft. Note the Martin bomber sales insignia on the vertical fin—a Martin star superimposed on a bomb. The B-10 currently displayed in the Air Force Museum was brought back from Argentina.

In the air the struggle was unequal, for the Martins had no armor or self-sealing tanks, and often fell victim to the Zero. The bombers did achieve a few aerial victories, however, some due to the sting of the Gotha-like tunnel gun in the rear.

The strength of the Dutch dwindled, and one day before the March 8, 1942 capitulation, the last Martin flew from Java to Australia, where it became *Miss Latrine of 1930,* serving for a brief while as a squadron hack before disappearing forever.

This was the Martin entry in the competition that was won by the Douglas B-18, and in which the Boeing B-17 got a token order. The Model 146 was clearly just a cleaned-up B-10, and while mildly competitive with the B-18, was no match for the B-17.

Two other countries used the Martin in combat. Nine Model 139WCs were purchased by China in 1937. These had Wright GR-1820-G2 engines of 850 horsepower, mated to Hamilton Standard constant speed propellers. Capable of 229 mph, the bomber could have been a potent weapon. However, their most spectacular effort proved to be a two ship leaflet raid over Japan, a feat which gained international headlines but little else. Ground strafing eventually eliminated them from combat.

Siam, which purchased six of the Model 139WSM in 1937, managed to use them in two wars. The Royal Thai Air Force used them against the French in Indo China in January, 1941, and then eleven months later used them in the one day struggle with Japan. The Thai Martins were similar to the 139WCs except for the use of a -3 engine.

As war approached, parts for older aircraft became scarce, but the airplanes were still needed. So if a B-10 was lacking a turret, you just faired it in and went on flying.

Two good customers fortunately never had to use the aircraft in combat. Turkey bought 20 of the 139WTs in 1937. These were identical to the Chinese aircraft except for equipment details, instrument markings and so on. Little is known of their subsequent employment.

Argentina bought 22 139WAAs in 1938 for its Army, and 12 139WANs for its Navy. One of the latter group was very graciously donated to the Air Force Museum in 1971. The prodigal Martin is in good structural condition, but is disassembled and minus most of its equipment. No details are presently known on the history of this aircraft, and it can only be hoped that some diligent Argentine researcher will someday come up with the full story.

Performance

Perhaps the best test of the basic worth of a design is its ability to maintain an acceptable international standard of performance for a long period of time, despite increases in gross weight and drag which seem to be an inevitable part of the development process.

The original XB-907 had a 197 mph top speed and a gross weight of 10,580 pounds. The ultimate development of the Martin, the Model 166C, had a gross weight of 15,894 pounds and a top speed at critical altitude of 255 mph. Initial climb rate improved from 1600 fpm to 1860 fpm, while landing speed decreased from 83 mph to 68 mph. Service ceiling climbed from the original's 20,000 feet to 24,800 and even endurance was improved, from 8 to 8.6 hours at 170 mph.

More spectacular than mere speed and altitude data was the increase in capability through improved equipment. In the six year development process there had been striking improvements in radios, oxygen equipment, auto pilots, de-icers, bombing equipment and so on. However, the two items which might have made a great deal of difference to the Dutch were never incorporated—armor plate and self-sealing tanks.

The B-10Bs were perhaps the most representative of the series, although all of the models were very similar. With an empty weight of 9,681 pounds and a gross weight of 14,887 pounds, the Martin was very comparable in size to the contemporary B-9. However, the generally cleaner design of the B-10 offered better performance, and permitted an overload weight capability of 16,400 pounds.

Normal maximum fuel load was 226 gallons, but an auxiliary tank of 365 gallons could be fitted in the bomb bay; in this configuration the B-10B had a 1,830 mile range. For the Alaskan epic, two additional tanks were fitted, a 165 gallon unit being placed aft of the turret, and a smaller 65 gallon tank located near the rear cockpit. With this extra tankage, the range was a respectable 2,500 miles at 170 mph.

The B-10Bs had a service ceiling of 24,600 feet, although they in fact seldom operated anywhere near that high.

Take-off performance was brisk; with proper technique the plane could break ground in 725 feet, and clear a fifty foot obstacle in 1,325 feet. Initial climb rate after take off was 1,345 feet per minute and this improved to 1,565 feet at the critical altitude of 5,400 feet. The plane could reach 10,000 feet in only seven minutes, phenomenal performance for the day.

Construction Details

The Martins were tough birds, due to their very excellent construction.

As previously noted, the wing and fuselage center sections were built as an integral unit, providing great strength at minimum weight. The tail and nose sections were of riveted aluminum monocoque construction. The corrugated sheet metal used along the dorsal and ventral exterior surfaces was handled in a much more cosmetic manner than previous efforts by Ford, Junkers or Dornier. The smooth side skin, stiffened by internal rings and bulkheads, carried both torsional and shear stresses.

The wing used a modified Gottingen 388 airfoil. Two tapered outer wing panels were bolted to the wing center section, which incorporated the nacelles, tanks and undercarriage. An aluminum alloy box girder spar provided torsional rigidity, while compression loads were carried by the corrugated sheets covered by the smooth outer surfaces. The lower wing skin and beam flanges took tension loads in flight.

The empennage was of all metal cantilever construction. All control surfaces

Another view of the GLM 146. It would be interesting to know what happened to this aircraft; Martin probably dismantled it.

This is the very first example of the Martin 139WH-3, or Model 166, as it was also called. The nose had a more rounded look, and a big greenhouse covered all the crew. It was the fastest of the series, with a top speed of 250 mph. Built for the Dutch, the aircraft fought valiantly against the Japanese.

(including the ailerons and split flaps) were fabric covered. The rudder and elevator had trim tabs controllable from the cockpit.

The front turret, which had been a joint Martin/Materiel Division effort, gave the airplane its characteristic pugnacious appearance. Looking not unlike a glazed bird cage, it provided the gunner with protection against the 200 mph wind blast.

The entire assembly rotated on ball bearings and the .30 caliber Browning was suspended in a vertical stainless steel track. Weight of the gun and air blast effect were offset by a simple but ingenious system of bungee cords which made aiming the weapon relatively effortless.

A flat panel was provided for the bombardier through which he could aim the standard M-1 bombsight. Later the super-secret Nordens were used, and the bombardier's accuracy was immeasurably enhanced.

Bomb bay doors were operated mechanically by means of a hand crank. The pilot could, in an emergency, salvo the bomb load right through the doors.

The Air Corps had insisted that a D-3 shackle be fitted under the right wing so that a battleship busting 2,000 pound bomb could be carried. As an alternate load, 2,100 pounds of bombs could be carried internally.

From the pilot's point of view, the Martin had an extremely well laid out cockpit, with a good field of vision in all quadrants. As a carry over from past practice, engine instruments, including oil pressure, oil temperature, cylinder head temperature and tachometer were mounted directly on the engine nacelles.

An auxiliary pilot's station was provided at the gunner/radio operator's position. Swing-away flight controls

This is a lineup of the early Dutch East Indies Air Force Martin 139WHs, which retained the B-10–style canopy. These sold for $50,000 each in lots of 50. A total of 189 were sold to foreign governments, more than the 154 bought by the Air Corps.

The Dutch flew a surviving Model 166 aircraft to Australia after the Japanese conquered the East Indies, where it was used by the USAAF as a "squadron hack." This is a very poor-quality photo, but it shows the unusual shape of the "greenhouse."

Aircraft Data Sheet

Type	Year	Qty	Normal Gross Weight	Engines	Top Speed	Service Ceiling	Remarks
Air Corps:							
XB-907	1932	1	10,580	1820-E	197	20,000	Prototype
XB-907A	1932	(1)	12,560	1820-19	207	21,000	Longer wing, long chord cowlings
XB-10	1932	(1)	12,560	1820-19	207	21,000	33-139
YB-10	1933	14	12,829	1820-17	207	21,800	33-140 to 153
YB-10A	1933	1	13,212	1820-31	236	25,000	33-154-turbo supercharged
YB-12	1934	7	12,824	1690-11	212	24,600	33-155 to 161
YB-12A	1934	25	12,980	1690-11	212	24,600	33-163 to 177; 33-258 to 33-267
YB-14	1934	1	13,560	1830-9	222	24,800	33-162
B-10B	1934	88	13,212	1820-33	213	24,400	34-028 to 115
B-10B	1934	15	13,212	1820-33	213	24,400	35-232 to 246
B-10B	1936	2	13,212	1820-33	213	24,400	36-347 and 348; built up from spares, Middletown AD
Model 166	1942	(1)	15,394	1820-G-102	240	22,000	Ex-Dutch East Indies AF
Foreign:							
139-WR	1936	1	14,364	1820-F-53	220	25,400	Sold to Amtorg
139-WH	1936	13	14,372	1820-F-53	220	25,400	First to Dutch
139-WC	1937	9	14,780	1820-G2	229	24,900	Leaflet raid, Feb. 1938
139-WSM	1937	6	14,607	1820-G3	236	23,700	Siam
139-WT	1937	20	14,915	1820-G2	224	23,700	Turkey
139-WAN	1937	13	14,856	1820-G2	227	27,910	Argentine Navy
139-WH2	1938	26	14,854	1820-G3	242	27,800	2nd batch to Dutch
139-WAA	1938	22	15,080	1820-G3	225	25,950	Argentine Army
139-WH3	1938	39	15,394	1820-G102	240	22,000	Long Canopy

Note: ( ) indicates conversion
Foreign performance figures from old Martin data; differences stem from use of different propellers, etc.

Engine Data:

Wright:

1820-E	600 hp @ 6000′
1820-19	675 hp @ 4000′
1820-17	675 hp @ 4500′
1820-31	675 hp
1820-33	750 hp @ 5400′
1820-G102	900 hp @ sea level
1820-F-53	750 hp @ 9600′
1820-G2	850 hp @ 5500′
1820-G3	850 hp @ 5800′

Pratt & Whitney:

1830-9	950 hp
1690-11	700 hp @ 6500′

Another photo of the sole surviving Martin of the Dutch East Indies Air Force was flown from Bandung, Java, to Australia on March 7, 1942.

plus the throttle, mag switch, air speed indicator and altimeter were sufficient to allow the person in the rear cockpit to control the plane.

Gear retraction was by an electric system, although a manual back-up was provided. It took 35 seconds to retract the gear electrically (compared to five seconds on a "modern" Convair) and 90 back-breaking seconds manually. Despite the ample warnings provided by (at first) a rudder bar shaker, warning lights, gauges, and later a horn, the gear system would be a cause of embarrassment to many young Air Corps pilots accustomed to fixed gear.

Three .30 caliber Browning machine guns were provided for defense, although in the earliest days of the B-10, there were few fighters which could have made a pass at it. In addition to the front turret gun, one fired from the upper rear cockpit, and one from a tunnel in the floor.

The earliest standard radio equipment for the Martins was a SCR-183 command set and the SCR-134, which also had an interphone position.

The Twilight Years

World War II called forth an endless stream of capable bombers—B-25, B-26, A-20, and so on—and the B-10s were relegated to ever less important tasks. Their demise was hastened by a previously undreamed of quantity of replacement equipment. In another time, they might have remained in the inventory longer, but by 1943, they had become totally obsolete, and an embarrassing drag on the supply train. They disappeared one by one, anonymously, and without a tear. It wasn't until years later, that it was realized not a single example was to be found anywhere in the world. Then, to the enormous satisfaction of bomber buffs everywhere, the Argentine B-10 was discovered and presented for restoration. When completed, the reborn B-10 will fill a very important spot at the great new Air Force Museum, located at the very same Wright Field where the program was developed forty years ago.

Everybody is a humorist, and someone had the nerve to put this on the nose of a very gallant aircraft after its combat with the Japanese.

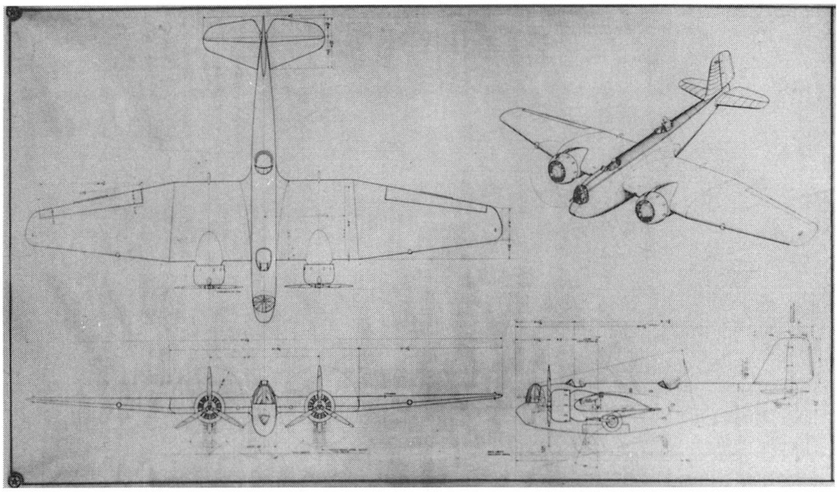

Martin tried to develop the basic B-10 into a multi-place fighter, but it was refused by the Air Corps because it was not built to fighter strength requirements.

14 SPEED MERCHANT

The Ultimate Racer, Howard Hughes' H-1

Airpower September, 1977

This beautiful airplane was the pride and joy of Howard Hughes, and deservedly so. He gathered a team of experts around him, as he always did, and the airplane they created with his leadership and the vision of Richard Palmer was a superb product for 1935. In the course of my work at the National Air & Space Museum, I came in contact with several of Hughes' close collaborators on the racer and on his massive flying boat. I spent a good deal of time with some, including Jack Real and Glenn Odekirk. Every one of them had nothing but positive things to say about their relationship with Hughes. They admitted that he had unusual working habits, but all agreed that when working on a design problem he was a reasonable man who understood other viewpoints and could even take a joke. His practice, however, was to deal with people only in their specialties, talking hydraulics only to the

Howard Hughes was a serious pilot with enormous self-confidence. He practiced for his Hughes H-1 racer by flying Jacqueline Cochran's souped-up Northrop Gamma to set a transcontinental record on January 13–14, 1936. He flew from Burbank to Newark, New Jersey, in 9 hours and 26 minutes.

This is a typical Hughes pose—reserved, impatient, but aware of the need for publicity. Note the steerable tail skid of the Hughes H-1, an anomaly in so sleek an aircraft, but still necessary for the grass fields of the day.

This was an extraordinarily advanced conception for 1935, and Howard Hughes exacted the best from his small team. Dick Palmer was the designer who executed Hughes' ideas, and Glenn Odekirk was the genius behind the construction. A little study of this view will reveal why many people contend that the H-1 was the inspiration for Kurt Tank's Focke Wulfe FW-190.

hydraulics guy, engines to the engine guy, and never crossing boundaries.

It's good to know that there is a flying replica of the Hughes racer being built, one that is intended to explore the full range of the beautiful aircraft's possibilities. It is being built at the Wright Machine Tool Company of Cottage Grove, Oregon, by a team led by Jim Wright and Steve Wolf.

Howard Hughes was a gifted pilot, and in airplanes as in all else he undertook, he wished to deal only in the superlative. Although he started flying at age 22, his interest in aircraft was undoubtedly intensified by his production of Hell's Angels, which placed him in continuous contact with a number of colorful pilots. It was almost certainly during this period that he decided that he would break the world's land speed record.

His first overt steps in this direction came in the form of the extensive modification of the two-seat Boeing Model 100A, which was the first of the famous Boeing 100 series to fly. (See June *Wings* 1977). It probably had a longer active service life than any of its military counterparts, 586 of which were built as P-12s and F4Bs.

Hughes, working with Glenn Odekirk and others, saw to it that the 1344 cubic inch Pratt & Whitney Wasp was tuned and tweaked to a maximum horsepower, probably near 700, and that the airframe was radically cleaned up. A huge, voluptuous cowling was added, the landing gear elaborately faired and panted, and the vertical surfaces greatly enlarged to offset the additional forward area.

All of this was not enough, however, for although definitive performance figures were never released, modern developments had already eclipsed the basic Boeing fighter design. Hughes flew the aircraft in some minor races, but it did not have the potential for development he required. By 1929, the Travel Air Mystery Ships were heralding the arrival of the low wing monoplane, as were the Wedell-

On the threshold of aviation immortality, a confident Howard Hughes is shown here just prior to his record-breaking transcontinental flight on January 20, 1937. He once again crossed the continent faster than anyone, this time in 7 hours, 28 minutes, and 25 seconds, at an average speed of 332 mph.

On September 14, 1935, Hughes brought a world record back to the United States by posting a new world's land speed record of 352.383 mph. It was a sensational flight, and very near the aircraft's computed top speed of 365 mph.

Happy and relaxed as only a man being honored with a ticker-tape parade in New York can be, Hughes has just set an around-the-world speed record in his specially modified Lockheed 14 *"New York World's Fair 1939."* He had taken off from Floyd Bennett Field on July 10, 1938, and circled a 14,672-mile route, returning 71 hours, 11 minutes, and 10 seconds later.

Williams and Gee Bee racers. In California, Hughes was already casting appraising eyes at the deeply filleted, low wing, all metal monoplanes emerging from the small Northrop factory, and the hot little Model 100A Alpha was sold to him, eventually passing through the hands of, among others, Art Goebel. It crashed in 1957, after almost three decades of service.

Another front view of the H-1, showing its wide-track landing gear, which retracted so smoothly into the wooden wings. The Twin Wasp Jr. engine was nominally rated at 700 horsepower, but Hughes flew it at power settings generating 1,000 horsepower. The bell-shaped cowling is especially beautiful.

Hughes had been serious about his apprenticeship as a pilot, and flew many types of aircraft to gain as much experience as possible. He learned to fly in California in 1927, and earned transport certificate No. 80. By 1942, admittedly long after his experience with the H-1, but the only record available to me, he had over 2,100 hours of flying time. It would be interesting to know his final total.

"Millionaire playboy" is one of the terms most often used to describe Hughes, but the playboy part was completely inaccurate. He was never a dilettante when it came to aircraft. People who worked with him admit to his idiosyncrasies, but none of the almost dozen I have talked to have anything but praise for his seriousness of purpose and his dedication. "Howard" as they almost inevitably refer to him, was always in deadly earnest, often to a degree beyond the comfortable or the convenient.

And so, when in 1934 he began construction of the Hughes H-1 in Charles Babb's hangar at Grand Central Air Terminal, the small group he gathered around him knew that they were challenged to produce the very best. Nothing was to be "adequate"! Everything was to be "superb"!

With a skill that was to become a familiar hallmark, Hughes picked two excellent men to help him lead the

The *"New York World's Fair 1939"* was mobbed when it landed. Hughes had carefully surveyed all possible contenders for the world flight, including a Douglas DC-3 and a Sikorsky S-43, but the Lockheed Electra was far faster and had a better range.

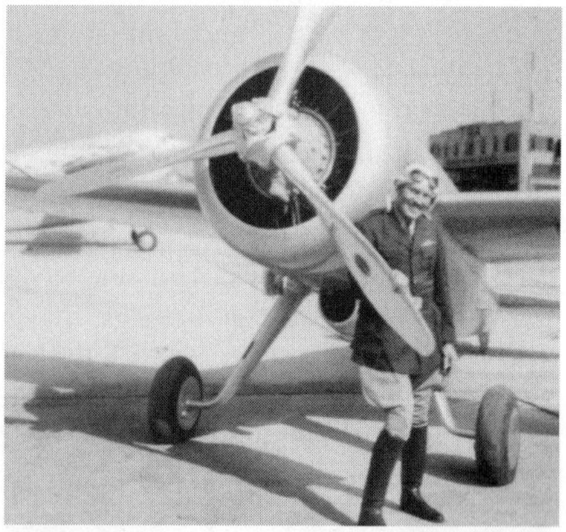

Hughes was in every way different from another aviation luminary of the time, Roscoe Turner, shown here with his famous Laird racer. The biggest difference, of course, was financial. While Hughes had virtually limitless money to finance his projects, Turner had to fight for every nickel. It would be nice to think that they get together in some airport in the sky and talk about the old days of racing.

As Hughes got older, he became more eccentric. Nonetheless, the people he worked with liked and respected him, despite his unusual hours and strange meeting places.

Howard Hughes will always be associated first and foremost with his massive eight engine flying boat, in which he made one fabled flight. The aircraft was constructed of wood fashioned in the patented Duramold manner, and was designed to fly over the menacing German U-boat fleet.

team. He shared design responsibilities with Dick Palmer and production responsibilities with Glenn Odekirk. Palmer had a Bachelor's degree from the California Institute of Technology, and a Masters from the University of Minnesota, had worked with Douglas, Fokker and the Aircraft Development Corporation. At 31, he was dynamic, sharp, and ready to try for the top.

Odekirk was 29, and had an equally broad background. He worked first for Bach Aircraft, then for Gilpin Airlines and Pacific Airmotive, before joining Hughes for the Boeing 100A project.

Other employees were selected with equal care. Apparently Hughes worked on an informal, first name basis with many, and when a man earned his confidence, the millionaire was able to delegate authority on a given project with ease. It was a happy shop, and the long hours and tight security were not too different from that experienced in similar groups around the country. The Travel Air "Mystery Ships" had earned their name from the secrecy which had shrouded them before race time, and most racing groups were not happy about strangers walking into their work area. The Hughes group, however, probably had stricter enforcement of security precautions than any others, a characteristic that would be intensified to the point of mania later in Hughes' career.

The task the group faced was generally the same as that of any design team seeking a record: how to obtain maximum thrust and minimum drag in a safely controllable airframe. Hughes knew exactly what the airplane should look like, and there was money in abundance to build it exactly as he wished. He determined, with Palmer, that the aircooled Pratt & Whitney Twin Wasp Jr., of 1535 cubic inch displacement, was more attractive than any liquid cooled engine available, because of its relatively low frontal area and high reliability. He sketched out the general outlines of the aircraft, and the team went to work.

This is the engineer's position on the Hughes flying boat. When Hughes made his one flight, he made sure there was no other pilot on board, so no one else could claim to have flown the aircraft.

What developed was the bold concept of a dual purpose airplane, one capable of breaking both the world's land speed record, and also the transcontinental record. The dual capability was obtained by designing two separate wings. One, a long span version of 32 feet, was to be used for the transcontinental event; the short wing, 25 foot span version, would be employed to break the world's land speed record. There was an immediate parlay for this combination—the long wing span version could almost surely win the cross country Bendix Race, and be at least competitive in the closed course Thompson Trophy race.

The design was tested in the Cal Tech wind tunnel, with an estimated top speed of 365 mph being predicted. Curiously, in view of his penchant for security, Hughes released this information to the public.

Hughes, who had himself studied briefly at Cal Tech as a very young man, did not have formal engineering training, but he was anxious to learn, and he exploited his contacts throughout the aviation industry, as well as in academic circles, to gain knowledge on aerodynamics. Palmer was of course extremely well qualified, and with Hughes leading, probing, and prodding, he was able to establish design parameters which led to both a safe and fast machine.

After making the engine choice, the principal concern was drag reduction. The aircraft's small frontal area and relatively slender fuselage were a good start towards this goal, but it was the subsequent succession of refinements that raised the aircraft to record setting caliber.

The first happy choice was the lovely, long chord bell cowling, which smoothly streamlined the air outside, while smartly directing the cooling air inside. The Twin Wasp Jr.

This is a drawing of the mysterious Hughes D-2, also an all-wood aircraft, which was intended to have a variety of missions, depending upon Hughes' vision at the time. These ranged from "Experimental Long-Range Multi-Gun Fighter" to a reconnaissance plane. Photos exist of this airplane, but they are hard to come by.

had a diameter of only 43.875 inches, obtained by arranging the cylinders in two rows of seven each. Two rows were naturally harder to cool than the standard single row, but excellent baffling solved the problem. A typical-for-the-time ring collector for the exhaust would also have added bulk, and the solution here was a complicated collection system which ducted the exhaust out of a series of rearward facing ports, and which probably provided a few extra pounds of thrust in the process.

The *Twin Wasp Jr.* was tuned for maximum output, which was very close to 1,000 horsepower, although the engine's nominal rating was 700 hp.

The next refinement was in the superb design of the aluminum monocoque fuselage, which was of circular section, tapering to a smartly upswept tail cone. The skin was butt-jointed and flush riveted, each section matched with a precision that would put a Rolls-Royce custom body shop to shame. The lines were relatively simple, with few protuberances, and where a compound curve was required—in the wing/landing juncture with the fuselage for example—it was done with a restrained elegance. Enormous strength came from a massive central keel, to which both the engine and the wing were attached.

A deep, almost flamboyant fillet faired the trailing edge of the wing into the fuselage, and Hughes' attention to detail was such that each of the hundreds of attaching screws had its slot aligned parallel to the wind stream. It was an esoteric item of drag reduction that Hughes insisted on even in later aircraft.

The cockpit, which was placed just about at the trailing edge of the wing, was strictly utilitarian, and had a functional look very similar to that found in later World War II fighters. An autopilot was fitted, but Hughes preferred not to use it. (There was some reluctance to having it installed when the airplane was brought to the Museum, for Hughes did not want people to think he used it on his record flights.) The cockpit is well laid out from a human factors point of view, if you consider only the various levers, switches and handles, but the instrument grouping leaves much to be desired. Rumor has it that Hughes largely taught himself instrument flying, thus it may have been arranged according to his individual preferences.

The cabin enclosure was of a type probably not used before or since. The wind screen was cranked forward for entrance or egress, and aft for flight; the sides of the canopy rolled up from a slot in the fuselage sides, joining at the top. The arrangement was simple, lightweight and effective, for it had relatively low drag, yet provided good in-flight visibility.

The D-2 concept ultimately evolved into the huge, powerful XF-11. This is a historic photo, for it shows Hughes preparing to taxi out for takeoff. He insisted on test-flying the very complex aircraft himself. He crashed when the propeller mechanism malfunctioned, and he was unable to get back to the field. His injuries were severe, and this may have been the start of his long dependency upon narcotics.

As important as the streamlined fuselage was, even more critical was the wing, where Hughes wanted the smoothest possible air flow. Somewhat surprisingly, Hughes selected a wooden wing rather than a metal one, so that he could obtain the glassy smooth surface he wanted. The long wing version used an N.A.C.A. 23012 airfoil, and had a very elaborate built up structure, with the fuel tanks sandwiched between two deep main spars. The wing was built in one piece, and fitted precisely into the fuselage keel. Reportedly it was covered with plywood that had been shaved from one inch to one-quarter inch thickness, sanded, sealed, covered with Wellington Sears HH Balloon Cloth, painted, rubbed and waxed. The ailerons were aluminum tubing, fabric covered, and were balanced and aerodynamically sealed. The flaps were built of metal, and fit perfectly; you cannot even see the line of demarcation between flap and upper wing surface.

The plumbing for the fuel tanks was complicated, as tankage for 280 gallons was built into the fuselage and wing.

While retractable landing gears were hardly new at the time, they were still not a stock item in aircraft part houses, either, and there were many different contemporary approaches to the problem in being or on the drawing board. The Seversky P-35 gear swung straight back, as had Boeing's P-29, and the wheel was allowed to protrude below the surface of the wing. Curtiss adopted a more sophisticated Boeing design for its Model 75, the wheels rotating as they retracted aft, to lie flat in uncovered wheel wells. There was a fairing for the landing gear. Grumman, of course, was tucking them up into fat fuselage sides.

In Europe, Messerschmitt and Supermarine fastened the main attachment points inboard, and swung the gear up and out, leaving the wheels largely unfaired. The Hawker Hurricane had a more modern arrangement, with the gear swinging inward.

The Hughes approach was far more advanced. The gear had a ten foot wide tread and was positioned to swing inwards, so that the fat wheels lodged just at the wing/fuselage juncture where space was greatest, and with the gear structure lying forward of the forward main spar. "Gear structure" is the right term, for instead of the classic Cleveland Pneumatic machined landing gear strut, Palmer had designed a rugged aluminum box which served both as the wheel strut and its fairing when retracted. A small hydraulic dampener was fitted in the bottom of the assembly, but most of the shock was taken by the fat tires. The gear was retracted by a relatively slender fork mechanism. It was a unique design, never used before or since to my knowledge, and it left the wing undersurface virtually drag free. Most remarkable of all for the time was the use of an engine driven hydraulic pump to operate both the gear and the steerable, steel-shod tail skid. There was a chain driven mechanical back-up system.

The plane was rolled out in its short wing configuration, and after relatively trouble free flight testing, achieved its first major goal on September 14, 1935, Hughes shattering France's Raymond Delmotte's nine month old record of 314 mph, while posting a new world's land speed record of 352.383 mph. The flight almost ended in tragedy when, during an insurance pass through the speed traps set up in Santa Ana, California, the engine quit cold due to fuel starvation. Hughes made a successful wheels up landing which resulted in so little damage that the record was allowed to stand. (A crash will void a new record.)

Utterly pragmatic, Hughes probably regarded the damage as of little consequence, for the aircraft was to be

The Hughes flying boat was exhibited for years next to the *Queen Mary* in Long Beach, and was later moved to the Michael Smith Education Center in McMinnville, Oregon, where it may be seen today.

immediately refitted with the 32 foot long wing for the transcontinental attempt anyway. This was no simple bolt-in/bolt-out project, for the wings were not interchangeable like spare tires. It would be 15 months before the H-1 was ready for another record attempt.

Meanwhile, Hughes prepared himself by setting a flock of records that a 1930's film would have shown as a series of newspaper headlines flashing in sequence upon the screen. On January 13/14, 1936, he flew a Northrop Gamma, which had formerly belonged to Jacqueline Cochrane, from Burbank to Newark in 9 hours 26 minutes and 10 seconds for the west-east record and the non-stop transcontinental record. He had modified the Gamma with more fuel and a big Wright Cyclone engine, and made the flight mainly on instruments, in very bad weather. Then, in the same plane, he set a new Miami to New York record, flying the distance in 4 hours 21 minutes and 32 seconds. Finally, on May 14, he took the Gamma from Chicago to Glendale in 8 hours, 10 minutes and 25 seconds for yet another inter-city speed record.

This demanding flying had him ready for the H-1's transcontinental attempt. On January 20, 1937, he retraced his record-breaking Burbank to New York route, completing the trip in the sensational time of 7 hours 28 minutes and 25 seconds, averaging 332 mph.

Thus, in 1937, the Hughes H-1 held two important records. Barely broken in, it was in prime shape, having less than 40 hours total flying time. A global war was clearly imminent. What would have been more logical than for Hughes to have developed a fighter plane from his beautiful racer?

We know in fact that the Hughes company prepared such a proposal for one of long time employee Bruce Burk's first jobs, was to draw up a three-view of the aircraft from engineering drawings. None had ever been done, and one was needed for a military proposal. And there is strong evidence that, much later, Otto Timm headed a group which tried to market the aircraft. There are also recurring rumors that the H-1 was tested at Wright Field; but this is doubtful.

No one knows, or will say what actually happened. All we know is that, in 1937, the aircraft was rolled into a hangar in Newark until it was flown, months later, back to California, where it was stored in a temperature and humidity controlled hangar until it was transported to the Smithsonian nearly four decades later.

Why? Was Hughes piqued because some rival pilots considered him to be "unfair competition" if he raced in the Bendix or the Thompson? Did the preparations for the forthcoming round-the-world trip preoccupy him? Or, more probably, did he see that the H-1 had already achieved the goals he had set for it, and that the more mundane problems of developing it into a fighter were unattractive? (It was obvious, of course, that a fighter version of the H-1 was possible, but only after a complete redesign for combat equipment and production ease. These were routine problems, and routine was anathema to Howard Hughes.)

In any event, in 1975, after a complex series of negotiations that are a story in themselves, the Hughes H-1 was prepared for shipment to the new National Air & Space Museum in Washington D.C. A small Hughes team did some necessary clean-up work, disassembled the aircraft, and placed it tenderly in a well padded, specially built shipping container. The container was a latter-day example of Hughes' craftsmanship. It could have been hit by a train or dropped from a crane, and it's doubtful that any damage would have accrued to the aircraft lashed so securely inside.

A smiling, good natured, ebullient Californian named Van Storm accompanied the aircraft, and his general demeanor was that of an F-16 salesman meeting a new prospect from Iran. He could not have been more helpful, more knowledgeable, or more enthused about his duties, and his expertise was invaluable in the subsequent assembly and suspension of the aircraft.

The Smithsonian team was led by Joe Fichera, whose 40 years of experience in aviation qualified him for the task.

The first job was to dismantle the boxes, and it took a three man crew two days to strip them down to the point that the aircraft could be inspected. The 27 foot long fuselage was prepared for lifting to the second story of the Museum, where it was to be installed in the fascinating Gallery of Flight Technology. A 30 ton crane, complete with an enormous handling bridge, swung the fuselage easily up on the balcony, where it was trundled into the Gallery on small basket dollies. The wings followed the same route. (The short wings, which accompanied the shipment were delivered to the Silver Hill restoration facility, where they are now in storage.)

Without question, Howard Hughes was a brave man. He recovered from his injuries and insisted on test-flying the third XF-11. (The number two aircraft was used for static testing.) This aircraft used four-bladed Curtiss propellers instead of the counter-rotating Hamilton Standard propellers that had malfunctioned on the first test flight.

To digress, the Gallery of Flight Technology is a most appropriate place for the Hughes racer, which is the only aircraft on display there. The H-1 is mounted in a circle of tall panels, each of which is devoted to the men and inventions which chronicle the progress of flight. Around the outer edge of the circle are a series of exhibits and shows which explain the basic technology of flight, and includes an amazing cutaway "dancing" R-985 engine. The entire hall is designed and lighted in such a way that the Hughes aircraft is perfectly set off. The designer of the Gallery is the talented Lou Lomax, and he deserves a great deal of credit for its stunning impact on the eye.

The left side of the Hughes racer's engine, with the cowling removed. You can see how "fully packed" the powerplant was.

After the wing was brought into the Gallery, there was a long conference on how best to assemble the aircraft. It was decided to place the wing on two suitably padded hydraulic stands, one stand centered between each tip and root. The fuselage was then lifted and placed above the wing. After the wing had been carefully checked and the landing gear retracted, the lifts were raised so that the wing and the fuselage came together.

But they wouldn't mate. The problem lay in the absolute precision with which Hughes had built the two parts, and the close tolerance of their fit. The fuselage had to be positioned at precisely 90 degrees to the wing; one tenth of a degree off, and the two sections binded. After a great many "ups and downs," and a lot of maneuvering, they came together, and once they were mated, it was impossible to get a sheet of ordinary bond paper between the parts. The parts mated so precisely, it really looked as if they would hold together without any of the attaching bolts.

But there were attachment bolts in profusion, 56 in all, each one specially tailored to its own required length. An afternoon was spent in sorting out which bolt went in which hole.

Once the wing and fuselage were together, everything else was expected to connect rapidly and well. It went well, but not rapidly, for the racer was not designed for ease of maintenance, and the final details of hooking up the plumbing, wiring and controls took a great deal of time. After this was completed there remained the final task of attaching the fillets and insuring that the screws lined up just as Mr. Hughes intended.

The prop turned the engine freely, and the latter was drained of oil and preservatives were applied. As with all airplanes, when the H-1 was suspended some hidden pools of oil materialized, and periodically a small yellow streak will drip from the engine and back down the belly. Somehow it makes the plane more realistic.

The lower part of the cockpit, showing surprising wear. Hughes stored the aircraft for many years in an air-conditioned, humidity-controlled environment.

Looking straight down into the cockpit, you can see cushioned seat, stick, and fuel controls.

The designer of the Gallery had called for the airplane to be suspended in a rakish climbing turn, as if it had just flashed across Newark airport. There were no built-in provisions for hanging the airplane, so these had to be fabricated and attached. The resultant fittings were then machined, magnafluxed and X-rayed for security.

Attaching the fittings to the airplane proved to be the most difficult job in the assembly process, for it was necessary for Fichera to drill through a heat treated aluminum casting in the landing gear trunnion. Joe used over a dozen carbide drills to get through. The drilling was done on a slight angle, but the material was tougher than any the veteran craftsman had ever worked with.

Finally, after the fittings were installed, the aircraft was lifted into its desired final position by running one of the hydraulic stands up higher than the other to "bank" the plane. Cables were attached to a special structure overhead, adjustments were made, and then the hydraulic stands were slowly bled down. As the cables took the weight, the plane became alive again, looking for all the world as if it were in flight.

(All of the aircraft suspended in the Museum have a curious quality of life imparted to them by the fact that they do move imperceptibly in the ever changing currents of air. All of the suspension fittings have a safety factor of at least four, and all are inspected regularly.)

Fichera, whose antique aircraft restorations have won many prizes, states that the H-1 is absolutely the best made airplane he has ever seen. He contrasts it to Roscoe Turner's famous Laird RT-14, which is contemporary with the H-1, and is on exhibit in another Gallery. The exterior appearance of the RT-14 is crude by comparison (even though it is itself a beautiful airplane), and the interior, with its hodgepodge of mutilated welded steel tubing, is painful when contrasted to the beautiful workmanship of the Hughes.

Before closing, let's take an imaginary walk-around inspection of the fabulous Hughes H-1, as it might have rested on the line in Newark after its transcontinental trip.

The first step in any walk-around is the cockpit, and a quick check inside reveals that the mag switch is off, the fuel is off, the battery is off, and the hydraulic pressure is up. The plane does not sit high off the ground, and there is a step on the right fuselage side, carefully faired with a spring loaded cover.

Glancing over the wing, you sense that it is smoother than any of the Spam-cans on the line, and more perfect than even the laminar flow wing of a P-51. Reach down

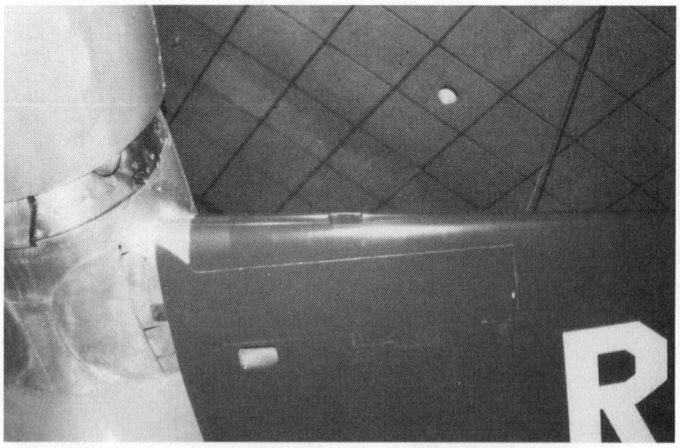

The landing gear retracted into the wing and fuselage so smoothly that you could not put a business card in the line separating fairing and wing. Very beautiful construction, available only at a very high price.

The left and right sides of the very spartan cockpit. No luxuries here—just good, solid design.

and feel under the wing root; the static port is clear. The flaps are up and flush, a much tighter fit than any private plane and tighter than most military jobs. Moving down the wing we check the ailerons; the fabric is drum taut, and the control surface moves easily in its closely fit, well sealed slot in the wing.

There are no scratches on the wing tip—Hughes put a few there on the short wing version—and the leading edge is clean and smooth. Underneath the wing, four inspection plates are barely visible.

The gear is down and locked, the right amount of oleo is showing, and the tires are inflated. And as this is an imaginary walk-around, let's imagine we fold the gear up. The fairings snap neatly into place, so smoothly that a business card cannot be inserted in the crack between fairing and wing. You wonder how it could possibly retract so exactly when under aerodynamic load, at perhaps 120 mph. A very simple, clean, clever design.

The cowling checks perfectly; no drips, no rags, no tools, no grease, all fasteners tightly snugged. The big Hamilton Standard prop is polished and free of nicks; its back side is painted a dark umber shade to prevent reflection.

Glance down along the belly; it is smooth and clean. Underneath the center section there are four access plates, two square and two round. The two round ones are marked "dump valve" in a fairly crude hand lettering. One of the square ones is marked "Hands Off Dump Valve", again hand lettered. The other one is blank. The shaky hand lettering is a jarring note for the H-1; one almost expects letter press printing.

Inspecting the left gear and wing is about like the right, except there is a small five by five inch vent port under the wing, and at the tip, a rather fat pitot tube.

The left wing is also smoothly polished, and its smooth fillet, as on the right side, is secured with all of the screw slots in line with the relative wind.

The instrument panel was very simple, no GPS in sight. Note cockpit padding.

The aft fuselage of the Hughes is more of the smooth, polished, butt jointed, flush riveted skin, tapering to a very jaunty upswept pointed cone. Almost at the very rear, the tail skid is retracted, with just enough of the edge of the shoe projecting to absorb any shock in case of a wheels up landing.

The horizontal surfaces are tapered, and have rather formidable looking fixed tabs mounted inboard. Neither tab has any sort of a bend in it.

The rudder, a forecast of later Palmer designs for Vultee, is rather petite, and the vertical fin has a spring attached antenna which leads down to a point behind the cockpit.

There it is; nothing left now but to make an imaginary leap into the cockpit, start the engine, and take-off.

Well, it's a dream, of course. The Hughes H-1 will never fly again, nor will its Twin Wasp engine ever roar. It didn't do much flying in its active career, but what it did was magnificent . . . significant. There will be no better memorial to Howard Hughes than this beautiful, completely successful aircraft, locked in an eternal climbing turn, banking into history.

15 Sky Tiger

Bell's Airacuda—Bomber Destroyer Without a Mission

Airpower September, 1971

When I wrote this article, not a great deal had been written on the Bell Airacuda, and most of what had been written was wrong. Part of the problem stemmed from the way Bell and the Army Air Corps had ballyhooed the aircraft when it first appeared, each for different reasons. Larry Bell, of course, wanted to interest the public and the service in the new company he had formed, and he knew that he had to have something unusual to attract attention. In the Air Corps there was a small group that favored multi-seat fighters, and they touted the Airacuda as a solution to a number of problems, including the need for a long-range escort fighter. The situation was not too different from the days when the proponents of the McDonnell Douglas F-15 were vehemently opposed to the idea of the "lightweight fighter" as embodied in the General Dynamics F-16. Writers had to rely pretty much on what the Air Corps and Bell said. I had the advantage of working closely with Brigadier General Benjamin Kelsey, a charming, intelligent man who exemplified the best of Army Air Corps officers. Despite a lack of promotions (if memory serves, Ben was a First Lieutenant for 11 years) and the low pay of the Army, Ben stuck it out because he loved the work. He easily could have gone into industry and earned triple his Air Corps salary, but he never gave it a thought.

By working with Ben and others who had participated directly in the program, I was able to get some facts about the Airacuda on the table for the first time. Since then, much more informative work has been done. One work that stands out was done by my good friend, the late Birch Matthews, who covers the story well in his fine book Cobra: The Bell Aircraft Story *(Schiffer, 1996).*

This is the airplane the Bell Airacuda beat out to win the contract—but just barely. Kelly Johnson and Hall Hibbard designed the Lockheed YFM-2, which scored 71.6 in the United States Army Air Corps "Measure of Merit" evaluation, compared to the Bell YFM-1's 72.0. The decision easily could have gone to Lockheed, but the Burbank firm already had the prospect of Hudson and P-38 contracts, and the Air Corps wanted more competitors in the field, so it selected Bell as the winner.

The YFM1-A Airacuda was outfitted with a tricycle landing gear, which made it look even more modern than the prototype. The armament was formidable on paper—a 37 mm cannon in each nacelle, paired with a .30 caliber machine gun. The two waist guns were .50 caliber, while the ventral and dorsal guns were .30 caliber. In actual practice, however, bringing such weaponry on an enemy fighter would have been very difficult.

In the early months of 1942, the U.S. Army Air Force was desperately drafting every kind of aircraft into service—plush Stagger-wing Beeches became UC-43s; tatty old Boeing 247 Ds became workhorse C-73s, and so on. At the same time, twelve powerful twin engine fighters, some with as little as 17 hours total time, sat mouldering at training bases, their Allison engines silent, their parts disappearing one by one.

There are many reasons why Bell's streamlined Airacuda received such shabby treatment . . . the most important was that it had too many undeveloped engineering innovations. Yet despite the fact that it never fired a shot in anger, the Airacuda was important to the war effort, and it was an undoubted merchandising triumph for Bell.

In point of fact, the XFM-1 can only be considered a whopping success, for it did exactly what Larry Bell had planned for it. He wished to become established as an aircraft manufacturer at a time when the limited military budget was dominated by giants like Boeing, Curtiss, Douglas, Martin, Grumman and others. The Airacuda accomplished this for him, carrying his fledgling corporation through its crucial transition period, and insuring its growth from a barewall plant in the fall of 1935 to a fully functioning producer that would build over 13,000 aircraft in the following ten years.

Further, the technological spin-off from the Airacuda in terms of gun mounts, prop shaft extensions and experience with cannons, Allison engines and tricycle gear, would benefit the entire armaments industry.

Thus if the bomber-gulping tiger of the skies, of 1937, fell into service test and ground school obscurity by 1942, it was only of sentimental consequence to Bell, who was planning greater things.

Lawrence Dale Bell's plans had a habit of working out. Born on April 5, 1894 in Mentone, Indiana, he was, at 16, an accomplished mechanic, serving two famous stunt pilots; one of these was his idolized older brother Grover, and the other was a young man named Lincoln Beachey. Bell joined Glenn Martin at a time when aircraft manufacturers were, for want of any better classification, listed under *Amusements* in the Los Angeles telephone book, and became shop foreman by the age of 18. His mechanical skill and legendary salesmanship took him to the rank of Vice President and General Manager by 1928. Reuben Fleet then lured him to Consolidated, first as General Sales Manager, and a year later, as Vice President and General Manager. When Fleet moved Consolidated to San Diego in 1935, Bell stayed behind in Buffalo, determined to make it on his own.

The Airacuda created quite a stir at the New York World's Fair in 1939. The aircraft had been shrouded in secrecy for more than two years, and now it was suddenly on display. To the crowds, this simply meant that the United States was so powerful and so confident that it could put its latest weapon on exhibit for all to see. For the knowledgeable, this meant that the airplane no longer had any secrets worth hiding and was probably at the end of its production trail.

He took over 1,200,000 square feet of empty floor space with little more than his own reputation and ability, plus the talents of Robert J. Woods, then the boy wonder of aircraft design. The company accumulated $150,000 in working capital, $35,000 in used tools and the design and manufacturing rights to the antiquated Great Lakes BG-1 dive bomber, hardly the hottest thing on wings, even in 1935. Sub contracts with Consolidated for PBY outer wing panels (60 in 1936, 144 in 1937) kept the wolf from the door while Bell and Woods addressed themselves to the main problem: they had to come up with a design so revolutionary that the Air Corps would be forced to buy it. Their solution was the Airacuda, a multiplace cannon armed fighter that looked like nothing else in the sky, before or since.

You have to consider the strategic climate of the mid-thirties to realize how the Airacuda's role as a long range bomber destroyer could have appeared plausible. Hap Arnold had, as early as 1933, expressed his disappointment in the performance of single place pursuit aircraft as a bomber interceptor. He wanted to see a heavily armed, multiplace fighter developed, one which could destroy a bomber in a single pass.

Air Corps thinkers responded by defining the multiplace fighter as one which could be capable of denying definite areas of airspace to the enemy, and would "undertake the sustained attack of hostile aircraft in flight." Very rigorous requirements were set. As a minimum, the new type

There is no denying that the Bell Airacuda was an impressive-looking aircraft, but it was an aircraft without a mission. There were other drawbacks, too: engine cooling, excessive drag, poor routes of escape for the gunners in the nacelles. But on the positive side, visibility was good, ground handling (except for cooling) excellent, and the armament both advanced and powerful. *Peter M. Bowers*

was supposed to have a speed of 300 mph at 20,000 feet, a service ceiling of 25,000 feet, and an endurance of 10 hours at 15,000 feet at 220 mph. Specified armament included two flexible 37 mm cannon, four machine guns and 600 pounds of bombs!

In 1935, this was more than formidable—it was impossible.

As World War II loomed closer, many strategists were apprehensive of possible surprise attacks by Japan on the Philippine Islands, Hawaii, Alaska and even the Panama Canal. The popular press, typified by *Liberty* magazine, went a step further and pictured German aircraft carriers launching attacks on New York City. The Pacific scenario, of course, proved to be only too accurate, and had the war taken a slightly more adverse turn, it is entirely possible that the stillborn German carrier *Graf Zeppelin,* or captured Allied carriers, might actually have attacked the Eastern seaboard.

So it is not altogether strange that on January 18, 1935 a young Army officer at Fort Leavenworth's Command and Staff College wrote a letter to the Chief of the Air Corps, advocating the adoption of a multi-place bomber destroyer. Captain Harry A. Johnson's experience with the Berliner-Joyce P-16, while in the 1st Pursuit Group had convinced him that the single engine, two-seat fighter was unsatisfactory. He pressed for a twin engine aircraft with four fixed .50 caliber machine guns, plus two gunners firing flexibly mounted weapons. Not intended for dogfighting, Johnson's superplane was to be used as a patrolling airborne interceptor and a long range bomber escort.

Instead of being thrown into the round file reserved for captains who want to tell generals how to run the service, the letter went up the chain of command, through the Chief of the Materiel Division at Wright Field, the Air Corps Board at Maxwell, on to Headquarters, GHQ Air Force at Langley and, finally, to the Chief of the Air Corps, in Washington.

All the way up to GHQ Air Force level, there had been virtually no support for the project. The idea was not new—

The Bell Airacuda was especially good-looking in aerial views, for it was unlike anything in the sky and seemed to bristle with power and potential. One drawback was that it did not take to the sky very often; most of the Airacudas that were sent to ground-training schools came with pitifully low total flying time. *Peter M. Bowers*

Perhaps the greatest advantage of the Airacuda's unusual layout was that it attracted attention to the newly fledged Bell Aircraft Corporation. As there was nothing like the Airacuda, it seemed worthy of investigating, and provided Bell with a reputation for innovative thinking that it certainly deserved. ***Peter M. Bowers***

at least two previous design studies had been accomplished. One (No. 301) had been made on a multi-seat fighter version of the then new Martin B-10, and the problem of carrying the required weight of fuel and ammunition in a structure stressed for pursuit design factors seemed insurmountable. The letter's endorsements also made highly unflattering reference to the European endeavors along these lines, noting that the resulting aircraft was a combination fighter, bomber and observation plane, almost equally inefficient in all three tasks.

At Langley, however, Brigadier General Frank M. Andrews expressed a totally different opinion in a letter dated August 12, 1935. He affirmed the necessity for defending areas like the Panama Canal at long range, and he clarified some of the design requirements. The multi-seat fighter did not have to be as maneuverable as a single place aircraft, so it did not have to be designed to pursuit factors. Attack loads were considered satisfactory, as it was envisioned that the heaviest concentration of fire would be delivered in Trafalgar like broadside attacks. (Boulton-Paul would later elaborate on this in their *Defiant.*) Andrews went on to state that such an aircraft should have a distinctive designation—to clearly differentiate it from the pursuit role—and thus was derived the code FM, for fighter, multiplace.

Less than a month later, the Chief of the Air Corps, Major General Benny Foulois, sent a detailed memorandum to the Assistant Secretary of War, requesting permission to proceed with the procurement of a multi-seat fighter aircraft. The memo was so comprehensive as to suggest that the requirement had been maturing for some time, and that Captain Johnson's letter had been used as a vehicle to bring a long desired project to fruition.

General Foulois indicated that proposals would be solicited from both the Lockheed Aircraft Company and the Bell Aircraft Corporation. It noted that Bell's designer, Mr. Woods, was responsible for the advanced Consolidated PB2 then entering service. He further stated that the company had already made a "rather complete" study of the multiseat fighter problem. Lockheed had also presented a preliminary study, although not in the same detail as Bell.

A very sophisticated three phase approach was devised for the development of the new fighter. Phase I called for preliminary engineering studies by both contractors, with $25,000 (that's thousand, not million) to be allocated to each. At the end of this phase, one contractor would be eliminated. Phase II Mockup and Static Test, was funded in the amount of $80,000. If warranted, $250,000 would then be made available for Phase III, Option for Construction. Cancellation clauses were embodied in each phase.

Lockheed's design was the little known YFM-2. (The photos which accompany the article are the first ever seen of the project, and are due to the sleuthing ability of Lockheed representative Phil Settlemyer, who located them in a private collection.)

Although details are lacking, the YFM-2 was essentially a Model 10D Electra, modified with Allison engines, tricycle gear and heavy armament. It appears to have been the first *Skunk Works* product, although somewhat subdued compared to the next Hall Hibbard design, the incomparable P-38 Lightning.

War Department Special Order No. 72 convened a Board of Officers to decide the Phase I results. It was a very close contest, as the following evaluation indicates:

Characteristics	Measure of Merit Maximum % Possible	Measure of Merit % Achieved Bell XFM-1	Lockheed XFM-2
Performance	30	27.5	27.0
Engineering	40	25.2	29.0
Military	30	19.3	15.6
Total	100	72.0	71.6

Thus by the slim margin of .4 of one percent did Bell manage to lock onto a contract that would give them publicity, income, reputation and inspiration until their just conceived second product, the P-39 Airacobra, could bear fruit.

The XFM-1

There was more than a touch of Consolidated in the radical new design that Bob Woods laid on for the XFM-1, not so much in planform as in engineering technique and detail. The Buffalo plant was fortunate in having large numbers of experienced aircraft workers to call on, personnel who had learned their trade with Curtiss, Consolidated or Hall-Aluminum. This backlog of experience accounts in part for the high quality of craftsmanship and finish in Bell's first product.

One of the many anecdotes about colorful Larry Bell concerns a tough bargaining session he was having with Air Corps engineers, who were pressing for the installation of rearward firing machine guns. Inwardly, Bell panicked, for the Airacuda was already overweight, and there was really no place to install tail defense weapons. Taking the offen-

Spectacular, revolutionary, imaginative, Lawrence Bell's XFM-1 Airacuda was all of these and more. It certainly was the most intriguing combat aircraft of the golden decade (1930–1940) and, perhaps, one of the most fascinating fighters ever built.

Unfortunately for Bell, the XFM-1 Airacuda was a brilliant application of design theory to a need that never arose. It was a formidable flying machine for a mission that did not exist. It was, in fact, the ultimate defensive weapon in an age which had conjured up the image of great bomber fleets bent on the destruction of America's cities.

By the mid thirties, the impact of the long range bomber was just being felt by farseeing warplanners. Since the gifted always spot a trend several years before the public, and even the War Dept. become aware of it, the performance of Boeing's YB-17s was not lost on Bell's young engineers. By 1936 they could see just how formidable the long range bomber was with its speed and heavy payload. They also realized that it would be most vulnerable out of fighter cover range of its own escorts, several hundred miles off the American coast, yet still far out to sea. It was at this point that a heavily armed, high flying, fast, long range defensive fighter could intercept and destroy them. Thus was born the Bell XFM-1 Airacuda, the bomber destroyer envisioned for the great intercontinental air wars of the future which men like Seversky, Douhet and Mitchell had been predicting for over a decade.

In an age when first line pursuits were just breaking the 200 mph. speed barrier and carried one or two rifle caliber guns, the Airacuda was an imposing proposition.

Aviation writers were ecstatic, laymen dumbstruck and, if the dispatches by the correspondents of the day are to be taken at face value, the "jaws of the European war lords dropped" when the Airacuda was rolled out. Moreover, in keeping with the aviation theories of the day, Lawrence Bell proclaimed: "Too long have our designers worked at bombers. The result is that the cities along the seacoast would have been helpless in the event of an attack by air. We had nothing capable of staving them off. We saw the need, conceived the plans, presented the idea, then built the Airacuda."

In 1937, the ringing speech made sense, but as time and WW II were to prove, the Airacuda was not needed by the Army Air Corps. First and foremost the aircraft was a bomber destroyer and was, in fact known as *The Destroyer.* Had the Germans possessed a similar aircraft during our 1942–1944 air strikes over Europe—before the advent of escort fighters all the way to and from the target—our losses would have been far heavier and unescorted bombing attacks would have proven prohibitive in terms of bombers lost. But the United States never faced the problem of air attacks on our cities, and the Airacuda could not be used in any other role.

History notwithstanding, its concept was brilliant in the mission it was designed for. With sufficient range to catch attacking bomber streams far from our coasts, a 50 mph. speed advantage and tremendous fire-power, it was to line up behind the enemy's formations and blow his aircraft to pieces, one-by-one, with its gyro-stabilized 37mm cannon which locked on the target. With a .30 caliber machine gun mounted with each cannon, the pilot could employ the lighter guns for ranging and direction, while .50 caliber weapons in waist blisters provided for any eventuality including defense against escorting fighters, an unlikely possibility.

Sitting two miles behind the bomber stream, the Airacuda would be immune to their defensive machine guns, flying with impunity, out of range, while its heavy

37mm shells tore up the attacking formation. On paper and even in metal, the idea seemed foolproof.

In its prototype model the XFM-1 nearly measured up to the stringent requirements projected for it. However, its top speed was only 271 mph. at 20,000 ft. and that was a few miles faster than the service test YFM-1s, 1As, and -Bs. It took ten minutes to climb to 15,000 ft. and although range with a full two ton load was a respectable 800 miles and service ceiling was 30,500 ft., with the aircraft capable of good altitude performance, the General Motors built Allison V-1710-13, -23, and -41 pushers, providing 1150 hp. and 1090 hp. in the -41, were not powerful enough for the aircraft.

Even so, the Airacuda featured some forward looking innovations. In place of engine driven instruments and auxiliary power units, the Airacuda relied on an all electrical system for gear, fuel pumps, etc. This caused numerous engine failures, since the new system tended to break down and the emergency backup did not have the power to run the aircraft until the primary system could resume operation. The overload on it was so great that it continually shorted out. In bad weather, when this occurred, the instrument panel would go, and two of three fatal crashes were caused by instrument failure. Sometimes the gear would not come down, or worse still, the electric fuel pumps would quit, all due to flaws in the electrical system. It, however, could have eventually been redesigned and the 50 amp. battery replaced with a more powerful unit, but there were other faults inherent in the Airacuda which made it a suspect, if not actually dangerous aircraft to operate.

You could not fly it hands-off, at any time. Stability about the longitudinal axis was poor. In a dive, the aircraft tended to continue nosing down. In a pull up, its nose continued to raise. In a tight turn, it wanted to roll over in the direction of the turn. This made it very maneuverable for such a large aircraft, but you were forced to hang on to it every second. You could not trim it and take your hands off the wheel, yet, ironically, this marginal stability with power on might have made it a rather remarkable bomber destroyer, even for close in work.

Oddly enough, with power off, the aircraft was extremely stable. It would almost land hands off on final approach, and power off stalls were clean, crisp, stable and gave ample warning. With the power on it was, again, unstable. However, rudder control was good, but you had to cut the power to recover from a spin. The aircraft landed smoothly, had no tendency to groundloop and reacted well on the brakes, which would stop it in just over 1,000 ft. on roll out. The approach was flown at 140 mph. and the aircraft touched down at just under 80 mph.

Climb rate was approximately 1,500 fpm., half of the proposed velocity, but the aircraft could clear a 50 ft. obstacle with a two man crew and no armament at 1,000 ft., 250 ft. longer than the proposal specified.

Probably one of the Airacuda's most interesting features, or lack of one, was the fact that the aircraft could not taxi. The engine did not have a cooling fan, thus as soon as it was fired up and the manifold pressure began to climb, the pilot took off. When the aircraft landed and completed its roll out, turning off the taxi way, it was towed to its parking place. While in the air the velocity of the machine cooled the engine, but on the ground, no provision was made for a cooling apparatus, since there was no room in the nacelle housing to position one.

This, however, did not hamper performance, and bore no part in the Air Corps' decision to drop the project. Despite the fact that the XFM and YFMs were revolutionary, extremely well built, and finished, cleverly designed and well armed, their guns fired by a centrally directed system, the gunners in the nacelles acting principally as loaders, the threat for which the aircraft was built, never materialized. What the Air Corps needed at the outbreak of WW II, were fast, single engined interceptors to fight first—a defensive war—close to the front, a mission the Airacuda was never designed for. What it was, in effect, was a bomber-sized fighter with tremendous fire-power. But like the bomber it emulated, it was too big, too slow, too vulnerable and too expensive. Even in May of 1938, when 13 service test models were ordered, an Airacuda cost $244,000 each, the price of ten P-36 fighters or two B-17s. Meanwhile, Bell had come up with a new, lightweight single seat fighter, the P-39 Airacobra, which nearly cracked the 400 barrier during its maiden test flights. As the threat of destruction to American cities by long range German bombers diminished after the Battle of Britain in 1940, it was obvious that the Airacuda was not needed. Nevertheless, despite its demise, it proved just how advanced and imaginative America's aircraft industry was during the golden decade of the '30s, even if in its search for new concepts and techniques it turned its talents to a superlative machine that was not needed.

This YFM-1B version of the Airacuda had a conventional landing gear, somewhat out of keeping with the advanced look of the design. This was changed in later models to a tricycle gear. *Peter M. Bowers*

This is the Bell YFM-1B, with one of its 37 mm cannon installed. The aircraft was more attractive in its later models when a tricycle gear was installed. *Robert F. Dorr*

sive, he snorted "That makes about as much sense as putting teeth in the ass of a lion. You put the teeth in the mouth." The earthy remark broke up the meeting and Bell had his way.

Allison V-1710-9 engines, driving a three bladed pusher prop by means of a 64-inch extension shaft, were mounted behind the gunners, and on each engine there was placed an old, but still troublesome device—a turbo supercharger. Boeing Fortress-style blisters protruded from the conventional rear section of the aircraft, each housing a .50 caliber machine gun.

The "teeth in the mouth" design philosophy was evident as the prototype began to take shape. The pilot was seated well forward in a rather hunnish style cockpit, flanked on either side by nacelles packing wicked looking, and yet to be designed, 37 mm cannon. Each cannon was served by a gunner, and could be fired independently or jointly from a central fire control device at the navigator's station. The gunner also had a .30 caliber machine gun.

The impact of the design on the press was tremendous. Here was an intoxicatingly different airplane, and while aero engineers might have been dubious about such mundane things as drag, weight and complexity, the public could recognize the Airacuda as a masterpiece of weaponry. True there were probably some bugs to be worked out, but in the meantime the aircraft's style and mystery compensated for the feelings of inferiority being generated in Europe by Hawker, Supermarine and Messerschmitt.

And for Bell Aircraft, the innovations, certainly provided some mysteries as testing proceeded. First flight came at the Buffalo plant on September 1, 1937, with famous Air Corps test pilot Lt. Benjamin S. Kelsey at the controls. Kelsey flew the aircraft for twenty-five minutes, and except for a backfire on take off which damaged one supercharger's intercooler, the trip was uneventful.

Kelsey, now Brigadier General, USAF (Retired), recalls that aside from some unusual asymmetric-power control reactions induced by the relationship of the propellers to the empennage, the aircraft was pleasant enough to fly. As Project Officer for Fighters at Wright Field from 1934 to 1943, Kelsey probably flew more new types of U.S. fighters than any other pilot, and Bell was understandably pleased to have him test fly the XFM-1.

The plane, serialed 36-351, had a somewhat star-crossed career as a test bird, however. On its second flight, the right landing gear collapsed, damaging the undercarriage, outer wing and propeller. Then, after its modification

While the Airacuda was not a big success, it established Bell in business and ultimately put it in a position where it could produce such aircraft as the Bell XS-1 (later the X-1), shown here with Captain Chuck Yeager, the man who broke the sound barrier on October 14, 1947.

to near YFM-1 standards, Captain Ernie Warburton had to make a forced landing on November 24, 1939, when a cooling jacket plug blew, spilling out all of the Prestone coolant. Still, the prototype was to acquire, by far, the most flying time of all the Airacudas before being relegated to Class 26. In forty-two months it would log 103 hours; not much by anyone's test standards, and certainly far too little to develop the many innovations crammed into the aircraft.

The most obvious difference in the Airacuda was the use of twin pusher propellers. Less obvious, but more troublesome was the fact that the Allison engine was relatively new, and the Airacuda would shepherd it through its earliest teething problems. Bell had the advantage of having made the very first installation of the Allison engine in an attack version of the PB-2, the Consolidated A-11A, and this experience was of great benefit. So was the sound approach to the extension shafts, which were tested exhaustively on the torque stand at Wright Field, and which were so trouble free in use that their design was carried over to the P-39. This preliminary testing revealed a potential problem area in the airplane—the vibration induced by the shaft and the propellers causing material failure of the light metal wing skins remedied in later aircraft by use of a heavier gauge aluminum.

A second important difference in the Airacuda, and one which would plague it throughout its career, was the use of an auxiliary power unit for the nine different electric motors which powered gear, flaps, prop control mechanism and so on. An Eclipse 3710X two cylinder gas engine of 13.5 horsepower was used to drive a generator which supplied 110 volt A.C. current. The 110 volt system was simply not powerful enough to meet peak demands, particularly during emergencies, and a 24 volt D.C. system was later substituted. The APU, however, was an important concept which would see use in many later multi-engine aircraft.

The third major innovation was the adoption of the T-9 37 mm cannon, adapted by Colt from their M1E1 anti-aircraft gun. As General Andrews had indicated, the multi-place fighter was expected to be a ship-of-the-line, lobbing 37 mm broadsides against incoming bombers.

Far fetched? Perhaps, until you compare the theory with the bitter air battles over Germany when multi-engine Luftwaffe fighters broke up B-17 formations with rockets fired from over 800 yards range. Different tools, but the same concept, certainly.

The Bell engineers had also devised a rigid mount for the 37 mm cannon, nestled in a flexible turret which was driven through a 25 degree cone of fire by electrically powered gear trains. As noted, the cannon could be fired either by the gunner, or by the navigator using a Sperry-built *"Thermionic"* central fire control system. In addition, an optical sight protruded below the lower left side of the fuselage, and could also be used as a bomb sight. This mechanism, however, was never installed on 36-351, even after its modification.

Lt. Kelsey conducted a 16-round firing test of the 37 mm during the spring of 1939. He recalls that there were no problems except for a peculiar visual side effect—if you *watched* them fire. It felt as if you were being blown out of the cockpit.

There were also some inherent design difficulties which would have had to have been overcome. The gun mounts were lightly built to save weight, and would undoubtedly have been a maintenance headache. Worse, the entire nacelle was moved by aerodynamic forces, and the pitching and twisting movements created a compensation problem for the central fire control system.

Getting the T-9 cannons redesigned for use in the Airacuda was a task in itself, and Bell spent almost as much time with Colt as he did in his own factory, trying to introduce aircraft production speed into the staid ordnance work pace. Thirty nine weapons were procured, 26 for the Airacudas, with first delivery coming on April 20th, 1939.

The familiar .50 caliber machine guns provided an unexpected problem; the first time they were fired from the fuselage side mounts, the recoil literally tore gunmount and aircraft structure to bits. Bell engineers, (believed to have been led by Fred Schoellkopf IV) invented a hydraulic shock absorbing gun mount which allowed the gun to recoil 5/8″ every time it fired. It was simple, lightweight, practically foolproof, and it worked. Whereupon an entire ordnance division of Bell Aircraft was set up in Burlington, Vermont to manufacture similar mounts for weapons in all branches of the service—another example of an Airacuda spin-off.

Construction Details

Modern but conventional structural techniques were employed in the aircraft, perhaps to compensate even better visibility. A flat, shatterproof, laminated glass removed some of the slight distortion found in the earlier XFM-1 installation. The picturesque but inefficient side blisters were replaced by flat sliding windows in which a swinging turret mounted a .50 caliber machine gun.

A retractable turret of formed plexiglass and aluminum framing was mounted in the top of the fuselage. The entire assembly could be retracted flush with the fuselage, reflecting the urgent requirement to reduce the Airacuda's considerable drag even at the expense of complexity. The .30

The rather portly designer of the Airacuda, Robert J. Woods, stands with another of his more radical products, the all-wood Bell XP-77. Woods was the very heart of Bell Aircraft at its start and masterminded the Bell P-39 Airacobra as well. Note the name on the cockpit—Jack Woolams was a famous Bell test pilot who lost his life in a post-war racing accident.

In flight the Airacuda was an elegant machine, with great visibility for the pilot. The name "Airacuda" was a masterstroke of marketing; Bell had wanted a barracuda image for its airplane, so the name was just perfect. *Peter M. Bowers*

caliber gun had a 360 degree field of fire, with interrupters to prevent firing into the propellers or tail surfaces. A ventral .30 caliber gun was provided in a sliding glass covered tunnel turret. This lower turret gave a notched appearance to the somewhat fuller lines of the YFM-1's fuselage.

The nacelles were more finely streamlined on the YFM-1, as the radiators and superchargers had both been installed in the wing. (Ground cooling remained a problem throughout the aircraft's short life.) But the nacelle armament was reduced by deletion of the .30 caliber gun.

A rather diminutive bomb bay was set into the wing center section. Twenty M-5 bombs could be hung vertically. Bomb bay doors were manually operated.

There were three basic YFM-1 models. Eight YFM-1s had conventional gear and V-1710-23 engines. Three YFM-1s had tricycle gear and -23 engines, while two YFM-1s had conventional gear and altitude rated -41 engines. The YFM-1Bs could be most easily distinguished by the small carburetor air scoop mounted on top of the nacelles.

The first flight of the YFM-1 almost ended in disaster when the right F-10 turbo supercharger let go, slinging turbine buckets all the way through the fuselage, and causing a forced landing to be made at the Buffalo airport. Ed Coffey of the National Archives staff made a special effort to have the previously classified photos of the damaged aircraft made available for the article.

The incident could easily have been a disaster, as control cables were severed on one side of the fuselage. The aircraft was subsequently repaired for $38,104. As a side effect, F-13 (B-1) turbos were recommended to replace the F-10 type which had failed.

On September 2, 1939, General Andrews made his own evaluation of the Airacuda, saying that: "While it was not all that was to be desired in the way of speed, it was the best thing available, and was in production: hence the procurement of an adequate number of the type without waiting for further development was indicated." He thought the type would be particularly useful in Panama, where the only bombers available to counterattack a hostile fleet were obsolete Martin B-10s and Douglas B-18s, which could certainly have made good use of a fighter escort.

Original proposals called for four aircraft to be sent to Wright Field, four to the Panama Canal Zone, and the remainder assigned for familiarization to various squadrons in the United States. As it happened, the initial distribution was as the chart on page 119 indicates.

General Kelsey says that there was no rush to fly the Airacuda, primarily because of the psychological as well as physical hazard of the pusher props during a bail out. Consequently no service test group of aircraft were probably ever flown as little as the thirteen YFM-1s. This general lack of enthusiasm resulted in no suitable tactics being devised, nor did anyone become an advocate of the type.

Bell had been concerned about the escape problem, and devised a primer cord ring which was designed to shear the propeller shaft to permit an emergency bailout. There is no evidence that this was ever used, although there were at least two successful bail outs recorded, both believed to have been from the fuselage door.

Aircraft record cards at the Smithsonian Institution reveal that four of the service test aircraft were involved in accidents. Major Paul T. Hanley had a forced landing in 496 on September 6, 1941, when an electrical malfunction (alas, all too common in the Airacuda) feathered both propellers. 38-497 was on its way to becoming a ground school trainer when it had an engine fire, crashing and burning. The pilot, 1/Lt James G. Reed was killed, but his crew chief parachuted to safety. 489 and 498 were involved in minor repairable accidents, the latter on two occasions.

Type	Serial Number	First Station	Total Flying Time
XFM-1	36-351	Wright Field, Ohio	103.0
YFM-1	38-486	Hamilton Field, Cal.	43.0
YFM-1	38-487	Hamilton Field, Cal.	61.7
YFM-1	38-488	New York World's Fair	16.9
YFM-1B	38-489	Hamilton Field, Cal.	40.8
YFM-1B	38-490	Langley Field, Va.	45.7
YFM-1	38-491	Maxwell Field, Ala.	7.0
YFM-1	38-492	Demolished at factory	—
YFM-1	38-493	Langley Field, Va.	42.3
YFM-1	38-494	Langley Field, Va.	68.3
YFM-1	38-495	Langley Field, Va.	42.4
YFM-1A	38-496	Hamilton Field, Cal.	48.5
YFM-1A	38-497	Wright Field, Ohio	64.0
YFM-1A	38-498	Orlando, Florida	15.4

John F. Strickler has written to me of the rather hair raising adventure he had while test flying 38-492, the Airacuda that was never delivered to the Air Corps. He and Bryan Sparks, then Bell's chief test pilot were flying at altitude on June 16, 1940, when their aircraft fell into a spin. Strickler, a graduate of Randolph Field's first class of Flying Cadets, and an ex 1st Pursuit Group P-6E pilot, wasn't too worried until he tried to apply opposite rudder to break the spin's rotation. The rudder was locked full over, and even with Sparks standing on the copilots controls, it simply wouldn't budge. Strickler tried everything—power on, power off, power against the spin—nothing worked. With the ground leaping up, he feathered both props and signalled Sparks to bail out. Immediately after Sparks jumped, there was a loud bang, and Strickler found that he had rudder control again. He decided to ride it out—when the spin was broken, it was too late to restart the engines, and he deadsticked it into a field.

Subsequent analysis revealed that the very long, sharp leading edge of the rudder would "unport" from behind the fin and lock hard over in the full rudder position. When Sparks had bailed out he had struck the empennage, breaking his legs, but disrupting the airflow enough for Strickler to regain control. Sparks recovered, and Bell redesigned the leading edge of the rudder to a blunter shape, solving the problem.

Strickler, who became Project Engineer on the YFM-1 after the original Project Engineer, Art Fornoff had suffered a heart attack, has many other, fonder memories of the Airacuda. Like General Kelsey, he thinks that the aircraft simply tried to offer too many novel features at once, at a time when interest and spending had veered to more conventional fighters. In a different environment, faced with different requirements, the YFM-1 could have been developed into an effective aircraft. In any event, whether a tiger or a turkey of the sky, the Airacuda served to establish Bell as a major contender in the aviation arena.

Data Sheet

	XFM-1	YFM-1	YFM-1A	YFM-1B
Wingspan	69′10″	70′0″	70′0″	70′0″
Length	44′10″	46′0″	46′0″	46′0″
Height	13′7″	12′9″	12′9″	12′5″
Wing Area	684 sf	688 sf	688 sf	688 sf
Empty Weight	13,376	13,630	13,962	13,023
Max Gross Weight	17,333	19,000	19,301	21,625
Engine, Allison	V-1710-9 (later -13)	V-1710-23	V-1710-23	V-1710-41
Speed (Max)	271 mph (@ 20m)	270 mph (@ 12.6m)	270 mph (@ 12.6m)	268 mph (@ 12.6m)
Normal Range	800 miles	940 miles	940 miles	650 miles
Landing Speed	77 mph	77 mph	77 mph	77 mph

16 Cry Havoc

The Douglas A-20, Part I

Wings June, 1976

Some aircraft designers have the knack of imparting their trademark to the very lines of the airplanes they work with. Compare the side views of an S.E.5a and a Gloster Gladiator, and you'll notice the unmistakable style of H. P. Folland. Examine a Hawker Fury and a Hawker Hurricane, and the name "Sydney Camm" will leap out at you. It was entirely different with the work of Ed Heinemann, who designed many great aircraft for Douglas, all of them differing significantly in appearance. The one thing that they had in common was that they were top performers.

Heinemann, working under Jack Northrop, began the design of the Northrop 7A in March, 1936. When Northrop was reabsorbed into Douglas, the design was enlarged to become the DB-7, one of the many American designs (including the Lockheed Hudson) that would greatly benefit from the interest of foreign nations as World War II approached. France, in desperate need for modern aircraft, immediately became interested in the DB-7.

Speaking of signature designs, one of the people working with Heinemann was Ted Smith, and one has only to look at his post-war Aero Commander, and even the hot Aerostar, to see the DB-7 ancestry.

About to land at 95 mph, a Boston III (Douglas DB-7B) shows off its clean and pleasing lines. One of 761 7Bs (built by both Douglas and Boeing), it was powered by Wright R-2600 engines. *Peter M. Bowers*

The success of the Douglas Aircraft Company during World War II is an incredible page in American aviation history, for while the California based firm had always done well, from its 1920 Cloudster through its epoch making DC series, its achievements from 1939 through 1945 were unexcelled by any manufacturer in the world. It turned out thousands of first class aircraft of many types while globally expanding its manufacturing and servicing organizations. The C-47s, C-54s, A-20s, A-24s, A-26s, SBDs and others, were more than just excellent planes; they were superior weapon systems respected by both air and ground crews.

The French had led the way in foreign orders for the DB-7A, and the country's collapse in 1940 meant that the orders had to be taken over by the British. The French aircraft had many modifications to American practice, including having the throttle operation reversed—forward to cut-off, back to full power. *Peter M. Bowers*

Part of this phenomenal success stems from Douglas' almost ideal indoctrination into the design and production methods which would serve it and the nation so well. By 1939 it had produced hundreds of the famous Douglas Commercial transports, and in doing so had acquired an enormous range of manufacturing skills and techniques. Substantial foreign sales had the additional advantage of providing the foundation for an outstanding service network, but even more important, the firm was endowed with such engineering geniuses as Jack Northrop, Ed Heinemann, R. G. Smith, Leo Devlin, Gene Root and others, and this fortunate combination of production capability and design talent was given a magnificent opportunity to mature by the fast developing requirements of the Western Allies for warplanes of all types.

There is an additional factor, often overlooked, that will receive special consideration in this article—the effect of British testing on American tactics and equipment. U.S. aircraft which were provided first to France and then to Great Britain served well in combat, but served even better as a means of indoctrinating American soldiers and civilians into the realities of war. The Douglas DB-7 series—known variously as the 7B, DB-7, BD-1, BD-2, P-70, F-3, O-53, A-20, Boston, Havoc, Ranger, Intruder, Turbinlite, Pandora, Moonfighter and (even) Helmore—was the major instrument in the maturing process. (See page 134 for a cross reference of types.)

By 1937, Douglas had long been established as a valued vendor to both U.S. services; it produced first class airplanes at reasonable prices, and was relatively easy to deal with. (This factor is often overlooked, for it is never mentioned publicly. Some firms are genuine pleasures to work with, while others seem to enjoy making life difficult. During World War II, Douglas and Boeing were good examples of the former, while Glenn L. Martin and Curtiss were horrible examples of the latter.)

Douglas had enjoyed a long, intimate, financial, engineering, personal and management relationship with the Northrop Corporation, having been a 51% shareholder since the latter firm's inception. A troublesome labor dispute caused the Northrop Corporation to be dissolved in the late summer of 1937, and when it reappeared it was known as the Northrop Division of the Douglas Aircraft Company. The Division produced some 270 of the single engine A-17 type which was serving as the Air Corps' basic attack plane, and whose major significance lies in its being the direct ancestor of the Pacific war-winning SBD. The A-17 also helped convince service planners of the inadequacy of the single engine airplane in the attack role. For despite herculean competitive efforts by both Pratt & Whitney and Wright, power plants were not generating enough horsepower for a single engine airplane to carry an effective load of bombs, at a reasonable speed, for a reasonable distance.

As a result, three aviation immortals—Donald Douglas, Sr., Jack Northrop, and Ed Heinemann formed a team to develop the initial concept of what would become the DB-7 series. Known as the Model 7A, the plane was intended to reach 250 mph with a full load of bombs, using two 450 horsepower Pratt & Whitney engines.

However, reports coming from Europe soon indicated that something far more formidable was required than the tame performance planned for the 7A. The modest goals somehow reflected America's 1936 naïveté, for the proposed bomber was underpowered, undergunned and underarmored. It may have been suitable for streaming smoke at war games, but hardly ready to face combat. As a consequence, the design was dropped.

Heinemann—who had the principal role in developing the series—went back to the drawing board and came up with a radical improvement, the Model 7B, which featured

It is difficult to imagine now, but Boeing was undergoing hard times in the prewar years when Congress elected not to buy large quantities of the new Boeing B-17. The Seattle firm was pleased to be able to manufacture Douglas DB-7s like this Boston III to fill in the gaps. Of course the tide was turned later, when Douglas was asked (along with Lockheed) to build B-17s. *Peter M. Bowers*

The basic DB-7 design was very adaptable and went through a long series of modifications. This is a Douglas A-20K Havoc attack bomber; note the revised nose and the rear turret. *Peter M. Bowers*

the new and potent Pratt & Whitney R-1830-C engines of 1,100 horsepower. The 7B was larger, with much more bombload and armament, yet it retained a significant portion of the original concept: an interchangeable fuselage nose section which provided optional attack or level bombing capability.

The 7B arrived at a time when almost every major U.S. manufacturer had a twin engine attack plane under development, responding to a series of extremely rigorous design competitions by the Air Corps. These were being conducted on an almost semiannual basis, with the performance stakes being raised each time, as new requirements became known, and as manufacturers' performance promises expanded. From these trials would emerge such stellar aircraft as the Martin Maryland, North American B-25, and of course, the Douglas A-20, but the road to perfectibility would not be easy.

Its hurried development was fostered by the increasing threat of a general European war, which seemed practically certain by 1938. The Western Allies, particularly France, were absolutely desperate not only to buy modern warplanes, but to obtain visible signs of American commitment to the Allied war effort. Those were days when the words neutrality, isolation and embargo were filled with real and bitter meaning, and overt support of either side was laden with political risk.

The heretofore covert French interest in buying airplanes was made public knowledge on January 23, 1939, when the prototype 7B crashed in Los Angeles, seriously injuring the representative of the French Purchasing Commission, Captain Chemidlin, and killing test pilot John Cable. Several versions of how and why the aircraft crashed exist, and perhaps none is more accurate than an account by the well known test pilot Melvin N. Gough. In his analysis, "The airplane passed over the field, apparently in cruising condition, wheels up, both engines running, at between 1200 and 1500 feet. As prearranged, the airplane was rolled from side to side by means of the ailerons to demonstrate to both the ground commission and the French observer in the airplane the lateral characteristics. It continued on past the field quite a way, made a 180 degree turn, and came back, this time with the right engine stopped and the propeller fully feathered. A demonstration of single engine performance, including full throttle climb, was to be started over the field. At what appeared to be 1000 to 1200 feet directly over the field, the airplane seemed to be moving quite slowly in comparison to the previous passage. It then did a violent roll to the right, much faster than had been seen when the ailerons were used, and much faster than had ever been seen in any of the maneuvers it had previously been put through. How far it went in this roll-off to the right is uncertain, but it was described in almost minute detail,

This snow-covered A-20C was also built by Boeing. Many changes had occurred since the first flight of the prototype in October, 1938. The aircraft had grown heavier and longer-ranged, and carried a wide variety of armament packages. *Peter M. Bowers*

Photographs of the undersurfaces of an aircraft are relatively rare in comparison to profile shots, but they often reveal some interesting details. Note that the wheel well doors in the left nacelle of this A-20G are open, the flaps are down, and the cowl flaps are cracked. The aircraft was probably photographed just after takeoff. *Peter M. Bowers*

The A-20A was a big addition to the U.S. Army Air Corps, and in these 1941 war games, they were observed with great interest. The Douglas designers had versatility in mind from the start and made the aircraft adaptable to several different noses for different missions. *Peter M. Bowers*

in one case, as appearing to be a complete barrel roll with the nose practically on the horizon, followed by a very tight spiral or spin nosing down. Either the one engine was on continuously or the power was decreased, then increased, because both observers said that the pilot was using the good engine as best he could. Undoubtedly, however, being trimmed for single engine flight, the reduction in power on the good engine would produce as much dissymmetry of control force with the good engine off as would be produced by aerodynamic dissymmetry with the good engine operating. In any event, at approximately 500 feet, Cable was seen to come out of the airplane, go over the fuselage and pass over the tail, with the airplane descending at very high speed. Cable struck the ground feet first with the parachute fully streamed out but not fully blossomed. He was killed instantly. The French observer, who must necessarily have been in the tail due to the very narrow fuselage, was carried from the wreckage on the vertical fin, which was torn off by a spectator."

By April, 1944, when this photo was taken, the A-20G had matured into an effective warplane, well liked by air and ground crews. The lines of the later private aircraft, the Aero Commander, are implicit in the A-20's layout. *Peter M. Bowers*

The incident received world wide publicity, from both the spectacular nature of the crash into a parking lot, as well as the wild domestic political troubles it created for a hapless Hap Arnold, who, as Air Corps Chief of Staff, sacrificially received blasts from Secretary of the Treasury Morgenthau and from President Roosevelt himself.

Despite the political brouhaha, France liked the aircraft, and it liked the improved DB-7 proposal even better, ordering an initial 100 on February 15, 1939. The accident was rare in that the pressure to buy was so great that the catastrophic crash did not terminate interest, but in effect gave it impetus. Further, it permitted Heinemann to undertake a completely fresh approach with the DB-7, incorporating many of the things learned in the 7B's relatively brief career.

Carl Cover had made the first flights in the 7B, and had complained of tail flutter and bad lateral visibility. (Cover performed something like the same test flight functions at Douglas that O. E. "Pat" Tibbs later did at Martin—always the first flight, and enough of the subsequent ones to make sure that the other test pilots would be able to handle the project.)

As a result of Cover's comments, Heinemann was able to get Donald Douglas' agreement to make drastic revisions, foremost of which was stiffening the tail structure and improving visibility. The resulting airplane was much more attractive to both U.S. and foreign buyers. It was, in effect, a completely new machine, its engines were now mid wing and underslung. Only the wing and landing gear remained of the 7B.

The U.S. Army Air Corps, which had contributed substantially to the 7A in the original formulation of requirements, and to the entire light and medium bomber fleets of World War II by the criteria stipulated in its Circular Proposals, soon ordered 63 of the aircraft as A-20s and then 143 as A-20As. These were essentially the same as the DB-7Bs being purchased by France and Britain, but with, of course, American equipment.

The DB-7/A-20 was a larger, more sophisticated aircraft than its 7B forerunner. The fuselage was deepened to permit an increased bombload and tankage, and the cockpit was stepped as a consequence. The increase in drag was partially offset by making the already slender fuselage even narrower, which though better aerodynamically, posed a morale problem of sorts by isolating the pilot, navigator/bombardier and gunner into three separate compartments. This was the exact reverse of German human factor philosophy, which called for all crew members to be as cozily grouped as possible, and would soon come in for criticism in later British reports. The arrangement created definite hazards for the bombardier in the event of a forced landing or ditching, for there was very little structure to protect him on impact, and nowhere to go.

There were numerous design differences in the 7B and the DB-7, although Heinemann's beautiful handiwork was obvious in each. The DB-7's nacelles were lowered to a racy underslung position on what were now mid-mounted wings, and the nose gear was lengthened to provide ground clearance. The undersurface of the 7B's fuselage had tapered quite sharply upward to the rear, and it is interesting to note how closely the aircraft resembles the post-war Aero Commander in general outline. It's probably just a coincidence, but it's just possible that T. R. Smith, who was the final Project Engineer on the DB-7 program, drew from the 7B when he designed the Aero Commander.

The DB-7's top speed of 305 mph was a vast improvement over the A-17's 220 mph, but more important were the maximum bomb capacity of over 2,000 pounds, and, with a lesser load, the 450 mile range. Four fixed forward guns and two flexible rear guns provided a significant punch for the time.

The basic rightness of the design was confirmed as it began to fulfill its growth potential. Just as the DB-7 had been a major improvement over the 7B, so did the DB-7A, with its more powerful Wright Cyclone R-2600 engines, improve on it, and so in turn were later variants better. Speed peaked early with the A-20's 390 mph, but armament, bombload and combat capability were increased throughout the life of the design. And, of course, all of the Havocs provided a development base for the immortal Douglas A-26 Invader, often called a scaled up A-20, which served in three wars over a twenty-five year period.

Going back (as we must, for it's difficult to recount the many varieties without skipping back and forth) the French order for 100 was completed in an amazingly short time. Unfortunately, the lassitude of the phony war prevented much participation by the DB-7s, only a few of which were operational at the front. Even though the *Armée de l'Air* did not energetically incorporate the relatively potent Douglas into frontline units, additional orders were placed, first for 170 DB-7s and then 100 DB-7As, and from this contractual base sprang the very first Boston Is and IIs for the Royal Air Force. The R.A.F. later purchased quantities of the aircraft, and eventually the joint British-French total exceeded 1150 aircraft.

The DB-7A's use of the potent new R-2600's 1600 horsepower permitted a gross weight of over 17,000 pounds. The larger engines caused a further redesign of the nacelles, which became positively sinister in their pointed slimness, and the increased power required that the vertical surfaces be enlarged.

The bell tolling for France in the summer of 1940 signaled Great Britain to salvage what was possible from the Continental disaster by taking over French war contracts. DB-7 aircraft, equipped with French instrumentation and equipment, including the "reversed" (back to increase power, forward to decrease) throttle set-up, were hurriedly incorporated into the R.A.F.

The Havoc was a pleasant aircraft to fly, with good single engine characteristics. In this photograph of an A-20B, the great visibility from the bombardier's position is evident. *Peter M. Bowers*

Although the fact was entirely overlooked in contemporary accounts, it was a real tribute to the airplane that it managed to satisfy the vastly different operational requirements of France, England and the United States. The French had seen the airplane as a general purpose level bomber, whose operation behind a fixed front line would not require excessive range. When France fell, England was faced with an immediate requirement for a far ranging attack plane to protect its sea approaches, and eventually to intrude upon the Continent. The U.S. requirement was traditionally for a long ranging, fast, hard hitting attack bomber combination, one that could fight its way to the target and back.

And even the Germans were interested, for despite the ineffective use of the plane by the French, the DB-7 had made a good impression on its enemy. Apparently all surviving aircraft of the type had been evacuated to either England or North Africa, and the following March 26, 1941 letter from *General de Flieger* Foerster, the principal German Air Force Officer on the Wiesbaden Armistice Commission to the French Authorities at Vichy shows how determined the Luftwaffe was to examine the DB-7:

"Subject: Sale of Douglas Aeroplanes

The French Government received from the American Government some time ago a considerable number of fighters (60 had reached French units) *Douglas D.B.7, fitted with the Bugrad-Fahrwerk tricyle undercarriage. The Chief of the German Air Force, as was intimated during former negotiations, wishes to get hold of planes of this model. Up to now the French Government would not entertain any such proposals on the grounds that America was aware of them, and that political complications would certainly arise. The German Armistice Commission insists, once again, on the necessity of contracting for the delivery of planes of the above types, and offers in exchange spare parts listed herewith for the Douglas D.B.7. In addition two further cases containing spare parts for Glenn Martin Type 167, F.3 can be offered. If the French Government fears political complications, insomuch as the American Government is aware of the proposals put forward by the German Government for obtaining delivery of Douglas D.B.7 planes, then the German Commission D'Armistice agrees that the French Authorities shall insist that this exchange was made under pressure of the Germans. If the spares offered are not sufficient to persuade the French Government to abandon its negative attitude, the latter should make known the articles she wishes to receive in exchange. The*

(continued on page 129)

The ability of the Havoc to have interchangeable noses made the transformation of the aircraft to the Douglas P-70 night fighter relatively easily. The ventral gun tray and the antennae caused the P-70's top speed to drop to about 330 mph, but this was still more than adequate for its mission. *Peter M. Bowers*

Crash Of The 7B Prototype

Eyewitness Account by Douglas Nile Vail, as told to Dan B. McCarthy

"On the day of the Havoc crash it was right at lunch hour and hundreds of us were out in the parking lot where we ate in those days."

Nile Vail was talking about that day in 1939 when the Douglas prototype 7B Havoc flat spun to a fatal crash landing in North American Aviation's parking lot at Mines Field, Los Angeles. Vail was with North American then, located right across the street from Douglas, working on engines.

"Douglas had taken over the El Segundo plant from Northrop, using the plant for experimental testing.

"The Havoc was the hottest thing we had seen at that time. An outstanding performer with a very good climb ability. Johnny Cable, an exceptionally good test pilot, apparently was doing most of the Havoc test flights.

"Every few days there would be some of this flight testing going on during our lunch break. That day Cable was flying with a representative of French aviation in the rear cockpit. Apparently the American military was blind to the potential of the Havoc, which Douglas produced as a private venture, not under government contract, and was trying to stimulate sales, for the French military were early customers.

"All of a sudden, there was this Havoc streaking by. Cable made single-engine passes, maybe twenty-five feet off the ground. Then he'd pull that thing up in tight spirals . . . Man, he'd go up like he was tied to a cloud! And he'd leave vapor trails up there.

"Single engine performance was remarkable. Cable would make these tight, climbing spirals right off the deck, up to six or eight thousand feet. Then he'd come again, buzzing the field, first one engine feathered, then the other, and on that last pass he took her up to I'd guess about six thousand . . .

"Suddenly there was this roar from one of the engines. The airplane did a couple of snap rolls out of this tight climbing spiral, and right out of that into a flat spin. Then, here's the airplane coming down in this flat spin.

"Well, the pilot's hatch flips open. We saw Cable standing up, ready to jump, but he was looking back to the rear of the plane. We didn't know it at the time, but as it turned out, this Frenchman was in back and he couldn't or didn't start to bail out. We saw Cable turning aft a couple more times.

"Then Cable disappeared back into the cockpit and the dead engine prop was turning slowly. He was trying to start that engine again, maybe hoping to recover from the flat spin. He'd had the power yanked off so it wouldn't increase the rate of spin. But the engine wouldn't start.

"Everybody was running out of the parking lot because this plane was coming down in our direction, covering a pretty wide course in falling. People would run this way, then back the other as the plane shifted direction toward the parking lot.

"I started running, too, but stopped, realizing there was no use running. One second it'd be over there, couple seconds later it was right overhead.

"Cable came back out, stood up, and at this moment I couldn't accurately tell you how high he was, maybe only two, three hundred feet now. But he jumped at the last and his chute just started to trail out when his body hit the ground. I was about 100 feet from where Cable impacted in that parking lot. His chute settled over him. He was dead.

"In the meantime the airplane hit the ground a couple hundred feet from Cable. The plane smashed about ten, twelve automobiles right flat to the ground, hitting flat, not nose first.

The A-20H had more powerful engines but was otherwise identical to the A-20G. This would be a good example for a modeler to copy, as it shows lots of wear and tear—as aircraft in the field always do. *Peter M. Bowers*

Even the early A-20As packed heavy armament for the time, with four forward-firing 0.30 inch machine guns and twin flexible 0.30 inch machine guns in an open dorsal position, and a third similar gun firing out a ventral opening. An unusual modification, not often seen, were two rear-firing machine guns, one in each nacelle, that were operated by the pilot via foot-pedal!

"Fire broke out and they got that extinguished fast. Somebody got to the rear cockpit. The Frenchman was jammed way back in the tail section, apparently thrown back during the spin. They removed him alive. He had some broken bones and bruises, but survived, and was presented medals for bravery from the French government when he came out of the hospital.

"Cable had plenty of time to get out at several thousand feet when the plane first went into the flat spin. But he did that superhuman thing when he saw that the Frenchman wasn't coming out to jump.

"He crawled back in there to try and restart the feathered engine. Cable was marvelous the way he tried to save his passenger and plane. We watched that Havoc crash and couldn't believe it because we had watched it in tests for several months.

"Douglas people swarmed into North American's lot, roping off the area, running people out who didn't belong there."

Shortly after the Havoc crash Vail went to work with Douglas, first as a flight line mechanic, later as inspector of power plants and fuel systems. His Douglas work included A-20s, SBDs, DC-3s and the B-19 heavy bomber. (An account of Vail's perilous flight aboard the B-19 during tests was carried in the March 1975 issue of *Airpower.*)

"That was the only real crash of the DB-7 in the testing program. But during the war we lost three A-20s in first flight and ferry work," Vail said.

"Every morning of the A-20 program we had 32 aircraft to test flight and every afternoon had 32 planes to ferry out to military bases. Every day, 64 of the A-20s were worked."

In one of the A-20 forced landings Sid Luft, Hollywood film producer and an ex-husband of the late Judy Garland, figured in one of the three emergency situations Vail mentioned.

"Luft was a Douglas test pilot during World War II. On one ferry flight to Daggett, near Victorville, California, Luft was on final approach when a fuel line fitting, we found out later, broke. It was the same type fitting used on the B-19, which also popped loose on number two engine during one of the big bomber's test runs.

"The A-20 hatch swings open to the right, but it was the left engine on fire, so Luft couldn't go out that way. He put the plane on the runway, flames trailing behind. When the plane stopped Luft had to go out the fiery side to clear it.

"His chute chest harness was unfastened but not the leg straps. When he went out the leg straps held him back and he tipped head first out the side of the cockpit. He had to crawl back into the cockpit to get free of the chute. How he did it I'll never know except a fire will make a person do lots of superhuman things."

The hardy structure of the Havoc made it suitable for operation all over the world. The demand for the aircraft was so great that Douglas built a new plant in Long Beach, California.

Sid Luft got away from the burning plane but suffered some burns in the accident.

Another A-20 mishap occurred at Santa Monica on a short field. Both engines had quit on takeoff. Vail continues:

"Lee Bishop, our chief pilot, was flying. Only thing we figure in that accident is that it was vapor lock. At the time we carried big, 50-gallon external tanks on the belly for ferry work. I used to fill them and run checks for performance.

"Well, some pilots would operate the belly tank on warmup to see if it was feeding, then go to mains for first flight. We think that in switching from belly tank to mains, well, maybe there wasn't that much gas in the belly tank as the pilot thought and he got a surge of air that didn't show up until full power takeoff. Bishop was lifting the nose wheel when the engines quit.

"Runways were coated with camouflage paint so it was like skis on snow trying to brake that plane. Bishop hit full brakes. The tires just slid forward. At the east end of Douglas Clover field there was a dropoff about seventy feet to the street below.

"Lee had presence of mind to lift his feet onto the instrument panel, trying to brace himself. The plane hit so hard that the bottom and nose folded back to the instrument panel. His legs might have been severed if he hadn't raised them as he did. He lost his upper front teeth when his head struck the control column."

The third A-20 mishap also involved a flat spin, like the prototype. Douglas pilot Johnny Martin got into that emergency near Santa Barbara.

"Regardless of the weather planes flew during World War Two," Vail said. "Martin was on instruments and suddenly he was in a flat spin. He remembered someone telling him to get out of a flat spin by dropping gear and flaps suddenly and shoving ahead on the control column.

"Martin did all that at the same time. The airplane snapped out of the flat spin just as he broke out of the overcast. In front of him were mountains. Martin made a tremendous pullout to keep from hitting a peak.

"The plane's aft section fuselage and wings bent. He almost lost his wings, the outer wing skin overlapped the center wing section and all castings were bent out of shape, giving more dihedral than the engineers had planned.

"Martin brought the plane home with the fuselage like a pretzel and the wings all bent up. That plane had to be scrapped. We lost three A-20s in that program of first flights and ferrying operations."

A fine study of an A-20A. The easiest way to differentiate the A and B models is to check the cowling; the B model eliminated the line of small oval exhaust ports that are evident here.

(continued from page 125)
German Armistice Commission expects delivery of the two Douglas D.B.7 planes at the earliest possible moment, and trusts that exchanges of this kind covering improvements in aircraft will be continued in the future."

signed
FOERSTER

The letter is a fascinating combination of persuasion, threat and naive presumption of complicity, and it would be interesting to know how the Vichy French responded.

The Japanese did not have to resort to such measures, for they captured several DB-7s, and apparently tested at least two. The number cannot be confirmed, but as photographs exist showing a Havoc in Japanese markings undergoing tests at both Navy and Army establishments, we can probably assume that at least two were test flown.

Meanwhile, in the United States, development and procurement of the A-20 paralleled the foreign interest. As noted, the first 206 aircraft were counterparts of the DB-7B, with American equipment and instruments. The potential of the new airplane excited Air Corps leaders all the way up to and including Hap Arnold, and documents of the period reveal that the German Luftwaffe was not the only service hypnotized by the potential of the dive bomber. Arnold very seriously labored to have the A-20 modified to have a dive bombing capability, and there are numerous tactfully worded reports recommending against the idea. One, signed by Brigadier General George H. Brett, flatly stated that the A-20 could not be used for dive bombing at angles of 30 degrees or more (i.e. not really dive bombing at all) without a complete redesign, but that it could carry 1,400 pounds of bombs in a glide bomber configuration. As an alternative, he proposed that 5BD-2s be procured. An angry penciled note from Arnold reads:

"*Flaws* The above does not and will not decide dive bombing question for Army, for our Air Force to be in being within 2 years. What next? HHA"

(As an aside, Arnold must have been at least a little difficult to deal with during the period. One report of June 23, 1941 reveals that he was considerably upset by the repair work being done on A-20s at El Segundo, California. The Air Corps had become the U.S. Army Air Force only three days before, and a harassed George E. Stratemeyer sent an urgent staff summary sheet requesting a rapid answer to Arnold, via General Spaatz, with the comment: "The above two items are of extreme importance at this time as the new Air Staff is starting today. It is therefore desired to impress General Arnold with the fact that he *must* operate (italics Stratemeyer's) to secure information and to give directives through the Air Staff."

Bureaucratically speaking, things haven't changed a whole lot.

The new service was not used to its burgeoning budget and zooming production schedules, and penny packet thinking was evident in the initial allocation and priorities decided on for the A-20 aircraft on the initial contract W-535-AC-12967. First priority naturally went to Wright Field, where the first seven aircraft were allocated; four were for test, and three were intended to form a special demonstration team. The remainder were to be parcelled out, in one, two and three plane increments to various pursuit groups as tow target tugs, for "a decision has been made that all A-20 airplanes will be equipped with tow target installations, and that, when installations have been made, they will be utilized to tow targets for pursuit units." (Routing and Record Sheet, Office of the Chief of the Air Corps. May 6, 1941).

Fate and common sense, however, were to hold a more honorable role for the A-20s. For instead of pulling a sock around the blue sky for novice fighter pilots to pepper, all but three were converted to the P-70 night fighter configuration, the odd three becoming F-3 photographic planes. The conversion required adding on a ventral pack with four 20 mm cannon, and changing over to a solid nose which concealed an early model radar set. The resultant P-70 was intended to provide an operational training airplane in anticipation of deliveries of the Northrop P-61 Black Widow, and ultimately 270 A-20s of various series were converted to P-70 types. (The U.S. took its lead from England, which provided the necessary technical knowledge for the airborne radar, as well as its experience in converting DB-7s to Havoc night fighers.)

In many respects, the development of the A-20 into a fast, well armed, hit and run attack ship, was due to the combat experience of its British crews. Although America had provided the hardware, eighteen months after the aircraft's initial introduction into combat—during the Battle of France—we were still not at war. True, the U.S. Army sent observers and delivered itself of voluminous memos and reports, but only the British were flying the Havoc in combat, and as we shall see in Pt. II of this story, they were the ones who made the decisions which turned the A-20 into the most dependable, sweet flying, versatile light bomber of WW II.

17 Cry Havoc

The A-20 Goes to War, Part II

Airpower July, 1976

The original French interest in the DB-7 resulted in a whole series of contracts for variants of the aircraft with France, Great Britain, and the Netherlands. As the war developed, most of these ultimately wound up wearing the colors of the RAF or of British Commonwealth nations. (One difficulty in all instances in which French contracts were taken over by Great Britain or the United States was the modification of the throttles. It was French practice for power to be applied by pulling the throttle back, instead of shoving it forward.)

The basic airframe lent itself to modifications for many different missions, including bombing, close air support, reconnaissance, night fighting, target towing and, oddest of all, sub hunting (the Turbinlite version used a Hel-

The American aircraft industry was given a jump start by the Anglo-French Purchasing Commission. The Allies, preparing for a war with Germany but terribly behind the Germans in air armament, were willing to spend the money that would enable American companies to invest in new plants as well as new designs. The investment paid off, for both the U.S. and the Allies. The British were very pleased with the Boston.

The XP-70 was a straightforward conversion of the A-20, of which only one was built. Unsupercharged Wright R-2600 engines were used, and a British AI Mk IV radar was fitted in the nose. All bomb racks and defensive armament were deleted. The armament package was a ventral tub with four 20 mm cannon. *Warren M. Bodie*

The new Douglas plant at Long Beach was soon churning out A-20s in great number. These are A-20Bs in the assembly area. *Warren M. Bodie*

more/GEC searchlight to seek out surfaced submarines). Pete Bowers has written great articles on the airplane, and the book to read is Rene Francillion's McDonnell Douglas Aircraft Since 1920 *(Putnam, 1979).*

After their initial reports from the British, concerned with improving the performance of the DB-7As and Bs, the U.S. Army Air Force continued to learn from the R.A.F. and from its own experience with the versatile new bomber, and orders for improved models followed swiftly. 999 A-20Bs were built at a new Douglas plant at Long Beach; and 948 A-20Cs were next, with 808 being built in Santa Monica, and 140 by Boeing in Seattle. This aircraft was almost identical to the R.A.F.'s Boston III. As usual, as equipment and gross weight increased, speed went down, and the 25,000 plus pound A-20C maxed out at a little better than 340 mph., still rather startling for a fully loaded light bomber.

The next production version, the A-20G, was produced in greater numbers than all the others, 2,850 being built. A Martin turret provided effective rear defense, and the solid nose contained much heavier armament. The first A-20Gs had four 20mm cannon and two .50 caliber machine guns, with the standard single gun rear armament. A later block of aircraft (A-20G-20D0) dropped the cannons, substituting four more of the dependable .50 caliber machine guns, and adding the Martin turret. The rear of the fuselage was widened a full six inches to accommodate the turret. The structure was determined to be strong enough to have the bomb load doubled from the standard 2,000 to 4,000 pounds, and additional tankage was provided. Maximum gross weight was 30,000 pounds, and speed naturally dropped, to 317 mph.

The A-20G was widely used and well liked, for it was considerably more sophisticated and better armored. The subsequent A-20H, of which 412 were built, was basically similar, using a slightly different engine—the -29 instead of the -23—which offered an additional 100 horsepower; 450 A-20Js were built, and these were basically A-20Gs with a bombardier nose. In a like manner, 413 A-20Ks were simply A-20Hs with a bombardier nose.

Ultimately almost 7,400 of the DB-7/A-20 type would be built, with more than 3,000 going via Lend Lease to Russia, where the plane was very well liked. Typically, however, Russian contemporary accounts make short shrift of the Douglas, preferring to laud the native Stormoviks, but the plane is often mentioned in German accounts of Red air activity, particularly against airfields.

The underlying success of the aircraft was gained from early and sometimes bitter experience. In December 1942, for example, the U.S.A.A.F was still having serious teething problems with the airplane. On a single squadron movement from the U.S. to Africa, a flight of 13 aircraft required 18 engine changes, causing consternation at both Wright Field and the Pentagon. A voluminous correspondence grew in which the blame was placed variously on "leaving in the running-in oil", operating with excessively lean mixtures, including reported instances of take-offs in auto lean (not recommended), poor maintenance and/or poor pilot technique. The problems persisted as the series developed, and in the fall of 1943 A-20G aircraft began experiencing severe tail buffet at airspeeds above 350 mph. Trim tabs were torn from two aircraft on high speed runs, and the buffeting was so severe that failure of the tail group seemed probable. All A-20Gs were temporarily placarded not to exceed 350 mph, and the trouble was soon discovered. A new non-ram air carburetor air scoop had been installed, and the variation in air flow created the buffeting.

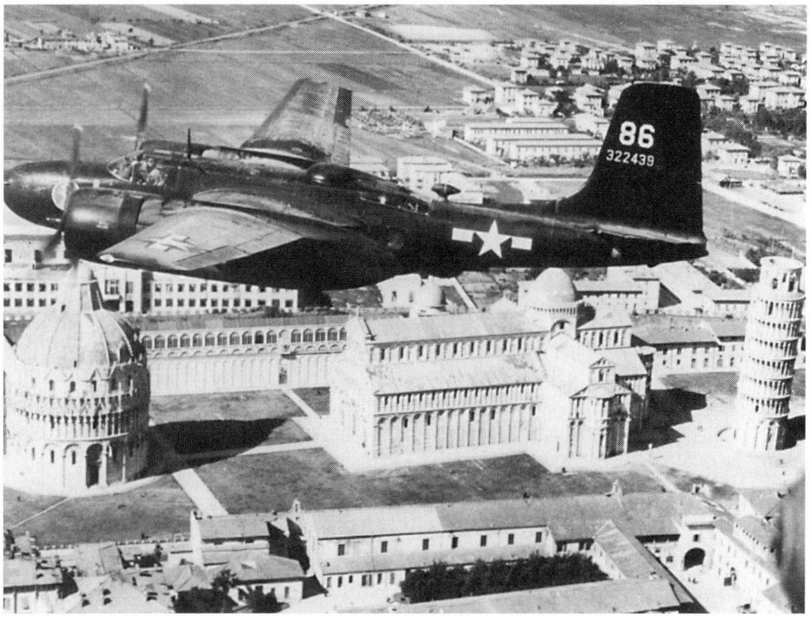

The Havoc's successor, the A-26 Invader, over the leaning tower of Pisa—what a shot! *Warren Thompson*

Yet, when all is said and done, the success of the type over a global range of operations and employment in every conceivable mission has to be in part due to the Royal Air Force's careful test and development program, which was begun during the time when the Luftwaffe seemed so close to victory, and continued right down to the end of the Boston's operational career. These tests included not only an exhaustive general survey and intensive tests of individual items of equipment, but also trials which revealed the most efficient methods of tactical employment.

Reports Number 30 and 45 from the Air Fighting Development Unit at R.A.F. Station, Duxford, give an incisive look at the British appreciation of the Boston. Report No. 30 covers a Boston II, serialed BK 883, which had the 1,200 horsepower Pratt & Whitney engines, while 45 is related to a Boston III with the 1,600 horsepower Wright Cyclones.

The British test crews were much impressed by the general luxury of the Douglas, for its interior "appointments"—padding, carefully routed wire bundles, extensive instrumentation, etc.—were far less spartan than the typical R.A.F. bomber. The cockpit layout was very well liked, but some complaint was voiced over the lack of a clear vision panel, a vital item when making a low level cross country in the marginal European weather. The rear gunner's compartment was considered exceptionally roomy and comfortable, with excellent visibility in the upper hemisphere, but poor in the lower, where the wings and empennage blocked the view.

The flying characteristics were particularly appreciated, for the Boston II was better in all departments than the Blenheim. Even with special flame dampeners that subtracted an estimated 20 mph from its top speed, the Boston was found to be 5 to 14 miles per hour faster than its Blenheim Mark IV counterpart. At the time, Blenheims were doing most of the R.A.F.'s bombing, and the Boston's superiority was welcome. All of the test pilots were especially pleased by the Douglas' night landing characteristics, for the then novel tri-cycle landing gear made it safer to brake "fiercely" and get off the flare path quickly.

The superb pilot visibility and precise handling made formation flying easy, although the relatively poor rear armament of two hand held Vickers machine guns made small compact defensive formations inadvisable. The test unit suggested that Bostons be used in pairs rather than in mass gaggles.

Combat trials were carried out against a Hurricane I and II, and a Spitfire I at altitudes up to 6,000 feet; the fighters carried camera guns, and one was fitted into the rear gun position on the Boston.

The pilots found that with enough muscle the twin-engine bomber could almost out turn a Hurricane if it used a little flap to help it along; unfortunately speed bled off so quickly that the plane was an easy target if the fighter broke out of the turn and made another attack. The rear gunner was ineffective, being unable to bring a gun camera to bear on the fighters.

The best maneuver seemed to be to break into the oncoming attack, and then use the Boston's relatively high speed to get away. Despite the fact that the Boston's four forward guns were usually unable to get in a shot, it was felt that the plane could evade almost all attacks except from dead astern.

Overall, the test pilots were inordinately pleased with almost everything about the airplane except for its relatively short range, which was computed to be just over 400 miles at a 230 mph cruise.

The Boston III covered in the later report was even more highly regarded, for it had an improved range and heavier rear armament. The single V.G.O. (Vickers Gas Operated) gun in the upper rear mounting was replaced by twin Brownings. While the single gun had used 100 round magazines, which took almost one minute to change in the air, the twin Brownings had a belt feed providing 500 rounds per gun. The single Vickers was retained in the lower installation, where its difficult access and poor visibility rendered it almost useless except against a positively suicidal attacker.

In the tactical trials of the Boston III, the test pilots found that it had retained all of its predecessor's maneuverability and had even better single engine characteristics. The additional power provided more combat capability, and tests showed that a single Boston presented an attacking fighter with an extremely difficult target, for it could maintain a high rate of turn, and be ready to pop off with its front guns if the opponent broke away. Against more than one fighter a corkscrewing movement was recommended; this consisted of a turn of at least 30 degrees combined with a dive of 500 feet, followed by a climbing turn of 500 feet in the opposite direction, all done as violently as possible. The corkscrew had the great advantage of permitting the airplane to work its course homeward, rather than be trapped in a tight-turning circle which might drift in the wrong direction.

The crews once again noted that formation flying was not the answer for the Boston, for even with the additional fire power, very little mutual support could be given. A

The shadow of the screaming Douglas A-20 does not frighten the camel caravan. ***Warren Thompson***

multiple corkscrewing maneuver was proposed, one that would have required a very high order of formation skill, but this was hardly comparable to the solid phalanx of .50 calibers possible with the larger medium and heavy bombers.

Because of the limited combat capability of contemporary escort fighters—Kittyhawks and Hurricanes—and because at least some Boston pilots called the airplane the "flying primus stove" (compare with the Luftwaffe's nickname for the Heinkel 177, the *Luftwaffenfeuerzeug* or Luftwaffe's Petrol Lighter) most combat flights in the African theater were flown at altitudes of 10,000 to 12,000 feet, and this was indeed the recommendation of the Duxford test crews. But the altitude prevented real bombing accuracy, and formations were not the best Boston defense; on the spot reports from the field recommended that the airplane be operated at much lower altitudes.

Combat reports also indicated that the firepower of the four forward guns could not be used effectively at 10,000 ft, for the airplanes were too high to strafe and could not bring them to bear in air combat. The Commander of the 12th Squadron, South African Air Force, attempted to make some use of the guns by reversing two of them so that they would fire to the rear, and would at least discourage an enemy fighter from sitting in the all too vulnerable 5 degree blind spot on the tail.

The Duxford test group recommended that bombing be done by individual aircraft, but that if any of the bombardiers was not satisfied with his own run in, he could bomb on signal from the leader. This was often the case in the South Pacific during the early days of the war, when there were simply not enough bomb sights to go around. Opening the bomb doors slowed the aircraft down by 15 miles per hour, and gave a nose up attitude which had to be compensated for early to obtain accurate bombing results.

The real testing of the beautiful little bomber, as with all warplanes, came in combat, and the "li'l Douglas racer" succeeded admirably in every theater. Its career with the French *Armée de l'Air,* was, as noted, inauspicious, through no fault of the aircraft. Later in the war the DB-7s fought again for France, this time in mixed company of Marylands, captured Junkers Ju-88s and other oddments, as the Free French forces were directed against beleaguered German "fortresses" on the Atlantic Coast.

In England, the DB-7s became stalwart night fighters, known first as Rangers, and then as Havocs, a name which the U.S. would adopt for its A-20s, but not, oddly enough, for the more equivalent P-70 night fighters.

The Havocs were fitted with very early airborne interception radar, and, over time, a mixed bag of armament. Initial aircraft had the standard four-pack of .303 Brownings, which was later increased to a truly formidable package of twelve. Still others had a ventral tray of four 20 mm cannon.

Sunny Italy! A Douglas A-20 hangs a protective wing over some RAF Spitfires at a waterlogged field in Italy. ***Warren Thompson***

Table One—Type Relationships

Type	Equivalent Type or Alternate Name	Distinguishing Features	Other Comments
7B		P&W R-1830 C, 1100 hp	Prototype
DB-7	Boston I	P&W R-1830 -SC3G, 1100 hp	Single speed
	Havoc I	P&W R-1830 -SC4G, 1200 hp	two speed
	Some Boston II		
	Intruder, Ranger		
DB-7A	Havoc II	Wright R-2600-A5B, 1600 hp	951 ordered
	few Boston III	Larger fin and rudder	
	A-20B		
DB-7B	Boston III, A-20, Intruder A-20A A-20C	Changed fuel system, hydraulics	300 diverted from U.S.A.A.C.
DB-7C	Boston III	Revised to DB-7B standard	Dutch ordered 48 French 480
DB-73	Revised French designation for DB-7C		
A-20	DB-7B (RA-20)	R-2600-7; turbocharger	390 mph; 63 ordered
A-20A	DB-7B, BD-1	R-2600-3	143 ordered
XA-20B	Converted A-20A	Three power turrets	one only
A-20B	DB-7A, BD-2	R-2600-11	999 produced
	Havoc II		8 to BD-2
A-20C	Similar to A-20A DB-7B; Boston III	Standard U.S. & British equipment; torpedo capable; R-2600-23	25,600 pounds 948 built; 140 by Boeing
A-20D	None Built		
A-20E	Converted A-20A	R-2600-11	Similar to A-20B
A-20F	Converted A-20F	R-2600-3; 37 mm cannon two G.E. turrets	
A-20G		R-2600-23; later models used Martin turret	2850 built; some with 4 20mm, some with 6 .50s
A-20H		R-2600-29; Gun Nose	412 built
A-20J	Boston IV Similar to A-20G	R-2600-23; Bomb Nose	450 built
A-20K	Boston V Similar to A-20H	R-2600-29; Bomb Nose	413 built
Boston I	DB-7	P&W R-1830-SC3G	
Boston II	DB-7, Havoc I	Mark IV A.I. radar Flame dampeners, armor	
Boston III	DB-7B, Intruder A-20C	R-2600-23	3 to Turbinlite
Boston IIIA		Different electrical system, flame dampeners	Boeing built
Boston IV	A-20J		169 total
Boston V	A-20K		90 total
XF, YF, F-3	A-20	T-3A cameras	3 total
F-3A	A-20J/K	Camera added	46 total

Type	Equivalent Type or Alternate Name	Distinguishing Features	Other Comments
Havoc I	Boston II, Ranger Moonfighter, Havoc IV, Pandora	A.I. Mark IV Radar L.A.M. (Long Aerial Mine)	31 to Turbinlite
Havoc II	DB-7A some ex French	80 had 12 m.g. R-2600-11	99 from DB-7A 39 to Turbinlite
Havoc III	Turbinlite, Pandora, Helmore	2.7 million candlepower searchlight	Searchlight, idea of Group Captain Helmore
XP-70	Revised A-20 prototype	R-2600-11, solid nose	4 20mm cannon, 2 crew
P-70	Converted A-20's	Trainers	59 total
P-70A-1	Converted A-20C's	Six .50 caliber m.g.	39 total
P-70A-2	Converted A-20G's		65 total
P-70B-1	Converted A-20G	6 .50 caliber m.g.	1 only
P-70B-2	Converted A-20G/J	Trainers	105
TA-20	Converted A-20H/J	Trainers	
TA-20H	Converted A-20H	Tracked undercarriage	1 only
O-53	Observation type	Cancelled, none built	1,489 scheduled
BD-1	Converted A-20A		1 only
BD-2	Converted A-20B	Used by Marines for tow target & utility	8 total

There were some exotic experiments which seem pretty naive today—31 Havocs received an incredible 2,700 million candlepower searchlight installation, called Turbinlite, with which to illuminate enemy aircraft which were to be shot down by accompanying Hurricane fighters. Less auspicious was the Long Aerial Mine, a device which was to be trailed at the end of a 2,000 foot cable, and into which, perhaps enemy raiders would run. It was Churchillian, but it was not modern war.

All of these developments occurred before the end of 1941, by which time the R.A.F. was receiving Boston IIIs, and was using them in the attack role. The greatest successes were obtained in Africa, where airplanes and crews were lauded by Montgomery, Alexander and the press.

In Europe, the Bostons were used as both intruders and bombers; in the former role, their 2,000 pound bomb capacity made them especially valuable. Still, the aircraft did not have the performance edge that it would enjoy in the Pacific. None-the-less, the bombing offensive of the mighty Eighth Air Force commenced in borrowed Bostons in which American crews flew the first official U.S.A.A.F. sortie over Europe on July 4, 1942. This attack, which is well covered in several accounts, saw a mixed squadron of six R.A.F. and six U.S.A.A.F. crews attack Luftwaffe airfields in Holland. Two American and one R.A.F. crews were lost, and one Boston, commanded by Captain Charles C. Kegelman, took direct hits, nearly flew into the ground, kept on going, and continued to strafe on its staggering trip back to England.

The Douglas bombers distinguished themselves in the European and African theaters, but it was in the Pacific that they played their intended role to the fullest. The Pacific was somehow more suited to the A-20s, for neither the flak nor the fighter opposition was equivalent to Europe. It was tough, but the Havocs were far more competitive dropping parafrag bombs from tree top level on jungle strips, than in beating up radar-alerted, heavily defended airdromes in France.

The Havoc's original level of effort in the Pacific was dismally small, for in August, 1942 there was a single unit—the 8th Bombardment Squadron (Light) of the 3rd Light Bombardment (Dive) Group—operational, and it was not yet equipped with guns or bombracks. From this miniscule beginning, A-20s would fight a brilliant war, strafing,

In January, 1941, Douglas felt the need for a follow-on aircraft, and a design by Edward Heinemann and Robert Donovan became the basis for the highly successful Douglas A-26 Invader. It was a sleeker, more powerful aircraft than the A-20 and would fight in three wars. The aircraft was to have three designations: first, A-26; after the war, B-26; in Vietnam, A-26 again. *Warren M. Bodie*

parafragging, laying smoke and interdicting jungle trails and ocean shipments to the point that Japanese troops in New Guinea and elsewhere literally starved to death in their positions. Ultimately, General George C. Kenney, Commander of the Allied Air Forces, South Pacific, was so eminently satisfied with the A-20 that he refused to have it replaced with the newer A-26s. He knew he could finish the war with a proven weapon.

The A-26 was a much more advanced aircraft, and when the war ended all A-20s, with very few exceptions, were retired, and the A-26 became the standard attack plane. In a way it was a fitting departure for the A-20, for it left the scene as it had entered, unsung and relatively unpublicized, but having acquitted itself well in every task assigned.

The A-26s used in the Vietnam War were much modified, but time had taken its toll, and they suffered wing-spar problems. This is an A-26 in flight over the Canal Zone in 1967.

Construction Notes

The construction techniques for the A-20 were as modern as the airplane's lines, and mark a distinct step forward in Douglas engineering, for the structure was not only sophisticated in its attainment of strength at a minimum weight, it was also easily adapted to mass production.

The combined goals of versatility, strength, light weight and production ease were met through breaking down the design into sub-units which could be produced in volume, and could be individually modified to meet new missions without impinging upon production as a whole. The most obvious case in point is the use of interchangeable nose assemblies. An armored bulkhead served as the dividing point between the main fuselage and the bombardier or attack noses. Six bolts secured the bombardier nose to the fuselage, while ten were required for the heavier attack package, which was also 8 inches longer. As there were several different attack noses, depending upon mission, there were other variations in structure, but from the bulkhead back, no changes other than in controls were necessary. Noses could be changed by field ground personnel with a minimum of hand tools and a simple fixture.

The fuselage itself was built up in halves, using the typical frame and longitudinal channel frame member construction of the period, augmented by extruded sections at stress points. Alclad 24 ST sheet was flush riveted to the frames.

The two fuselage halves were joined together in a semi-monocoque whole, comprising five major sections—nose, pilot's compartment, bomb bay, gunner's compartment and tail. The cockpit was exceptionally comfortable, with a good field of vision in all directions except downward and to the rear. Entry was via hinged panels on the

It is hard to believe that the same company that built the SBD, C-47, C-54, A-20, and A-26 had been competing with this B-18 just a few years before.

top of the cabin, the panels capable of being jettisoned in an emergency. The pilot exited across the fuselage, over the wing, and under the tail, if time and control permitted; but it was considered generally better to roll the aircraft on its back and drop out of the hatch.

The bombardier nose was built up of formed channel sections and plexiglass, which was excellent for normal operation but exceedingly vulnerable to a ditching or crash landing. The bombardier had a choice of emergency exits—either through a lower door (preferred) or out of an upper panel. Either option was better than riding out a crash landing.

The rear gunner's compartment was commodious. Crewmen entered by a door in the bottom of the fuselage, which also served as the primary emergency exit.

The 61 foot 4 inch wing was made up in six sections, and used a NACA 23018 airfoil section at the root, changing to a modified NACA 23010 at the tip. The main sections were the inboard panels, which extended from the fuselage juncture to 60 inches beyond the nacelle center line. These were connected to the main fuselage by aluminum alloy fittings and steel bolts. Outer wing panels ran to within thirty inches of the end of the wing, which was made up of an easily replaceable wing tip assembly.

The wing structure was complex to look at, but was broken down into elements that were relatively easy to manufacture. It consisted of a single Wagner spar and two sheer webs, with densely spaced ribs and formers extending to leading and trailing edges. The skin was flush riveted. Typically, fuel was carried in four wing tanks, two outboard and two inboard, for a total capacity of 540 gallons. Bomb bay tanks could be fitted, and later versions of the aircraft had form-fitting, jettisonable fuel tanks installed.

The tail surfaces were of conventional all metal construction, distinguished by the fact that the horizontal stabilizer was interchangeable left and right. Elevators and rudder were made up of fabric covered riveted aluminum alloy frames.

The tricycle landing gear was probably the most advanced feature of the aircraft at the time of its appearance and was, as we have seen, sufficiently novel to fully intrigue the Luftwaffe. The main gear had a tread of almost seventeen feet, which made landings relatively easy. The combination of Bendix oleos and the large 44 inch smooth tires cushioned all but the most violent touchdowns.

In general, the Douglas DB-7 was easy to build, easy to fly, and easy to maintain; at the same time it was an effective, versatile performer, capable of almost any task assigned to it. It grew up with Douglas, and in a large measure, Douglas grew up with it.

Douglas also built the huge XB-19 and submitted proposals for the competition won by the B-29, but did not have success in the heavy-bomber field. The XB-19 had a wingspan of 212 feet, weighed 162,000 pounds at its maximum weight, and had a top speed of 224 mph. At the time there were not engines of sufficient power to make the aircraft useful.

18 AIR JEEP

The Curtiss AT-9

Wings February, 1974

The rapid expansion and contraction of firms in the aviation industry led to mergers, and this was the case with the Curtiss Wright Company in St. Louis. In 1932, the great George Page came from Buffalo to St. Louis to supervise engineering operations in the new company, and under his guidance a whole series of aircraft emerged, from the stately Curtiss Condor to the C-46 Commando to the AT-9 Jeep.

Page was a remarkable individual, able to work within a very limited budget to create totally new ideas. I knew him in the early 1960s. George would come to an American Aviation Historical Meeting with a 15-inch stack of 8 × 10 photographs—photos of airplanes, plants, people, parties, and even plans. He would slap one after the other in random order on an overhead projector. Then he would discuss each one, citing the date and the project, identifying everyone in the picture, telling humorous anecdotes about them, and then revealing the underlying engineering rationale behind whatever project it happened to be. It was always a tour-de-force, one that any witness would never forget.

The AT-9 had rather beautiful lines if viewed from any angle that hid the truncated nose of the airplane. The large vertical surfaces were effective at low speeds and high angles of attack, an advantage over some of the other competing twin engine training aircraft of the time. *Author's collection, courtesy Peter M. Bowers*

Aviation buffs have an unrelenting tendency to romanticize aircraft rather than realistically regarding them for what they are: mere inanimate tools, pieces of metal, rubber, plastic, and cloth joined together to do a job—only this and nothing more.

Unfortunately, when you come across a real inanimate

This was the prototype of the AT-9, built—in accordance with Air Corps instructions—out of nonstrategic materials, i.e., steel tubing and fabric. The plane was overweight and had very poor flight characteristics. The Air Corps relented and allowed Curtiss to return to designing a standard all-metal structure, of which it was a master. *Author's collection, courtesy Peter M. Bowers*

The snub-nosed appearance of the AT-9 becomes noticeable in a side view. You can see how the propellers clear the nose section here. No danger of nosing over from a too-hard application of the brakes in this airplane!
Author's collection, courtesy Peter M. Bowers

tool like the humpbacked Curtiss AT-9, there is a decided temptation to look the other way. This isn't fair, for although the Jeep, a twin-engine knock propellered crew trainer, came into being as a tool, served as a tool, and retired with the moving ceremonies accorded a used hacksaw blade, its story still deserves telling. The hot little trainer from St. Louis did exactly what it was supposed to do for the people for whom it was supposed to do it, turning thousands of green kids into accomplished pilots in just a few months.

In the early 1940s, Air Corps planners were becoming all too aware that some very hot items were about to enter the inventory, despite the fact that flight training was still strictly of Beirne Lay's "I Wanted Wings" vintage. Of particular concern were two new airplanes with blistering performance and high landing speeds, the Martin B-26 and the Lockheed P-38. Neither would be an easy transition from BT-9s, or even AT-6s; some intermediate step was required.

It's probable that the planners would have thrown in their cards and gone to Canada if they had been aware of the true scope of the training problem facing them. In 1939, the Air Corps had a total strength of 26,000 men and 800 first-line combat aircraft. There were 2,000 pilots. By 1944, 5 years later, the new U.S. Army Air Force had over 2,400,000 men, with tens of thousands of combat aircraft, and an unbelievable surplus of pilots. From a simple training system centered at Randolph Field, there had grown a gigantic complex of civil and military flying schools turning out polished professionals who would not enter combat with less than 250 hours of flying time. Meanwhile, the Germans were sending green pilots directly into combat with 100 hours or less, their training plagued not only by fuel shortages but by marauding Mustangs which frequently shot down scared kids on their initial solo flights.

All of this was, of course, unknown to the men at Wright Field, who had many worries collateral to the training problem. In late 1940, Germany was on a seemingly unstoppable march to world dominance, her formal alliances with Italy and Japan backstopped by a Russian détente, and her borders stretching from Norway to Poland. The U.S.'s new war was clearly going to be a long one, and no one knew what, or how much raw material would be required.

Consequently, Brigadier General K.B. Wolfe sent his personal representative, Captain William N. "Nelly" Morgan, to the Lambert Field-based Curtiss plant with a specific set of instructions. Morgan, who retired as a Major General, laid a series of tough demands on Curtiss. The new transition trainer was to embody as nearly as possible the flight characteristics of the coming generation of multi-engine aircraft; it was to be powered by two Lycoming R-680 engines of 295 horsepower and to have a maximum speed of at least 200 miles per hour; it was to be made of nonstrategic materials, and last but not least, it was *not* to be easy to fly or to land.

Relatively few of the Jeeps were painted. This aircraft, photographed at McChord Field in Tacoma, Washington, in 1942, had received a camouflage paint-scheme for some reason. Note the window in the cabin, which was often left open in flight when the weather was warm. ***Author's collection, courtesy Peter M. Bowers***

An AT-9 with the simple standard markings of the day, taken at Mather Field, California, on May 9, 1942. The AT-9s were sometimes used to train pilots for the Lockheed P-38. Pilots who had flown both have said that approach was backwards—the P-38 should have been used to train people to fly the AT-9!

Trust the ardent photographer to take the great shot, even at night. This dramatic photo makes the AT-9 look like it's on a dive-bomb run on a Japanese carrier.

(Wolfe and Morgan are among the handful of key figures whose wisdom, foresight, and willingness to take a chance made it possible for the U.S. to win the war in the air. Most of these people are unknown to the general public, for unlike the combat leaders—Spaatz, Weyland, LeMay, Doolittle, and so on—they labored away anonymously at Wright Field or the Pentagon. Their rise in rank was sometimes meteoric, in some cases zooming from Major in 1939 to Brigadier General in 1944, but in the main they never received their proper share of thanks from the American public. A relative handful of men—Kenneth B. Wolfe, Howard Z. Bogert, Oliver P. Echols, Franklin O. Carrol, and Benjamin W. Chidlaw, to name only the most prominent—found themselves in positions where gigantic decisions had to be made. Under their stewardship, U.S. aircraft production rose from a custom-built total of about 4,500 aircraft per year to a staggering annual capacity of over 110,000 by 1944. Almost 300,000 planes were produced for the Army, the Navy, and the Allies, at a cost of more than $45 billion. Amazingly, 158,800 were accepted by the Army Air Force, and the very existence of the vast majority of these was due solely to the genius and the guts of the men mentioned above.)

No matter what the temperature was outside, you know that the student pilot inside is already sweating as he taxis out for a check ride. The name "Jeep" derived from the fact that the airplane was manufactured in St. Louis, and the mascot of St. Louis University was the Billikin—which is a Jeep. Maybe you had to be there to appreciate it.

But back to the AT-9. George A. Page, Jr., then Director of Engineering and now a vital, cheerful engineer emeritus at a very young age of 82, laughingly recalls that "I probably caused the next mistake." Mr. Page, whose Curtiss background extends to Hammondsport, and who designed (among a great many other airplanes) the Curtiss C-46 Commando, is an absolutely fascinating aviation raconteur. Apparently gifted with total recall, he can work without stop through a foot-high stack of 8 × 10 glossies, calling out names, dates, specifications, and occasional ribald anecdotes.

Page took Morgan at his word and suggested that the new plane might be constructed primarily of tubing, with appropriate fairings to render the desired airfoil and fuselage shape, and a fabric covering.

Data Sheet

Curtiss AT-9 Jeep

Wing Span	40′3.7″
Length	31′8.0″
Height	13′1.2″
Wing Area	249 square feet
Gross Weight	6,062 pounds
Maximum Speed	197 mph
Max Diving Speed	230 mph

Serial Numbers:

AT-9:	41-5745 through 41-4895
	41-11939 through 41-12279
AT-9A:	42-56853 through 42-57152

The prototype outside the Curtiss Wright hangar at Lambert Field in St. Louis (which would become the home of McDonnell, then McDonnell Douglas, and now Boeing). The similarity of the fuselage and tail to the earlier Curtiss Wright CW-21 fighter is evident here.

Herb Perkins and Carl Scott immediately began detail design work. The plane which emerged could have been called "the blind date," for it was ugly and overweight, with flying characteristics to match.

Edwin A. "Ned" Warren, currently assistant to the President of Aeronca Corporation, made the first flight on November 17, 1940, and he was markedly unimpressed. In Page's still delicate phrasing, they had "overstretched the capability of the structure."

Scott, who was to function with outstanding success in a long, rewarding career with Curtiss, made the hat-in-hand journey to Wright Field to sell the idea of using a sheet aluminum structure, as the time required to improve the tubular prototype could well have extended into World War III.

Wright Field acquiesced to the change, and the St. Louis engineers fell with relief upon a material and a manufacturing discipline in which they were expert—good old sheet metal.

The "new" AT-9 rapidly took shape, ultimately resembling a Quasimodian Curtiss Wright-CW-21. The tail surfaces, wing planform and landing gear retraction mechanism were all similar to the earlier lightweight fighter, and a blood test would have revealed many other design detail similarities. The forward fuselage was bulged to provide accommodations for four, and the nose was chopped off. The two engines were set so close together that the arc of the propellers seemed to overlap.

Warren was again test pilot on the 30 July 1941 first flight, and while the airplane was vastly improved over the tubular terror, it still did not meet the V max requirements, nor did it possess the smoothly harmonized control characteristics for which Curtiss aircraft were famous. Yet, Warren describes the AT-9 as a great aerobatic airplane, so much so that test pilots had to be disciplined for doing "nip ups" in it.

The latter was not entirely to its disadvantage, for the Air Corps still did not want an airplane that was too easy to fly. If you stop to think about it, almost all prototypes (except for a few weirdos like Northrop's XP-56) are pleasant to fly. After all, the designers are looking for contracts. It isn't until the user hangs on various bulges and boosts gross weight that a new plane begins to behave like a dog. In that sense, Curtiss had achieved a design breakthrough by producing canine qualities in the prototype.

Air Corps reservations about the airplane were overcome by Captain Morgan's insistence that they needed exactly what Curtiss offered, and by the manufacturer's ready agreement to remedy the flaws on the production line, with appropriate retrofit action.

The first of three Wright Field contracts, AC 15707, was approved on September 13, 1940, for 150 aircraft. This was followed by AC 16007 for 341 more AT-9s on

The Curtiss AT-9 served well as an intermediate trainer, although it was not particularly beloved by either instructors or students because of its relatively hot performance and less-than-docile handling characteristics.

September 24, 1941, and by AC 26982 for 300 AT-9As on June 22, 1942.

After the initial shock of seeing the new trainer, onlookers were usually struck by its deceptive innocent charm. The plane was not handsome, nor even lethal looking, but it did have the certain dopey élan possessed by the strange and wonderful animal of the Popeye cartoon strip, the Jeep. It just so happened that the Jeep was a Billikin, which is the mascot of St. Louis University, and many alumni of this university were employed at Curtiss. Someone mentioned the name jokingly, but it caught on. Later, Curtiss valiantly tried to dignify the title by associating it with the famous ground combat vehicle as "the Jeep of the Air." It wasn't—it was a Billikin.

Pictures of the plane give an appearance of large size. Not so, for Page's engineers had in fact turned out a very compact, if heavy, 6,062-pound 40′4″-wingspan airplane.

Student and instructor pilots were seated side by side, and there was room for two passengers in the rear, although the airplane had little appeal as a cross-country vehicle. One big drawback was that the Jeep's cockpit was hot as blazes on a summer day in Yuma or Williams, Arizona, or wherever else it served. The multiple windows didn't do nearly so much for visibility as they did for insolation, and the sun raised temperatures to the boiling point.

The instrument panel was rather simple, with one exception noted below. Flight instruments were presented on the left in the semi-standard display of the day, while huge duplicate engine instruments were mounted on the right.

A very unusual and advanced item was the "Tell-tale" indicator, which today would be called an annunciator panel, and can be found on everything from a Continental Mark IV to an F-111. This device was mounted in the upper right center of the panel, and told an intricate story of what was right and what was wrong with the aircraft. If all was well, the panel was black. If something—damn near anything—went wrong, it began to light up. The nosy little monster not only monitored the condition of vital parts, such as oil temperature, pressure, and so on, but it also kept track of cockpit procedures and would blink at you if you came back too far on the throttles if the gear was not down.

The AT-9 handbook has almost two full pages of possible "tell-tale" indications, and these must almost surely have been made "memory" items to bedevil the poor Kaydets. Nothing could describe system operation better than the handbook itself, and I quote:

"Operation. Below is given the Tell-tale system operation showing the various warning lights and the conditions governing their operations for both lights "on" and lights "off." Normal airplane operation for takeoff, flight and landing requires all lights off; for single engine operation, with other engine idling, horn release switch will stop horn but lights will burn until correct engine operation is resumed. For single engine's operation with 1 engine dead, the dead engine's throttle should be half opened so tell tale signals will operate correctly from running engine's throttle."

Sure! Remember, this is not a translation from the Japanese.

It goes on to say, in part, "For landing, both gears must be locked down, and either the throttle must be closed to maximum of 1/3 open, or the flaps must be down hence the lights are controlled from the locked down switch and relay through throttles and flaps."

This was only a small part of the dense instruction on the device, and I feel certain that the first button pulled on entering the aircraft was the circuit breaker deactivating it.

The rest of the airplane was much simpler, with good design flair being shown for ease of production and maintenance. The semi-monocoque fuselage was built in three sections,

The great George Page was lead engineer on the AT-9, as he was on so many Curtiss Wright aircraft, and he tried to achieve increased maneuverability by reducing the propeller moment-arm. To do this, he mounted the engines as close as possible together (their center lines were only 11 feet apart). It was this that led to the "bob-nosed" look of the AT-9.

This famous photo showing hot-shot pilots in AT-9As peeling off from their formation flight was used in many publications. Note the retractable landing light, and the reinforced area in the wing center section, where the integral fuel tank was placed.

with the entire snub nose just forward of the windshield, removable for easy servicing of the controls and instruments. The tail section was similarly detachable, about 1 foot in front of the vertical stabilizer. Car-type doors, generously hinged, provided entrance into the cabin, and occasional thrills when they weren't secured properly prior to flight.

The wing center section was built integral with the fuselage and contained the single 145-gallon gasoline tank. The jaunty thrust out engine nacelles were built into the outer wing panels, to which detachable wingtips were attached. Two spars carried the considerable loads generated during student training. The thick, heavily filleted wing root had an N.A.C.A. 23016.7 airfoil, tapering to a 4410 at the tips, which had considerable washout.

The ailerons, which like the elevators were affixed in position by continuous "piano" hinges, were statically and dynamically balanced. Some of the Jeep's handling problems may have stemmed from the shape of the aileron, which had an unusual angled taper at the wingtip.

The rather generously sized flaps were built in three sections and were hydraulically operated. There were some split-flap problems with early airplanes which contributed to its mystique as a nondocile bird. The flaps were all metal (as were the control surfaces) and could be deflected through a full 50 degrees for landing. If a pilot had sufficient confidence (that's spelled guts), he could slow the AT-9 down to 75 or 80 mph for landing. Instead, with the normal conservative approach of adding 5 mph for safety, 5 for mother, 10 for the girl friend, and 10 for luck, pilots usually approached at well over 100 mph—a practice which contributed to the plane's hot reputation. Carefully flown, with positive, accurate air-speed control, the Jeep was no harder to land than other tail draggers, and easier than the Beech C-45.

The pugnacious look of the airplane on the ground came from its nose, which appears to be both bobbed and pointed skywards. The big bulky nacelles, set well forward on the wing, added to the aggressive demeanor.

The landing gear, as noted, was similar to other Curtiss aircraft, retracting the 30″ diameter Hayes wheels straight back into the nacelle, from which they peeked out. The gear was a maintenance problem during the early service life of the AT-9, with fractured forgings causing a series of groundings. Mishaps of this type were perfectly natural, seeing that the airplane had been custom designed for a new requirement, without the period of development that had been accorded other equivalent types.

In an effort to increase maneuverability by reducing the propeller moment arm, the engines were mounted as close together as possible, with their centerlines being only 11 feet apart. The earlier airplanes used an 8′6″-diameter Hamilton Standard two-bladed constant speed propeller; later aircraft used a 7′9″ prop by the same manufacturer, for reasons which will appear below.

Primary difference between the AT-9 and AT-9A was in the engines, with the R-680-9 being fitted to the former and the R-680-13 to the latter. This was really a production-line distinction only, for either aircraft could take either engine, provided only that they were fitted in matched pairs, as there was a considerable weight difference between the two. Both engines had the same rated power—295 hp at 2,300 rpm and 28.3 inches of manifold pressure for takeoff, and 280 hp for maximum continuous power. The AT-9A's hydraulic system was slightly modified, and there were some other minor detail changes.

One of the great rivals of the AT-9 was the Cessna AT-17 Bobcat, also known as the "Bamboo Bomber." Despite the conventional fabric-covered construction of the Bobcat, many more survived after the war because their handling characteristics were considered better than those of the AT-9. The government withheld sale of the AT-9 to the public because they were considered "too hot to handle" for the average private pilot.

Curtiss engineers kept trying to bring the Jeep up to the guaranteed performance specified in the contract, but with very little success. PhDs were a comparative rarity in the aircraft industry in those days, and Curtiss committed all they had employed to solve the vexing problem of why the AT-9 couldn't reach 200 mph maximum speed in level flight. Then there came a report from a small Midwestern airfield of a modification which had upped the little trainer's speed by 5 mph, so that it was just touching the magic 200 mark.

The Curtiss team sent to investigate was stunned with the simplicity of the fix. It seems that a transient AT-9 had nicked one of its props while landing at the field. The shop had no spare AT-9 props on hand, but it had bins full of Beechcraft paddles, which used the same basic hub but had a 7′9″ diameter. In those happy un-management-ridden times, the flight line mechanics simply pulled both Curtiss props, substituted the smaller Beech version, and cleared it for a test flight. It worked just fine, and speed picked up.

The Curtiss people went back to St. Louis and proceeded to "replicate" the experiment, as the scientific types say. Sure enough it worked, although a careful calibration of the speed indicated that the improvement was only to about 198 mph.

Two things remained to be done. The first was to figure out why the smaller props added speed (for engine power settings remained substantially the same), and the second was to sell the fix to Wright Field.

After a little inspection and introspection, the slide-rule experts decided that the large fuselage had blocked out some of the propeller slipstream, reducing its efficiency. The smaller props churned in cleaner air and thus achieved more speed.

Warren flew back to Wright Field, and not only sold the concept to Wright Field, but talked them out of any penalties whatever, although the plane was still just shy of V max requirements.

The AT-9 was a comparatively simple airplane, and Curtiss completed its production run without any unusual problems for a completely new model. Despite the fact that pilots grew to like it after they had flown it for a sufficiently long time, the Jeep did not earn any general lasting affection, and no further orders were placed, nor did any go to foreign governments. In 1944 and 1945, an enormous crush of letters started pouring in on the Pentagon from citizens who were correctly anticipating that there would be a big post-war selloff of airplanes.

The governing powers decided that the AT-9 would be withheld from sale as it was too hot for the average private pilot. It was not a popular plane for administrative use, and there were scads of the much more tractable Beechcraft AT-11s and C-45s around, so the AT-9, a proven but no longer needed tool, was consigned directly to the scrap yard. To my knowledge, no example remains today.

The end of the line—a surplus AT-9 awaits destruction. For many years it was thought that no AT-9 had survived, but the Air Force Museum found sufficient parts to create one, which may be seen in the fantastic Dayton facility.

19 McDonnell's First Fighter

The XP-67 Moonbat

Wings December, 1973

When the aviation industry was small, and especially during the dark days of the Depression, aeronautical engineers followed the contracts from one company to the next. They were aided in this by government policy, which tried to spread out the few available procurement dollars among as many firms as possible to maintain a manufacturing base. Thus from 1924 to 1938, James S. McDonnell went from Huff-Daland to Consolidated to South Metal Aircraft to Airtransport Engineering Company to Great Lakes to Glenn L. Martin. When he was between jobs, he formed his own consulting company.

He formed the McDonnell Aircraft Corporation in 1939, an auspicious year, and prospered by making components for established aircraft companies such as Curtiss and Douglas, who for the first time had more work than they could handle. But McDonnell wanted to build airplanes, and he knew that to win a contract he would have to come up with something unusual. He did so with the XP-67, and had adequate engines been available, he might have gained a large production contract for the aircraft. The XP-67 did not go into production, but it paved the way for one of the most successful lines of jet aircraft in history.

A previously unpublished photo of the XP-67 in the McDonnell factory, still unpainted. What a great-looking airplane! But if Mr. McDonnell had come in he would have raised hell about all the debris on the floor; he was a stickler for a clean factory. *Robert F. Dorr*

Most giant industrial aggregations are founded on a smashing success—Ford looks back to its T-model, Rolls to its Silver Ghost, Wrigley's to its Spearmint—but the McDonnell Aircraft Corporation, as it was known prior to its merger with Douglas, was different, for it owes its existence to a complete and utter failure; the beautiful but fireprone XP-67 Moonbat.

This sleek twin-engine fighter was the very first of the St. Louis-based firm's attempts to gain a production contract. James McDonnell, the founder, had paid his dues in the aircraft-manufacturing fraternity by working under that stern and usually difficult taskmaster, Glenn L. Martin, and like so many others, ultimately got a belly full and left to start his own firm. (Martin's martinet disposition should be regarded as a national asset, for it was the indirect inspiration for Douglas, McDonnell, and Bell aircraft, whose founders all left Martin in fits of pique and went on to compete.)

Starting out in St. Louis in subcontract work, McDonnell realized that breaking into the aircraft bigtime would require something new and different, which in 1940 was exactly what the Army Air Corps was looking for. This sudden need for the novel was embodied in Request for Proposal R-40C, a brand new concept which called on aircraft manufacturers to pull out their imaginative stops and produce really radical aircraft. For the first time there was sufficient money not only to expand and reequip the Army Air Force, but to experiment in an effort which would hopefully catch up and pass European standards, and American aircraft manufacturers responded

This, as the photo indicates, is November 29, 1943, and the XP-67 is clearly years ahead of its time, with a blended wing and fuselage that presages the much later General Dynamics F-16. *Robert F. Dorr*

In 1943, the McDonnell plant in St. Louis, pictured here, had not yet grown to the colossal size it achieved before becoming McDonnell Douglas and then, later, part of Boeing. Bailing out of the XP-67 might have been a problem, although the dihedral in the vertical surfaces might have allowed the pilot to clear it. *Robert F. Dorr*

with no less than 23 designs. The Vultee XP-54 "Swoose Goose" won the first two places, with "Figures of Merit" of 817.9 and 812.9. Curtiss' radical XP-55 "Ascender" placed third and fourth, with totals of 801.2 and 770.6. Northrop's lethal XP-56 "Black Bullet" was fifth, with a total of 725.8. Far down on the list, below even such relatively tame entries as Continental engine-powered P-39s, was the McDonnell Model I, in 21st place, with a point total of 466.4.

The McDonnell entry was conventional in every respect except for its power train, which featured a buried Allison V-3420 engine and a complex and still undeveloped right-angle drive gear for the wing-mounted pusher propellers.

McDonnell's estimated performance figures for the Model I were unexciting, and the plane really didn't seem to offer much. Still, the Army wanted to encourage imagination, and so a $3,000 (that's three thousand dollars) contract was awarded for procurement of preliminary engineering data. It was perhaps the best investment the Army Air Force ever made, for it was the down payment on thousands of the best fighters ever built, the F4 Phantom jet.

McDonnell, a great engineer and an even greater salesman, drove his entire staff—all 10 or 12 of them—back to the drawing board. On 30 June 1941 they submitted a revision to the Model I and a more conventional new plane, the Model II. Both were rejected, but the Army Air Force expressed continuing interest, and 10 months later, on April 24, 1942, the Model IIa was submitted. It would ultimately be the XP-67.

In the Model IIa, McDonnell had dispensed with the center engine and drive train and developed a twin-tractor engine fighter whose lines were a sinuous combination of curves and fillets bespeaking speed and deadliness. Ironi-

The shadow of the XP-67 emphasizes its unusual shape and proportions. Had the proper engines been available, the XP-67 might well have been a winner. As it was, McDonnell's advanced thinking on this aircraft made the company a contender when the jet engine came along; McDonnell took advantage of the new engine with the first McDonnell Phantom. *Robert F. Dorr*

cally, these flowing graceful lines would both create and conceal aerodynamic flaws which would result in its rejection by Air Force test pilots.

While McDonnell had impressed one faction of the Air Force with the beauty and potential of his design, he was having a much tougher time with others. Major (later four-star General) Benjamin W. Chidlaw was adamantly opposed to letting McDonnell even bid, for he felt with some justification that they simply didn't have an adequate engineering staff to develop a completely new plane. There were plenty of full-time manufacturers ready to build for production, and there was a desperate need for competent second-tier subcontractors, where McDonnell already excelled.

The head-on view shows the closely cowled engines, and blended wing and fuselage aerodynamics. This was a well-thought-out aircraft. *Robert F. Dorr*

McDonnell knew, however, that to survive in the postwar world he was going to need his own product, bearing his own name, and he made a whirlwind tour of Washington and Wright Field offices, finally getting a go-ahead first from Brigadier General O. P. Echols, and later from Hap Arnold, himself. Major Chidlaw went along.

As the project matured, interest and excitement mounted at both the plant and Wright Field, for the new firm was producing an airplane which had a sexy, functional styling worthy of Raymond Lowey, combined with a speed range and firepower punch all but unknown in 1940. On May 5, 1940, Model Specification 23-A was submitted, and the Model IIa was now a single-place, pressure cabin interceptor, armed with six .50-caliber machine guns and four 20-mm cannon. Furthermore, McDonnell guaranteed a high speed of 472 mph and an estimated gross weight of 18,600 pounds.

Time was running out for peace, but there was still time for conferences, and Air Force planners, some of whom had witnessed the recent German bomber assault on England, wanted even more firepower. As a result, the armament package was changed to six 37-mm cannons (yes, six!) with an alternate plan for one 75-mm big gun installation. (You have to remember that this was a time when the Philippine Islands were being defended by fixed-gear Boeing P-26s and recently arrived Seversky P-35s, each armed with two .30-caliber popguns.) In the process of armament changes, the design gross weight of the airplane grew to a somewhat more realistic 20,000 pounds.

A mock-up inspection was held in mid-April 1942, and the usual number of changes were processed, the most noticeable of which was a 15-inch extension of the fuselage nose to improve gunsight installation. The airplane was even more beautiful in the three-dimensional mock-up than it had been on paper, for McDonnell's idea of carrying the laminar-flow airfoil throughout the aircraft, including the nacelles and fuselage, conveyed a sense of speed and style that had been seen previously only in Bill Barnes' Lancers.

Right from the start, McDonnell had made every effort to secure maximum wind-tunnel time for the aircraft, both at company and Government expense. The XP-67 would stand or fall on its performance, and drag reduction was a paramount consideration. As the tests proceeded, one harsh aerodynamic fact of life became increasingly apparent. Unless manufacturing tolerances were rigidly con-

The prettiest view of the XP-67 was in flight. E. E. Elliot was the test pilot, just visible behind the propeller disk here.

trolled to produce a supersmooth skin finish, the advantages of a laminar-flow air foil were lost, while the disadvantages (loss of low-speed lift, higher stall speed) remained. In one sense the new firm was at a disadvantage, for most of its working force was at the top of the learning curve and was unaccustomed to such precision work, especially in matching sheet metal surfaces. On the other hand, the XP-67 provided a training ground for methods and techniques that would catapult the firm into the first rank of manufacturers—one has only to visit the superbly automated St. Louis facility today to see how far this initial effort has carried it.

Throughout its life, the project was closely compared to the Lockheed XP-49, the advanced model of the famous P-38 Lightning. The aircraft were generally similar in size, and both were intended to be powered by Continental X1-1430-1 engines. As Lockheed was regarded as a well-established firm, with good engineering methods and a working knowledge of weight-control techniques, the Air Force felt that the XP-49 would be a good gauge by which to judge the relative validity of McDonnell's estimates. On paper, of course, it was the XP-67 all the way, with a projected speed 14 mph higher than the Lockheed, more armament and almost twice the range. As it turned out, neither aircraft achieved production status nor specified performance.

McDonnell's cost figures were attractive, with a cost-plus fixed-fee contract No. W 535 AC 21218 being entered into on September 30, 1941, and calling for two aircraft, one free-spinning wind-tunnel model and data for $1,508,596, plus a fee of $86,315.76.

Despite the avalanche of war orders, the XP-67 then entered that protracted period of change characteristic of every advanced design. The changes stemmed from three primary sources—first, the wind-tunnel data, of which more later; second, a continually vacillating armament requirement; and third, the ever-shifting problem of engine availability.

The three-fold wind-tunnel effort undertaken jointly by McDonnell at the University of Detroit, the NACA, and the Air Force generated tons of data, much of it alarming. While general aircraft stability and control characteristics were adequate, it was evident that there were going to be manifold cooling problems inherent in the unusual wing-duct design.

Models, Inc., of North Bergen, New Jersey, was responsible for delivery of the ultimate wind-tunnel model, a huge ¼-scale detailed version of the XP-67 upon which would depend many of the final lines of the actual airplane. The original delivery date had been November 8, 1941, but changes came with such regularity that the firm complained to Wright Field on September 5, 1942, that "every component part of this model has been completely changed". Naturally, work

The very long, streamlined nacelles are evident here. The armament package was intended to be six 37 mm cannon, with an alternate plan for the installation of one 75 mm cannon. Wind-tunnel tests on models revealed that the closely cowled engines would have cooling problems, but McDonnell was able to redesign them. *Robert F. Dorr*

A close-up view of the cockpit shows the excellent visibility afforded the pilot. The engines were the aircraft's weak point, and an engine fire ultimately destroyed the prototype.

The XP-67 made its first flight from Scott Field (now Scott Air Force Base), Illinois, on January 6, 1944. After a pleasingly short takeoff roll, the test pilot, E. E. Elliot, saw the engine gauges begin to show excessive heat, so he returned and landed after only 15 minutes' flying time. The Continental X-1430 engines were just not going to work out. *Robert F. Dorr*

on the prototype was stalled until the model could be delivered.

Other problems reared up in a mind-bending sequence which only a man like Jim McDonnell could have handled. While he was tearing from one crisis to the next—getting engines allocated from Continental, curing radiator-manufacturing problems, and helping expedite exhaust manifold deliveries, he was still able to exert an almost hypnotic spell on the Materiel Command, convincing them not only that the XP-67 would meet specifications, but luring them into new versions of the aircraft, including attack, bomber, and photo-reconnaissance. But his greatest feat was talking his way into 51 additional hours of testing at the vastly overloaded NACA wind-tunnel facility at Langley, and this bit of amazing promotion came at a time when many projects were flatly cancelled simply due to the projected unavailability of the huge wind tunnel.

The XP-67 wasn't the only airplane swamped with trouble, however, for the Air Defense Branch in the Pentagon had also recommended cancellation of the Bell XP-69 (original pusher piston version), and the 75-mm armed Curtiss XP-71. Somehow the XP-67 survived this onslaught, partly due to McDonnell's irrepressible salesmanship, but primarily because of the aerodynamic possibilities in the new wing planform which seemed to have application for the upcoming and supersecret jet engine.

Nevertheless, the word from Langley was far from encouraging and confirmed that the XP-67 would have extensive cooling problems as a result of the leading edge duct design. McDonnell wanted to redesign it on the spot, but Chidlaw, now a Brigadier General, demanded that the plane get airborne as soon as possible, reasoning that there were undoubtedly other problems to be uncovered and solved. Colonel C. F. Green from NACA advised that relatively minor changes in the ducts and adjacent leading edge areas could result in a 25-percent drag reduction and an increase of over 200 percent in cooling potential, and design of the Number 2 aircraft was revised accordingly.

The 689 inspection of the aircraft took place on the first of December 1943, with everything essentially complete except for the armament, pressure cabin, oxygen, and the proposed means to droop the ailerons. The armament compartment was rather wisely filled with CO_2 bottles. Taxi tests filled the following week, until December 8th when fires started in both nacelles during an engine runup. Exhaust manifold slip rings had failed, igniting the self-sealing oil tanks. Fortunately, the fire was quickly put out, but it was an omen for the future.

The XP-67 was repaired and trucked in secrecy to Scott Field, Illinois, where it was groomed for its first flight on January 6, 1944, 2 years and 3 months after the contract had been signed. E. E. Elliot was the pilot, and he had a handful of problems. After a pleasingly short takeoff roll, Elliot entered a gradual series of turns which confirmed the fact that the airplane would be easy to fly. Then it began. The heat gauges began to shoot up, gradually at first and then, alarmingly, right off the clock, and Elliot made a hasty return to the field, terminating the flight after 15 minutes.

In a manner that should have been familiar to the Air Force, McDonnell began to dangle new and juicier plums before them while the XP-67 overheat problem was being investigated. It was now official that the Continental engines were not going to be available, but McDonnell saw this as merely another opportunity to excel. Instead of the relatively tame X-1430s, why not go for either the two-stage Allison (shades of Don Berlin) or a Rolls Royce Merlin, and with either of these, install a Westinghouse 9.5-inch jet unit in the aft nacelle? (In those early days, you sort of specified jet engines by the inch and by the cluster, almost as if they were rockets you could stack side-by-side.) Old Mac didn't want to experiment either, but stated that he could put this new version directly into production with an estimated sea-level speed in excess of 500 mph.

But it was 1944, and the Air Force was becoming more sophisticated. Jet aircraft were clearly the coming thing, and General F. O. Carrol proposed that while the best available engine should be placed in the second test XP-67, no production commitment was justified.

The second and third test flights, on January 26 and 28, were successful and gave further indication that, while the aircraft was absolutely delightful to fly, it was seriously underpowered.

Elliot almost bought the farm on his next flight, as the main center bearing of the left engine burned out just after takeoff. The right tachometer failed, and, simultaneously, the canopy blew off. A more easily panicked man might have abandoned ship right there, but Elliot grooved it once around the field, making a smooth emergency landing.

The censor brushed out many of the distinctive features of the XP-67, but he could not hide the beautiful shape of the airplane. *Robert F. Dorr*

The plane was trucked back to Lambert Field for repairs and modification, the most noticeable of which was raising the horizontal stabilizer 12 inches for better stability.

Meanwhile, McDonnell made yet another hard sell to re-engine the second XP-67, using the Allison/Westinghouse combination, but the Air Force stalled, demanding more definitive test results.

In an attempt to get a better grasp of the plane's potential, the Air Materiel Command sent Colonel Marcus F. Cooper, Lieutenant Colonel Osmond J. Ritland, and Major F. A. Barsodi to test fly it during the period May 11–13, 1944. (Cooper and Ritland subsequently rose to the rank of Major General; Barsodi was killed in England on a test flight of the fourth or fifth P-80 to be sent abroad.)

Their combined test report was generally positive, but hardly enthusiastic, and it revealed some facts that had not been too prominent in the previous test reports.

Elliot briefed them thoroughly on the cooling characteristics, which required specific techniques during takeoff and climb to avoid overheating. For it had been determined that the duct entry lip was at such an angle to the airstream that cooling air was pushed only toward the outboard half of the radiator.

Cooper recalls, however, that there was very little information given on the handling characteristics of the aircraft at the stall, and that almost nothing was known about spin characteristics. The test flights would reveal why.

All three pilots considered the cockpit layout to be fair, and the taxi characteristics of the three-wheel landing gear setup to be good. As expected, the takeoff roll was excessive, and the acceleration to the 140-mph safe single-engine speed was uncomfortably slow, all of which confirmed the general assessment of a lack of power.

While the plane handled very well in gentle turns at normal cruising speeds and was stable in almost all regimes, certain awful truths began to show themselves at speeds approaching the stall. During an accelerated turn it would begin to feel very tail heavy, and then begin to buffet at a speed far in excess of the expected stall speed.

Cooper, noting the peculiar characteristics with some alarm, initiated a normal stall series. The gross weight called for stall to occur at about 95 mph; instead, a buffeting began at about 135 mph, with the nose having a tendency to tuck up. (This was a phenomenon that would haunt later swept wing aircraft and would be cured only through the use of complicated electronic sensing and control devices.) Facing a completely unknown spin characteristic, Cooper let the plane fly into the buffet for a little while, then accelerated out of it.

The other pilots agreed that there were far more aerodynamic problems to work out than just the cooling. In comparative flights with a North American P-51B, the Mustang proved to have a much better rate of turn and general maneuverability, hardly surprising, but still a factor to be considered when determining future production requirements.

Other Air Force pilots flew the aircraft a few more times while it was being groomed for the official performance tests, all of them privately agreeing that the program was at a dead end. On September 6, 1944, Elliot took off for a functional test flight from Lambert Field. At 10,000 feet he noticed a loss of power in the right engine. He chopped the throttle and dropped toward the field, watching nervously for flames, which appeared at about 3,000 feet. With the guts and loyalty typical of test pilots, Elliot again stayed with the airplane and had a presence of mind enough to choose a cross-wind runway so that the flames would be blown away from the aircraft. He made a good touchdown, but the right brake failed and the XP-67 turned sharply to the left, presenting the growing fire for the wind to fan. Elliot jumped out unhurt, but the flames mounted, burning the fuselage almost in two before the fire brigade could put it out. The aircraft was a shambles. The left wing and nacelle were badly damaged, and the entire wheel well area was burned out.

An accident investigation team attributed the accident entirely to engine failure, caused by a broken rocker arm at the exhaust valve of the No. 1 cylinder. No rebuild was possible, and the XP-67, with a total flying time of 43 hours, was no more.

A hold order had been placed on the No. 2 airplane in October 1943, and, as it was only 15 percent complete, it was decided to terminate all future effort. Total cost of the project, including a fixed fee of $108,549, was $4,742,476. When you consider that but for the XP-67 there would almost certainly have been no Phantoms, no Banshees, and no Eagles, it was money well spent.

Construction and Performance

Although construction was generally typical for the period, it was characterized by unusual attention to dimensional accuracy. The 55-foot span wing was of all-metal stressed skin, full cantilever type, with each side being built in two sections. Area was 414 sq. ft. Each two-spar inner section contained the nacelle, the armament compartment and the flap. The outer section also had two spars.

The fuselage was of semimonocoque aluminum alloy construction, covered with Alclad. The cockpit was designed for pressurization, and would have taken a Lockheed system.

The less than reliable Continental XI-1430 (-17 L, -19 R) engines had a 6.50 to 1 compression ratio, and D-23 turbo chargers. Maximum takeoff power at 3,300 rpm and 63.5 inches of manifold pressure was 1,350 horsepower, and was limited to 5 minutes duration. Using 55.3 inches and 3,000 rpm, 1,150 horsepower could be maintained from sea level to 25,000 at normal power. Two 10′8″-diameter Curtiss, four-bladed, opposite rotating propellers were installed; these would have later been replaced by Aeroprop Model H-20 units of 11-foot diameter.

The cockpit of the XP-67 was standard for the period, although a yoke control instead of a stick was a bit unusual. Helter-skelter instrument grouping was encountered in all aircraft of the period. *Robert F. Dorr*

At military power of 25,000 feet, with a 22,000-pound gross weight, the XP-67 achieved a disappointing 405 mph, according to the Official Performance Summary. Range at cruising speed was 2,385 miles, although as much as 4,000 miles could have been obtained in the ferry configuration. Service ceiling was 37,400 feet, while absolute ceiling was 38,000, according to the manufacturer's estimates. At 20,000 pounds weight (maximum gross was 22,114), the plane would clear a 50-foot obstacle in 3,018 feet with 15-degree flaps. Landing with 45 degrees flap required 1,583 feet.

While the Moonbat's performance was disappointing and the development period long, the United States really achieved a bargain, for a new and potentially most successful manufacturer had been trained. On March 7, 1945, a production contract was let for a hundred McDonnell FD-1 Phantoms, the first pure jet aircraft to operate from a carrier, and the first of a since unending stream of quality combat aircraft. The Phantom only faintly resembled the XP-67 in planform, but there were striking similarities in construction and production techniques which more than proved the worth of the first fighter from McDonnell.

20 The Custer Channel Wing Story

Airpower May, 1977

One of the rare pleasures of my life was getting to know Willard R. Custer, the creator of the Custer Channel Wing aircraft, and one of the most persuasive talkers I've ever met. Even though we met later in his life, when the main chance for development of the Channel Wing had passed, he was as enthusiastic as ever, able to convince an audience that the Channel Wing was the only way to fly. There is no little irony in his enthusiasm, for it probably created problems for his concept. Willard's tendency was to ascribe every virtue to the Channel Wing and never admit that there might be the engineering trade-offs that are inherent to every aircraft.

Because he claimed a tad too much for too many things—speed, range, altitude, takeoff distance, fuel economy, and so on—people did not believe the very real advantages the Custer Channel Wing had in certain flight regimes. Had he been a little less aggressive, Custer might have been able to get his aircraft into production and prove his ideas in the field. The aviation world is a poorer place because he did not.

Willard R. Custer is a man straight out of American folklore. He is the prototype Yankee inventor, smart, tough, resourceful, unafraid of the machinations of big government, big business, or fate. He believes in his invention, and he *knows* that sooner or later he will prevail.

Custer is a genuine innovator, for although designers have tried virtually every combination of wing size and shape, and every permutation of engine/propeller placement, it remained for him to combine the two elements in his famous Custer Channel Wing.

The inventor is a friendly, persuasive, energetic, singleminded man who has pursued a fifty year dream with a charming tenacity that has weathered many disappointments. He is convinced that he is right, that he has been right, and that the world has been denied the benefits of the Custer Channel Wing by a combination of misfortune,

Willard R. Custer's view on life and aviation paralleled the Wright brothers' in many respects, for he was determined to create aircraft his way, by pragmatic experimentation, without regard to established rules. Extremely personable and a born salesman, Custer believed passionately in his patented "Channel Wing."

Having built a successful model and two successful flying prototypes, Custer selected the very attractive Baumann Brigadier as the platform for his first attempt at a five-passenger, full-size aircraft. The Brigadier was quite advanced for 1950, and featured pusher propellers, unusual for the time.

lack of vision, and, sadly in some instances, simple bad faith.

It's hard to be around Willard Custer for more than a few minutes before beginning to believe with him in his concept. He is so evidently sincere, so deeply convinced and so determined to win through that he converts even the most ardent skeptics—at least temporarily. He's an exhausting man to interview, for he flies around his small but neat shop/laboratory, grabbing an air hose to "fly" a screwdriver around to prove a point, picking up a 40 year old model, shoving a jet engine test rig out of the way, all the time telling you of the fundamental simplicity of his own science—"aerophysics"—and never tiring of the main topic of conversation, his patented channel wing.

In some respects these engaging characteristics may work against him in today's cold business climate. Times have changed, and aviation is more sophisticated, more finance oriented, and its engineering requirements are vastly more extensive. It may be that the very qualities which have sustained him in his battle against convention are not the ones which persuade a modern businessman to put up the necessary financing.

No matter; he has succeeded in his own mind, and the minds of many qualified engineers. More important, there are current indications that his concepts may yet be recognized.

The Custer saga began during a near-hurricane. A young Willard R. Custer was taking shelter in a barn, when suddenly the roof sailed off. Instead of being frightened, Custer wondered where the power to lift the roof came from. He'd been fascinated with aircraft for a long time, and knew that they had to accelerate down a runway to generate enough lift to take-off, while the barn roof, a poor airfoil, had lifted off "just sitting there".

Custer soon came upon a distinction that has eluded other inventors, postulating that when air passes over an object, as in the barn roof incident, that is "speed of air". However, when an aircraft flies through the air, that is "air speed".

Now don't just put this off as semantics, not just yet, anyway. It is Custer's theory, and it is best to use his words to describe it, i.e. "it is the speed of the air and not the speed of the object which counts. The conventional airfoil was designed to obtain a reaction from the air mass *through which it is moved*. The channel airfoil was designed to obtain a reaction from the *air mass moved through it.*"

In essence, Custer says that in his wing, the movement of air through the channels reduces air pressure in those channels, and that atmospheric pressure on the bottom of the channel airfoil then creates lift in direct proportion to the pressure reduction in pounds per square foot.

After converting the Brigadier to Custer Channel Wing configuration and flying it, Willard Custer had established enough confidence in the investing community to build a production version, the CCW-5, rolling it out on July 4, 1964. Willard and Mrs. Custer are on the right. Mrs. Custer supplied the strength, the encouragement, and often the basic common sense that all great inventors seem to need.

Other engineers have said it better for Custer, but his comments are essentially correct. In stricter terms, an engineer might say the following: "Greater lift coefficients are obtained by the effect of the propeller slipstream deflecting the air mass through which the wings are moved, by suppression of the flow separation of the wing's upper surface by energizing the boundary layer with high velocity slipstream, allowing the wing to fly at higher angles of attack before stalling, and by the vertical lift component due to the inclination of propeller thrust at high angles of attack."

I like Custer's way better.

Speaking again in more practical terms, the pusher propeller, tailored closely to almost touch the lip of the channel (Custer has experienced "channel shaving" in some of his experimental propellers) sucks air through the big half-tubes, and the Bernoulli principle does the rest. The propeller/channel juncture is critical, and some of the most efficient results have been obtained when the juncture was temporarily sealed by pouring water into the channel.

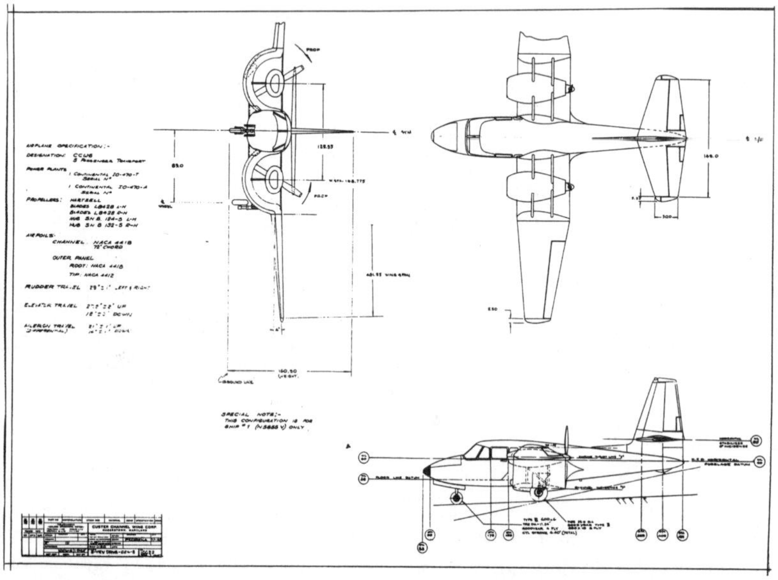

This three-view drawing of the Custer Channel Wing CCW-5 shows the placement of the propeller in the rear of the channel, a very critical detail in the operation of the aircraft. Flight performance was startling; in films of the aircraft, it seems certain that the CCW-5 is going to stall out on both takeoffs and landings, so slow is its speed, but it doesn't.

All of the above might sound like double talk, *if* Custer had not demonstrated his principle in several models and four full size aircraft, or if extensive testing had unquestionably refuted his claims.

Unfortunately, the testing has been ambiguous, and while it has not refuted the claims, neither has it sustained them. Part of the problem is that the tests have not been designed to prove or disprove the ability of the channel wing aircraft to perform, but have only investigated certain aspects which were amenable to contemporary testing techniques. Another part of the problem is that Custer has understandably maintained such tight control over his patents that full development programs have not been possible.

There are additional factors which will be covered in the second part of the article, which are more difficult to define. On the one hand, government reaction to Custer through the years has ranged from mildly patronizing to outraged; it is fairly evident from the correspondence that Willard Custer's native engineering talents didn't receive the same respect that would have been accorded an established manufacturer.

On the other hand, Custer has probably been too optimistic about the potential of his invention, while soft-pedaling some of the real problem areas. His reluctance to let professional engineers tell his story in objective, conventional, engineering terms, clearly delineating both advantages and disadvantages, has undoubtedly cost him some credibility.

As we shall see, engineering opinion is still divided about the Custer Channel Wing, but that doesn't inhibit an examination of the airplanes themselves, which constitute a unique line in American aviation.

Custer had translated his hurricane/barn roof idea into a working model by 1928, and obtained his first patent by 1929. At about the same time he coined the word "aerophysics" to use instead of "aerodynamics" to emphasize his concept that it was the removal of air pressure above the channel rather than the movement of the airfoil that was important.

In 1937 Custer built a single engine model which demonstrated vertical lift, and by 1939 he had formed a corporation, the first of many business entities which would sustain the idea over the years.

In 1940 he was able to demonstrate a twin engine model to his potential stock holders, obtaining enough financing to begin construction of the first full size channel wing, the CCW-1.

This aircraft was (is, actually, for it is now in storage at the National Air & Space Museum's Silver Hill facility) an

The CCW-5 was manufactured in Hagerstown, Maryland, using former Fairchild workers for the most part, so the fit and finish of the aircraft was excellent. The workers wanted the project to succeed as much as Custer did, for it would have meant many jobs in the area.

amazing combination of futuristic lines and modest test expectations. Custer is an excellent woodworker, and the streamlined fuselage and carefully built channels are beautiful examples of the art.

The airplane had 202.5 square feet of wing area, spread over a most unusual surface. Semi-circular, detachable wing tips were added to a straight chord wing surface, for a total length of nine feet four inches; a six foot channel was attached between the outer panel and the fuselage. Total wing span was 32′ 10½″. The channels were hung under the wing like huge nacelles, and the two Lycoming 75 horsepower four cylinder air cooled engines were mounted about midway in the channel.

The 19′11″ egg shaped fuselage seemed disproportionately short, and the aesthetics were not helped by a low aspect ratio "T" tail empennage. The stumpy landing gear looked like an afterthought.

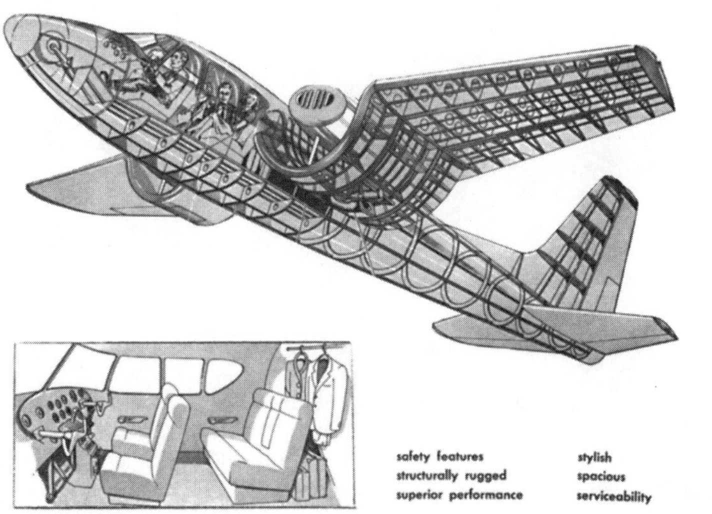

One of the things that Custer did very well—perhaps too well—was to project the performance of the channel wing concept into the future, imagining its use in all sorts of civil and military designs. Had he concentrated, even for a while, on just getting the first production line rolling, things might have been different.

Yet, despite this unusual appearance, the CCW-1 logged more than 300 hours in a restricted test program aimed primarily at learning how the channels worked, and what new flying techniques were required to guide the channel wing.

Curiously, Willard Custer made the first flight in the aircraft on November 12, 1942, entirely inadvertently. Custer is not a pilot and his test pilot, E. Kenneth Jaquieth was not in town on the day financial backers came to the Custer laboratory to see the airplane. The backers wanted to take some pictures, and asked Custer to taxi the CCW-1 to the small field where Jaquieth had been conducting taxi tests.

The field was only about 200 feet away, up a slight hill, and Custer felt qualified to move the plane. He applied power to get up the incline, and was somewhat disconcerted to see the trees on the horizon disappear. He was airborne, a non-pilot on the first flight of a brand new kind of aircraft. Custer throttled back abruptly, and the CCW-1 settled in, bending the landing gear.

Instead of being upset, the backers were delighted, for their dark horse had flown, albeit briefly.

The CCW-1 was later flown in demonstration for the military at the Beltsville, Maryland airport, where gruff, hard boiled Brigadier General W.E. Gilmore was excited enough to authorize a test program. Custer recalls that Gilmore actually phoned Orville Wright, who was in Washington at the time, urging him to come out and witness the new development.

The testing program which began on June 6, 1944 proved to be typical of the entire series of government tests of the channel wing concept, generating mixed conclusions, controversy and zero satisfaction to anyone.

The report, Army Air Forces Technical Report No. 5142, concluded that the lift generated by the channel was similar to the increment of lift generated by normal slipstream velocity in conventional wing/propeller arrangements. Unfortunately, the conclusion did not

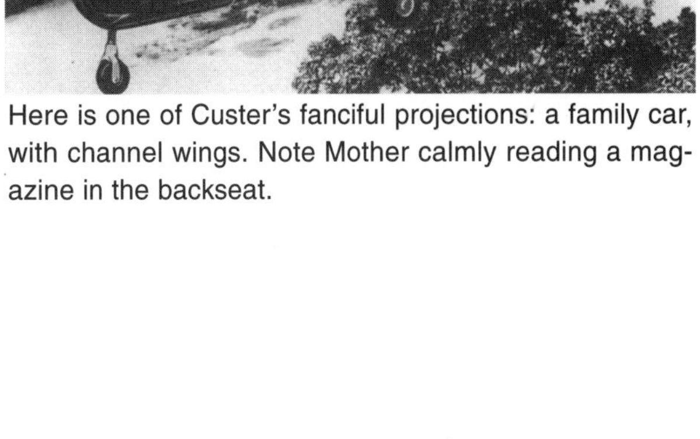

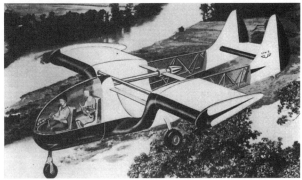

Here is one of Custer's fanciful projections: a family car, with channel wings. Note Mother calmly reading a magazine in the backseat.

The CCW-5 demonstrated its ability in public and received national attention, including articles in *Aviation Week.* One of Custer's papers was titled "How to Fly Slow and Hover in a Fixed Wing Aircraft." Given the problems the V-22 Osprey is having, perhaps it might be time to take another look at the channel wing concept!

The CCW-5 demonstrated its ability to hover in a relatively slight head wind, something that few airplanes other than the Fieseler Storch have been able to do.

restate the point made in the report that the channel generated *more* lift than the conventional arrangement. The report stated further that while the channel was markedly inferior to the helicopter in producing static lift, it was superior to conventional wing-propeller arrangements in this regard, and in producing lift with forward velocity.

The final conclusion was startling, for the report stated that "the device does not show sufficient promise of military value to justify further development by the Army Air Forces." This is surprising in that the improvement of static lift over a conventional wing/propeller arrangement was marked, and high lift devices in the form of flaps, slats and slots were under intensive development at the time.

The verdict typified the testing process, which never validated or denied what should have been the basic question, i.e. "Did the channel wing have characteristics of sufficient value when compared to other high-lift devices to warrant further development?"

Instead, the government denied that the channel wing was as good as a helicopter, and Custer compounded the problem by insinuating that it was indeed as useful as a helicopter.

Custer made an immediate and lasting interpretation of the test results, one which did not help the controversy. He inferred that perhaps the results were *too* good, and might actually be a threat to the then infant helicopter industry, which was receiving tremendous backing from the armed services. The first reaction to a charge like this is to shrug—it sounds too much like the stories of "60 miles per gallon carburetors" which have allegedly been suppressed over the years. Yet there are other arguments which makes one wonder.

Earlier models were tested in the Langley full-scale wind tunnel. Unfortunately, the report written on these tests was not correctly focused and failed to note the positive aspects of the configuration.

The most cogent of these are the later Wright Field tests, conducted in 1945 and 1947, which were cautiously optimistic about the channel wing concept. There is also the testimony of the Wright Field engineer, Don Young, who conducted the tests. He testified in a Washington Federal District Court that the channel wing was in fact capable of direct lift, and largely as a result of his testimony, Custer was granted additional patents.

These optimistic test interpretations are reinforced by results from independent engineering firms which have investigated the theory and found it to have merit.

The brutal truth is that the government would have rendered itself and Custer an inestimable service if it could have structured tests which would have proved, beyond any shadow of a doubt, that the channel wing was either (A) absolutely worthless or (B) had some promise. In case A, Custer could have turned to other things, while in case B, he might have been able to obtain adequate capitalization.

Custer persisted, however, and built an engineering test vehicle, the CCW-2, in response to some of Young's test report recommendations. The CCW-2 used a Taylorcraft fuselage and empennage, with six foot channels in lieu of wings. Conforming to Young's suggestions, the channels were shorter, and the propeller was placed at the extreme rear edge of the surface. The CCW-2 was extensively tested in free flight, tethered, and in the NACA wind tunnel.

Harold R. Custer, Willard's son, made the first flight of the new aircraft on June 3, 1948. Harold is as energetic and determined as his father, and has the unique distinction of having logged more channel wing time than any other pilot—over 1,000 hours.

Harold totaled 100 hours flying time in the CCW-2, which could take off in 45 to 65 feet, and land in the same distance. Lateral control of the wingless vehicle was obtained by differential use of the throttles.

The flight test program was not without its highlights. The C.A.A. insisted that wings be mounted on the test bed, and short stubs were attached. These neither helped nor hindered the aircraft, according to Custer, but did mollify the bureaucracy. More significantly, the aircraft demonstrated vertical lift in zero wind conditions, while tethered.

The wind tunnel tests at Langley are another subject of controversy and conjecture. Apparently the tests were well conducted, and the results reported accurately. Unfortunately, the conclusions seem to have been erroneous. Critics of the report indicate that it stated the primary increment of lift came from thrust, rather than from the lift, due to increased velocity in the channels, even though the plotted data showed this not to be the case. Also, the conclusions dealt with the CCW's hovering characteristics, rather than its STOL (short takeoff and landing) characteristics, an unfortunate view, for the channel wing was clearly designed for STOL, not helicopter style operation.

During the whole arduous process of design and testing, one thing definitely was not happening. Willard R. Custer was not making a lot of money; he had invested not only all of his own funds, but all of his life in the channel wing, and the material rewards to date have been small.

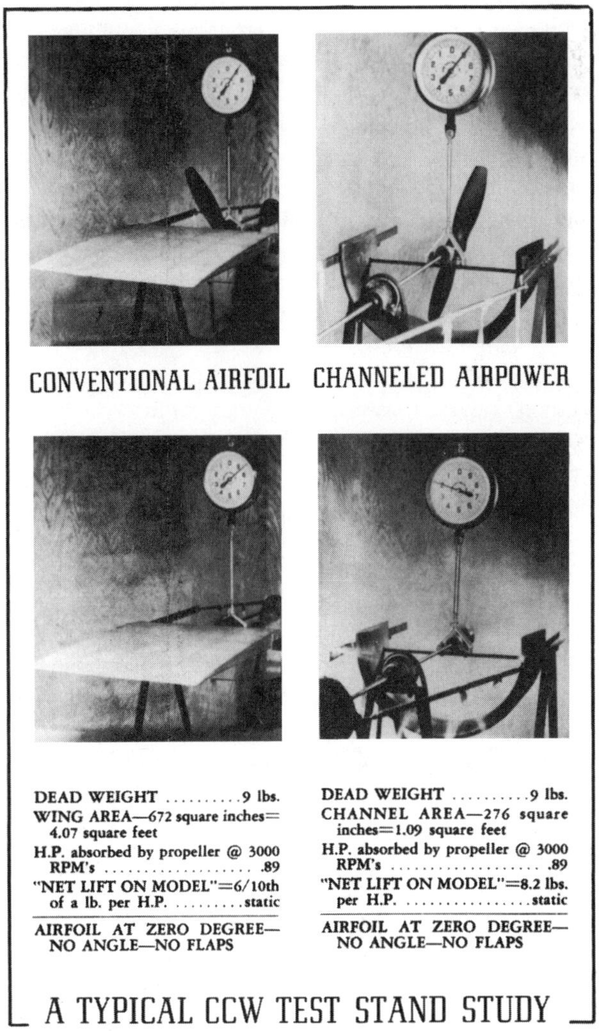
CONVENTIONAL AIRFOIL
CHANNELED AIRPOWER
DEAD WEIGHT ....9 lbs.
WING AREA—672 square inches=4.07 square feet
H.P. absorbed by propeller @ 3000 RPM's .... .89
"NET LIFT ON MODEL"=6/10th of a lb. per H.P. ....static
AIRFOIL AT ZERO DEGREE—NO ANGLE—NO FLAPS
DEAD WEIGHT ....9 lbs.
CHANNEL AREA—276 square inches=1.09 square feet
H.P. absorbed by propeller @ 3000 RPM's .... .89
"NET LIFT ON MODEL"=8.2 lbs. per H.P. ....static
AIRFOIL AT ZERO DEGREE—NO ANGLE—NO FLAPS
A TYPICAL CCW TEST STAND STUDY

The pragmatic, Wright brothers-like approach of Willard Custer can be seen in this simple "typical CCW test stand study."

But Custer's tenacity and his almost messianic belief in his program enabled him to secure backing from a series of investors, and in 1951 he was able to employ the Baumann Aircraft Corporation to modify a Baumann Brigadier to the CCW configuration.

The result was the prototype CCW-5, a rather handsome five place aircraft using two Continental 0-470-A engines of 225 horsepower each. The standard Baumann fuselage and empennage were retained, and a 41 foot span wing with two seven foot wide channels was attached.

First flight of the CCW-5 took place on July 13, 1953, with Walker J. Davidson at the controls. The company then spent the next several years performing demonstrations for civil and military audiences. These demonstrations consisted largely of maximum performance take-offs, with a terrifyingly steep climb out, using steep turns to the right and left at a high angle of attack and at speeds well below the stall speed of conventional aircraft to impress the audience. Motion pictures of the demonstration are heart-stopping; you know that an aircraft in that attitude, at that altitude and airspeed, is going to crash—but the CCW just keeps on turning.

Slow flight was a specialty, with speeds as low as 22 mph being measured. On August 27, 1954, in a remarkable display of the channel wing's ability, the CCW-5 was actually hovered against an 11 mph wind. The demonstrations would then conclude with a steep approach, an incredibly short landing, with the turnoff not at the first intersection, but at the approach end of the runway.

Take-off technique is critical in the CCW-5, for the pilot has to rotate sharply after the first 100 feet of roll, so that the high velocity air stream passing through the channel does not bounce off the runway against the undersurface of the horizontal stabilizer. If this happens, the nose can be forced down, considerably lengthening the take-off roll.

The prototype CCW-5 had an empty weight of 3,000 pounds, a gross of 4,925 and a maximum gross of 5,400 pounds. Maximum speed was quoted at 200 mph, with a 180 mph cruise; these were probably optimistic figures, but most manufacturers tend to err on the bright side.

The performance of the aircraft was good enough to interest several firms in its manufacture, the most promising being the Custer Channel Wing (Canada) Ltd., which secured the rights from the Custer-Frazer Corporation, and planned to build the plane in association with Norduyn Aircraft, Ltd. The short field capability of the CCW-5 was attractive to bush pilots, and an initial production run of 100 was planned.

This operation, like several other potential manufacturing plans, fell through, primarily because of problems synchronizing FAA approval of the aircraft, and SEC approval of the financing.

Custer undertook to build the 1st production CCW-5 at Hagerstown, Maryland, using Baumann Brigadier drawings as a start point, but modifying these as necessary to suit the different construction and stress requirements of the channel wing configuration. This, the fourth channel wing airplane, was rolled out on July 4, 1964, and it appeared that after many years of struggle the Custer Channel Wing was finally going to be marketed.

Fate intervened in the form of the Securities and Exchange Commission, which took exception to the manner in which the corporation stock had been issued, and the rug was pulled out from under the venture.

The production aircraft was outwardly similar to the prototype, but building it from the ground up rather than converting existing Baumann components permitted improvements to be made in the channel/fuselage juncture, considerably reducing drag. There were external differences, too; the engine nacelles were more streamlined, the wing had 2″ less span, the nacelle strut bracing was simplified, the ailerons were moved further outboard on the wings, and rudder and aileron travel was increased slightly.

In the steps toward FAA certification, it became necessary to raise the position of the horizontal surfaces, which impaired STOL performance. As previously noted, the CCW pilot has to get the horizontal surfaces below the vectored slipstream as soon as possible for optimum results.

Performance figures for the production CCW-5 varied little from the prototype, with the same top end performance indicated. Power on stalling speed was listed at 22 mph, initial rate of climb, 1,600 feet per minute, with a 22,000 foot service ceiling.

A single engine service ceiling of 5,000 feet was obviously a limiting factor in performance, and Custer planned to remedy this with improvements in the propeller/channel trailing edge juncture. A moveable sleeve has been suggested, one which would maintain a tight seal at the channel for STOL work, but which could retract for higher cruise performance.

And so engineering rears its ugly head again—if the advantages of the CCW derive from the channel section with its relative lack of mechanical complexity compared to slots and flaps, what does the addition of a moveable surface do? This and other similar questions will be covered in the engineering discussion.

Where does the program stand now? It still has its advocates, and there have been proposals for putting channels on everything from Curtiss C-46s to Fairchild F-27s, to executive jets. As indicated above, there is a real possibility that full scale testing of the production aircraft by a government agency will take place. But whatever occurs, you can be sure that Willard R. Custer will not stop fighting the good fight, nor will he be convinced that his discovery is not, still, the coming thing.

This is as close as Custer came to financial success with his project; if things had worked out differently, the Channel Wing might have made a great bush airplane. There is no question that the Custer Channel Wing made a very attractive appearance. Its flight performance in the STOL regime was very impressive. It would have cost much less than a helicopter, and only slightly more than a conventional twin-piston engine aircraft. Did the aviation public miss something here? I think so.

The Engineering Side—Pros and Cons

It is surprising to discover how sensitive and controversial the Channel Wing is today, after all its many years in the public eye. In an attempt to determine what the real merit of the Channel Wing is, I went to several engineers who had taken part in the testing and development of the device over the years. I interviewed participants of three different kinds, First were government representatives who had either conducted or interpreted the official tests. Second were engineers who had seen development potential in the channel wing, and who had a positive interest in its commercial success. Third was an engineer who was completely objective having neither a financial or government interest.

Because of the controversy, and because some legal action may still be forthcoming, I've been asked not to name the participants involved.

The Pro Side: Proponents of the Custer Channel Wing say that first of all, the true capabilities of the idea were not susceptible to test because appropriate engineering theory had not yet been developed to explain its demonstrated performance. In other words, the airplane was physically doing things for which aerodynamic formulas had not yet been evolved at the time of testing. Such formulas have since been developed, and further testing could be done in a more scientific manner.

This was a good-looking aircraft; even the bulk of the channels do not detract from the overall appearance of the airplane. In flight it was simply beautiful, for it could perform in the low-speed regime as no other twin engine aircraft of the day could do.

Because adequate theory was lacking, the CCW was tested for features and modes of flight which were in reality peripheral to its main intent, simply because there *was* theory to test *these* items.

The pro-channel wing faction maintains that the channel wing's pusher propeller arrangement not only forces circulation over the airfoil, taking advantage of the Bernoulli principle, but it also minimizes loss due to reverse flow around the trailing edge, and then across the ventral surface.

The NACA tests, they say, erroneously failed to reveal that the principal source of lift is due to the increased velocity in the channels, and further, the tests should have highlighted the findings that the static lift exceeded the weight of the test vehicle. This basic fact underlies the most salient advantages of the Custer Channel Wing, its simplicity, and its ability to operate in the STOL mode without expensive high lift devices.

The initial cost of the Custer Channel Wing aircraft—of any type—is probably slightly greater than a conventional aircraft of the same type, but less than that of an equivalent STOL aircraft using flaps, slots, etc. Its advantage stems from the fact that its operating costs would be far lower than those of the STOL alternative, because of the lessened maintenance requirements. Its greatest advantage, however, lies where it can be employed in helicopter operations, i.e. those situations in which helicopters are presently used, but with suitable modification in technique or landing area, a CCW could be substituted. The reason for this, of course, is the horrendously high cost of helicopter operation.

The CCW could be used for larger aircraft, and with jet engines. The increased drag of the channel wing undoubtedly would reduce top speeds, but in the correct application this would not be significant. "Correct application" includes STOL airline transportation over relatively short stage distances; use in remote areas where the ability to fly in and out of short airstrips with heavy loads is important, or where revenues dictate against the use of a high operating cost vehicle.

In sum, the CCW proponents say that the concept provides an economic, efficient solution for certain applications that are not presently met by conventional STOL aircraft or helicopters.

The Con Side: Those who take a negative view of the Custer Channel Wing do so persuasively and authoritatively. Their initial reaction is usually: "Oh no, not the channel wing again," followed by a measured explanation that there is not and never has been any emotional or economic prejudice against Custer's ideas. If, they say, the Channel Wing had shown merit, it would have been in the national interest to develop it, and it would have been so developed.

In more specific terms, the opponents of the Channel Wing say that it has less potential now than when it was first evaluated and found to be inferior to other approaches to STOL performance. The anti-Custer group concedes that the channel wing's lack of flaps results in a simpler, more economic system, and that the generation of high lift by the configuration is accompanied by a low pitching moment compared to conventional wing/flap arrangements.

The virtually viceless stall of the CCW is also acknowledged, as is the fact that ground personnel are exposed to less hazard by the propellers shielded by channels than by conventional propellers.

These are about the only advantages, however, and there are more than off-setting drawbacks, which the anti-CCW view lists as follows:

(a) Higher aerodynamic drag due to the increased wetted area resulting from the channels and, particularly, from the juncture of the channel to the fuselage.

(b) The very simplicity of the CCW arrangement prevents changing the wing aerodynamic characteristics to different modes of flight. In other words, the thicker CCW is optimized for one mode, while a wing with a well designed flap can be optimized for slow flight, cruise and higher speeds.

(c) The requirement for cross shafting of the engines to avoid uncontrollable asymmetric forces in the event of an engine failure when at a low airspeed, high angle of attack flight condition. (Custer concedes that production aircraft will be cross shafted.) This requirement of course dilutes the CCW claim for simplicity.

(d) A substantially lower power-off lift coefficient compared to a conventional wing/flap arrangement. This means a higher landing speed is required for a power-off landing. (Custer counters this with statistics on the relative infrequency of power off landings in any multi-engine aircraft.)

(e) Increased structural complexity of the wing.

(f) A lack of engineering investigation into problems of stability and control, and the use of rather simplified engineering theory to explain the complex CCW aerodynamics. (This, as noted above, is a two-edged sword.)

So there you have it. Two points of view, both basically honest, and both vulnerable to the assertion that the CCW has not been amenable to really valid testing.

What is the answer? Perhaps the future will tell, for more testing, presumably this time with more sophisticated techniques, is in the offing. It will be interesting to see, after all these years, who is really right.

21 GM's Flying Frankenstein

The Fisher XP-75 Eagle

Wings February, 1973

The basic idea behind the Fisher XP-75 was so sound and so simple that it seemed like a perfect way to procure an advanced new fighter at low cost. Simply take key components of aircraft already in mass production, combine them with a powerful new engine, and voila, you have a world-beater.

It would take engineering talent to do so, of course, and who was available but the remarkable Donovan R. Berlin, who had left his position as chief engineer of the Curtiss Airplane Division of Curtiss Wright? His career path was similar to so many: engineer at McCook Field, then successively more important posts at Douglas Aircraft, Northrop, and then Curtiss Wright. Berlin was a big man with a charming personality. He used to come to my office periodically to talk about his career and to lament that Curtiss had been so pigheaded in refusing to let him improve both the XP-37 and P-40 aircraft with better engines and his low-drag radiator scheme. Berlin seemed to be the perfect man to manage the XP-75, but sadly even he could not overcome the inherent design problems and the shifting mission requirements, and the Eagle never achieved production.

The Fisher XP-75 prototype, with the original canopy and with the landing gear still lacking the streamlined fairings. On the whole, not a bad-looking airplane.

One of the most valid precepts of aviation lore is that an aircraft which looks right will fly right, and vice versa. This truism applies to concepts as well, and if there was ever a conceptual approach to aircraft design which didn't look, sound or smell right, it was the one that led to the Air Force's first Eagle, Fisher's ugly XP-75. (The second Eagle is of course the beautiful and potent new McDonnell Douglas F-15.)

The basic idea for the XP-75, advanced by the same Don R. Berlin whose Curtiss P-36 and P-40 designs were fighting on several fronts, was ostensibly a fundamental, down to earth approach to the Army Air Force requirement for a fast climbing interceptor. Airframe parts from existing aircraft—a wing here, a tail there—were to be combined with a Fisher designed body which mounted the new Allison V-3420 engine. The first experimental aircraft was supposed to fly six months after the contract was signed.

In some respects, the proposal was attractive. It was known that the Fisher Body corporation had an excess of engineering talent which needed to be applied to the war effort; the proposed parts to be incorporated in the aircraft were in mass production and would be available; and, certainly not least, Berlin's reputation was such that any proposal from him had to be given serious consideration.

To General Motors, of course, the prospect of using Fisher Body aircraft to provide a market for Allison engines and Aero-product propellers was more than attractive—it was downright fascinating.

Within the Air Force, the initial reaction to Berlin's 24

The aircraft had a distinctly unusual profile, with the long, pointed nose, the bulky radiator aft of the wing, and the proportionately too-small vertical surfaces. The latter were derived from the Douglas SBD and were just too small for so big an airplane with so big an engine and propeller system.

The Curtiss P-40 wings and Douglas SBD tail surfaces are evident from this angle. Note the double-bubble scoops for the coolant radiators, borrowed from the North American P-51. It would be interesting to know what effect of having the two radiators side by side had on drag.

September 1942 proposal was justifiably skeptical. Still, at that early date in the war there was really not a single U.S. fighter which could be considered a roaring success. The first Merlin-powered XP-51B Mustang was only just ready to fly; the P-47Bs were starting to equip the 56th Fighter Group, but there were lots of problems to be worked out; Bell's P-39s were proving to be disappointments as they were called on to perform roles for which they were not designed; it seemed that only the first Lockheed P-38Es were beginning to show promise. If the truth were known, the bulk of the fighter work was still being done by the valiant, but aging P-40.

So it is not altogether surprising that the contractor's formal proposal of October 7, 1942 received a go-ahead only three days later—not bad even for war time. Letter contract W535-AC-33692 was issued later in the same month.

The very first proposal called for P-51 outer panels in an inverted gull wing arrangement; P-40E windshield, sliding canopy, and instrument panel; and SBD (Douglas Dauntless) landing gear and tail surfaces. These were to be married to a rather portly new fuselage which carried the hush-hush double Allison V-3420 engine amidships, the twin, counter rotating propellers of which were driven by a pair of drive shafts running under the cockpit.

Colonel M. E. Gross of the Office of the Director of Military Requirements specified the following characteristics: top speed, 440 m.p.h. at 20,000 feet; 5,600 feet per minute initial rate of climb; 38,000 foot service ceiling, and a wing loading of only 35 pounds per square foot.

The Eagle would try hard, but it would never achieve these requirements.

Elated over the quick response to their proposal, the Fisher engineers were as optimistic on cost and schedule as they were on performance. The first aircraft was to roll out on April 10, 1943, and the second, ninety days later. The total price, including a five per cent fee, was to be $428,271.48; the Air Force could scarcely afford not to buy the airplane.

The first of the seemingly endless series of modifications occurred almost immediately. A straight wing, using P-40 outer panels, was substituted for the gull arrangement, and the SBD gear was dropped in favor of the huskier Vought F4U Corsair units. Two mock-up inspections held in March and May, 1943, resulted in a host of delay inducing changes.

That savvy old war horse, Major General Barney W. Giles, was already beginning to have reservations on the project. He knew that it was running late, and he strongly questioned the wisdom of developing a new aircraft and a new engine simultaneously. Brigadier General F. O. Carroll, Chief of the Engineering Division at Wright Field, was well experienced in the hazards of aircraft development, and had probably never really expected the original promises to be kept. He knew that all new projects had delays built in, and that the Fisher program probably had more than most. First of all, the XP-75 required more than its share of government furnished equipment, a continuing source of dis-

This excellent view of the lower surfaces of a production Fisher P-75A shows how the "double-bubble" radiator housing appeared, as well as the Curtiss-style retractable landing gear. This is perhaps the best view of the Eagle. *Robert F. Dorr*

appointment and frustration then and now. In addition, he felt that the Fisher organization was not experienced in aircraft work, and its geographic separation (engineering organization largely in Detroit, and construction in Cleveland) was bound to work against the program. However Carroll felt that the Eagle per se had sufficient promise to be continued, for there was a new requirement looming on the horizon.

By early 1942, reports from every theater of war emphasized the need for greater range in both fighters and light bombers. In June 1943, General Arnold himself specified that an escort fighter *had* to be built; for by January 1944, all bombers leaving the United Kingdom for Germany would have fighter escort. (Given the circumstances, no one can be blamed for not foreseeing the amazing success to be achieved by the Air Force "Fighter Airplane Range Extension Program" which would give undreamed of legs to the P-51.)

On June 6, 1943, there was a conference in General Oliver P. Echols' office with top Air Force personnel and the Fisher brass, including Berlin and E. F. Fisher himself. It was decided that the XP-75 would be modified to meet the escort fighter requirement by adding internal wing tanks. The old letter contract was modified into a new cost-plus fixed-fee contract for eight experimental aircraft. More important, it was decided to order 2,500 production versions; this go-ahead would enable Fisher to order materials, establish a subcontractor network and build the required organization.

Fisher, once again optimistic, said that production deliveries would begin in May, 1944, and reach 250 per month by October—the firm was just unable to refrain from using its automotive time scales in estimating the aviation program. On the minutes of the meeting, a more sober, even ominous note was penciled in by Hap Arnold. He wrote "The entire production of P-75s depends upon performance of the 1st article. If it does not meet our requirements, all orders may be cancelled. Everyone must understand this."

The first and most apparent result of the new decisions was that the original $400K plus contract was going to be vastly exceeded. A formal cost-plus fixed-fee contract, W 535-AC-33692 was approved in October 1943 for eight XP-75s at a total cost of $2,836,271.00. This had to be bumped by $1,539,772.40 early the following year, because the estimates had been far too low. The production contract for 2,500 planes was set at $325,000,000, a tidy sum even for General Motors. When the fixed-price contract W 535-AC-41011 was negotiated, however, the estimated price was reduced to $258,966,750.

At a time when the laminar flow wing was becoming accepted practice, the crude fairings on the XP-75's wing are strangely out of place. The distinctively weird canopy shape shows up well here.

Fisher immediately moved to acquire the production facilities they had been planning on, the Fisher Body-Cleveland Plant No. 2, also known as Government-owned Aircraft Plant No. 7. This 320-acre giant had been committed to B-29 production, and it was necessary to make an agreement on July 24, 1943 to terminate some B-26 production at the Martin-Omaha plant to permit transfer of the B-29 production from Cleveland. This was to have later political repercussions.

Wright Field's Engineering Division followed the XP-75 project closely, reporting the status of each major sub assembly directly to General Echols. Despite the fact that by August 5, 1943, only fourteen of the big new -3420 Allison engines had been produced, it was felt that the program was generally on schedule.

The aircraft's center-mounted engine is revealed in the exhaust stacks on the upper surface and the side. The SBD tail seems both too small and too frail. *Robert F. Dorr*

The Engine—Double Trouble

Perhaps the chanciest element in the entire Eagle project was the twenty-four cylinder Allison engine. A huge 3,175 pound mill with a 5.50″ bore and a 6.00″ stroke, the engine was made up by assembling the power sections of two V-1710 engines onto one crankcase, maintaining an included angle of 30 degrees between the inboard banks of the two sections. The two power sections, down to and including the geared-together crankshafts, were interchangeable with standard V-1710 engines. The six throw, seven bearing, counter-balanced crankshafts rotated in opposite directions, and transmitted power through two counter-rotating drive shafts to a set of reduction gears in the nose. To construct it, P-39 experience was called on extensively.

A gear-driven, two-stage supercharger provided the necessary boost at altitude. Takeoff power at rated (3,000) rpm was 2,600, while normal rated engine power at sea level at 2,600 rpm was 2,100 hp.

The Aeroproducts propeller consisted of two three-bladed, constant speed, contra-rotating units, each with its own hydraulic system for pitch changes. The first twelve airplanes had 13 foot diameter props, while later examples were fitted with one of 12′7″ diameter.

An upper view shows the multiple exhaust ports for the Allison V-3420-19 engine. It was housed amidships and had one exhaust port for each three cylinders.

Considering the Germans' near disastrous experience in the Heinkel 177 with the Daimler Benz DB-606 (essentially the same idea, two DB-601 engines coupled side by side—see *Wings,* August '72) the Allison product fared comparatively well. It had its problems—intercooler difficulties, vibration, carburetion, mixture settings, etc.—but in general the engine performed well. It did not, however, develop the power expected of it early in the program and, of course, the jet engine had cast an ominous shadow across its future.

Aircraft Construction Details

There was a considerable change in aircraft configuration from the first XP-75 to the last production P-75A, but the internal construction details remained largely the same. The wing was a full cantilever type, using a stressed skin construction consisting of a straight center section and two five spar P-40 outer wing panels. Airfoils at the root and tip were NACA 2215 and 2209, respectively. The 49'4" span (in all but the first aircraft) had 347 square feet of area, and featured huge split trailing edge flaps, which were fully 27 feet 5 inches long. The ailerons, which were extensively studied and modified, but never fully satisfactory, were originally standard P-40 type, but were later lengthened and changed in shape.

The fuselage was of conventional 24 ST aluminum alloy, semi-monocoque construction and was built in three main sub sections. The forward and aft sections were bolted to the center wing section, which carried the engine and its principal accessories. As with most high powered aircraft, induction was a tremendous problem, one that was never fully solved in the XP-75.

The airplane perhaps appears best in a head-on view, where its wide-track landing gear can be appreciated. It had to be easy to land, or at least to taxi!

The original concept of using existing components was materially diluted when it became apparent that the original A-24 tail surfaces were inadequate both aerodynamically and structurally, and that a bubble vision canopy would be more desirable than the rather curious first approach to the problem. Still, the parts continued to flow together, and soon it was time for the Eagle to get airborne.

Equipment, Armament and Fuel Loads

While the P-75 never received the full complement of equipment standard for an operational aircraft, it was tested extensively with a variety of different gear. A type N-6 gun camera was installed in the leading edge of the right wing, just outboard of the center section splice. In the cockpit, a type N-9 gun sight was fitted.

Radio gear included an MN-26C radio compass, BC-1206A marker beacon, and SCR-522A command radio set.

Fuel load and range could be varied widely by alternate combinations of gasoline and armament. The "normal" mission called for a gross weight of 13,543 pounds, with 1,260 pounds of fuel and four .50 caliber nose guns, each with 300 rounds of ammunition. Maximum range for this configuration was 1,130 miles.

With maximum fuselage fuel of 435 gallons and the same armament, gross weight went up to 14,972 pounds, and range was increased to 2,240 miles.

Maximum internal fuel plus 203 gallons in wing tanks, boosted weight to 16,190 pounds and range to a lengthy 3,180 miles. An additional six .50 caliber wing guns, with 235 rounds each, could be added, boosting gross weight to 17,217 pounds, and reducing range to 3,010 miles.

The maximum gross weight condition called for all ten guns, 3,828 pounds of internal fuel, and 1,424 pounds of external tanks and fuel. Thus laden, the Eagle was supposed to stagger off at 18,665 pounds, and fly for 3,850 miles, a very creditable capability.

First Flight

The first aircraft, 43-46950, flew on 17 November, 1943, piloted by famous racer Russell Thaw. His comments were generally favorable, tempered only by some cautious

The contra-rotating propellers show up to good advantage in this shot; they would often give trouble over the life of the aircraft.

As the development of the aircraft progressed, it moved steadily away from the original concept of using components from other aircraft to using components designed for it exclusively. With the move came delays and rising costs. Nonetheless, the production P-75A was a relatively good-looking aircraft, with vertical surfaces in reasonable proportion, and a bubble canopy.

remarks on the stability under conditions of yaw. The airplane was flown intensively, and the fourth flight, on 24 November, was made by a possibly more objective pilot, Colonel Ernest J. Warburton. Warburton reported that stability and control forces in the XP-75 were flatly unsuitable for a fighter. Taxi and take-off characteristics were good, and the aircraft, with its huge 19′11⁵/₈″ tread, was easy to land. The problem was that it was also too easy to fly—control forces were heavy and the huge fighter did not respond as it should. Overall performance was below expectations, probably because carburetor heat was excessive throughout the flight. Stalling characteristics were not poor, as has been previously reported, but instead were rather good.

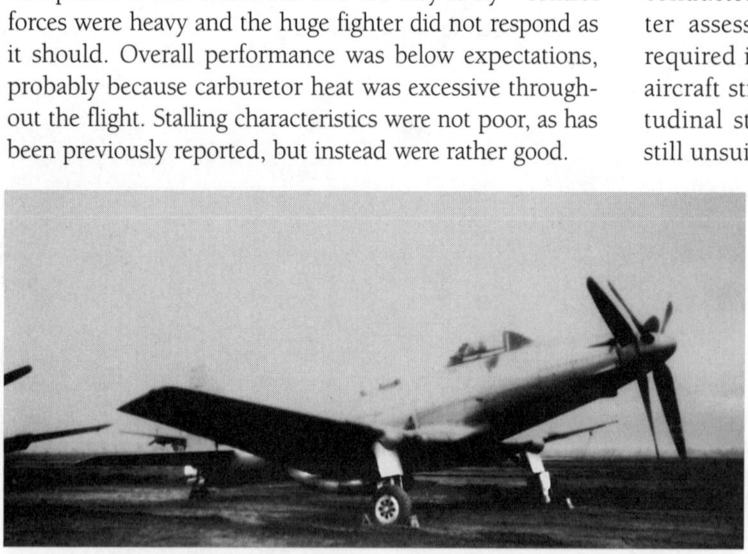
The one area that was not troublesome in the Fisher Eagle was the complex drive shaft connecting the engines to the propellers. For some reason, they worked well.

The main problem centered around lateral control. The aileron forces were too heavy, and apparently the ailerons themselves were somehow not adequate, and could not be harmonized with the general control characteristics of the plane.

Fisher immediately set to work with a host of design improvements, some of them major. The tail surfaces were to be revamped, ailerons extended to the wing tips, aileron booster controls installed, dive recovery flaps added, nose lengthened to improve c.g. (for which an embarrassingly incorrect calculation had been made) and cooling system drastically reworked.

The impact on design effort and production tooling can be imagined, and a wave of pessimism enveloped the Wright Field engineers. The basic premise of the original concept—the use of readily available existing components—was already hopelessly lost, and the future value of the continually changing hybrid was questionable.

Eagle

As usual, the most immediate solution for improving performance was to call for an immediate attainment of an increase in horsepower. On November 25th, a little over a week after the first flight, General Echols sent a memo to the Materiel Division demanding that the full potential 3,000 horsepower of the V-3420 be available for the P-75's official performance tests.

By April 6, 1944, sufficient flight tests had been conducted on the second XP-75 (43-46951) to get a better assessment of the Eagle's worth. Almost all the required improvements had been made to 951, but the aircraft still did not perform up to expectations. Longitudinal stability was unsatisfactory, the ailerons were still unsuitable, engine cooling was still inadequate, the propeller was throwing oil, and a decent speed could not be coaxed from the aircraft. On July 26th, the third XP-75 (44-32161) had obtained a speed of 420 m.p.h. at 22,000 feet at an estimated 2,200 b.h.p.; rate of climb, however, was only 3,000 f.p.m., compared to the original 5,600 f.p.m. requirement.

The status of the program was not enhanced when, on April 8, 1944, the fifth aircraft (44-32163) was destroyed and its pilot killed after some low-level acrobatics which reportedly exceeded the placarded limitations.

The cumulative effect of the poor test results and the accident threw the entire program further into jeopardy. In an

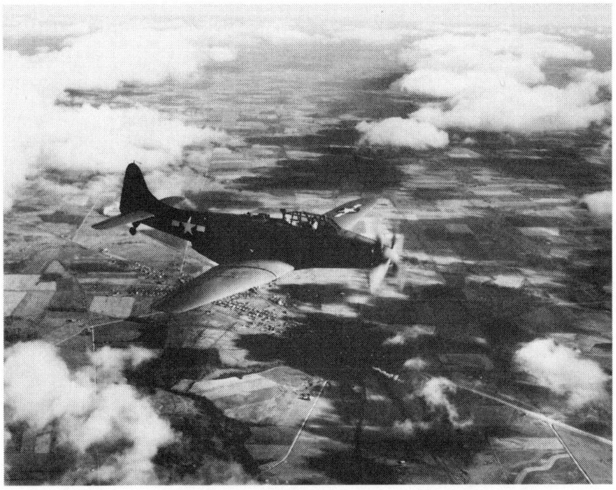

In flight, the Fisher Eagle looked like a world-beater. Unfortunately, it did not do much flying. *Robert F. Dorr*

attempt to counter the generally negative attitude that had grown at Wright Field, Colonel J. F. Phillips, Chief of the Materiel Division, advised the Development Engineering Branch in Washington that most of the objections to the Eagle were subjective and not supportable, and that the aircraft was probably no further behind its test objectives than any other similar type. He felt that the plane had promise, and that production plans should be accelerated.

Unfortunately a whole series of unrelated events combined to cast a further pall over the program. Major General B. E. Meyers, Deputy Assistant Chief of Air Staff, Materiel, Maintenance and Distribution, submitted an analysis on May 8, 1944, which called for immediate reductions in production of certain aircraft to avoid "abnormal excesses" of aircraft beyond forecast Air Force and Lend Lease requirements. The U.S. was cutting back. In a little less than three years, the giant American industrial machine had grown from a small, custom-built base to a position where it had to avoid producing too many planes! Meyers listed the P-75 as a possible candidate for the axe, requesting that a close examination be made of the requirement for the Eagle after tactical suitability tests had been conducted at Eglin. General Arnold approved Meyers' recommendation.

Next, the War Production Board expressed misgivings as to the availability of manpower in the Cleveland area to achieve a

This, the fourth production aircraft, was sent to Wright Field for storage. You can see an example of the P-75 in the Air Force Museum at Wright-Patterson Air Force Base.

250 aircraft production rate for the Eagle, even if it was ordered into production.

Then a disgruntled Fisher employee wrote letters to the Truman committee, the F.B.I., General Arnold and others, charging Fisher with "colossal fraud against the government". A thorough investigation failed to substantiate the alleged irregularities, but the harm had been done, with both public and government confidence shaken.

Almost in conformance with the otherwise uniformly bad publicity, the tests at Eglin were not proceeding favorably, primarily as a result of the continuing failure of the engine to put out the required horsepower.

As a final straw, the third XP-75, 44-32161, crashed on August 5, 1944, after an explosion and fire at 23,000 feet, the pilot bailing out at 4,000 feet.

Despite a growing list of miscalculation and acci-

By the time all the fixes were in—better propeller setup, bubble canopy, new vertical surfaces—the airplane looked pretty good, but there was no longer a requirement for it. The Mustang was doing everything it could do and more. *Robert F. Dorr*

From this rear view, the aircraft is now somewhat reminiscent of the much-later Westland Wyvern. Close to $50 million had been spent, and the result was a production run of six aircraft, with the sixth never made flyable. Only in America, and only in wartime!

dents, Fisher pressed on, and the first production P-75A (44-4549) flew on September 15, 1944. Colonel Phillips passed the bad news to General Echols on performance—top speed was 404 m.p.h. at 32,000 feet, and 2,300 h.p. Rate of climb at sea level was 2,400 f.p.m. The plane was immediately sent to Eglin, where it flew seven flights before a landing gear failure put it temporarily out of commission.

By now, time had run out for the Eagle. The Aircraft Requirements Board met on October 3, and recommended that no more than thirty P-75As be produced. Two reasons were given. First, the testing of the P-75 had not been satisfactory, and second, the P-47H and P-51H both seemed to be better aircraft. They were proven, available, and both would have the capability to serve in the escort fighter role. As an anticlimax, the first P-75A crashed on October 10th. The propellers apparently lost oil, and Major Bolster, the pilot, attempted a dead stick landing back to Eglin. It crashed on the approach, and Bolster was killed.

An analysis of Fisher assets revealed that five production aircraft could be put into flying condition with little additional work. Fisher quoted $6,000,000 for the job, however, and it was decided to acquire them "as is" and let the Air Force do the work. On 27 October, a letter was sent to Fisher cancelling all but six of the 2,500 production aircraft.

Of these six, the first had already crashed, and the second (44-4550) was flown to Moffett Field for wind tunnel tests. The third (44-4551) was provided to Allison on a no-cost bailment contract for ten hours of flight testing. The fourth (44-44552) and fifth (44-44553) planes were sent to Wright Field for storage, for possible use if interest in the engine should be revived. The sixth aircraft (44-44554) was never made flyable, and was to have been a spare parts bird.

There is little doubt that with sufficient time and testing, the P-75 could have been developed into a serviceable war plane. Unfortunately, the $9,099,073.06 spent on the experimental contract and the $40,930,010.45 spent on the production contract did not buy the United States very much in terms of airpower. The basic idea was unsound, as many engineers knew intuitively that it would be. Don Berlin would have been unquestionably better off if he had designed an entirely new airplane, one whose lines, proportions and details would have reflected his usual harmonious genius. Yet the need at the time was great, and a nation newly involved in a war cannot be expected to always make the best choice. In retrospect, it was fortunate that the United States could develop its Mustangs and Thunderbolts at the same time it discovered that its Eagle would not fly.

Data Sheet
Fisher P-75A (XP-75 in parentheses)
Wing Span: 49′4″ (No. 1 XP-75—49′1″)
Length: 41′4″ (No. 1 41′6″, others 40′5″)
Height: 15′6″
Wing Area: 347 sq. ft. (No. 1 342 sq. ft.)
Weight Empty: 11,255 lbs. (11,495)
Maximum Gross Wt: 19,420 lbs.
Max. Speed: 404 mph @ 32,000 ft.
(Mfr. estimate: 433 @ 20,000)
Cruise Speed: 250 mph
Service Ceiling: 36,400′
Maximum Ferry Range: 3,850 miles
Serials:
XP-75
43-46950*
43-46951*
44-32161 to 32166

P-75A
44-44549 to 44554

*Assembled in Detroit; remainder built at Cleveland Plant

22 Return of the Swallow

The Messerschmitt Me 262

Wings April, 1980

Few myths are so persistent as the one in which Adolf Hitler is blamed for the late arrival of the Messerschmitt Me 262 on the combat scene. Many writers, including me, have for years demonstrated that it was Germany's failure to properly develop jet engines that was the cause of the delay. Despite this, scarcely a month goes by without someone proclaiming Adolf's guilt about the aircraft. Adolf made plenty of other mistakes—he doesn't need to be blamed for this one.

Working on the Me 262 article was a pleasure, because it enabled me to interview some of the legendary figures of World War II aviation in Germany, including Adolf Galland, Waldemar Voigt, and many others. I put a lot of time and effort into the article and into my book Messerschmitt Me 262: Arrow to the Future *(Smithsonian Press, 1980); at the time of publication the book was probably as good as anything that had been done on the subject to that date. However, in recent years the popularity of the Me 262 has brought forth a host of books, many of them exhaustively researched, and these present substantial new information that was unavailable to me at the time. Perhaps the most significant of these are the four volumes by J. Richard Smith and Eddie Creek, who know more about the 262 than Willy Messerschmitt ever did! (Airtime, 1999)*

The Messerschmitt Me 262 was the world's first operational jet fighter; it was also the most advanced fighter aircraft of World War II. It had everything: good looks, tremendous performance, heavy firepower, easy maintainability, overwhelming pilot approval, but although 1,443 were built, and perhaps 300 reached com-

The first jet aircraft to fly successfully was this Heinkel He 178, flown by Erich Warsitz on August 14, 1939. The engine had been designed by a dear friend of the author, the late and greatly missed Hans von Ohain. The He 178 was just a technology demonstrator, but it served to pique the curiosity of the Luftwaffe about jet aircraft.

After an agonizingly long development process, delayed by the difficulties in creating a reliable jet engine, the first Me 262 emerged with conventional landing gear. The tail-down attitude caused problems with the runway surface being burned and with long-takeoff rolls.

This is the first aircraft to have the hydraulically operated, fully retractable tricycle landing gear. It was this aircraft that test pilot Gerd Lindner demonstrated to Adolf Hitler at Insterburg on November 26, 1943.

bat, the Me 262 was never a significant problem for the Allies.

The lack of impact by the arrow shaped fighter has been obscured for many years by a series of myths, the most pervasive of which was that only Hitler's obdurate stupidity prevented the Me 262 from entering service in 1943 and sweeping the Allied bomber forces from the skies.

Actually, Hitler's interest in the program helped, far more than harmed, it. And it is very possible that the notorious *Fuhrerbefehl* (Fuhrer's decree), that the Me 262 be employed only as a bomber, may have been, in great part, the result of overzealous sycophancy on the part of his Nazi toadies.

The basic facts of the matter are these: The Me 262 could not have entered combat much earlier than it did because the Junkers Jumo 004 engines which powered it were not available earlier. When it did enter combat, it was not as effective as might have been expected because the Luftwaffe's impoverished leadership was unable to devise effective tactics for it. Finally, it entered production on the relatively large scale that it did because Hitler had expressed interest in the aircraft, and Albert Speer, his Minister for Armament, gave the program the necessary priority.

None of this detracts a whit from the aircraft's reputation; it was an engineering masterpiece, a truly giant leap forward in aircraft design which ultimately affected concepts of aerial combat for at least the next three decades.

It was incredible that the Me 262 was able to reach combat at all, given the most hysterical state of Nazi politics during the last two years of war, and given the unbelievable ferocity with which Allied air power savaged the German homeland day and night.

Producing a modern jet fighter is a difficult task under peacetime conditions, even when you are not pioneering by constructing the first of its kind. Imagine what it must have been for Messerschmitt, with the British bombing the workers at home every night and the Americans coming by day to plaster factories with deadly precision; with machine tools always in short supply, and with materials that were not only short in quantity but sometimes disastrously poor in quality. Jigs and special tools were scarce to unavailable; transportation of sub-assemblies was difficult, due to marauding Allied *Jabos* (Jagdbomber fighter bombers) that considered a push cart a target of opportunity. Even when, by dint of unrelenting effort, twelve hour shifts and continuous innovation, a completed Me 262 was finally towed out the factory door, it would probably be shot up by a freelancing Mustang within a few hours.

Labor shortages were continually worsening; it was almost impossible to obtain engineers, and many of the assembly line workers were foreigners from occupied countries whose fondest hope was the final destruction of the Third Reich, and whose work had to be constantly supervised.

Add to this the constant flow of orders, counter orders, changes in mission and so on, and you have a completely deplorable set of circumstances. Even worse was the utterly wretched state of morale. Every thinking person knew that the war was lost, that the Nazis were an abomination for Germany, that the best they could hope for was occupation by the West instead of by the Russians. And yet in this worst of times, one of aviation's crown jewels, this supreme masterpiece of World War II flying, the Messerschmitt Me 262, was not only designed, built and introduced into combat, but was the subject for numerous proposals for modification which would have extended its primacy for years.

The success of this ill-starred program, whether we like to admit it or not, was due to the German technician, who with characteristic skill and industry labored to produce the best weapons possible under the circumstances. Common to the engineers who conceived the aircraft, to the factory workers who built them, to the "blackbirds" (ground crews, so named because of their black workers coveralls) who maintained them, and certainly to the pilots who flew them, there was a curious pride which said to all: "No matter that the war is lost, nor even that the cause is not a good one—we can still make better airplanes than anyone".

Development History

The history of the Me 262 parallels the history of the jet engine, which was being developed simultaneously in many countries in the world, including England, Sweden, Hungary, Russia and Italy. The principles of the turbine engine had been understood for years, but, for the most part, designers had correctly assumed that the jet engine would not really be required until aircraft speeds of about 500 mph were necessary, and incorrectly assumed that jet engines would weigh about the same as piston engines.

Flight Officer Frank Whittle, in England, and physicist Hans von Ohain in Germany, felt differently. Both agreed that the jet engine would be efficient at speeds slower than 500 mph, and both perceived that the jet engine could not only be much lighter, but, after development, much more reliable than the piston engine. (See *Airpower,* July 1978) The difference in weight was extremely important, for it was an offset to the increased fuel consumption of the jet. The weight and space necessary for a piston engine and its attendant liquid cooling accessories could be converted to tankage for the fuel gobbling jets.

The basic layout of the Me 262—swept back wings and engines placed in pods suspended on the wing—set the format for jet planes to this day.

Ohain sold Ernst Heinkel on his concept of a jet engine in 1937, and began development work on a hydrogen powered test engine to prove his ideas. Heinkel was relatively easy to sell, for he was fascinated by speed, which the jet promised, and he was desperately anxious to set up his own engine manufacturing facility, so that he could sell aircraft powered by his own engines, as Curtiss had done in the U.S., Bristol had done in England and Junkers was doing in Germany. The jet engine offered easy access to the new industry, for it didn't require the heavy casting machinery, foundries, and so on that piston engine manufacture did.

Heinkel had a jet plane designed for the HeS-03, von Ohain's first flight engine, and on August 14, 1939, Erich Warsitz took off from Marienehe airfield in the Heinkel He 178, for the world's first jet flight.

The Luftwaffe took note of the event which coincided with a burgeoning interest within the German Air Ministry in jet engines as a long range development option for the future. Within the operational side of the Luftwaffe, however, there was relatively little interest, primarily because the problems of meeting Hitler's constant demand for expansion kept them entirely occupied elsewhere.

In order to spur interest in the field of jet aviation, the Air Ministry set up complementary programs for the development of engines and airframes. In October, 1938, the Messerschmitt firm was invited to begin studies for a fighter capable of 528 mph, (850 kmh), with an endurance of one hour. This became Project 1065 at Messerschmitt and led directly to the Me 262.

Both single and twin engine concepts were pursued, but it soon became apparent that a single engine fighter could not meet the performance demands, while a twin engine fighter might exceed them. Accordingly there emerged a straight wing, all metal fighter with a conventional tail dragger landing gear, its engines buried in the wing roots.

Luftwaffe training was hurried, because of the war, and varied with the degree of experience of the pilots. Some were given a day or two of classroom instruction and then turned loose. Single-engine fighter pilots were given some time in a multi-engine type aircraft, such as the Bf 110, before trying the 262. Bomber pilots, accustomed to flying at 220 mph, had trouble handling the speed of the Me 262.

Airframe development was easier than engine development, and the original BMW 003 engines intended for the 262 encountered tremendous problems almost from the outset. Fortunately for the Me 262, a dedicated 39 year old engineer, Dr. Anselm Franz, had begun work at Junkers on a comparatively straightforward axial flow engine, the Junkers Jumo 004. It would save the program.

As in any air force, it was the enlisted men who worked hard keeping the aircraft airborne. (Enlisted *men* is politically and historically correct—the Germans did not use women as line mechanics.) Called "blackbirds" because of their black fatigues, ground crew members preferred working on the 262 as opposed to a piston-engine aircraft—it was easier to repair.

(Dr. Franz, who went on to a distinguished postwar career with AVCO, lives in retirement in Connecticut and is an absolutely delightful gentleman of the old school, with a perfect memory and an engaging manner of story telling.)

The relative ease of airframe design permitted Messerschmitt to accommodate the endless changes in engine development. First the BMW engine experienced a growth in size which ruled out the use of wing roots for engine installation; next the design was revised so that engines were located in mid-wing nacelles not unlike those planned for the later English Electric Canberra. But the increased size and weight of the BMW engines gave the Messerschmitt Me 262 center of gravity problems. The twin solutions were to house the engines in sleek underwing nacelles (which would also make any further engine changes easier to cope with) and to counter the center of gravity problem by sweeping the outer panels of the wings back 18½ degrees.

Even though it was more advanced than the BMW engine in its development, the Junkers Jumo 004 continued to have teething problems, and Messerschmitt decided to gain test data on the first Me 262 airframe (Me 262 VI PC + UA) by installing a Junkers Jumo 210G twelve cylinder piston engine of about 750 horsepower. *Flugkapitan* Fritz Wendel made the first flight on April 18, 1942, and despite the long take-off run, natural for the underpowered fighter, the aircraft flew quite well. It was capable of 260 mph in level flight and was a perfectly suitable test vehicle for the airframe.

BMW finally delivered flight-rated engines in late 1941, and these were fitted on the number one Me 262; but the piston engine was retained as insurance. This proved to be remarkable foresight, for when Wendel tried a tri-motor take off on March 25, 1942, both jet engines flamed out, and it was only the piston engine, straining against the drag of the two inoperative jets, that dragged the Me 262 around the field for a safe landing.

This setback removed the BMW engines from the 262 program for all practical purposes, and the following flight trials were conducted with pre-production Junkers Jumo 004A engines rated at 1,850 pounds thrust, fitted to the third prototype Me 262 V3 (PC + UC). Touchy as these early, almost hand made, engines were, Wendel made a successful take-off and landing on July 18, 1942, the first pure flight of a Me 262.

Wendel's first flight filled him with enthusiasm, for despite some drawbacks, it was evident that the twin jet fighter offered potential performance beyond any piston engine aircraft's capability.

The most immediate problem for the designers, was the conventional tail dragger arrangement, which not only permitted the jet engines to blow great chunks out of hard surface areas, but also resulted in the elevators being blanked out during take-off. Wendel had to apply brakes at about 100 mph, just below unstick speed, literally interrupting the take off roll, so that the aircraft would tip forward and allow the elevators to "bite", and while he had the piloting skill to do it, it was not something you could live with in the field.

To overcome this, a fixed tricycle gear was fitted to Me 262 V5 (PC + UE) and the first pre-production aircraft, Me 262 V6 (VI + AA) had a hydraulically operated, fully retractable gear.

Wendel also discovered during flight that the inboard sections of the wings, which had not been swept, caused severe turbulence in banking flight. Therefore, it was decided to extend the leading edge sweep across the inboard section, and the result was the classic swept wing which not only foreshadowed the future, but which also proved to have tremendous aerodynamic values as well.

Generalleutnant Adolf Galland flew the aircraft on May 22, 1943, and enthusiastically endorsed it. The number six aircraft, VI + AA, was demonstrated to Hitler and Goering on November 26, 1943.

A story has grown up that Hitler immediately ordered that the Me 262 should be built only as a "blitzbomber", and not a fighter, nor even a fighter bomber. Yet there is evidence to support the fact that he intended only that the

As the Allied Air Forces relentlessly bombed the German aircraft factories, desperate measures were taken to maintain production, including moving production lines into the forest. It was incredible—the most advanced aircraft on earth were being manufactured in the most primitive aircraft factory.

Production continued under the primitive system, but as might be expected with such a factory using foreign workers, quality fell off and most of the Messerschmitt Me 262s built never saw combat.

Officially, the Me 262 was called the *Schwalbe* (Swallow), but *Sturmvogel* (Stormbird) was the name Adolf Hitler preferred. Most pilots called it the "Turbo."

aircraft be used in a dual role, fighter bomber and fighter, which was perfectly reasonable. A letter, classified "Secret" at the time, from Dr. Ludwig Bolkow (of postwar Bolkow-Messerschmitt-Blohm fame) to Brigadefuhrer von Shultz-Tratzig indicated in its attachments that the notorious *"Fuhrerbefehl"* had been totally misinterpreted and that Hitler never intended that action should be taken to build the aircraft as a bomber only.

Irrespective of the intent or the validity of the *Fuhrerbefehl,* Hitler had helped the program more than he had harmed it, for his interest in it had led Albert Speer, the Minister for Armaments, to devote the necessary manpower and materials to the program in late 1943. If this had not happened, both material and manpower would have been used in other German aircraft programs, and the Messerschmitt Me 262 would probably never have become operational.

While the overall effect of Hitler's order was perhaps not great, the immediate effect was dramatic. Messerschmitt was plunged into a serious development effort to determine how bombs could be carried and dropped effectively, and by October, 1944, 239 of the first 337 planes delivered had been completed as Me 262A-2a *Sturmvogel* (Stormbird) fighter bombers. In November, production shifted to exclusively Me 262A-1a *Schwalbe* (Swallow) fighters.

This division of the limited production capability into fighters and bombers had other effects as well. Two separate training programs had to be set up, for the performance of the Me 262 in either fighter or bomber role was so advanced that pilots had learned new tactics.

Unfortunately for the Germans, the Third Reich had become a land of make-shift, improvisation and do-without. Instead of the normal Luftwaffe method of thoroughly testing an aircraft, and then delivering a limited quantity to a service test unit for work-up prior to acceptance of production aircraft by operational squadrons, the exigencies of war forced the shipment of pre-production aircraft directly to units for pilot training and the development of tactics.

A fighter school, of sorts, was set up in Lechfeld, and the test detachment (Erprobungskommando 262) under *Hauptman* Thierfelder undertook operational sorties against high flying Allied reconnaissance aircraft.

Similarly, a special *Kommando Schenck* was set up to develop bomber tactics, and to make pin-prick attacks against the invading forces in France.

The amount of training a German pilot received in the 262 varied widely; at best it was a two-week, ten hour course in which he got to practice take-offs and landings, a few limited acrobatics, a cross country trip and some gun-firing passes at a ground target. Many pilots received less—a walk-around in the morning, a solo flight in the afternoon, and an operational mission the next day. But one must remember that only the best veterans were posted to the Me 262 and all of these men were highly experienced.

It was not that flying the Me 262 was so difficult—when all was going well it was actually easier to fly than the Bf 109—the real problem was adopting tactics which would permit the jets to bring the maximum weight of fire to bear on the Allied bombers without exposing them to attack from the escorting Mustangs and Thunderbolts. This problem was never solved, and the postwar memoirs of Galland, Joseph "Mackey" Steinhoff and others clearly reveal that they were still experimenting, still trying to find a way to use the Me 262's flashing speed more effectively.

The training difficulty resulted from the general deterioration of the war situation. By October 1944, when the brilliant Major Walter Nowotny reformed the remnants of *Erprobungskommando* 262 into *Kommando Nowotny,* the 1000 year Reich had shrunk to almost its prewar size and German training bases were under constant attack from marauding Allied fighters.

The archives are filled with bitter memoranda from both Messerschmitt and service personnel decrying the misuses of the aircraft and demanding better training and tactics. Even *Kommando Nowotny,* which became JG 7, and the even more famous *Jagdverband* 44 of Adolf Galland, the "Squadron of Aces", had only limited success.

Oddly enough, as the war degenerated for the Germans, the quality of pilots and quantity of machines available to the few Me 262 formations rose. The best pilots were ordered to JG 7 and JV 44 in the closing months of the war, simply because there was nowhere else to send them, and no other planes to fly.

In the field, the Messerschmitt Me 262 was well liked by both pilots and mechanics. Contrary to some reports, it required less maintenance than most of the contemporary German aircraft, and a well run unit usually had a high serviceability rate, given the conditions and the times. The Junkers Jumo 004 engines had only a 25 hour life expectation, and often achieved less than that, but this was only to be expected considering that the engine had been frozen for production in June 1944, long before its designer, Franz, considered it ready. (Gerd Lindner, famous 262 test pilot reported that late in the war, an engine was inspected after 25 hours, and if it was in good shape, was cleared to run for 25 hours more. He himself achieved a record of 70 hours on an engine, but admitted that he had nursed it carefully.)

The biggest anomaly of the Me 262 program was not the late production start, nor even the use of the fighter as a bomber, but the fact that the Luftwaffe required Messerschmitt to simultaneously pursue a whole host of experimental efforts, just as if it were peace time. Thus while the production lines suffered from a lack of manpower, parts, drawings, jigs and tools, the advanced design teams toyed with a dozen different concepts which could not have been brought to service in less than two to three years. One was the rocket boosted Me 262 *Heimatschutzer* (Home Protector) which had a Walter rocket motor mounted in the aft fuselage that provided it with a thrilling, but distinctly risky climb rate of more than 9,000 feet per minute. Another idea whose time wasn't right was the use of towed bombs or fuel tanks, the *Deichselschlepp,* which envisioned an aircraft taking off towing a tank or a bomb to which V-1 buzz bomb type wings had been affixed. (Waldemar Voigt, who was chief of Preliminary Design, maintains that the towed bombs failed because the center of gravity was too far forward, resulting in the towed vehicle pressing down on the tow-bar junction, causing porpoising.)

There were other far out projects including one aircraft built with a 35 degree wing sweep (it never flew, being destroyed by a landing aircraft), four aircraft fitted with a mammoth 50 mm cannon; the big gun worked, but it had a slow rate of fire and belched great clouds of smoke; and several high speed and recce versions, some of which featured wing-root buried engines, three crew members, *Schrage-Musik* cannon installations and so on. In addition to all of these type variations, numerous equipment changes were proposed including the installation of a pressurized cockpit, ejection seat, windshield wipers, and so on.

The pressures of war also forced the rapid development of even less orthodox but more effective means of increasing the 262's lethality. Perhaps the most dramatic was the installation under each wing of wooden racks for launching twelve R4M rockets. These 55 mm rockets weighed a little over eight pounds and carried just over one pound of explosive. They proved to be extremely effective and had the war lasted a little longer, and had more *Schwalbes* been introduced into conflict, they might have given the bomber formations a very rough time.

Similarly, a two seat trainer (the Me 262B-1a) evolved into a night fighter (Me 262B-1a/UI), and both proved to be very successful, even though built in small numbers.

Neither the innovative planning for aircraft which would never be built, nor the brave and sometimes sacrificial use of the airplane in combat made any difference in the long run, for in Germany's lost war no single weapon could stem the tide on either front.

Performance and Handling

The *Schwalbe* had a top speed of 540 mph at about 20,000 feet, easily 120 mph faster than the Mustang. Even more impressive, perhaps, it was 60 mph faster than the British jet, the Gloster Meteor, which turned in 483 mph at 30,000 feet.

Initial climb rate was not too spectacular for the time, approaching 4,000 feet per minute, but the difference over piston engine aircraft was that the *Schwalbe* could sustain a high rate of climb at altitude, being capable of close to 1,100 feet per minute at 29,000 feet.

The range of the aircraft varied with its load, and with the altitude and airspeed at which it was flown, but with a full gross weight, and clean, it could fly as far as 650 miles at about 30,000 feet. At lower levels, fuel consumption went up drastically and range was much reduced.

Gerd Lindner reported in a June 1945 interrogation that a perfectly functioning Me 262 could achieve 565 mph at 16,400 feet, but that there was as much as 25 mph variation between individual aircraft. Service ceiling was around 33,000 feet, although the absolute ceiling was higher. German pilots tended to limit their ceiling because of the difficulty encountered with the sensitive jet engines at altitude.

In a normal, full gross weight take off, a fifty foot obstacle could be cleared with a run of about 3300 feet; with two 500 kg bombs, the distance increased to about 5700 feet, but a 1000 pound rocket to assist take-off reduced this to about 2200 feet.

Both German and Allied pilots agree that the Me 262 handled very well. It had very good stalling characteristics, the excellent stall warning coming in the form of heavy elevator buffet, with a maximum loss of only 100 feet altitude for all configurations tested.

Aileron controls became very heavy as speed built up and Messerschmitt introduced a simple "quick fix" which increased the length of the control column and hence its leverage. The *Schwalbe* was never intended to be a dog fighter, and smart pilots used hit and run tactics which took advantage of the heavy fire power and speed. If a German pilot, through combativeness or inexperience, tried to dog fight with a section of attacking Mustangs, he was bound to lose.

Landing approaches had to be made with some caution as the axial flow jets were slow to accelerate and prone to compresser stall if the throttles were not handled carefully. If a little excess rpm was carried on the approach, however, a go-around could be made as easily as in a piston-engine fighter.

The principal advantage of the new jet fighter was not so much its speed as the confidence it restored to its pilots. The German pilots who flew the airplane report that it gave them pride again, and the feeling that they once more were invincible. Generalmajor Erich Hohagen, a 57 victory ace called it "the absolute fulfillment of a flying career". Another pilot, Generalmajor Walter Windisch termed it "life insurance", for it took him out of the cockpit of a Me 109, where he was the hunted, and made him a hunter again.

The source of this confidence, of course, was the *Schwalbe's* blistering speed, which enabled it to engage in or break off combat at will. Unfortunately for the Luftwaffe, however, the skies over Germany were so crowded with aggressive Allied fighters that a Me 262 could inadvertently flee from one disadvantageous situation only to find itself directly embroiled in another.

The Me 262s were most vulnerable during take-offs and landings, and the Allies tried to maintain standing combat air patrols over known 262 airfields. The Germans responded to this, first by providing piston engine fighters to cover the fields, and then by building "flak alleys" on the approaches to the airport; these literally blanketed the sky with an explosive canopy under which the jets could land or takeoff safely.

The early months of 1945 saw the Me 262 units reach their greatest strength, with formations of as many as twenty-four or thirty-six aircraft engaging the countless Allied formations. In Joseph Goebbels' diaries for the period he notes these attacks with some satisfaction, even though he is recording at the same time that the Allies were launching two *thousand* heavy bombers and three *thousand* fighters in a single day's operations. Against this avalanche, even two hundred Me 262s could not have done much.

The end came swiftly in 1945 and as the war closed the Schwalbes were spotted around the airfield of a dying Germany, unable to participate in combat because of the lack of pilots and fuel. Forest assembly lines were clogged with partially completed aircraft, and the whole vast network of dispersed industrial sites came to a complete breakdown for lack of ground transport.

Both the U.S.A.A.F. and the R.A.F. hurried in to round up flyable examples of the latest Luftwaffe equipment. The U.S. effort, codenamed "Operation Lusty", was headed by Colonel (later Major General) Harold E. Watson, and it succeeded in rounding up ten Me 262s plus a host of other fascinating aircraft including Arado Ar 234s, Heinkel He 162s, Dornier Do 335s, a Heinkel He 177, and even a gigantic four engine Junkers Ju 290, the famed "Alles Kaput" (All is Lost!).

Watson's team was immensely successful, and his scourings were taken to the United States for test. Preliminary trials, essentially post-maintenance shake-down flights, were undertaken at Freeman Field, Indiana, with more rigorous tests being done at Wright Field, Ohio and (to a lesser degree) at Muroc Dry Lake, California. The Navy also conducted test work at NAS Patuxent in Maryland.

After the test work was completed, many of the captured aircraft were scrapped. Most of the rest were sent to Park Ridge, Illinois for storage and eventual display in what was to become the National Air & Space Museum. A full accounting was never made of all of the aircraft, and, almost overnight wonderful examples from both Germany and Japan simply disappeared, probably disposed of as a base was closed, or as part of a scrap drive, or simply on the whim of some unthinking person who had a directive that required the expropriation of the storage site of "some old German wreck".

Technical Details

The Me 262 was a low wing, all metal, semi-monocoque jet fighter characterized by its swept back wings and underslung Junkers Jumo 004 engines.

Not unnaturally, the jet fighter followed traditional Messerschmitt practice, but there was tremendous effort placed on making it suitable for mass production at small sites ranging over an area that spread from Stuttgart to Linz in northern Austria, and from Nurnberg south into the Bavarian Alps. Subassemblies were made in caves, in tunnels off the Autobahn, clearings in forests, homes, small buildings and so on. Many assembly lines consisted of just a small steel building with one pair of rails for conveying and an overhead crane. In the end, as metal became scarce, even the rails were replaced by a corduroy road of small trees, cut and trimmed to serve as rollers.

Under construction west of Munich, near Landsberg, was a semi-subterranean vault, 270 feet wide by 900 feet long with an arched roof, which was to have been covered with earth and trees. This vast chamber was to have contained half a dozen sub floors and was to have produced Me 262s from start to finish. The roof would have been impervious to any existing bombs. Jigs and machine tools had been moved in, although the excavation under the poured concrete was yet far from complete. (Does this structure still exist? Has it been converted to some peacetime use?)

Despite all the talk that Hitler destroyed the Me 262 program by demanding that the aircraft be built as a bomber, most were built as fighters. This is the Me 262A-1a fighter version.

Ludwig "Willie" Hoffman, a former Messerschmitt test pilot, helped train the American pilots who arrived as a part of Operation Lusty. The pilots, who called themselves "Watson's Whizzers," were personally picked by Colonel Harold E. Watson to spirit the new jets back to the United States.

The end of a German forest production line, and the end of the line in general. The aircraft were built from components shipped in from all over Germany.

Fuselage

The fuselage was broken down into five sub-assemblies, the nose cone, armament and nose wheel section, forward fuel tank and cockpit section, rear fuel tanks and radio section, and empennage section.

The fuselage stringers were heavy gauge hat sections riveted with one row of rivets, and spaced twelve inches

Here are "Watson's Whizzers" who carefully broke the propellers off their standard U.S. Army Air Forces uniform lapel insignia. In this photo compare Colonel Watson's insignia (he is third from left) with the others. Pictured from the left: First Lieutenant James K. Holt, Captain Robert J. Anspach, Colonel Watson, First Lieutenant William V. Haynes, Captain Kenneth E. Dahlstrom, First Lieutenant Roy W. Brown, First Lieutenant Robert Strobell, and Captain Fred L. Hillis. These men would get a brief orientation, and if they were lucky, a flight in a two-seat Me 262. Then they were on their own, with the task of flying the new jet to a pickup point.

The *Schwalbe* was fitted with a 50 mm cannon, at least partly at Hitler's insistence. Hitler was a big gun fan, on tanks and in airplanes.

Another view of the 50 mm Mauser MK 214 A cannon. The cannon installation was said not to impair the Me 262's performance very much. Only one round could be fired at a time. Note name *"Wilma Jeanne"* painted on the aircraft by the exuberant American captors.

Repair work was done in the German hangars to prepare the captured aircraft for the flight to the port where they were to be shipped home.

While not so advanced as the bubble canopy on the Mustang or the later model Thunderbolt, the Me 262's canopy did provide relatively good visibility, especially when compared to the Bf 109.

The aircraft were cocooned and shipped home for testing and evaluation, and after that, for an uncertain fate.

apart on the fuselage side. The cockpit was a separate entity (the "*fuhrerraum*") designed for eventual pressurization and simply inserted in the metal fuselage opening like a cork into a bottle.

Construction was mixed duraluminum and steel, which resulted in corrosion problems during the postwar period of storage, but which was the most economic solution for the Germans at the time. All through the aircraft it is evident that the primary consideration was given to ease of manufacture and assembly, at the expense of weight saving and even smoothness of fit. If the Me 262 had been built according to American standards, it probably would have been several hundred pounds lighter, but it would also have required more than the 12,000 man hours that it took the Germans to complete the aircraft. (The German design aim was 6,000 man hours, but this couldn't be achieved because of the shortage of tools and jigs. Much handwork had to be done on the Me 262 at all stages of its production and for the whole period of its manufacture.)

Among the other aircraft shipped were the Arado Ar 234 and other choice examples of the latest in German technology.

Here is Colonel Watson at Freeman Field, Indiana, where many of the German airplanes were tested. He is putting on a high-speed, low-pass demonstration flight that left onlookers convinced that the 262 was the wave of the future.

Wing

The "accidental" sweeping back of the wing to correct a c.g. problem caused by a growth in engine size and weight has already been described. The resultant sweep

My good friend, Dr. Guido Mutke, flew four years of missions in the Bf 110 before transitioning to the Me 262. On his final mission, he became lost and landed this one in Switzerland, where it remained for many years. Later it was returned to Germany and may now be seen in the fine Deutsches Museum in Munich. Mutke still visits it there. He convincingly maintains that, in another Me 262, he actually exceeded the speed of sound in a dive.

offered aerodynamic improvements by delaying the onset of compressibility and raising the critical Mach of the Me 262 to a respectable .86. (For comparison, the postwar Republic F-84 had a limiting Mach of .82, and the rocket powered Me 163 had a limiting Mach of .83.) Even though the theoretical advantages of sweepback had been known since the middle 1930s, it took the flight success of the Me 262 to convince engineers all over the world of its critical importance.

The airfoil section of the Me 262 was not laminar flow for two reasons. First, Germany no longer possessed the time, manufacturing skill and quality of materials to produce a laminar flow wing, and second, the use of sweepback and slots mitigated against the use of a laminar flow section. The full span slots, which derived from Messerschmitt's patent exchanges with Handley Page before the war, operated automatically, as in the Me 109.

The wing was built up with two spars, although it was for years considered to be a single spar wing. The second spar was a small member near the trailing edge. The main spar used steel cap strips, and the wing had heavy, actually overdimensioned aluminum skin for strength, varying from 3 mm thickness at the root to 1 mm thickness at the tip. Made in two halves, the wing was joined together by steel plates and heavy bolts, before assembly with the fuselage.

The fuselage attachment is typically Messerschmitt; a 20 mm bolt in single shear at the forward end of the wing is very accurately fitted, and positions the wing to the fuselage. A similar bolt near the rear spar has a much looser fit, making assembly easier. Additional smaller bolts reinforce these main attachments, and most of these had to be individually fitted to the aircraft by reaming, as there was no jig available, yet, to permit jig drilling of the parts.

The wing also had hydraulically operated flaps, run on internal tracks, and actuated by a single hydraulic cylinder in the right wing and a system of bell cranks and push rods.

Empennage

The tail group was of conventional construction, except a great deal of thought had been given to the ease of assembly and maintenance. The horizontal stabilizer was adjustable by means of a commercially available geared electric screw actuating strut, and this feature was greatly liked by the pilots, who could trim the aircraft very precisely with it.

All control surfaces, including ailerons, had tabs built in for trimming, but only the rudder tab could be operated in flight, a few turns being enough to compensate for asymmetrical forces if an engine failed.

Engines

The Junkers Jumo 004B engines had a static thrust of about 1970 pounds, and weighed only about 1670 pounds. Somewhat difficult to start, and very sensitive to throttle movements at low rpm, the powerplant was, nevertheless, very satisfactory when one considers that

After testing, some Me 262s were simply junked or used as landfill. A sad sight.

Howard Hughes obtained an Me 262 and cleaned it up with the intention of racing it and of establishing some speed records in it. The aircraft was beautifully finished, far better than any German production aircraft, but the USAAC did not want records set by an enemy aircraft, and no attempts were made. The other airplane in the photo is his Sikorsky S-43 that he once intended to use for a world flight, but subsequently crashed in.

For a while, Me 262s were popular exhibits at post-war celebrations on military bases. Then they began to deteriorate and were left for junk or assigned to museums.

The Junkers Jumo 004 engine designed by Anselm Franz was the heart of the Me 262. Production models of the engine had a lifespan of only about 25 hours, but they were rapidly improved, and by the end of the war, 100-hour engines were beginning to come off the production line. It sounds laughable today, when commercial jet engines run without problems for thousands of hours, but then everything was new!

it was introduced into production long before its designer thought it was ready, that it was built of rather inferior materials by Western standards, and that the skilled labor necessary to build and maintain it was usually not available.

Once started and brought to full rpm, it ran well and its lack of vibration and noise was almost disquieting to the pilots. Had it been allowed an adequate development time, it would have been truly outstanding. Even so, its advanced features set the stage for many later engines, for it was the first axial flow type to go into mass production, the first jet engine to engage in combat, and the first to be capable of using an afterburner.

Maximum rpm was 8,700, while idle was 3,080. It consumed fuel at a prodigious 2750 pounds per hour rate, at max. power. The starting drill was immensely complicated, and was often interrupted by a flash engine fire. The starting motor was a 10 horsepower, two cylinder Reidel gasoline engine, not unlike an outboard motor. This could be pull-started like a lawn mower by tugging on a lanyard housed in the nose cone of the engine if the regular electrical starter failed.

Standard fuel was an evil smelling synthetic coal derivative, termed J-2; but the engine would also run on a variety of other mixtures, including diesel fuel.

The National Air & Space Museum restored its Me 262 at the renowned Garber Facility. This is a "before and after" comparison of the cockpit area.

Landing Gear

The tricycle landing gear was hydraulically operated by a rather slow acting 18 liter per minute pump; it was planned to install a second pump in the aircraft to speed up the sequence. The undercarriage was the aircraft's weakest point, accounting for 34% of all accidents. Unlike most aircraft of the time, the main gear members were made up from drawn seamless steel tubing, and while this was excellent from a production standpoint, it was not strong enough for field conditions.

The brakes were unsatisfactory by American standards, being inadequate in size and too quick to overheat and fade. The expander type brakes were operated from the rudder pedals for the respective mainwheels, and by a car-type handbrake for the nose wheel.

Armament

After lagging behind Allied standards for most of the war in weight of metal thrown, the Germans caught up with a vengeance with the Me 262. The standard armament of four MK 108 30 mm cannon, after some initial difficulties, proved to be a potent combination, and when this was supplemented by the 24 R4M rockets carried under the wing, the *Schwalbe* became extremely formidable. There were other weapon combinations tried, including a six cannon package on the A-1a/UI and the *Schrage Musik* installation on the B-2a, but these were only variations on a theme. The biggest, a 50 mm cannon, actually 5.5 centimeters, installed experimentally on four aircraft worked well enough, and paralleled Hitler's ideas of big cannons on tanks, but the war was too far along for any real development of several Rhinemetall cannon of this size.

The *Sturmvogel's* basic bombload was either a single 1100 lb bomb or two 550 lb bombs, although there were experiments with other stores.

Restoration

The Me 262 had long been a popular attraction for visitors at Silver Hill, for even in its spurious markings, and somewhat the worse for wear after years of storage, it was still an attractive aircraft. The master craftsmen who do the restoration work were delighted when they learned that the Schwalbe was going to be restored, even though they knew that the bimetallic construction used in the aircraft was bound to have created severe corrosion problems.

Part of the adventure and challenge of restoring an aircraft at Silver Hill is watching the detective work that goes on to determine exactly what the original markings were, what the serial number was, what unit operated it, and, if possible, which pilot flew it. The Museum's aircraft proved to be a mystery, for there was no clear cut "werke number" (constructor's serial) in evidence, nor did any records indicate what it might have been.

The careful hand sanding by Mike Lyons, a skilled craftsman and master model builder revealed full details on the original paint scheme and markings, but did not uncover the werke number. Because the number 500491 was found in each engine nacelle, and had also been found in the nose wheel door, and was a logical sequence for the aircraft, it was tentatively adopted as the werke number.

Similarly the pilot's identity was hinted at by the markings of the aircraft, which showed that it belonged to II Staffel, JG 7, and by the individual 42 victory insignia located on the aft section of the fuselage. Working with the German Embassy and with the German Society of Fighter Pilots, it appears that the plane might have been flown by *Feldwebel* Heinz Arnold, a 42 victory ace who was reportedly killed on April 15, 1945.

Before sanding or any other work is done at Silver Hill, however, a complete restoration package is made up which details what work is to be done, how it is to be done, what parts are missing and, most important for this aircraft, what the final configuration will be.

Like most of the Museum's collection of former enemy aircraft from World War II, the Me 262 had undergone a number of changes from the time it left the German production line as a standard Me 262A-1b *Schwalbe* fighter. First of all, it had received a series of non-standard coats of paints and markings, and second, it had been given a complete "nose job" at Freeman Field after the war.

The Air Force had made a decision to test the Me 262 against the Lockheed P-80 in carefully calibrated performance trials. There were several aircraft to choose from, and the well known Messerschmitt Me 262A-2, werke number 111 711 and FE 4012, and an Me 262 A-1a/U3, were selected. The first aircraft, 711, was one which the ex-Messerschmitt test pilot, Hans Fay, was to surrender to the Allies on March 30, 1945. It was the first Me 262 to fall into American hands, and it was extensively photographed. It flew for twelve flights for a total of ten hours and forty minutes flying time before it crashed on August 20, 1946. Lt. Walter J. McAuley bailed out after an engine failure and the plane crashed near Xenia, Ohio.

FE 4012 was one of the aircraft brought back by Watson's Whizzers, and, except for its photo recce nose, was deemed to be in the best condition for test. Someone made a decision to swap its nose section with that of FE 111, a rel-

The entire cockpit was built as a "bathtub" sub-assembly and plunked in on the production line. Clever manufacturing technique!

Views of the completed masterpiece.

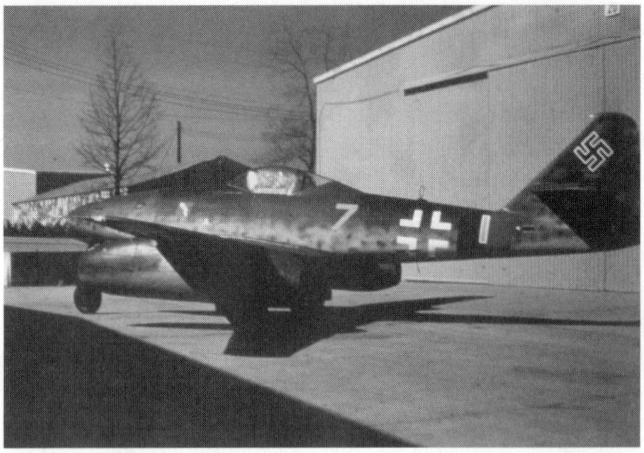

atively easy task as the accompanying photos indicate. The newly nosed FE 4012 then flew four hours and 40 min. in the comparative test program with the Lockheed P-80A.

After 711 went in, and FE 4012 had made two single engine landings, it was decided to stop the test program. The test results showed, however, that the Me 262 despite a 2000 pound weight disadvantage, was superior to the average P-80 in acceleration and speed, and approximately equal in climb performance. The handling characteristics were poor, but German tests had indicated that this came primarily from the poor fit and contouring of the Me 262's fin and rudder, which caused handling difficulties at high speeds.

FE 4012 was then sent to Hughes Aircraft for a complete rebuild and subsequent testing at Edwards Air Force Base. Howard Hughes reportedly expressed some interest in the aircraft, either for a film ("Jet Pilot"), or for a speed record attempt. In any event it went first to a now defunct ground school, and then to Ed Maloney.

There were two schools of thought at Silver Hill on the restoration configuration. One felt that since the nose was original, even if it belonged to another aircraft, it should be preserved. Others felt that since the majority of the Me 262s had been fighters and that this aircraft had started life as a fighter, it should be reconfigured as a fighter. A decision was made to modify the aircraft back to fighter standard, for the present owner of FE

Another brilliant example of German wartime technology, the Arado Ar 234 was the world's first operational jet bomber.

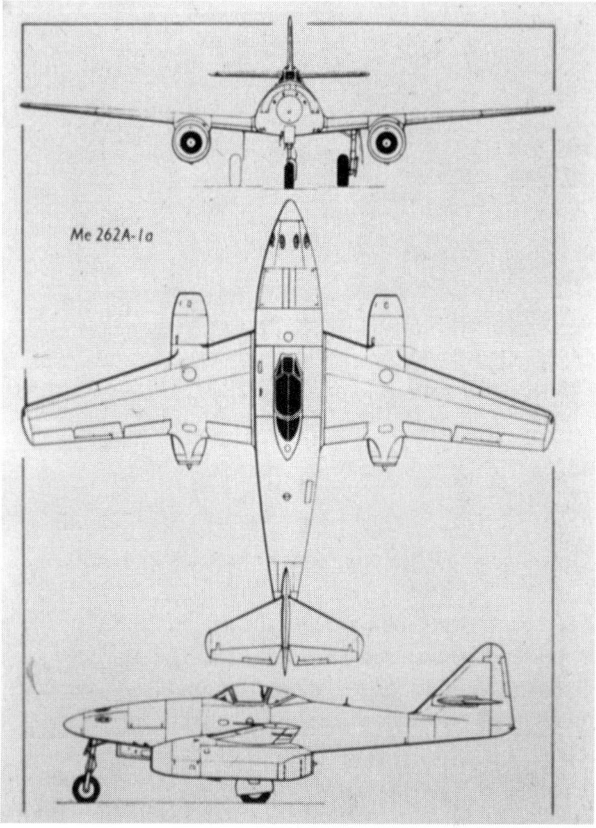

A three-view drawing of the 262.

4012, had, quite understandably, declined to trade noses back.

Disassembly of the airplane revealed that corrosion was far worse than had been feared. Even though the plane had been in indoor storage for most of its life, the electrolytic corrosion in the bimetallic areas was extensive.

Typically, the Silver Hill workers turned to with a will; Mike Lyons constructed a plastic tent over the fuselage, armed himself with a respirator and an air gun that spewed ground walnut shells and spent ten days removing corrosion from the inside of the fuselage.

Bill Stevenson and Bob Padgett constructed a jig which kept the wing aligned as they removed alternate skin panels by drilling out the old rivets. They arrested the corrosion, applied preservatives, and reinstalled the panels, then went back and repeated the process on the panels that had been left in place. It was an arduous, time consuming, knuckle busting delicate task, and perhaps most curious of all, one that won't be repeated for perhaps a hundred years, when it may be necessary to again inspect for corrosion. Knowing the work of Bill and Bob, I suspect that none will be found.

The reconstruction of the nose involved both tremendous corrosion control efforts, and the fabrication of a host of new parts. When the airplane was being made in Germany, the aluminum and steel parts used in fabricating the nose had been turned out in mass by machinery which shaped the hat sections, channels and so on. None of this material or the machinery which made it remains, of course, so it was up to Silver Hill craftsmen to reproduce it by hand. George Genotti, an intelligent, articulate man who can make anything from delicate springs to massive machined parts, patiently built the male and female dies from which the formed aluminum parts could be coaxed with repeated blows from a mallet.

Some of the sheet metal was missing, so Dale Bucy used modern techniques to reproduce it. An upper section of the left nacelle, a complex piece with lots of compound curves, was no longer with the airplane. Dale took photos of the matching right nacelle part, reversed the negative, blew it up, and made a pattern, from which he handformed the missing part.

This sort of creative, innovative craftsmanship was used wherever a part was missing or needed repair. Close attention was paid to applying the correct preservatives to avoid corrosion in the future. Wherever steel and aluminum came together, epoxy was applied to prevent electrolysis, even though the airplane will probably never again experience inadequate storage conditions.

As noted before, life was not easy when the 262s were rolling down the production line, and the aircraft was designed to accommodate to both poorly fitting parts and inexperienced labor. The German wartime equivalent of

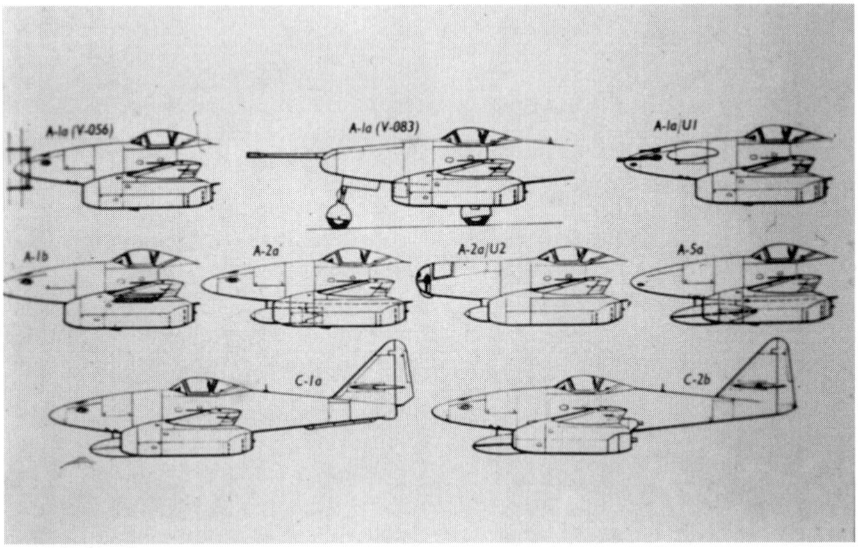

Drawings show the progressive changes in the 262's design.

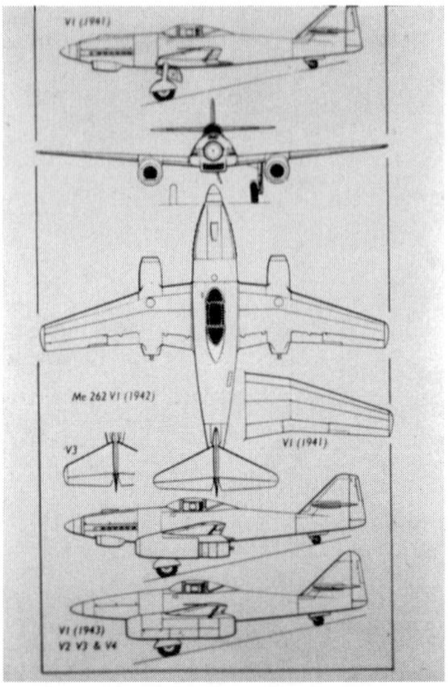

Early versions of the Me 262.

body putty and tape were liberally used to fill in gaps, low spots, seal seams and so on. Add to this the inevitable hangar rash that a stored aircraft accumulates over thirty years and you'll recognize the task that Silver Hill people had.

One of the most rewarding aspects of the restoration is how, after months of effort in which seemingly nothing happens, the aircraft suddenly starts to "come together". When all the corrosion control and metal work had been completed, and all of the supplementary work like the painstaking detailing of the cockpit interior, the building up of the engines, the patient rejuvenation of the misshapen tires has been done, it becomes evident that you have an airplane, and not just a miscellaneous collection of parts. The long hours of sanding, filling, resanding and priming are over, and it is time for finish work.

Due to material shortages, the nose gear of the Me 262 was manufactured of less than the highest-quality steel, and frequent failures resulted.

The markings of the aircraft had been uncovered from the many layers of postwar paint by Mike Lyons' intricate, tedious, and delicate hand sanding. A fanatic about quality, and about the Me 262 in particular, Mike patiently hand sanded away all of the multiple layers of non-standard paint to reveal the markings, insignia and camouflage pattern of the aircraft as it had flown during its operational life.

After Mike sanded the aircraft, he then took "pounce paper", a light translucent material not unlike a dress maker's pattern paper, and applied it over each one of the markings. These were then copied meticulously by hand, their general position on the aircraft identified by certain rivet patterns, seams, etc. The pounce papers were then laid away until it was time to finish the aircraft, when they were brought out and copied carefully so that the aircraft's appearance would be as it was in April 1945.

The markings Mike uncovered revealed the Schwalbe to be plane 7 of Staffel II, Gruppe III of Jagdgeschwader 7 (III./JG7), and that the camouflage pattern was somewhat unusual in its outline and colors. Curator of Aircraft, Robert C. Mikesh, made his customary astute analysis of the colors and came up with the nearest available equivalents to Luftwaffe standards.

The final result was a remarkably beautiful aircraft in pristine condition, which will be the absolute star of the soon to be opened Gallery of Jet Aviation in the National Air & Space Museum. It is a fitting tribute to a great aircraft and an even greater restoration.

23 ATTACK!

The XB-51, Martin's Phantom Strike Ship

Airpower July, 1978

It is tough publishing a magazine every month, and tougher still to think up titles for the articles. But this is one title that I would have changed if given the chance, for there was nothing "phantom-like" about the XB-51. It was a good, solid airplane with fine flying characteristics that would have become a useful part of the USAF if a little more development had been allowed. The argument is often made that the Canberra's range and loiter time gave it the advantage in Air Force thinking, but neither I nor many of the Martin engineers who worked on the airplane will ever be convinced that Glenn L. Martin's political problems were not the real reason that the XB-51 did not enter production.

This article was, for many years, about as comprehensive a history as one could find of the XB-51, for I had the opportunity to talk to many of the men who designed it and some who flew it. In 1998, however, Scott Libis wrote a monograph for Ginter Books called The Martin XB-51, *and it has more photos and more information than I was able to provide at the time. It's a great buy.*

This photograph tells more about the Glenn L. Martin Company than it does about the aircraft, despite the XB-51's striking appearance. It is roll-out day—September 4, 1949—and there is no one there to celebrate. A few workers take part, but where are the crowds, the dignitaries? Boeing would never have rolled out a new warplane with so little fanfare. *Scott Libis*

The Martin XB-51 was a fast, effective airplane that met every requirement for which it was designed, incorporated dozens of advanced features, was loved by its pilots, had one of the most trouble free test programs on record—but was rejected by the U.S. Air Force for reasons that seemed doubtful at the time and which have become even more suspect over the years. Looking back over nearly 30 years, sifting test data and reports, I believe that it was a truly great aircraft, one that should have been put in production. That it was not, was due solely to political pressure.

That is a pretty bald statement, one that would be very difficult to prove; yet it reflects not only my own bias, but the results of years of frustrating research. It also represents the beliefs of a large number of people who were deeply involved in the program, and whose opinions must be respected because of their stature in the field. The ultimate choice of the English Electric Canberra as a light bomber for the USAF has been well documented in Bob Mikesh's three part story on the B-57 (See *Wings* Aug. & Oct. 1977 and *Airpower* Sept. 1977). In it he relates how a change in Air Force requirements led to a competition in which the Canberra was selected as a type for Martin to build. I believe that the decision not to buy the XB-51 was made long before this competition, before the requirements were changed, and after the Martin aircraft was well along in a highly successful test program.

The fact that the Canberra ultimately did a fine job does not detract one bit from the XB-51. However, there are other managerial and production considerations which indicate that the cost to Martin and to the Air Force of choosing the foreign product may have been far greater than could have been imagined when the go ahead decision on the Canberra was made.

Years of delving into formerly classified files at the National Archives, the Air University at Maxwell Air

This airplane was loaded with innovations, including three General Electric J47 jets, variable incidence wings, snug canopy, "T" tail and rotary bomb bay. It should have grabbed headlines all around the world. *Scott Libis*

Like all early jet engines, the J47s churned out a smoke trail. The XB-51 had a remarkable takeoff performance and a 5,100-foot-per-minute climb rate, sensational for the day. Martin's famous Middle River plant is in the background. Famous Martin test pilot O. E. "Pat" Tibbs was at the controls of the 34-minute first flight on October 28, 1949, only 18 months after the contract had been signed. *Scott Libis*

Force Base, the Air Force Museum and the National Air & Space Museum have revealed a situation peculiar to the XB-51 when compared to the XB-42, XB-43, XB-45, XB-46, XB-47, XB-52 and a host of other aircraft of the period, and that is that the material is simply not there on the XB-51. It was and remains a ghost plane, faintly outlined in the records.

The histories of the other bombers are well detailed, and there is much contemporary correspondence on everything from contract changes to ground orders. In the case of the XB-51 there is very little, and much of what is found is usually innocuous stuff, not the meaty day-to-day decisions which make reading the other files so fascinating.

There are a number of possible explanations. One is that all of the material relating to the XB-51 was pulled together for some purpose—a report to the Congress, for example—and then either deliberately or accidentally lost. Another is that some person or persons, for private motives (either to conceal or to expose something) gathered the material and then either disposed of it, or retained it. Another alternative—that the material never existed—is implausible, for it is inconceivable that the vast DOD paper work machine would have somehow skipped over an amazing and important machine like the XB-51.

My own gut feeling, based not only on facts, but also on intuition and inferences I've made interviewing advocates of the program, is that the Air Force was continuing to "punish" Martin for both its troublesome management

Note that the third engine in the tail has a fairing over the entry. The tip gear do not quite reach the ground, but they could under heavy load. Two crewmen were carried. *Scott Libis*

behaviour during World War II, and for the more recent political activities of its famous founder and chief executive, Glenn L. Martin himself.

The World War II difficulties included not only Martin's reluctance to introduce changes into the B-26 Marauder, changes which ultimately converted the plane from "widow-maker" to workhorse, but from the company's real failure to brace up to the later manufacturing effort required to build Northrop's XB-35 "Flying Wing", when it had been selected for production over the Martin XB-33 "Super Marauder".

After the war, still smarting not only from criticism but from some pretty healthy contractual costs, the great Glenn L. Martin apparently decided to cast his primary fortunes first with the U.S. Navy, his historic bread and butter client, and then with commercial aviation. He did not do badly with the former, but his 202 and 404 aircraft were financial disasters. Furthermore, as a result of his Navy bias, Martin took a stand against the Air Force in a number of situations, but most notably in the carrier versus B-36 controversy, and he cost his company dearly. General Hoyt Vandenburg, Chief of Staff of the Air Force, was reported to have vowed that "Martin would never build another airplane of its own design for the Air Force".

This article is not an expose, nor does it suggest that other aircraft and other manufacturers have not experienced similar problems with other Air Forces, including our own. The point is, however, that personalities—Martin's, Vandenburg's and others—were allowed to cloud the picture, and the country lost a fine aircraft that many believe could have been employed profitably and proficiently as late as the Viet Nam war. But much more important than that, the country lost the potential services of Martin's well balanced, innovative management and engineering team forever, as far as building aircraft was concerned. Disheartened by the XB-51 and the XP6M cancellations, the grand old Martin company soon shut down its military aircraft development programs. Its engineering personnel drifted to other firms or into Martin's missile and space activities, and an era which had begun with the Glenn Martin Bomber, soared with the MB-1 and the B-10s, and served brilliantly with the Maryland, Baltimore and Marauder types, quietly and sadly came to an end.

Test Pilot Comments

When you want to find out the true facts about an airplane there is no better source than the *retired* test pilots who flew it. I stipulate retired, because you remove the natural reluctance of an active pilot to knock a product, either his own company's or a competitor's. But a retired test pilot has lived through a lot, and generally says exactly what he thinks. His opinion is valuable, not only for his engineering and flying expertise, but because his thousands of hours in hundreds of types give him a basis for judgement.

O.E. "Pat" Tibbs was Martin's chief test pilot for many years and made the first flights in many Martin aircraft. Russ Schleeh retired from the USAF as a Colonel after ten years of experimental test flying at the Flight Test Division located at Wright Patterson Air Force Base and ten years with the Strategic Air Command. Guy Townsend, Brigadier General, USAF (Retired), now works for Boeing but was a brilliant test pilot who did most of the flying on the XB-47.

These three men, top professionals in their field, are absolutely unanimous in their praise for the XB-51. Each was interviewed separately, without prior knowledge of his colleague's remarks, and their comments were almost identical. Schleeh said the XB-51 was one of the finest preproduction airplanes he had flown. Townsend said it was the best prototype he'd ever flown. Tibbs commented, as did the others, that it had the most trouble-free test program of any airplane he'd ever flown, and that the biggest mistake the Air Force ever made was not putting it in production.

Townsend recalls that the big 85-foot long, 53-foot wing span, twenty-five ton airplane was only one or two knots slower than contemporary F-86 fighters, and that its speed and agility made it very difficult to fly chase on.

Schleeh stated that the XB-51 was a delight to fly. Take-off characteristics were similar to take-off characteristics of all bicycle-type landing gear aircraft with the exception that lateral control was greater on the XB-51 at all speeds (especially very high and very low speeds) because of the highly effective lateral spoiler system. The elevators on the XB-51 appeared to have more power while the aircraft was still on the runway and within 10% of take-off speed than the elevators of other bicycle-type landing gear aircraft. The pilot didn't have to be too concerned about the aircraft once the brakes were released as direction was maintained with the nose-wheel steering control connected to the rudder pedals, and wings-level attitude was easy to maintain during the take-off roll. The aircraft became airborne from the two-point position with ease. Gear retraction was fast, and climb-out was comparable to the climb-out of a jet fighter of that time period.

The B-47 was similar to the XB-51 in take-off and landing characteristics and was also a very enjoyable airplane to fly, but the ailerons on the B-47 were not as effective as the spoilers on the XB-51. Consequently, it was more difficult to keep the wings level during the ground roll in gusty crosswind conditions. Since the larger B-47 had an engine located close to each wingtip and more mass had to be overcome, the lateral response of the B-47 was also slower than that of the XB-51.

Another factor which made the B-47 slightly more difficult to land was the design of the high-lift, low-drag flap system which necessitated the use of a drag chute as well as a brake chute. The two chutes helped the B-47 decelerate and gain positive ground control.

The most outstanding feature of the XB-51 during maneuvering flight was the lateral control system which permitted high rates of roll and made the aircraft a joy to fly. Performing aileron rolls was comfortable at any altitude.

Landing technique was similar to that of other bicycle-type landing gear aircraft; a normal approach was established and touchdown was made either on the two main gears or on the aft gear first, either being acceptable and comfortable. The deceleration was quite good due to the high drag in the landing configuration. A brake chute was also deployed once the aircraft was on the ground, and very little braking was generally required. In addition, the XB-51 had a most effective Westinghouse air-brake, anti-skid system which allowed it to stop in a very short distance.

The engines on the XB-51 were located close to the centerline; therefore, during an engine-out condition, little asymmetric trim was required. With the No. 2 (middle) engine inoperative and the inlet door closed and streamlined, the XB-51 was still a high performance airplane. As a matter of fact, the No. 2 engine-out condition was noticeable only in take-off or climb.

Schleeh's love for and mastery of the XB-51 was demonstrated a number of times, but never more convincingly than on his first flight. Ralph Draut, the Project Engineer, recalls that Schleeh climbed in the airplane, took-off, and disappeared over the horizon. A few minutes later there was a thundering noise, and the XB-51 roared back over the field at low altitude doing a series of impeccable aileron rolls.

On another occasion, Schleeh was at the Glenn L. Martin Field in Baltimore when he received a message from Tactical Air Command Headquarters specifying a bomb-load configuration to be carried to Langley to demonstrate the reaction time.

Before arrival at Langley, the tower granted approval for a high-speed, low-level pass. As the XB-51 reached the boundary of the field at 600 mph, Schleeh opened the patented, revolving bomb door, which exposed the bombs, and at mid-field pulled up in an Immelmann turn. Upon reaching the inverted position at approximately 10,000 feet, his pleasure with the maneuver was cut short by a terse voice on the radio saying, "The Commanding General directs you to close that bomb bay door immediately, get those *bombs* out of sight, and return to Baltimore!" Schleeh reported that he had the last words: "Yes, sir!"

Program History

In late 1944, the successful use of the new jet engine by the Germans in the Messerschmitt Me-262 and Arado AR-234 generated an immediate requirement for comparable USAAF aircraft, and a whole series of projects were set in train. The first American jet bomber, the Douglas XB-43, was a quickie conversion of the static test article of the piston engine XB-42 "Mixmaster." It was a successful airplane, but the Air Force decided that other projects had more promise. As the war was obviously in its last stages, it was decided to concentrate on a later generation of more efficient, specially designed jet aircraft.

A new competition resulted in some very advanced concepts. Convair fielded the radical XA-44, a three-jet aircraft with swept forward wings and a canard surface. It became the XB-53 during the welter of designation changes in the late 1940s, and was ultimately cancelled, its funds going into the XB-46. (See *Airpower* Sept. 1976.)

North American, which had become the "Sweetheart of the AAF" with its P-51s and B-25s, provided the four-jet B-45 "Tornado", which had a long, useful, but not spectacular service life. Curtiss offered the XA-43, which emerged through a series of budget jugglings and requirement changes as the four jet XF-87, the Blackhawk, and the last fighter from Curtiss. (See *Wings* Feb. 1975.) Martin proposed the XA-45 to the Air Material Command on April 1, 1946. It was a 70,000 pound, 525 mph airplane, carrying 8,000 pounds of bombs over a tactical radius of 800 miles. The XA-45 was to have a six man crew and be powered by two TG-110 turboprop engines and two I-40 turbo jets.

The Martin design was chosen over competing entries from Consolidated, Douglas, Curtiss and North American, but a few months later the Air Force changed its mind about what it really wanted. Martin was advised that

The XB-51 handled beautifully in the air. The first time the veteran Air Force test pilot Russ Schleeh flew the airplane, he took off, departed the area for a few minutes, then roared back over the field doing impeccable low-level rolls, demonstrating both his competence and his confidence in the experimental airplane. *Scott Libis*

although their design met or exceeded the original requirements, a smaller aircraft was now desired. As of January 31, 1947, they wanted a plane with a 640 mph top speed, a 500 mph cruise, able to carry a 4,000 pound bombload over a 600 mile radius of action.

1946 had been a bonanza year for American aircraft engineers as they assimilated captured German technology. By February, 1947, Martin was ready with an engineering proposal that met the new specifications. It weighed only 52,000 pounds, had a two man crew and was powered by three jet engines. It had a variable incidence swept wing, tall "T" tail, revolving bomb door, and was capable of dive or Shoran bombing. It packed a formidable nose armament, and incorporated a host of other modern features.

On September 13, 1947, Martin was directed to proceed with basic engineering and a mock-up. Work was done by Martin's novel New Design Section, headed by W.D. Van Zelm; R.K. Wentz was design engineer.

The important mock-up inspection was held during February 24–27, 1948, and on April 23 the Air Force directed Martin to proceed with Phase II design of what was unquestionably the most advanced bomber in the world, the XB-51.

Ralph H. Draut is a soft spoken, modest man now living in retirement in Florida. He was named Project Engineer and continued in this capacity for the life of the all too short program. Ralph speaks of the XB-51 program with both pleasure and regret, for he enjoyed it to the hilt, but feels, as so many do, that its cancellation was a great mistake. It was exhilarating at the time, however, for an extraordinary number of simultaneous studies were carried on, reflecting the advanced management concepts of both Martin and the Air Force.

Draut and his group correctly anticipated that "Dutch roll" problems were probable in such an advanced design, and the results of both theoretical analysis and wind tunnel studies were fed into the program from the outset. These had some immediate effects on configuration, and the empennage was moved aft by five feet, wing anhedral (reverse of dihedral) was increased from 3 degrees to 6 degrees, maximum wing incidence was decreased from 10 to 7½ degrees, and the flap and variable wing incidence mechanism had a load relieving device built in.

Even these relatively radical changes did not eliminate the Dutch roll problem, but it did reduce it to manageable proportions.

Martin had, unlike its old competitor, Curtiss, recognized that its management of prototype programs in World War II had been poor, and in the XB-48 program had drastically revamped and simplified its engineering organization. These improvements were carried over to the XB-51, with the result that there was a close harmony between engineering and manufacturing personnel. While tools

Only two prototypes were built. Both flew very well and both were lost in crashes that were attributed to pilot error. You can see the variable incidence arrangement of the wings on the aircraft at the left. *Scott Libis*

Note the extended slot on this aircraft—a sizeable surface! The arrangement of the low-slung podded engines had an effect that was not understood for some years. Quite inadvertently, their placement in relation to the wings and the fuselage had, in effect, "area-ruled" the fuselage, anticipating Richard Whitcomb's later "coke-bottle" fuselage. As a result, the aircraft was extraordinarily fast for its 25 tons, hitting 585 mph. *Scott Libis*

The marvelous build-quality of the aircraft fairly leaps out in this photo. The seams are perfectly smooth; there are very few ripples. Note the angle of the wing incidence in this photo—it could be varied between three and seven degrees. *Scott Libis*

were being made and metal being cut, Martin was developing and testing many of the key components of the XB-51. The famed XB-26H "Middle River Stump Jumper", which had developed the tandem bicycle gear used so successfully on the XB-48 and XB-47, was brought back for tests of the "decelostat" (anti-skid) system for the XB-51.

Meanwhile, a full scale mock-up of the advanced Martin revolving bomb door was built and tested, a system later applied to the Martin B-57 "Canberra".

A complete fuselage nose section, from forward of the cockpit, was built and the heavy armament installation of eight 20mm cannon tested, over 84,000 rounds being fired.

Similarly, a complete righthand engine installation was built and tested. Emergency egress tests on the canopy and ejection seats were also completed.

In short, it was a dead serious attempt by Martin to get back into the Air Force's good graces by providing a clearly superior jet bomber. Things went smoothly, and the first airplane, 46-685, was completed on July 29, 1949. It was devoid of tactical gear, but filled with test instrumentation, a Martin strong point. Taxi tests began on September 17, and Pat Tibbs made the first flight on the morning of October 28, 1949, only 18 months from the date the Air Force directed that construction begin.

Tibbs, veteran of many first flights, used both water injection and JATO to get the 48,000 pound gross weight XB-51 off on its maiden flight.

The XB-51 broke ground cleanly after a 3,000 foot roll and Tibbs climbed to 10,000 feet where he made a series of clean and dirty stalls. The dive brakes were tested successfully, and he then climbed to 20,000 feet for the uneventful cruise down to Patuxent Naval Air Station, Maryland. Guy Townsend was flying chase in a Lockheed P-80. Pat had just started a series of normal checks when Townsend called, "Pat, you better do a 360 degree turn; I'm at full power and I can't stay with you". Obligingly, Tibbs started the turn, but Townsend came back—"Never mind, I've lost you!" The big XB-51 had, at cruise, outstripped the P-80.

Tibbs went on to land, where he amazed onlookers by using a brake chute stopping the plane in less than 3,000 feet. This was the first of 233 contractor flights during which slightly more than 211 flight hours were logged.

The Phase I testing by Martin pilots was productive and not without incident. There were two engine failures and one hard landing that occurred because of an inadvertent gear retraction. The most serious problem, however, was an unsatisfactory lateral trim condition at Mach .87 at 10,000 feet, or at speeds above 550 mph at 5,000 feet.

Martin worked hard to solve the problem and by the time Phase II testing was completed on November 10, 1950, the Air Force considered the plane's performance to be excellent, equaling or exceeding all of the contractor's guarantees.

The number one prototype had an eventful career after the Phase II testing. It was used in a special program to evolve a prototype for a supersonic bomber, but encountered another bad landing accident on February 28, 1952 and had to be transported back to Martin for a complete rebuild. It was then sent to Edwards Air Force Base for high speed bombing tests, and while there appeared in the William Holden film *Toward the Unknown,* where it masqueraded as the "Gilmore fighter". The big bomber's amazing maneuverability was convincingly demonstrated in this picture, filling the screen with lots of aileron rolls.

In March 1956, on a flight from Edwards to Eglin, it crashed on take-off from Biggs Field, El Paso, Texas. Amateur films taken of the crash reveal that the pilot rotated the aircraft far too early in the take-off roll, got behind the power curve, and was unable to take-off.

The second aircraft, 46-686, made its first flight on April 17, 1950, and was accepted by the Air Force on December 8, 1951. F. E. "Chris" Christoffersen did most of its 64 hours and 13 minutes of Martin testing.

The head-on view reveals more of the XB-51's striking innovations, including bicycle gear and outriggers, rotary bomb bay, and the huge flap area. On the right is another unsung Martin product, a four engine, jet/piston hybrid, the Mercator. It did yeoman work in secret reconnaissance flights.

The airplane was used for gun, rocket and bomb tests, with the rotating bomb door proving an outstanding success. Further high speed tests were conducted at Edwards, but the aircraft augured in on May 9, 1952, and was totally destroyed after only an estimated total of 151 flying hours.

The Aircraft Described

The XB-51 was perhaps the most radical assemblage of innovative ideas in bomber history, and it is a tribute to the Martin Company that not only the pilots, but the engineers, mechanics and support personnel all regarded it with deep affection throughout its career.

Unphotogenic from some angles, particularly on the ground, the XB-51 was most attractive from others. Part of the photo problem came from the contrast between the relatively short 53 foot 1 inch wings and the long 85 foot 1 inch fuselage. In normal flight the wing rested at a three degree angle of incidence, but on take-off and landing it was changed by a relatively simple but ingenious mechanism to as much as seven and one half degrees.

For stability reasons, the wing had an anhedral of 6 degrees. This aspect, combined with 35 degrees of sweepback provided a shape not previously seen in the sky.

The wing was an extremely sophisticated piece of engineering, for in addition to the variable incidence, it had

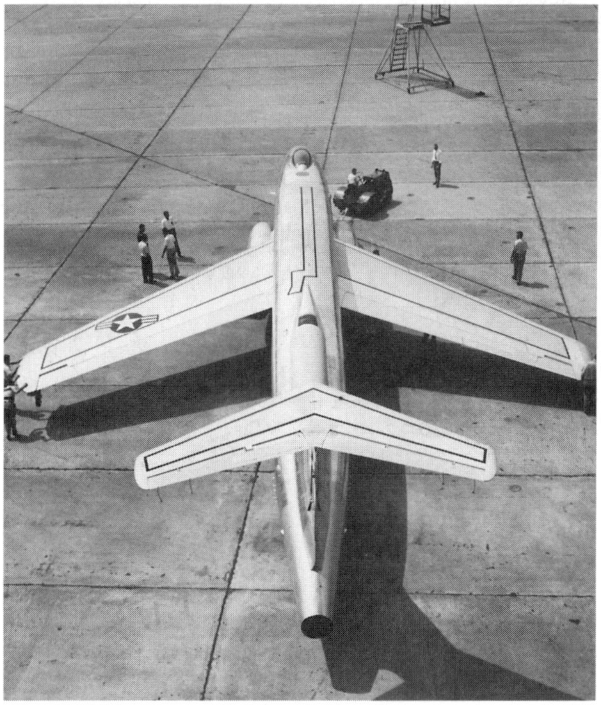

The striking proportions of the aircraft are evident here—55 foot wingspan, 85 foot long fuselage, "T" tail, and a third engine positioned as the Boeing 727's would be, high on the fuselage with an S-shaped duct to the exhaust nozzle in the tail. *Scott Libis*

The two XB-51s did not get to fly together often, but they make a striking picture as test pilots Russ Schleeh (later a champion power-boat driver) and Lee Horn flash by for the camera. The XB-51 appeared as the "Gilmore XF-120" in the William Holden film *Toward the Unknown.*

full span, single slotted flaps, partial span automatic wing leading edge slots, spoilers and thermal anti-icing.

The tail surfaces were also radical, for this was not only among the first of the "T" tails, but it also had a variable incidence mechanism for trim control and dive recovery.

The long lean fuselage was equally unusual. The pilot sat under a very low drag canopy which seemed almost disproportionately small. The second crew member, whose principal task was the operation of the Shoran bombing equipment, sat behind the pilot and had no exterior view. Both men had ejection seats, and the cabin was, of course, pressurized.

At Edwards Air Force Base, where most of the tests were conducted, the crowd gets a good look at the XB-51, one of several unusual airplanes displayed there at the time. *Author's collection, courtesy Warren Bodie*

The thin swept variable wing ruled out the more conventional jet nacelle location pioneered by Boeing. As a result, two of the engines were mounted on pylons on the underside of the fuselage while the third was tucked into the tail, very much in the manner of the later Boeing 727 transport.

The axial flow General Electric J-47-GE-13 engines weighed only 2526 pounds, but they provided a maximum sea level thrust of 6000 pounds at 7950 rpm. Military rated power was 5200 pounds of thrust, while normal rated power was 4320 pounds at 7370 rpm. Four ATO bottles were provided; each gave 1000 pounds of thrust for 14 seconds. ATO was used on a surprisingly high percentage of take-offs during the test program.

The table on the facing page gives the best illustration of the versatility and performance of the XB-51. At 55,923 pounds, the plane could get off the ground, with ATO, in 4340 feet, climb to 20,000 ft. in 5.4 minutes (initial rate of climb was 7130 feet per minute!) and then cruise at 434 knots to the combat area. Military load was 4000 pounds of bombs and a prodigious 1280 rounds of 20mm ammunition. Combat radius was a respectable 516 miles, a distance that would have been very useful in the Korean War.

What Might Have Been

If the XB-51 had been ordered into production, the chances are that the very capable Martin design team would have solved the limited range and marginal high altitude performance problems during the same period of time that it took to convert the very English Electric Canberra into the very American Martin B-57. A number of options were available, including increased tankage, e.g. a slipper tank built onto the fuselage spine, improved specific fuel consumption of the engines, better tactics and so on. The B-51 design could have been stretched, as all designs are, for a longer service life.

More important, however, the fertile inventiveness of the Martin team could have been maintained, and the company might well have developed a later supersonic bomber that would be in service today. But it was not to be; politics intervened, and the Martin Company was put to work building another manufacturer's design. It was not very much later that the company stopped building aircraft entirely, and when it did, a fine tradition disappeared from the American scene.

Loading and Performance—Typical Mission

			Basic	Attack Missions		High Altitude Missions			Ferry
Conditions			**Mission**	**Radius**	**Radius**	**Radius**	**Radius**	**Radius**	**Range**
			I	**II**	**III**	**IV**	**V**	**VI**	**VII**
TAKE-OFF WEIGHT	⑦	(lb)	55,923	55,923	54,137	55,923	58,238	62,452	56,662
Fuel & Oil		(gal)	2835/12	2835/12	2835/12	2835/12	2835/12	2835/12	3535/16.2
Military Load		(lb)	4000	4000	1120 ⑨	4000	6384	10,494	None
Total Ammunition		(rds/cal)	1280/20mm	1280/20mm	1280/20mm	1280/20mm	1280/20mm	1280/20mm	1280/20mm
Wing Loading		(lb/sq ft)	101.7	101.7	98.4	101.7	105.9	113.6	103.1
Stall Speed (power off)		(kn)	133	133	131	133	136	140	134
TAKE-OFF DISTANCE SL									
Ground Run (no wind)	④	(ft)	4340	4340	4010	4340	4790	5965	4480
To Clear 50ft Obst	④	(ft)	5590	5590	5190	5590	6200	7835	5790
CLIMB FROM SL									
Rate of Climb at SL	②⑧	(fpm)	5100	5100	5340	5100	4890	3960	5030
Time to 10,000 Feet	②	(min)	2.2	2.2	2.1	2.2	2.4	3.0	2.3
Time to 20,000 Feet	②	(min)	5.4	5.4	5.3	5.4	5.7	6.3	5.6
Service Ceiling (100 f.p.m.)	②	(ft)	32,900	32,900	33,700	32,900	31,600	27,200	32,500
COMBAT RANGE		(n.mi.)	934	—	—	1044	—	—	1401
COMBAT RADIUS		(n.mi.)	378	331	332	516	502	446	—
Avg. Cruising Speed	⑥	(kn)	463	440	440	466	466	463	467
Total Mission Time	⑥	(hr)	1.82	1.68	1.70	2.40	2.33	2.12	3.08
Cruising Altitude (1000 ft)	⑥	(ft)	32.8 to 43.2	10.0	10.0	32.9 to 43.2	31.7 to 43.3	27.6 to 43.2	32.8 to 43.0
COMBAT WEIGHT		(lb)	41,457	41,958	43,118	40,747	40,571	40,289	—
Combat Altitude		(ft)	S.L.	10,000	10,000	35,600	34,300	29,700	—
SPEED									
Max Speed (combat alt)	②	(kn)	560	552	552	503	506	519	—
Max Speed at S.L. Ft	②	(kn)	560	560	560	560	560	560	—
CLIMB									
Rate of Climb (combat alt)	②	(fpm)	6980	5270	5080	1360	1600	2350	—
Rate of Climb at SL	②	(fpm)	6980	6900	6650	7130	7160	7190	—
CEILING									
Combat Ceiling	②	(ft)	38,900	38,600	38,100	39,200	39,300	39,400	—
Service Ceiling	②	(ft)	40,500	40,300	39,800	40,900	41,000	41,100	—
Service Ceiling	③	(ft)	39,900	39,700	39,100	40,200	40,300	40,400	—
LANDING WEIGHT SL	⑥	(lb)	34,267	34,267	35,361	34,267	34,198	34,302	34,962
Ground Roll	④	(ft)	2355	2355	2425	2355	2350	2360	2400
From 50′ Obst	④	(ft)	3240	3240	3325	3240	3235	3245	3295

24 BOMBER 47

How Boeing's B-47 Brought America into the Jet Age

Wings August, 1981

I've been accused of repeating myself too often about the Boeing B-47 being the most important multi-jet aircraft in history, but I cannot stop myself because it's true.

The importance of the B-47 in the development of both civil and military aircraft is indisputable, for virtually every large jet aircraft you see flying today shares its basic characteristics of swept back wings and podded engines. It was a veteran Cold Warrior, serving as a bomber and in reconnaissance, and it participated briefly in the war doing electronic reconnaissance in Southeast Asia. Yet because it never dropped a bomb in anger, it has been largely overlooked by the public. Today, however, the large and growing B-47 Stratojet Association is doing its bit to preserve the memory of the aircraft and of the men and women who built, flew, and maintained it. For information, contact the association at 23 Oak Ridge Road, W. Lebanon, NH 03784. Good books on the subject are The B-47 Stratojet: Boeing's Brilliant Bomber *by Jan Tegler (McGraw Hill, 2000) and Al Lloyd's* A Cold War Legacy: A Tribute to the Strategic Air Command *(Pictorial Histories, 1999).*

Nothing conveys the raw power and speed of a Boeing B-47 better than the rocket-assisted takeoff (ATO), when the power of rockets is added to the churning General Electric J47 engines. These takeoffs were a thrill and not without hazard, for the ATO bottles were rockets, with all the heat and danger that implies. On the first B-47s, 18 of the bottles were mounted internally; later models used an external collar that could accommodate 33 bottles. When the technique was first used it was referred to as JATO for "Jet Assisted Takeoff."

Although the Boeing B-52 Stratofortress is undoubtedly the most important jet bomber of all time, there are many who would argue that its predecessor, the Boeing B-47 Stratojet, may well be the most important jet plane ever built.

The difference, of course, is what each airplane spawned. The B-47, revolutionary as it was, was less important for its own role as a bomber as for the aircraft which derived from it, the billions of dollars worth of military B-52s, KC-135s, and commercial 707s, and later, on this solidly established foundation, the jet transports of our own time, the 727s, 737s, 747s, 757s, and 767s. On the other hand, the B-52, great warplane that it is, was the end of the subsonic bomber line.

While the design influence has been greatly expanded upon, the fundamental contribution of the B-47 to Boeing's engineering and its competitive position in the market place is unassailable. It might even be said that the B-47's influence spilled over beyond the Boeing stable, for certainly the elements it pioneered—swept wings and podded jet engines—are to be found in many of the world's aircraft.

The origins of this multi-billion dollar flying empire, which stretches across all the airlines of the world, began with a project originally budgeted at a mere $10,000,000, but before we examine just what that $10 million bought, let's take a look at what it was like to be a B-47 pilot.

Flying the B-47

The B-47 brought joy to the hearts of bomber pilots. After years of listening to garrulous fighter pilots spieling endlessly about their responsive mounts, of enduring their witless barroom jibes about aerial truck drivers (you can guess that I flew bombers), we bomber pilots suddenly had in the B-47 a plane that was almost fighter-like in its flying qualities.

It was pure pleasure to fly the slim, six jet B-47. Despite the myths that surrounded it concerning its unforgiving ways; its requirement for airspeeds to be flown with impossible precision; its inevitable flight to the "coffin corner" where high speed stall and low speed stall were just knots apart, the B-47 was a lovely airplane to fly, particularly for veterans of the B-29 and B-50.

The B-47s poured into the SAC fleet in ever increasing numbers, and scenes like this were soon common at Air Force bases around the country. In this photo you can clearly see the ATO bottles on the rear of the fuselage, just aft of the aft landing gear. The wing and tail sweep are also evident. No one will ever be able to pay sufficient tribute to the way the enlisted ground crews worked and sweated to keep the B-47s airborne. They were the true heroes of the SAC, as they are of every air force and every service.

The sleek lines of the airplane gave one a first impression of speed and liveliness that familiarity did not dim. The fighter-like cockpit with its blown canopy and tandem seating added to this feeling. But most important was the fact that the B-47 was responsive in almost all flight regimes. At very heavy weights, on hot days, and at high altitudes, it was sluggish on takeoff and runways did tend to seem very short. I can remember taking off at Kirtland Air Force Base, New Mexico, on warm summer days and watching the first runway markers go by in a lazy fashion. The speed lagged until long past mid-field, then slowly accelerated so that you would be airborne just where you predicted—damn near the end of the runway.

But even under these conditions, once airborne, the B-47 assumed almost regal characteristics. Its speed was exhilarating; for pilots brought up on four flailing piston engines, the climb speed of the B-47, starting at 310 knots indicated airspeed, was heady. Its rate of climb was fantastic, and its high cruising speeds, normally .74 Mach, or 425 True Air Speed, made cross-country flight a pleasure.

The XB-47 was a compendium of radical features, most of which can be seen here: 35 degree swept wing and tail, bicycle landing gear, engines hung in pods, and approach chute. The radar observer/bombardier had considerably more visibility in the XB-47, but the glazing was eliminated on later models.

The Stratojet, as it was never called by pilots, demonstrated this early in its career. The Air Force wanted it shown to a gathering of distinguished Congressional guests at Andrews Air Force Base, Washington, D.C., and Majors Russ Schleeh and J. W. Howell were assigned to fly the prototype from Moses Lake, Washington. They took off on February 8, 1949, and set an unofficial transcontinental record, arriving at Andrews three hours and forty-six minutes later. Perhaps even more remarkable than the speed was the fact that it was Schleeh's second flight in the airplane and Howell's first.

The visibility from the B-47's cockpit was superb; and at altitude, in the early days, you had an exclusive. You were the only ones there. If you saw a contrail, it had to be another B-47.

Tactical operations were a pleasure. The radar observer in the three man crew was kept busy all of the time, sharing duties with the aircraft commander and the pilot. Bomb runs, navigation legs, instrument let downs, all became precision tasks in which the crew cooperated and coordinated. A less obvious, but very real advantage, was the small size of the crew; there is nothing more frustrating for an aircraft commander than to get ready to brief only to find that the waist gunner, or the radio operator, or somebody else has forgotten his lunch and is on his way back to base operations. In the B-47, discipline was easier and better.

Inflight refueling at high gross weights was somewhat dicey when the tanker was the piston-engined Boeing KC-97. These tankers, perfectly suitable for a B-50, often had to refuel in a full power descent in order to keep above the B-47's stall speed, which naturally increased as it took on fuel. The entire refueling process with the KC-97s was inefficient because the B-47 used almost as much fuel to descend, rendezvous, refuel, and climb back to cruising altitude as it was able to take on from the tanker. When the turbine powered KC-135A tankers came into service, refueling became a much more productive task.

The B-47 was the first of a totally new generation of aircraft where airframes rather than powerplants became the limiting factor on speed. Much has been written about the critical requirement to maintain exact airspeeds in the descent and landing phases of B-47 operations. The requirement was there, but so was the capability to fulfill it; a caress of the throttles would result in a minute flickering on the percentage calibrated RPM counters, and airspeed could be controlled exactly as desired. In a crosswind, a slight differential between the number one and number six engines would keep you right on track all the way down an ILS approach.

The B-47 was flown in formation on occasion, usually for show purposes, and at lower altitudes was relatively easy to keep in position. At higher altitudes, however, the aircraft was so clean that station keeping was more difficult. I'll never forget a twelve ship formation from the 93rd Bomb Wing at Castle, formed up in four elements of three, at about 25,000 feet near the Sierra Nevadas. A new hotshot major had just joined the 330th Bomb Squadron, and he was, for some reason, late and hurrying to catch up with the formation.

He came barreling in out of the west, and fighter style, whipped his B-47 up on one wing to allow aerodynamic braking to slow him down for a stylish join-up. Even in what seemed to be a 60 degree bank, he didn't slow down a knot, and the B-47 sailed through the formation in knife edge flight, missing the second element lead by just a few feet, before steaming on out toward Nevada with a unanimous stream of animated curses following in his wake. He joined up in a more conservative manner a few minutes later, and was pretty quiet around the squadron for a few days.

There were losses with the B-47 in the early days, primarily due to the rapid roll rate, caused by the yawing tendency of the swept wing. If an outboard engine failed just as you became airborne, you had just three seconds to apply sufficient rudder forces (15 degrees) to maintain directional control. This was a particularly hard lesson to learn, for the normal tendency in a jet is to minimize use of the rudder and to pick up a wing with aileron control—which was exactly wrong in this case. Later in its service, as we shall see, there were fatigue and other problems which caused a series of accidents.

When the B-47 fleet was at its peak in the mid-1950s and early 1960s, the United States enjoyed a measure of strategic superiority greater than any nation had enjoyed before—or since. In those halcyon days of the Strategic Air Command, the B-47s were virtually immune to attack. At altitude they were almost as fast as the North American F-86s, Grumman Panthers and other fighters that vainly tried to intercept them, and it would not have been any different with MiG-15s. With more than 2,000 B-47s built, and perhaps as many as 1,500 ready to launch in the event of a war, the United States enjoyed a dominating deterrent and could have destroyed any aggressor in a matter of days, with relatively few losses. It is worthy of note that this awesome power, this incredible fleet of virtually invulnerable aircraft, was never used. With absolute strategic superiority, with very little risk of a counterattack, the United States chose not to exercise its awesome power, a remarkable show of restraint that no other nation has ever matched.

As time went on, and the century series fighters and their foreign counterparts came into service, the B-47's measure of superiority faded. When it came, the end was sudden. After years of orbiting pre-selected sites, talking fighters in for an intercept attempt, we were cruising along one sunny morning when, from nowhere, a North American F-100 Super Saber barrel-rolled around us. We knew then that the B-47's heyday was over.

Development and Test

The B-47 saga began in 1943 with the crucial awareness that the Germans and the British had startling new powerplants in production and were building jet fighters. The jet fighter, and its inevitable follow-on, the jet bomber, spelled the end of the piston engine bomber just as surely as the *Merrimac* (*Virginia* for the purists) spelled the end of the wooden man-of-war, and by April 1944, the U.S. Army Air Force was calling for a relatively large aircraft with a 500 mile per hour top speed.

Five designs were tendered, ranging from the conservative to the radical, and for once the radical was to emerge triumphant. North American offered the straight wing XB-45, which became the first U.S. jet bomber to go into production, and which served operationally as the Tornado for several accident-filled years. (See *Airpower* Sept. 1973) Convair developed the most elegant appearing of the lot, straight winged also, but possessing an almost feminine beauty. It was the XB-46, but despite its magnificent looks and adequate performance, there was never a chance that it would go into production for the firm already had a large contract for B-36s and, as in all post-war periods, the Air Force's policy was to spread the wealth. (See *Airpower* Sept. 1976) The B-36, called the Peacemaker, would lumber along on its six piston and four jet engines for years, flying missions of interminable length. The B-36 was the capstone of the past in bomber development, while its partner in peace, the B-47, was the foundation stone for the future.

Martin offered the least attractive design, the boxy XB-48, which shared only one thing with the B-47, its bicycle type landing gear. Martin had insisted on using a large cowling for each of its two sets of three engines, and these created enormous drag. Although it was to build the English-designed twin-engined B-57 Canberra, Martin would shortly cease producing aircraft. The XB-48 was one of its last. After the demise of the XB-51 project, Martin's name would appear only on rockets and missiles.

Northrop adapted its XB-35 flying wing to the eight jet YB-49 configuration and, as radical as the design was, it offered excellent performance, but politics and the potential of the B-47 combined to kill the all-jet flying wing.

All of these aircraft flew in 1947, beginning with the XB-45 on March 17, the XB-46 on April 2, the XB-48 on June 14, and the YB-49 on October 21. However, when the Boeing XB-47 first flew on December 17, 1947, it was evident that a radical new era had dawned and that Boeing had no real competition.

The nature of the B-47's mission did not require it to fly in formation often; it was intended to fly solitary nuclear strike missions deep within the Soviet Union. Nonetheless, it was an easy aircraft to fly in formation, for it responded instantly to control and power inputs, even at fairly high altitudes. In this photo you can clearly see the vortex generators on the upper surface of the wing, put there to smooth out air-flow anomalies. These are RB-47Es, distinguishable by their slightly longer noses.

The XB-47's configuration—long, slender fuselage, narrow, high aspect ratio swept back wings, six engines arranged in underslung pods, and a bicycle landing gear—was arrived at only through a long and sometimes anguished process at the Boeing design desks.

The first Boeing jet design, the Model 424, was not promising. It looked like little more than a B-29 fitted with four jet engines paired in nacelles under the wing. One version followed another, all unacceptable, as more was learned about the problems associated with jet flight, problems which included high fuel consumption, the danger of fire resulting from failure of the all too brittle turbine blades of the day, and the effect of drag that conventional airfoils and wings had at the high speeds which the jet engine promised.

One model, 432, retained a straight wing and had engines arranged about the fuselage center section, right over the fuel tank area, with bulbous air intakes located beside the cockpit section. Model 432 was an almost classical expression of the 1944 dilemma facing aero engineers. The L/D (Lift to Drag) ratio of straight wings fell off drastically at Mach .6 because of the vastly increased drag due to Mach effect. On the other hand, at speeds below Mach

Even on the ground, the B-47 gave an impression of speed and capability. On the ground the wings drooped, especially when the aircraft was heavily laden. In flight they assumed an upward curve, and in turbulent weather they would literally flap up and down, sometimes in a disconcerting manner! The outrigger gear and the landing lights are evident in this photo.

This is B-47 serial number 51-2222, from the 4925th Nuclear Test Group at Kirtland Air Force Base. The 4925th was responsible for dropping nuclear test weapons, both live, in actual nuclear tests, and "shapes" as the dummy bombs were called. The author flew this airplane for three happy years with some of the wildest, craziest, most hard-drinking and best-flying pilots in the Air Force. Note the long bomb bay, changed in most production B-47s but useful at Kirtland for test purposes. Sad to say, "Triple Deuce" was scrapped in May, 1960.

Another shot of an assisted takeoff; you can differentiate the smoke from the rockets with the black smoke from the General Electric J47 engines. The author was entering the landing pattern at Little Rock Air Force Base some 40 years ago when the ATO rockets on a B-47 that was taking off somehow malfunctioned and turned inward, blasting a hole in the fuselage and blowing the airplane up.

.6, jet engines were only about two-thirds as efficient as contemporary reciprocating engines. One solution, tentatively essayed in Germany, favored for civil use in England, held in second class status in the U.S. and vastly labored over in Russia, was the turboprop. Not as fast as the pure jet, the turbine engine/propeller combination seemed to be the only feasible solution to the drag/efficiency quandary.

Robert T. Jones, of NACA, believed that a better solution to the problem was to use swept back wings. His paper on the subject was turned down for publication on the grounds he lacked experimental proof, even though swept wing aircraft were already flying in Europe. (The Messerschmitt Me 262, which had 18½ degrees of wing sweep and was the first operational jet fighter, had its wings swept for structural and center of gravity reasons rather than as an attempt to delay the critical Mach.)

In the closing days of World War II, the U.S. Army's Scientific Advisory Group under Theodore von Karman went to Europe to investigate the latest German aeronautical developments. George Schairer, Boeing's Chief Aerodynamicist, accompanied the group which included such luminaries as Frank Wattendorf, Hsu Shen Tsien, Hugh Dryden, and others. They found in German records sufficient material to validate Jones' theory. Interviews with German engineers, including Adolf Busemann, who had first proposed the theory of swept wings in Vienna in 1935, caused Schairer to write Seattle and recommend the adoption of sweepback.

As a result, the next model in the progression towards the B-47, Model 448, retained the rather rotund fuselage of the Model 432, but featured swept back wings. The very thinness of the high aspect ratio swept wings caused other problems, however. The thin wing did not allow fuel, engines or landing gear to be stowed within it, and these obstacles were only overcome in the Model 450-1-1, which looked almost like the final B-47 configuration. In it, the inboard engines were suspended in pods to avoid interference with the clean wing, and both fuel and landing gear were concentrated in the fuselage.

The suspended pods were one of those happy engineering circumstances where better aerodynamics also meant better structure. The weight distribution of the engines along the span permitted the wing to be made lighter, and in an additional side effect, they also made maintenance easier and added a margin of safety for, in the event of fire or damage, suspended engines were less likely to spread the condition to the wing. As a final unforeseen advantage, the inboard nacelles helped to induce a stall over the section of the wing next to them, while the outboard tip mounted nacelles tended to delay the stall. This permitted greater aileron effectiveness near the stall, but more importantly, delayed pitch-up, the nemesis of swept wing aircraft of the time.

A mock-up inspection was held in Seattle in April 1946, and the Air Force was impressed. Boeing was given the go-ahead in May, with two prototypes being ordered and $10 million budgeted. Further study of the mock-up resulted in the wingspan being increased to 116 feet, and the outer engine also being placed in pods. When the Martin-originated "Stump Jumper" bicycle undercarriage was adopted, the shape of the first XB-47 was finalized.

This radical, streamlined airplane, so unlike any previous bomber, made its first flight nineteen months after go-ahead with Bob Robbins and Scott Osler at the controls. In retrospect, it is probable that the Air Force did not fully understand the weapon it had been given, just as Boeing could not have realized that the basic cornerstone of a multi-billion dollar bomber and commercial transport business had been laid. From the B-47, Boeing marched on to become the dominant figure in multi-jet aviation for the next several decades and remains so today.

George Martin was Project Engineer for the B-47, and today he recalls it to be the most satisfying period of his engineering career. George can talk at length about the B-47, and although he was also intimately involved in the B-52, it is evident where his affection lies. He insisted from the start that the B-47 program be focused on the two major challenges: The aerodynamics of the new swept wings, and on the jet engines themselves. This is where most of the money was spent. Working within a limited budget, Martin adapted some readily available components for use in the B-47, including elements of the B-29 landing gear, a low pressure hydraulic system, and an obsolescent 28 volt D.C. electrical system.

Even with this off-the-shelf gear, the B-47 was precedent shattering. It was not a perfect weapon, for the early jet engines consumed fuel in enormous quantities. Solutions to the range problem were perceived through the use of inflight refueling and, eventually, the B-47 would routinely fly bone-tiring, 24-hour missions. While its speed was phenomenal for the time, its altitude capability was not startling, but at lighter, "over the target" gross weights, it was certainly respectable. Most of all, it was ideal for marriage to the remarkable new bombing and navigation systems which were then coming into being, and with the rapidly developing U.S. atomic arsenal.

Structurally, the aircraft was far more sophisticated than anything Boeing had ever built. The leap from the tubular aluminum alloy bridge truss construction of the B-17 to the webbed wing technique used in the B-29 was great, but the follow-on transition to the thick skinned B-47 was even greater. The 116 foot span wing, with its 9.3 to 1 aspect ratio, the highest to date of any jet bomber, was extraordinarily flexible and capable of a 17½ ft. deflection, tip to tip in static tests. (Watching those wings bob around in turbulence, with the pods twisting up and down, was worrisome in the extreme in flight—but that capability made for a very comfortable ride.)

The wing was also flexible chord wise, and at speeds above 425 knots indicated, the ailerons acted as a tab, twisting the wing rather than causing the ailerons to initiate a bank. At 456 knots the ailerons became absolutely ineffective, the wheel was like a rock in your hands, and you were devoid of lateral control. In the normal operating envelope, however, there was plenty of lateral control at all speeds.

As so often happens in aircraft design, solutions to one problem created others. The bicycle gear, adopted because there was no room to stow the undercarriage in the wings, dictated that the aircraft take off and land in a fixed attitude, rather than with the customary rotation or flare of conventional aircraft. The gear arrangement also required some new techniques for taxiing, but pilots quickly adapted to it.

Despite its size and speed, the B-47 was quite maneuverable. It could be rolled and of course performed what was essentially an Immelmann turn in the LABs, or toss-bombing maneuver. The white paint on the undersurfaces was intended to reflect the flash and radiation from a nuclear bomb drop. It is worth noting that the basic layout—swept wing and tails, and podded jet engines—can be seen in most modern jet transports, from the 707 to the 777 and beyond. *Author's collection, courtesy Fred Johnsen*

The huge Fowler flaps chosen for the B-47 were designed to give maximum lift and low drag. Because the early jet engines took a long time to "spool-up" for acceleration, it was advisable to carry power during the landing approach so that a go-around could be made if necessary. But carrying power in the super clean B-47, even with full flaps, made it very difficult for the pilot to put it down exactly on the end of the runway, where he had to be in view of the relatively short runways of the time. The solution to this was the approach chute, which permitted the pilot to carry power to keep the engines in an rpm range where he could rapidly accelerate for a go-around, but still provided enough drag to permit spot landings. Spoilers were also considered as a possible answer to this problem, but a trial installation on the prototype revealed that they had disastrous impact on the stall speed. A second brake chute and an anti-skid braking system helped get the airplane stopped once on the runway.

For an important period of time in the 1950s and early 1960s, the Boeing B-47s constituted an important part of the United States' offensive power, and, in fact, may fairly be said to have been the dominant aircraft of the period. In the early years of the B-47, it was almost immune to interception by the jet fighters of the time. Later, as the Century Series of fighters was introduced, this was no longer true, but it was still very effective.

With only a three man crew, it was possible to group the men all together in a small pressurized compartment. The triple-threat radar observer (radar observer/navigator/bombardier) sat in a dark cubbyhole unrelieved by windows in later models, while the two pilots had an unrestricted field of view.

Yet, despite its formidable performance, the Air Force did not continue to evidence a great deal of interest in the plane, for it seemed to fall midway between the requirements for medium and heavy bombers. General K.B. Wolfe, who had masterminded the B-29 program and was continually urging Boeing on in the B-50 program, was one of those not particularly taken by the B-47. He made an almost perfunctory trip to Moses Lake, Washington where the XB-47 was being tested.

Major (later Brigadier General) Guy M. Townsend had taken over the test program by then, and Colonel Henry E. "Pete" Warden, of Wright Field, who would be perhaps the single most important Air Force figure in the B-52 program, wanted Wolfe to take a trial flight. Wolfe wasn't interested, but Warden kept at him for almost forty-five minutes before he finally agreed to make a short flight. Townsend made a spectacular takeoff, climbed at a speed which made a skeptical Wolfe inquire if the instruments were reading accurately, and then let him fly it. When they landed, Wolfe called Warden over and said: "You'd better come see me about this." From then on the Air Force was fully behind the B-47.

The original XB-47 had been powered by 3,750 pound static thrust Allison J35-2 engines, which were so primitive that they actually used farm machinery bearings. Consequently, bearing temperatures became a critical factor in their use. The total of 21,500 pounds of thrust delivered by six of the J35s was marginal even for the 125,000 pound maximum gross weight of the prototype, but the second prototype had six General Electric J47-GE-3 engines, each with a thrust of 5,200 pounds static, more than adequate. These engines were also retrofitted to the number one prototype and the development accelerated rapidly, soon leading to a contract for ten B-47A aircraft on September 3, 1948. These were essentially test aircraft, as important for the lessons they taught about production of a sophisticated jet bomber as for their trial results. All were fitted with the J47-GE-11 engines of 5,200 pounds static thrust.

The B-47A was built at Boeing's Wichita facility, which had turned out as many as four B-29s a day during the war. Located in the heart of Beech and Cessna country, and on the same site as McConnell Air Force Base where B-47 training would take place, the plant responded to the challenge of the new aircraft, in spite of atrocious weather conditions. No one who was there will forget the numbing Kansas winters with the wind whistling mournfully, or the excruciatingly hot, dry summers, where cockpit temperatures sometimes exceeded 160 degrees Fahrenheit. Under the blast furnace sun, the McConnell ramp would be a noxious ocean of unburned J-4 fumes, waves of mirage inducing heat, sticky asphalt, and sweating crew members. After hours of searing pre-flight activities, there was almost miraculous relief after takeoff when the aircraft's air conditioning system would bang into action, filling the cockpit with a chill fog that looked unnervingly like smoke. It was better than a cold beer, although you had to calm anyone on his first flight, for he was usually ready to abandon ship because of the "fire."

There were many historical forces at work which determined the extent of the B-47 program. The Berlin Airlift (June 24, 1948 to May 12, 1949) had called worldwide attention to the escalating cold war, and there followed a series of similar crises which shocked the U.S. Congress into appropriating enormous sums of money to buy the swept wing bombers.

The lessons of the A model having been somewhat digested, 87 B-47Bs were ordered in November 1948, and this aircraft featured the absolutely indispensable inflight refueling capability. Boeing had solved the low fuel rate delivery problem of the existing probe and drogue systems with its innovative flying boom, and inci-

The external rocket racks provided 33,000 pounds of thrust on takeoff. The collar-type rack could be jettisoned after use, cutting down on weight. At left is Ed Hensley, a Boeing test pilot, and Merle Carder, a flight-line mechanic.

After its flying days had ended, old 51-2222 from Kirtland still served. It was used as a radar target, mounted inverted from this rig. It was subsequently scrapped, as noted, but not before this one last bit of effort.

dentally sewed up future sales for KC-97 and KC-135A tankers.

The B model was greatly improved in other ways, including a structural beef-up and a change in load limit factor from 3 to 2, which permitted the all up weight to go to 200,000 pounds. The B-47 still didn't have ejection seats, however, a dreadful defect that made SAC crews nervous for two years before the B model was turned over for training purposes.

A total of 399 B models was ordered, and these not only provided the basis for training and tactics, but also underwent structural and development revisions for the later programs. They also provided the entry for Lockheed and Douglas in the sudden acceleration of B-47 procurement. Lockheed built eight B-47Bs and Douglas ten, the basis for their later full scale participation in the B-47E program.

The B-47C and D models were experimental only. The B-47C was a paper study of a four-engine B-47 with much greater range; it was dropped at General LeMay's insistence because it was a threat to the B-52 which was being developed almost concurrently. Two B-47Bs were converted to XB-47Ds to serve as test beds for a turboprop installation. A Wright YT49-W-1 turboprop was placed in lieu of the two J47s in each inner nacelle; the outer nacelle retaining the J47 jet engine. The airplane was fast, faster than any other propeller powered airplane at 597 mph, but engine out conditions rendered it virtually uncontrollable, and the project was dropped.

The B-47E was the definitive Stratojet; General Electric J47-GE-25 engines of 6,000 pounds of thrust were augmented to 7,200 pounds by water injection, and new rocket-assisted takeoff racks consisted of thirty-three 1,000 pound thrust units in a jettisonable horseshoe collar fitting. Tail armament was improved with the addition of a General Electric radar-directed rear turret fitted with two M-39 20mm cannon. To enhance this new defensive capability, the copilot's seat would swivel 180 degrees, and he could then pick up at a limited range and azimuth any enemy fighter obliging enough to make a lengthy stern attack. The guns worked well enough in training, but their use in combat would have been problematic.

The biggest improvement from the crew's point of view was the installation of ejection seats. The aircraft commander and pilot ejected upwards, while the radar observer ejected downward. One radar observer used to regularly ask, in a somewhat plaintive manner, that if we had an emergency takeoff and had to eject, would we please roll the plane as much as possible so he wouldn't be fired downwards into the runway. A reasonable request.

Orders continued to flow for the B-47s, so many that all three manufacturers, Boeing, Lockheed, and Douglas, began essentially wartime production efforts on the B-47E. Before production concluded, Boeing had built 931, Douglas 264, and Lockheed 386 of the E model, and SAC had the most formidable unchallenged strike force in history.

Operational Use

The Strategic Air Command grew almost ten fold in size from the time of its formation in 1946 until 1959, when it reached its peak in terms of numbers of personnel and aircraft assigned. At the same time, safety records and all measures of performance—gunnery, navigational accuracy, bombing accuracy, pilot proficiency, maintenance, etc.,—were improved enormously.

Within SAC, the B-47 program flourished between 1951 and 1958; there were four wings equipped with 45 aircraft each in 1952, seven by 1953, seventeen by 1954, twenty-two by 1955, twenty-seven by 1956, and a peak of twenty-eight by 1958, with four additional wings of reconnaissance RB-47s.

SAC could muster 1,367 B-47s in 1958, along with 176 RB-47s and 380 B-50s. These were operated by highly trained crews who could fly as much as they needed to in order to maintain superlative standards in bombing, inflight refueling, and the hundred other tasks by which Headquarters—and this meant LeMay—evaluated efficiency. Fuel prices were low, morale was high, and operational use was limited more by maintenance and crew factors than anything else.

The onus for nonperformance was placed squarely on unit commanders; if an enlisted man got drunk and had an accident, it was assumed that his Squadron Commander was directly responsible, and this made for a tightly-knit unity.

These glowing years of American airpower were studded with individual feats which grabbed headlines and characterized the business-like growth in efficiency. The first operational B-47 was delivered from Wichita (where all of Boeing's production aircraft were built) to MacDill Air Force Base on 23 October 1951, to the 306th Bomb Wing. Colonel Michael N.W. McCoy made the delivery flight; he was later killed in a B-47 crash resulting from aileron ineffectiveness in a high speed turn. Pinecastle Air Force Base was renamed for him.

In 1953 the 306th initiated a five year program of rotating B-47 wings throughout England, where the pres-

A blurry photo, taken from an accompanying photo plane, showing the author on a bomb-run over the Salton Sea. The bomb doors are open, and within seconds the "blivet" will be dropped.

This is just after the most critical point in the flight of a B-47—the last few seconds of the takeoff roll. An outboard engine failure just before the airplane was airborne, or even immediately afterward, meant that the pilot had just a few seconds to apply the correct control inputs, or lose control of the aircraft. And, because of the swept wings and the placement of the engines, those control inputs were different than in the past. Many more than one B-47 was lost in an accident at this point in a flight. This aircraft is from the 306th Bomb Wing, en route to Fairford, England, for a three-month tour of duty.

ence of American nuclear power would be even more visible to the Russians. From June 1953 through April 1958, one or more B-47 wings was on station in the United Kingdom.[1]

The 22nd Bomb Wing, whose roots run from the bloody combat of the South Pacific in 1942, appropriately made the first flight of B-47s to the Far East. On June 21, 1954, three B-47s flew nonstop from March Air Force Base, California, to Yokota Air Base, Japan, in fifteen hours, covering the 6,700 miles with two inflight refuelings. This flight was alluded to in the Jimmy Stewart film "Strategic Air Command." Later in the same year, a combination of bad weather and recognized opportunity induced Colonel David A. Burchinal, Commander of the 43rd Bomb Wing, to establish a distance and endurance record in the B-47, flying 47 hours and 35 minutes and covering a distance of 21,163 miles, back and forth between Fairford RAF Station and Sidi Slimane, French Morocco.

The demonstrated success of inflight refueling, and the prospect of the introduction of the turbine powered KC-135 tanker fleet, permitted a revision of SAC's planning. Instead of deploying to overseas bases and conducting strikes from there, B-47s would in the future make their strikes directly from the United States, and either return to the Continental U.S., if sufficient refueling capability was available, or make a post-strike landing at a friendly foreign air base.

The entire achievement of the SAC force was based on the long hours of intensive work put in by every level of personnel. All over the country, an eighty hour work week was nothing to comment on; if it was required, it was done. There were curious anomalies in the system as it grew. I can remember when hand tools were in such short supply that crew chiefs shared them, one set between each two B-47s. It was crazy to have two $3,000,000 airplanes sitting side by side with a $400 tool kit between them, and two master sergeants arguing over whose turn it was to use a rachet wrench, but that's the way it was. Funds for tools came out of one pocket, funds for airplanes out of another.

LeMay made his personality felt down to the newest airman; he was symbolically looking over your shoulder at all times, and often enough he was actually there looking. The *esprit* was magnificent; the morale numbing

[1] In the summer of 1958, special B-47 Reflex Squadrons were stationed at USAFE's newly opened Spanish bases.

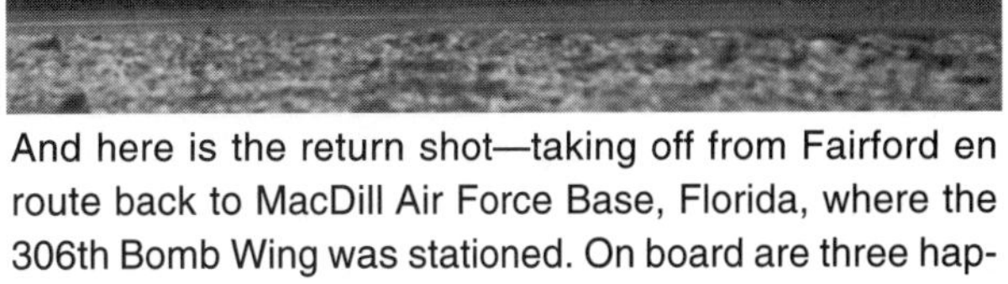

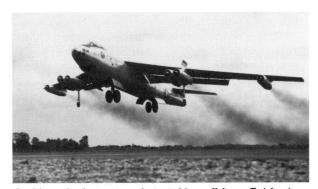

And here is the return shot—taking off from Fairford en route back to MacDill Air Force Base, Florida, where the 306th Bomb Wing was stationed. On board are three happy guys, anxious to get home to their families, and bearing a bomb-bay-load of gifts.

ground alert system had not yet been initiated, and the full capabilities of the B-47 were just being proven, so everyone had a feeling of direct participation.

The high morale was reflected in a number of ways. Crews began sprucing up; instead of the sometimes rancid flying suits of the past, clean flying clothes with nattily colored scarves became the order of the day. One affectation that many pursued was a LeMay-like cigar jutting out from the jaw; no matter that it made you sick, or that it made the cockpit smell bad, if LeMay did it, it was bound to be right.

The requirements for mobility and flexibility were uppermost in SAC planning, and entire combat wings and air refueling squadrons would rotate to England, Africa or Alaska. Enormous amounts of thought were placed into what "fly-away" kits would carry so that maintenance could be carried on with a minimum of interruptions. Similarly, new concepts in maintenance resulted in changes in inspection methods and times, overhauls, inventory systems, and so on. The SAC budget, while large, was finite, and the operation of more than 3,000 aircraft called for great quantities of fuel, spares, and even such ordinary commodities as parkas, sunglasses, boots, dog food for K-9 corps watchdogs, and so on.

All of this effort reached an operational peak with two simulated combat missions during December 1956. More than 1,000 B-47s and KC-97s flew missions all over the Northern Hemisphere; in many respects it was the contemporary war plan applied to the West. More than anything else it proved that with the B-47, SAC was able to execute its mission with a precision never before achieved by a peacetime air force, and with a thousand times the potential firepower than had been expended in all the wars of recorded history.

This was the zenith of America's relative military advantage over Russia, which after 1957 was steadily eroded by the Soviet missile build-up. SAC strength would increase, but not at as rapid a rate as that of the Russians'. Meanwhile, the B-52 strength was rising; by 1962, only ten years after its first flight, there would be 639 Stratofortresses available. The B-47 phase-out program incredibly had begun in 1957, the same year that the 100th Bomb Wing became the last to equip with the B-47. The phase-out stemmed from a number of factors, including the limited life expectancy of the B-47 airframes, the increased capability of the B-52 units and, not least, the requirement to change operational techniques so as to be able to have one third of the force on ground alert. This strategy, in which one third of the SAC fleet was on alert at all times, ready to take off in 15 minutes, was required because Soviet ICBMs could now target all SAC airfields.

Once the B-47 phase-out began, it continued with increasing rapidity. B-47 bombers fell from their 1958 peak of 1,367 to 880 in 1962, 391 in 1964, and 114 in 1965, the last year of their operational use. They soldiered on for a year in the EB-47 electronic ferret role, and then performed a variety of test and other duties, but their once invincible numbers were soon reduced to aluminum ingots at the Davis-Monthan Air Force Base disposal site. One of the saddest sights ever seen by an old B-47 pilot was the row upon row of beautiful aircraft being guillotined to pieces by massive chopping blades and then melted down. The B-47 deserved better.

Operational Problems

The B-47 was an effective weapons system, but it is only fair to mention that the aircraft encountered some very serious problems in the course of its service.

Many of these stemmed from the fact that it was a radical design, operating at speeds and altitudes that no heavy bomber had been capable of before. The original 125,000 pound gross weight had been increased steadily to 230,000 pounds for taxi, and a maximum inflight weight of 225,958 pounds.

The B-47 was limited to two positive "Gs" at maximum gross weight, 1.5 Gs with flaps down, and no negative (a proper double negative, for once) "Gs." With the great speed of this 193 ton airplane, its power controls, and the capability to enter fighter-like banks, the "G" limits were doubtless often exceeded. In addition, some pilots could not refrain from rolling the aircraft, although all aerobatics were strictly forbidden.

Not surprisingly, the aircraft had shown some routine fatigue problems early in its operational career. One involved replacement of the fuselage-wing drag angles, and the other the replacement of some panels which cracked near the outboard engine. New tactics, required to offset the increasing threat from ground-to-air missiles, imposed inordinate new strains on the aircraft however, and catastrophic problems began to occur.

The tactics involved two separate maneuvers. One, called "pop-up," required the bomber to fly low, just off the ground, then pull rapidly up to 18,000 feet to release its weapon before turning violently away and dropping back down to ground level. The second, called LABS, for Low Altitude Bombing System, involved the aircraft roaring in on the deck, pulling up in a half loop, releasing the bomb at the top of the maneuver, then rolling in an Immelmann

If you saw the great picture *Strategic Air Command,* with all its wonderful visuals of SAC bombers, you'll remember Jimmy Stewart's long flight to Japan. Well, this is one of the real B-47s that made the trip in June, 1954. It was a 15-hour flight, with several in-flight refuelings between California's March Field and Yokota, Japan.

The author after giving a speech at McConnell Air Force Base, Kansas, at the dedication of this Boeing B-47 "gate guard." McConnell was the training base for B-47 crews, and no one who trained there will ever forget the hot summers, cold winters, and friendly people.

turn to provide clearance from the impending nuclear explosion.

It was not an exceptionally difficult maneuver to do, except the aircraft was large, bomber pilots were not used to aerobatics, and it was easy to exceed "G" limitations.

Much more serious, however, was the fact that the maneuvers induced fatigue, and there were a series of failures in 1958 which rocked SAC just as the failures in the Vickers Valiant would rock the RAF in 1964. Between March 13 and April 15, 1958, six B-47s crashed, and these triggered a fleet-wide investigation. The inspection revealed widespread fatigue problems, ranging from fatigue in the lower wing skin at buttock line 45, and failure due to stress corrosion of the "'milk bottle pin," the main fitting holding the wing to the fuselage. (See *Airpower,* Jan. 1979)

There ensued a nightmare of fixes, new problems, further fixes and further problems. After an immense amount of effort in a close approximation of wartime urgency, Boeing, Lockheed, and Douglas succeeded in an enormously complicated, immensely expensive program that ultimately contained the problem.

The B-47s had another six years of service remaining, so the Milk Bottle Program, as it became known, was worthwhile on its own merit. Even more important, it pointed out previously unconsidered problems inherent in the use of what were then considered exotic, high strength metals for jet aircraft construction. There had been very little information available on possible fatigue problems with these metals, and the unknown ground being charted proved to be fraught with hazard.

On the positive side, the B-47 fatigue and stress corrosion problems led to improved maintenance and inspection methods which would enable the B-52 to endure even more severe challenges.

In retrospect, the B-47 was a supreme aircraft for its time, and its shortcomings were minor compared to the tremendous advance it offered in performance. It was fun to fly, and although often uncomfortable and occasionally dangerous, most crews felt an affection for the aircraft that would not be transferred to its longer lived successor, the B-52.

This is the last B-47 to take to the air, refurbished and flown to then Castle Air Force Base in Merced, California, to be in the museum there. The base has since closed, but the Castle Museum still is going strong.

25 The Fable of Able Mable

The Martin AM-1

Airpower July, 1974

Aircraft companies are not only made up of humans, but they often act just like human beings themselves. Take, for example, the different ways that they grow old. Like some fortunate older people, the Boeing Company has managed to stay young, reinventing itself as conditions demand, and remaining not only competitive, but premier in the aerospace industry. Other firms, however, did not learn the technique of rejuvenating themselves so that they could stay competitive. Such was the case with Curtiss, which became managerially senile during the course of World War II and was never able to land a production contract for its own aircraft after the great P-40.

It was somewhat the same with the Glenn L. Martin Company, which went from full World War II activity into a decline that saw its share of the aircraft market continually diminish. Unlike Boeing, it was unable to save itself with new aircraft designs, not even those as clever as the AM-1 or the XB-51. Instead, the company survived by merging with American Marietta to form Martin Marietta and by shifting company emphasis from aircraft to space. Later, of course, it reentered the aircraft business with an even larger merger, this time with Lockheed.

The Martin AM-1 Mauler was a heavy-weapons carrier, without a doubt. As such it was part of the long tradition of powerful Martin naval aircraft. Here it carries three one-ton torpedoes plus 12 five-inch rockets. A good-looking airplane.

For the early part of its career, this was a weak spot in the Mauler structure; the tail sometimes was torn away.

The unusual "comb-tooth" dive brakes extended. The aircraft could be dived to 400 mph, the drive brakes extended, and there was no effect upon trim. When the two sections were closed, they could be lowered to form an effective flap.

In the swiftly paced three years following Pearl Harbor, the industrial machine of the United States reacted to its war emergency challenge far more spectacularly than anyone, especially its adversaries, could have imagined.

There was no energy crisis—fuel or human—in those days and nowhere was this more convincingly demonstrated than in the arms and tactics of U.S. Naval Aviation. From a crippled force limited to hit and run tactics with largely ineffective aircraft like the Douglas TBD Devastator (*Airpower* July 73) it had become a relentless giant, pounding the outmanned Japanese wherever they were found. The almost embarrassingly ample forces provided close air support, attacked land installations and completely suppressed the merchant shipping life blood of the island empire, right down to the harassment of individual fishing trawlers.

So complete was the technical and numerical superiority achieved in the air that veteran naval aviation planners were able to depart from restrictive custom and launch totally new concepts in carrier aviation. Heretofore, the planes actually fighting the war had been limited to the performance parameters available from engines of 1,000 horsepower; now they could command a host of new power plants of two to three times that output, as well as new propellers, instruments, airfoils, and construction techniques. Even better, the Navy's comfortable command of the air permitted the employment of a new breed of attack plane, one which could serve as an aerial dump truck, a load hauling marauder pouring the maximum weight of explosives on a tenacious but fast expiring enemy.

The new concept of the single place attack plane, initiated with the Pratt & Whitney R-4360 powered Curtiss XBTC-1, would call forth four new designs in 1944—the Curtiss XBT2C-1, Kaiser-Fleetwings XBTK-1, the Douglas XBT2D-1, and the Martin XBTM-1, forerunner of the AM Mauler. Outwardly similar in appearance—single engine, single place (tail gunners no longer being necessary) all-metal monoplanes—the four aircraft varied extensively in engines, armament, and performance, the four designs representing different approaches to essentially the same requirement. Curtiss had been assigned to develop a successor to its famous (or infamous, depending on your point of view) SB2C Helldiver, using the Wright R-3350. This aircraft, the XBT2C-1 (Experimental Bomber, Torpedo, Second Type, Curtiss—first model), was slightly smaller than their long-delayed XBTC-2. Kaiser-Fleetwings, on the other hand, a firm whose production performance on the stainless steel BT-12 had been little short of disastrous was, nevertheless, given a contract for a smaller plane using the P&W R-2800. The Douglas entry was a totally new start after an unsuccessful attempt to develop the XSB2D-1/BTD-1 (Experimental Scout Bomber, Second Type, Douglas—first model/Bomber, Torpedo Douglas—first model) design as a successor to the workhorse SBDs, while Martin, which had both engineering and production capability available, as a result of the impending phaseout of the B-26, was asked to provide a backup for the R-4360 Curtiss-powered design, already months behind schedule. No small part of this last request was the general dissatisfaction with the status of Curtiss production and products, particularly the prolonged teething troubles, prior to operational employment, of the SB2C Helldiver.

The Martin Baltimore company was delighted with the chance, for it faced the unpleasant and less profitable prospect of building someone else's designs. After all, it had been Martin which kicked dive bombing off in the Navy with its famous and long-lived biplane XT5M-1 (later BM-1), and Project Engineer Wally Symington had an eager crew ready to challenge Curtiss.

While the Curtiss XBTC-2, as it was now designated, had incorporated many experimental features, in addition to the first single engine use of the big R-4360, including a preposterous looking counter rotating propeller, Martin was urged to build as simple and "unexperimental" an aircraft as possible, one which would get the new engine into the air in the minimum time.

As a result, Procurement Directive Number 4701, dated 7 January 1944, called for the purchase of two model XBTM-1 airplanes and a static test article for $2.8 million; this was subsequently confirmed with a cost-plus fixed-fee contract.

Martin's genuine interest was demonstrated by the celerity with which a mockup of the Model 210 (Martin's company designation) was presented for inspection on 7 February, one month later to the day. Captain L. C. Stevens chaired the board, and he liked what he saw: a clean, simple design promising production and maintenance ease, with few potential flight problems.

The Mockup Board, however, did note three "unknowns": The first of these had been built in by the specified use of the 28-cylinder R-4360, and was in fact the prime reason for the aircraft's existence. The second was the radical new type of intermeshing finger dive brakes, which opened on both top and bottom of the wing-trailing edge, and also used a cheese-grater variety airbrake under the fuselage. The last unknown was the stability and control problems posed by putting such a high-density heavyweight package into the restricted overall dimensions demanded by existing carrier elevators.

The Martin plant, built especially for the construction of the famous B-26 Marauder, was sadly underutilized after World War II ended, and these workers were delighted to have the rugged Mauler to build.

The biggest problem the Mauler was supposed to have was the engine. This was not the case.

Encouraged by the warm response of the Mockup Board, Martin pressed on, confident that it could deal with problems two and three, while working hand-in-hand with the engine manufacturer to solve number one.

Ironically, the first two unknowns caused relatively little trouble. The final production engine configuration was very successful. With the exception of some minor cooling problems, the installation was a triumph of the uniquely diverse American subcontractor system. Ryan, in far off San Diego, had been given the task to develop a suitable stainless steel exhaust system for the R-4360-4W engine, one which would fit between the bristling rows of cylinders and the sleek, skintight cowling. The West Coast firm came up with an arrangement that was as much sculpture as it was engineering, and which provided an extra 100 horsepower through the ejection of the hot gases.

As will be related, the dive brakes proved to be no problem at all, but the stability and control area was a progressively worsening nightmare. Unfortunately, there was a fourth unknown, an almost unforeseeable engineering enigma which delayed testing and production and ultimately contributed to the selection of the Douglas entry, the AD Skyraider, as the standard Navy attack plane. Of this, more later.

Construction and design proceeded with true concurrency, some parts actually preceding the paperwork. Actually, it wasn't until June 7, 1944, that all engineering drawings necessary to put the first airplane into flying condition had been released to the shop, although the first flight was scheduled for July 15, 1944, a little more than six months after the release of the Procurement Directive.

There had been minor manufacturing problems, however, and an August 1, 1944, status report noted that *"the airplane is on the ramp minus outer wing panels, the rudder and the elevators, while the engine is being ground run. The outer wing panels are in the shop undergoing last minute installations and were scheduled to be assembled to the airplane July*

All AM-1s were transferred to reserve squadrons in early 1950 to permit the Navy to concentrate on one attack type for the fleet, the Douglas Skyraider. The reservists enjoyed the novel experience of having a virtually brand-new aircraft whose performance exceeded Navy standards in many respects.

26th. The ailerons are complete and the dive flaps should be completed very shortly. The airplane looks very good and workmanship on the skinning of the cowl, fuselage and wing is excellent. However, the skinning on the control surfaces is quite rough."

The first flight took place on August 26th, slightly more than five weeks behind schedule, but still the shortest time in which an experimental dive bomber had been built for the U.S. Navy.

O. E. "Pat" Tibbs, Martin's Chief Test Pilot and a legendary figure in aviation, was at the controls for the initial lift-off. This was no circuit and "thank God" bump affair, but a full sixty-eight-minute wringout. A highlight of the first flight was a "race" with a Marauder chase plane. The B-26 was flown at full throttle, with the XBTM-1 easily keeping formation at 67-percent power.

Tibbs' comments were as follows: *"Control on the ground during takeoff was good, stability about all axes was good, engine overcooled, elevator control was marginal, cockpit is very windy on the ground with the hood open and the wheels retract and extend very rapidly."*

The seemingly unending four years of testing which followed the first flight are the heart of Able Mable's story, for rarely has so much effort gone into perfecting an aircraft whose production had been curtailed and whose intended mission was being ably fulfilled by another aircraft.

Things started at a leisurely pace, for by October 1, 1944, only eight flights totaling 10.5 hours had been flown. All test flights had been conducted at a maximum gross weight of 18,500 pounds, and a survey of the Martin test pilots participating in the program confirmed Tibbs' initial impressions. They agreed that stick forces were heavy, but with a good gradient, while emphasizing that elevator control was so marginal that both hands had to be used to get the tail down for landing. Engine operation was satisfactory except for a tendency to overheat on the ground. Wave-off tests *at altitude* appeared satisfactory.

During October the number one aircraft, BuNo. 85161 was returned to the shop for a variety of fixes, including installation of the dive brakes. In addition, an alternate design had already been prepared for the fin, rudder, stabilizer, and elevator; and it was hoped that these changes would improve stick forces and general handling.

(The second prototype, 85162, would not make its first flight until May 20, 1945, and would then incorporate the many improvements developed on the first plane. The most apparent of these were a reduction in wing dihedral and the revised empennage.)

BuNo. 85161 reached the Naval Air Test Center at Patuxent River on December 11, and Navy test pilots put fifteen hours on it in the next five days. They were on the whole enthusiastic about the XBTM-1, but did report three major deficiencies, for each of which Martin had a proposed fix. The first was rudder reversal in level flight, which occurred in a clean condition at about 160 mph and resulted in a violent yaw. Martin had already built a dorsal fin in anticipation and agreed to incorporate it in the design.

The pilots also complained that the rudder was not sufficiently effective for carrier takeoffs, and Martin in this case promised to modify the rudder trim appropriately. Finally, aileron forces were considered too high at low speed but too low at high speeds—conditions easily remedied by making the aileron seals less effective.

Recognizing the prototype for what it was—a little overweight, somewhat roughly finished and operating with an interim propeller, the Naval Air Test Center gave the production program additional impetus by indicating that the plane would meet or exceed its requirements except for a slightly low top speed and a slightly high stall speed.

A letter of intent for 750 BTM (Bomber Torpedo Martin) airplanes was released on January 15, 1945, and the relatively slow testing program became a subject of official concern, leading eventually to some sharp words between the Navy and the contractor. Additionally, the airplane became a *cause celebre* within the Navy, having advocates who were determined to bring it into service regardless of test problems and opponents who felt that enough was enough, and it was time to switch to other things. The two sides would, ultimately, both win and lose.

The first XBTM-1 resumed testing on January 25, 1945, and opened its unique new dive brakes for the first time. Tibbs recalls that "The dive brakes were the greatest I have ever flown. They could be opened at 400 IAS, and there was almost no effect on trim. I have done vertical dives from 24,000 to 3,500 feet and never exceeded 360 IAS." Nevertheless, despite this praise, a slight tail shake was noted on the first flight, a harbinger of things to come, and the opening was temporarily restricted to a few degrees of travel.

Martin had completely instrumented the single prototype flying and was gathering reams of data. The very thoroughness of their approach was a direct cause of program delay; a management decision had been made to gather complete data even at the expense of time. In terms of the aircraft's later problems, it was unquestionably the right decision; in terms of the competition with Douglas, it was probably a mistake.

In contrast, the Douglas XBT2D-1 had been ordered on July 21, 1944, and first flown on March 18, 1945, with production deliveries of what was now called the AD-1 beginning in December 1946. (The BTM designation had been similarly changed to AM-1.)

The AM-1's testing process was unusual in the manner in which problems were sequentially revealed. In the beginning there seemed to be only minor problems common to every prototype. As these were solved, others, more serious, manifested themselves, but never in such a way that the program *had* to be cancelled.

The testing pace had accelerated through September 1945, but with the end of the war there was a natural dropoff in intensity. Still, there was an enormous commitment to the program, with at least 18 aircraft ultimately taking part in the flight testing.

The first production aircraft, 22257, incorporated 17 modifications determined to be necessary from the testing of the XBTM-1. These ranged from crew comfort items like increasing the height of the control column by two inches to major engineering changes like moving the engine forward six inches and adding two degrees of right thrust.

As the many facets of the testing program proceeded, simultaneously, there occurred a frenzied updating effort which saw selected test aircraft receiving almost continuous changes as modifications occurred. These were also incorporated into the production line where possible, although the 100th aircraft (122394) was usually considered the "break point" for the addition of engineering changes, with the preceding 99 aircraft usually slated for updating during the first regular overhaul cycle.

Of all the enormous number of changes which ultimately turned the Mauler into a highly reliable warplane, four stand out. Three of these were concerned with stability and control problems of varying degrees of severity, while the fourth, and most difficult, was a mysterious lack of structural integrity.

The term mysterious is apt, for examination of the Mauler would have revealed the usual excellent Martin workmanship on an airframe of tanklike solidity. Yet the carrier suitability trials conducted from 12 February through 27 August 1948 revealed ominous deficiencies.

The trials consisted of 100 launches from the hydraulic H4B catapult at aircraft gross weights ranging from 21,670 to 23,590 pounds. There were also 34 taxi-in and 222 fly-in engagements with the Mark V arresting gear.

Pilots had become understandably alarmed about a violent tail shake that occurred during engagements, with vibratory loads that sometimes reached 40 Gs. An assortment of fixes were tried, including "detuning" the natural frequency of the airplane by placing lead shot in various key areas to dampen the vibration. The nadir of the entire test program was reached when BuNo. 22279, the twenty-third production airplane, came in to make the fifty-first engagement. Apparently weakened by previous stresses, the entire aft section of the fuselage, including the empennage, tore off completely.

Martin immediately began a massive strengthening program, with fuselage longerons and the arresting hook carry-through structure being reinforced to carry *300* percent of their previous design load.

It soon became obvious that almost anything short of a solid stainless steel billet fuselage was going to fail, so attention was directed to the arresting hook itself. After a succession of trials, a new roller type was installed and the problem was largely resolved. This hook featured a sheave rotating on a vertical axis at the throat of the hook, allowing the hook to literally roll sideways along the arresting cable and preventing transmission of sideloads between the hook and the cable. Other modifications were made to the engaging equipment, but these were relatively minor. There apparently had been a totally unforeseeable resonant frequency problem with the airframe and the standard hook—the sort of improbable "glitch" that turns engineers gray.

The stability and control problems were more persistent and less susceptible to dramatic solutions. In every case the problems were of the sort that might well have been endured in the prewar and early wartime situation; however, test standards had been significantly raised during the war years, and the refinements which ensued would soon become commonplace on jet aircraft.

The airplane had an unfortunate tendency to yaw in response to certain changes in pitch, and this made formation flying difficult and night carrier approaches downright dangerous. Martin aerodynamicists' painless fix for this was to have the sheet-metal shop bang out an angled aluminum strip which was placed adjacent to the inboard end of the elevator to contain the flow of air. This "stabilizer air dam" solved the yaw problem.

There also had been continuing complaints about the lateral control available near the stall, and the roll rate in the landing configuration. The trailing edge of the wing was completely taken up with ailerons, flaps, and dive brakes, so Martin developed a "spoiler aileron," mounted just inboard of the conventional surface. This hydraulically operated section operated with the normal control movements and served to reduce adverse aileron yaw as well as increase roll response. Many later aircraft would use essentially similar devices.

The marginal elevator control Tibbs had noted in the first test flight had persisted and was perhaps even less desirable in the production aircraft. There was a disagreeable tendency for the plane to pitch down suddenly from an altitude of about 20 feet, far faster than the pilot could control. This made for some interesting porpoising hops which would send Able Mable yo-yoing into a go-around. It was a physics problem, as there was not enough leverage for the pilot to apply sufficient elevator pressure to control the phenomenon. The stiffness also manifested itself during takeoff, although this was not so troublesome.

The answer here was a relatively complex, variable demand, hydraulic-assist mechanism—power steering if you will—which provided the needed muscle and completely normalized takeoff and landings.

Other Trials

The other trials didn't have as much tribulation (sorry), and the rugged testing encompassed guns, rockets, torpedoes, bombs, and electronics in a fairly routine manner. Not all results were satisfactory, of course, but there were no really unsolvable problems.

BuNo. 22269 was used for the test of the four forward-firing 20-mm (M3) cannon, which were mounted in pairs in the port and starboard center wing panel, just inboard of the wing fold. The guns were fully accessible with wings folded, but couldn't be serviced with the wings spread. Ammunition was carried in four cans, each holding 200 rounds. The guns were charged hydraulically through a Bendix solenoid-operated gun-charging system, and were fired by means of an AN-M4 electric trigger. After 28 separate NATC trouble items were resolved, the weapons functioned in a satisfactory manner, being tested in all conditions of attitude, velocity, and acceleration, including firing tests in vertical dives and 5.0 G pullouts.

Eight aircraft of VA-17A fly in echelon formation. Most of the pilots were experienced World War II veterans.

The rocket tests ran into immediate trouble when the blast from 5.0″ HVARs damaged the ailerons; a switch from Mark 9 Mod. 2 rocket launchers to the Mod. 3 version was

These Maulers were based at Quonset Point, Rhode Island, in June, 1948. Even though they were new airplanes, they were obviously very well maintained, as the sparkling undersurfaces of the wings show.

This is a purposeful-looking, competent aircraft; had it been able to avoid testing problems, it might well have given the Douglas Skyraider a run for its money in procuring production contracts.

a cure, and the rest of the tests, including rapid firing, were successful.

By contrast, the bombing, torpedo, and electronic trials proceeded almost effortlessly, with no major discrepancies.

One glaring defect in the Mauler was not rectified until the 100th production airplane; this was the appalling cockpit layout which made instrument flying impossible, and had in addition the usual human factors problems. The redesigned cockpit, which was tested on BuNo. 22297, was significantly better, and proved to be very acceptable for service use. This was not an uncommon problem for the time, and indeed persists today.

The aircraft could carry three one-ton torpedoes. One problem it faced, however, was that the world situation had changed, and the demand for torpedo delivery was almost nonexistent.

The AM-1Q

Contract NOa(s) 5400, as amended by MCR No. 53, called for the procurement of one prototype and 11 production AM-1Q radar countermeasure aircraft, while Contract NOa(s) 8523 covered the conversion of six production AM-1s to AM-1Qs.

BuNo. 22296 was converted to AM-1Q for tests which were limited to electronic aspects only. The main fuselage tank was deleted and a second crew member's position installed just behind the pilot's seat, along with the requisite radar countermeasures equipment. Other modifications included an entrance hatch, oxygen equipment, and heating and ventilation controls.

The test AM-1Q was totally unsatisfactory, and 18 pages of writeups spelled out why. Martin was apparently unaware of the appropriate specifications governing the installation of electronic gear and had committed one engineering *faux pas* after another. The human factors considerations were hopeless, as the position, besides being claustrophobic, was unbearably hot, with ground operations approximating a sauna. Even at 26,000 feet, where the outside temperatures ranged from 50° to 70° below zero, ordinary flight clothing was totally adequate for comfort.

Six AM1-Qs were ultimately delivered (BuNos. 122388 through 122393), but they made little impact on the EMC scene, though one was assigned to each of the two CVGs whose VA squadrons were equipped with AM-1s.

This was the Mauler's real problem: The Douglas AD did almost everything it could do equally well and had experienced few problems in its test programs. It was also less expensive.

Introduction to Operations

Attack Squadron 17A at Quonset Naval Air Station, Rhode Island, was the first operational unit to receive the AM-1, taking first delivery on March 1, 1948. Lt. Commander Robert E. Farkas was skipper of the VA-17A, and he divided the squadron into teams to develop procedures for operational employment of the Mauler. Farkas made the first carrier landing on the U.S.S. *Kearsarge*.

The uncertain test program had long since forced the cancellation of the majority of the original 750 aircraft order; only 2 XBTM-1s, 143 AM-1s, and 6 AM-1Qs were finally delivered, the last one being turned over in November 1949. The success and versatility of the Douglas AD Skyraiders had long since become apparent, and it didn't make logistic sense to have two attack aircraft with such similar performance throughout the Navy. AMs were therefore assigned to Atlantic Fleet squadrons, and after a short period were relegated to the Naval Reserve. The last fleet aircraft, an AM-1Q assigned to VC-4, was withdrawn in October 1950, less than a year after the production line closed.

Eighty-two of the Maulers were initially issued to reserve units at Atlanta, Georgia, Glenview, Illinois, Grosse Ille, Michigan, Floyd Bennett Field, New York, Squantam, Massachusetts, and St. Louis, Missouri. Pilots were happy with an airplane that had been so thoroughly tested and which had, in many respects, a performance superior to its first-line Regular Navy counterpart.

Structural, Performance, and Flight Details

Much of the experience gained in the construction of thousands of Martin B-26s was evident in the beefy structure of the Mauler. The flush riveted fuselage was of conventional semimonocoque construction, with the center section of the wing and fuselage being built as an integral unit, a Martin technique that went all the way back to the B-10. The Baltimore firm was adept in the use of large forged sections, and these added to the rigidity and ruggedness of the plane.

The commodious fuselage provided plenty of room for either a 150-gallon tank or the electronic countermeasures operator position. There were various proposals which would have capitalized on this space, including a transport version (ala the later Douglas AD-5) and a twin-tandem engine Model 210-M, which was reminiscent of the Kawasaki Ki-64.

The wings consisted of the center section and two outer panels which folded upwards for stowage and service. The box spars formed a strong basis for the ribs, riblets, and corrugated stiffeners which lay beneath the smooth flush riveted exterior surfaces. Each of the all-metal slotted ailerons had trim and balance tabs and was mounted immediately outboard of the dive brakes. A spoiler aileron was situated just forward of the wing flap on the upper surface and augmented lateral control.

The empennage was a completely conventional all-metal cantilever structure.

Power was supplied by the new and versatile Pratt & Whitney R-4360-4W Wasp Major, a 28-cylinder four-row radial that developed 3,000 horsepower for takeoff. The first 99 production aircraft used a 14′8″ diameter Curtiss electric propeller; the last 50 were fitted with a Hamilton Standard of the same diameter.

As noted, the dive flaps performed remarkably well despite their novel configuration. The dive brake and wing flap controls were mechanically interconnected so that dive brakes could not be opened when the flaps were extended, nor could the flaps be extended with the brakes open. The brakes could be positioned at any point between full open and full close by means of a control lever.

After the various stability problems had been ironed out, the Mauler was a joy to fly, particularly at light weights. Stall warning in the form of a light buffet occurred at 3 to 4 knots above the stall, which was characterized by a fairly sharp break and a moderate turn to the right. Aileron control was available all through the stall, and a gentle dip of the nose to the horizon restored the aircraft to normal flight.

While intentional spins were prohibited, recovery was conventional and presented no problem. Almost all other acrobatic maneuvers were allowed, although abrupt aileron action was cautioned against.

The overall performance of the completely vetted AM-1 was truly excellent. It's ironic that the plane which had so many testing problems might well have been a potent factor just a few years later, and, conceivably, could have been useful two decades later in Vietnam.

And here was the end of the road, as it was for so many aircraft. One Mauler still exists at the National Museum of Naval Aviation in Pensacola, Florida.

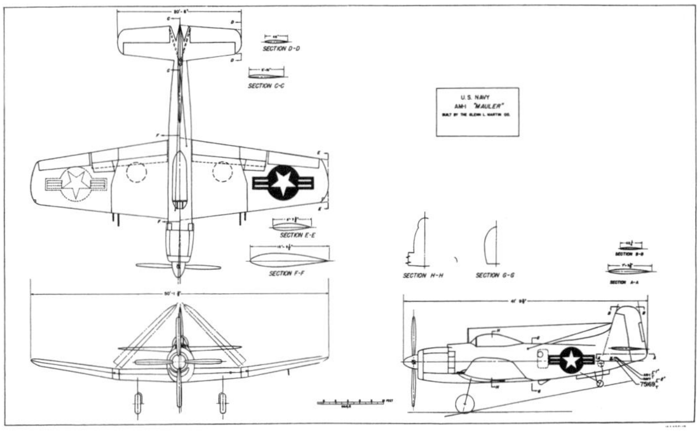

A three-view drawing of a handsome aircraft.

26 BOEING B-52

Emperor of Airpower

Airpower March, 1982

It is not easy to imagine the 1908 Wright Military Flyer continuing to engage in reconnaissance duties in 1988. Nor does it seem likely that the SPAD XIII of 1918 would have served any useful military role in 1998. Yet the Boeing B-52 is now projected to have just such a lengthy career, for it will almost certainly still be the backbone of the United States Air Force bomber fleet in 2032, on the 80th anniversary of its first flight.

No one in the Air Force or at Boeing would have predicted such a long career for the B-52; in the past, everyone was conditioned to bombers having roughly a 10-year service life before being phased out as obsolete. But the B-52 came to be perceived not as a bomber, but as a platform, *one that could be modified to carry ever new equipment, including cruise missiles and smart weapons. Thus, with good mainte-*

The Boeing XB-52 in flight. The most obvious difference from later production B-52s was the tandem cockpit, like that of the B-47. Curt LeMay was absolutely opposed to the idea, even though the canopy reduced drag. He wanted the closest possible coordination between aircraft commander and pilot, and you got this with side-by-side seating. He got his way, of course!

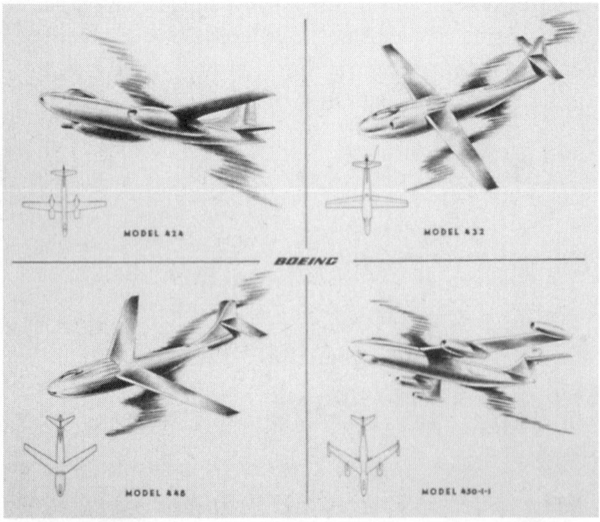

The Boeing engineers went through many iterations, from straight wing turboprops to swept wing jets, before arriving at the winning formula for the B-52.

The Boeing YB-52 actually flew before the XB-52, taking off on April 15, 1952. It is entirely possible that the USAF will be flying a B-52 on April 15, 2052, giving the aircraft an honest 100 years of service. (Possible but not likely—but it is almost certain that they'll be flying until at least 2032.) No one gathered at Boeing Field in Seattle to watch this takeoff would have believed it possible that their creation would serve so well for so long.

nance and ample modification funds, at least 50 B-52s could serve in new roles as they evolve for the rest of the 21st century. Economically this is wonderful, no doubt, but to those of us who remember the Strategic Air Command at its 1,600-bomber prime, it is more than a little sad.

The bomber has long been of special importance to American military thinking. It was a natural complement to early American ideas on isolation, for it promised to keep threatening fleets from our shores. Later it became vital to the preservation of post World War II American interests around the globe. Of all the bombers ever to enter service, none has been so important for so long as the legendary Boeing B-52.

This huge, angular, eight engined airplane, affectionately called BUFF (for Big Ugly Fat Fellow in mixed company and Big Ugly Fat Something Else in less polite society) by its crewmembers, was designed in story book fashion in a hotel room in Dayton over a single weekend. It transcended the role of simple bombing plane and became a factor in world politics. The small crowd that watched it lumber into the air for the first time on April 15, 1952, could not have known, and would have in fact been shocked to learn, that they were witnessing the start of what may well turn out to be a *half-century* of front line service.

At this writing, the B-52 has already served thirty years. There are already men who have served an entire military career solely with this airplane, and there are young pilots flying the same plane their fathers flew. Never in the history of modern warfare has a major weapon system been so long lived. It is as if a Wright biplane of 1911 had served until Pearl Harbor, or as if a P-26 Peashooter was to fly combat in Viet Nam.

But longevity does not imply lack of change. The airplane was improved continuously from the XB-52 on, so that while the external configuration is substantially the same, it is a vastly different machine under the skin. Three major elements have combined to give the B-52 its unprecedented lifespan. The first is the soundness of the original design, which provided a clean spacious airframe. The second is the cooperation between Boeing and the U.S. Air Force in predicting the modifications that have kept it viable; and the third is the Strategic Air Command's crew concept, where the integrity of crews maintained throughout years of training and combat, in effect, supports the aircraft and substitutes for modernity.

The B-52 began as a traditional high altitude heavy bomber, capable of carrying strategic nuclear warheads anywhere in the world. When the development of accurate ground-to-air missiles ruled out incursions at high altitude, the B-52 was adapted to the low level mission, a regimen which introduced entirely new factors of fatigue, stress and wear on the aircraft and required new levels of skill and courage from the crews.

During the Vietnamese conflict, the B-52 was adapted once again, this time to the role of conventional "iron bomb" carrier. What had been conceived as the deliverer of a searing nuclear stiletto to the enemy heartland was now rumbling flying artillery, dropping barrages more reminiscent of the Somme than Hiroshima. The crews, trained to be razor sharp in their precision delivery of a nuclear weapon on an urban target, were just as proficient delivering 750 pound bombs on enemy troop concentrations. They called themselves "coconut knockers" and other names but they did the job. And when it became time for them to take on the most intensive air defenses the world has ever seen, the SAM-studded skies of Hanoi, they performed superbly.

Yet the accomplishments of the B-52 are too often related to its magnificent airframe and the powerful Pratt & Whitney engines which power it, obscuring the massive pyramid of effort which underlies its success. If you analyze these factors, they spread across the country and around the world in a network of men and women and enterprise that involves hundreds of thousands of people. You can trace this network by beginning with the original principals, the handful of engineers and managers at Boeing who conceived the aircraft, and the Air Force leaders who spelled out the requirements calling for its conception.

This photo clearly shows the difference in the shape of the nose when the tandem canopy was abandoned in favor of a conventional crew-cabin layout.

We should never forget that the B-52, B-47, F-111, B-2, and all the other combat planes depend upon this aircraft to be able to complete their missions. The Boeing KC-135 is one of the unsung workhorses of the United States Air Force, and it and its crews should be saluted for almost 50 years of superb work. They'll be working for another 30 years, too!

Originally designed as a high-speed, high-altitude nuclear bomber, capable of penetrating the Soviet Union alone and dropping nuclear weapons there, the B-52 proved adaptable to many tasks. In Southeast Asia, the B-52, shown here, became a close-air support aircraft conducting tactical bombing raids with huge quantities of conventional weapons.

At the next level, we find the hard core engineers who translated these requirements first into drawings and then, with the talented Seattle team, into metal. Their Air Force counterparts in Dayton and elsewhere spelled out the equipment requirements—new and better radar bombing systems, inflight refueling systems, power generation equipment, electronic countermeasure equipment, and more powerful engines. Again the industry responded, managing each time to provide the essential new equipment to keep the aircraft serviceable in ever-changing environments, and with ever-changing missions.

In parallel fashion, workers were trained at Boeing to manufacture the aircraft while airmen were trained in the Air Force to service it; weapons were developed to be dropped from it; pilot training programs were set up, repair centers established, spare parts lists computed and stocks acquired.

As the aircraft began to leave the production lines for operational service, problems were encountered. Some were fatal, sad, savage accidents relating to equipment failures; others were routine, the ordinary process in a weapon system's development.

The final delivery of the 744th aircraft, a B-52H in October 1962, was made at a time when the whole industry associated with the plane was in full operation. Thirty-six SAC wings were operating the aircraft at bases all around the U.S.; two factories were equipped for the repair and modification of the fleet, and for the control and manufacture of updating kits. An entire bureaucracy of record-keepers meticulously tracked the hours on the fleet, noting the maintenance that needed to be done and the number of spares that must be purchased.

Yet despite the enormous human back-up, the B-52 has retained its own grudging personality. A monster on the flight line capable of consuming innumerable maintenance hours for each flight hour, with a history that includes every mechanical headache from an untraceable fuel leak to complete equipment failures, the B-52, nevertheless, always lumbered out to meet its takeoff times, wings drooping, brakes squeaking, its cockpit permeated with the smell of JP-4 and two decades of indigestible inflight lunches, sweat and smoke.

The engine runups bring the pounding vibration of eight powerful engines shaking and rattling at their pylon mounts. The skin oilcans, and everything on board, from tool kits to ashtrays, vibrates and chatters. The power is brought up and the aircraft lurches forward, a dumb mechanical giant lurching along at a snail's pace. But soon there is a change. The noises seem to lessen and the airplane becomes lighter, faster. The wings—just the wings—begin to fly as the airspeed builds and runway markers begin to race by. Finally, there is that precomputed moment, that balance of weight, temperature, air density, speed and hope where the airplane lifts from the runway into its own element. The smoke boils past, the noise swells and falls in Doppler fashion, and it is airborne for yet another mission.

The B-52 does not fly like a fighter. Nor is it a truck. It does things its own way, more crisply than you would imagine, but inevitably with the inertia and the space required for 450,000 pounds hurtling at 300 knots indicated air speed. It is a pilot's airplane, but only in the sense that pilots that fly it are also engineers, commanders, arm wrestlers and, when necessary, bronco busters. The B-52 does what it is supposed to do, from flying in close formation with a Boeing KC-135A tanker to blistering along in hopeful uncertainty over low level routes, or performing specialized tasks like dropping research aircraft and launching missiles. But it does this at a cost of much maintenance, and with the buttressing of very underpaid but highly skilled airmen, who literally have been asked to take the cost of national defense out of their own hide.

The importance of the B-52 to national defense has been inestimable and its contribution to civil aviation is often overlooked. It provided Boeing, in conjunction with its predecessor, the B-47, with the jet experience to launch the 707 program, which in turn carried the firm to a position of dominance never before achieved by any aircraft manufacturing company. Not least of its contributions, as we shall see, was the calling into being of the Pratt and Whitney J-57 engine, which in civil guise was the JT-3 which powered a generation of jet transports.

The Indispensable Forerunner—the Boeing B-47

As the readers of the August issue of *Wings* know, the Boeing B-47 was perfect preparation for the design and construction of the B-52. Though there was almost five years separation in their first flights, the B-47 flying first on December 17, 1947, and the B-52, as noted, on April 15, 1952, their development was still somewhat concurrent. Fortunately for the B-52 program there was enough time separation for many lessons to be learned.

The first and foremost of the lessons was that the wings need not be as thin as they were on the B-47. Boeing engineers learned that the critical place for wing thickness was not at the wing/fuselage juncture, as they had thought, but rather about a third of the way out on the span. This meant that the B-52 wing could be made much thicker, and this in turn meant that it could not only be made lighter, it could also be used to carry fuel.

Boeing also learned a great deal about metal fatigue in modern jet structures, even though the B-52 would teach them more. As a result, the B-52 was designed with fatigue and corrosion much more in mind than was the case with the B-47.

Because the drag of the B-47 had been much less than predicted, it was possible to stretch the performance capability of the B-52; typical of Boeing conservatism, though, was the fact that each B-52 version came in at less drag than had been predicted.

In the case of the B-47, Boeing engineers had been primarily concerned with learning about jet engines and swept wings. Systems were kept simple and, for a variety of reasons, wing area was kept low. By the time the B-52 was on the drawing boards, the Boeing engineers could take greater risks, to achieve greater speed and range. To do this they called for new systems, previously unheard of, for weight reduction. The electrical power systems, hydraulic systems and pneumatic systems were entirely new, and subcontractors had to strain their resources to meet Boeing demands for performance at minimum weight.

The B-47 had had only 1,428 square feet of wing area; for the B-52, a whopping 4,000 square feet was called for. This, coupled with the size of the aircraft, would permit a growth in weight and equipment that a lesser airplane could not have accomplished.

All in all, Boeing had made optimum use of the data streaming from the B-47. It was a far more sophisticated aircraft to build than the B-29s and B-50s had been, and it laid the manufacturing basis for production of the B-52.

A Weekend in Dayton

In a single October weekend in Dayton, Ohio, a whole series of separate events, each of which had followed a complex development path of its own, would come together under the guidance of a small Boeing and Air Force team and result in the B-52 bomber. These were the events, some with very long histories, which gave birth to the XB-52:

1. Major improvements in in-flight refueling, especially the Boeing designed flying boom system, made extremely long range possible for fuel hungry jets.

2. So much work had been done on the basis of lessons learned in the B-47 program, that a successor to it, the

This was the author's home base during the Vietnam War—U Tapao Royal Thai Air Force Base. It was built by cutting off the top of a mountain and placing the rocks in the nearby swamp, creating the best and most modern air base in the Far East. U Tapao and Andersen Air Base in Guam launched almost all of the B-52 strikes during the Vietnam War.

XB-55, had been selected. This aircraft had thicker wings and four jets.

3. The turboprop engine which had been planned for the heavy long range bomber requirement was having development problems which promised to take as long as four years to solve.

4. Major leaders in the Air Force had been convinced by the B-47 that the swept wing jet bomber was the wave of the future.

5. There was within the Air Force and the Boeing company sufficient flexibility to drop existing aircraft and engine programs and gamble on a better solution.

During the week of October 22, 1948, Colonel Pete Warden, a hero of both the B-47 and B-52 programs, suggested to senior Boeing officials that they stop work on their proposed series of turbo prop straight wing aircraft and plan to develop a swept wing jet. At the same time, Warden persuaded the Pratt & Whitney engineers to stop development of their turboprop efforts and instead build a large jet engine. (It would become the J57.)

The Boeing group consisted of Edward C. Wells, George S. Schairer, H.W. "Bob" Withington, Vaughn Blumenthal, Art Carlsen, and Maynard Pennell, all distinguished engineers who would do much for Boeing and their country. The six men distilled their wisdom into an entirely new aircraft design, creating a thirty-three page proposal calling for a large bomber with 4,000 square feet of wing area, 35 degrees of wing sweep, eight Pratt & Whitney J-57 engines in B-47-like pods, and a slim low drag angular fuselage with the pilots seated in tandem. Called the Boeing Model 464-49-0, it had a design gross weight of 330,000 pounds, a high speed of 572 mph and a range of 8,000 miles with a 10,000 pound bomb load. They made three view drawings and built a balsa wood model to present to Col. Warden on the following Monday morning.

Warden was ecstatic with the proposal, despite the fact that it combined a new airframe with a new engine and a new method of inflight refueling. Acting on his own authority, he authorized Boeing to terminate work on the turboprops and promised to deliver new funding for the XB-52 within a few months. (Today a Colonel making similar promises would become a prime candidate for attaché duty in Teheran.)

XB and YB-52s

The XB-52 and YB-52 aircraft rapidly took shape in a highly classified area of the Seattle plant. Contrary to previous accounts, there was basically no difference between the two aircraft, the YB designation being given solely to permit the Air Force to allocate an additional $10,000,000 in production funds on the experimental aircraft.

The B-52 landed on a massive gear consisting of four trucks, each with two wheels and two outriggers. The forward gear could be positioned to permit a crosswind landing (the B-52's wings were too wide to permit dipping a wing to approach in a crosswind).

The B-52 was utterly unique, on the ground or in the air. On the ground it creaked and groaned as it moved along the runway, its nose magically moving from side to side as the crosswind gear was tested. On takeoff, the wings began flying first, and you flew them with the ailerons until the rest of the airplane caught up and the machine began to fly as a unit.

The XB-52 was rolled out in tarpaulin shrouded secrecy on the night of November 29, 1951. During preparation for flight, a massive failure of the pneumatic system ripped out the whole trailing edge of the wing and it was secretly returned to the construction area for what was officially called "equipment installation" but was, in reality, repairs to the wing. As a result, the YB-52, which had rolled out on March 15, 1952, was the first to fly. The XB-52 did not make its first flight until October 2, 1952.

Paul Higgins and Vaughn Blumenthal, the aerodynamicists, were worried about the possibility that aileron overbalance might be encountered and they set control forces at a very high level for the first flight. A.M. "Tex" Johnson and Lt. Col. Guy M. Townsend were the first flight pilots, and they found the airplane truck-like to control in the flight from Seattle to Moses Lake, Washington. Adjustments were easily made, and within a week the aircraft was adjudged to be so "bug free" that it was returned to the Seattle area for further testing.

The Air Force was impressed with the prototype and promptly issued a letter contract for thirteen B-52As in February 1951, and these received the most extensive configuration change of all the aircraft down to the G model. The tandem cockpit was changed at Curt LeMay's request to the now familiar side by side type, and the fuselage was lengthened by four feet. Improved J57-P-9W engines were fitted outboard on the wings. These provided additional fuel as well as load relief to the structure.

The first A model flew on August 5, 1954, and a few days later a contract was let for 50 B and RB-52s, the latter having a reconnaissance capability. Later the order for 13 A models was reduced to three, the other ten becoming B-52Bs. The three A models entered development, and after serving as test beds for B-52 systems, did a variety of work in other capacities, including service as launch vehicles for the X-15, lifting bodies and other craft.

The B-52B was outwardly identical to the A model but had an increased reconnaissance capability and the MA-6A bombing system, considered truly revolutionary at the time. With a maximum gross weight of 420,000 pounds, the B models were fitted with a variety of uprated

The interior of the B-52 received far more changes than did the exterior, with new equipment of every kind being installed over the years. Even the cockpits gave up their familiar round analog dial gauges and received cathode-ray installations. This is a B-52G, one of 100 that had the new equipment installed as part of a $220-million modification project.

The B-52 took many maintenance man-hours per flying hour from the very start and continues to do so. There is no way that adequate praise can be given to the enlisted crew members who slaved outdoors in all sorts of weather, from freezing Arctic conditions to the "sweat and swear" heat of Southeast Asia. They did it for very little money, but with a great deal of patriotism, and the airplanes could not have flown a single mission without them.

The B-52 fleet has undergone continuous modification from the day the first one rolled off the production line. One of the most dramatic was the "Big Belly" series of modifications to the B-52D which enabled it to carry no fewer than 84 500-pound bombs or 42 750-pound bombs internally, plus additional bombs on the wing pylons, for a total of 65,000 pounds of bombs.

J57 engines, delivering as much as 12,100 pounds of thrust with water injection and 10,500 pounds without.

Twenty-seven of the series became RB-52B, using a two man pressurized capsule in the bomb bay which could perform electronic countermeasure ferret work or photographic reconnaissance. The two men who climbed into the capsule were of a special breed, for their's was a dark and remote world cut off from all but radio communication and extremely vulnerable to any sort of low altitude emergency where their downward ejection seats would be at a disadvantage.

A B-52B, 52-8711, was delivered with a flourish to Castle Air Force Base, Merced, California, on June 29, 1955. Within a few months the 93rd Bomb Wing had converted from B-47s to B-52 without losing their nuclear capability, and had set up the 4017th Combat Crew Training Squadron which became the focal point for all B-52 training for the next few years.

Fuel leaks caused some serious problems during the first year, but all of the training requirements were met. By 1957, SAC was so sure of itself that it sent three aircraft from the 93rd on a non-stop air refueled trip around the world. The 24,235 mile flight was completed in 45 hours and 19 minutes, and was within two minutes of the predicted enroute time, and within ½ of 1% of the predicted fuel consumption. All 24 engines were still running, and the only maintenance requirement was the replacement of an alternator. It was a stunning triumph for SAC and for the Castle crews.

As additional crews were trained, new and better model B-52s appeared. The first of 35 B-52Cs made its first flight on March 9, 1956, and it featured huge 3,000 gallon drop tanks. The gross weight was increased to 450,000 pounds, and there were improvements in the fire control system.

The Air Force eventually decided to open a second production source at Boeing's Wichita facility, which rolled out its first B-52D on December 7, 1955, that aircraft making its first flight on May 14, 1956. Seattle also produced D models. These became the backbone of the nuclear fleet for several years, and then had a renaissance as "iron bomb" carriers in Viet Nam. Originally not much different than the C models, the Ds were the recipients of many changes which enabled them to alter their role from classic high altitude bomber to the dropper of conventional weapons.

Meanwhile, the Russians had not been idle, building their radar and anti-aircraft systems with a beaver-like intensity. The B-52Es were therefore designed to use new low altitude equipment necessary to pierce these Soviet defenses. The B-52E also incorporated improved bombing and navigation equipment. More important, it adopted the use of constant speed drives for the electrical generating systems, thus obviating the air driven turbines which had caused some tragic losses. The turbine wheels, driven at extremely high rpms, had disintegrated on some of the earlier model aircraft, sending red hot fragments slicing into fuselage fuel cells with catastrophic results, that turned the B-52 into an airborne inferno.

Boeing built 100 E models and followed this with 89 F models, which featured J57-P-43W engines of 13,750 pounds of thrust. By the time the last B-52F had made its delivery flight from Seattle on February 25, 1959, SAC's bomber fleet had reached an intimidating size, with a worldwide destructive delivery capability that had never been matched before. As early as 1956, however, the need for even greater range and flexibility was seen, and production of the B-52G had been authorized. Outwardly the G model resembled its predecessors except for a shorter vertical surface and an absence of ailerons. Internally, however, it was almost an entirely new aircraft, one in which Boeing would pull off the spectacular engineering hat trick of lowering basic empty operating weight while increasing gross operating weight. However, some perplexing problems had to be solved first.

The Gs and Hs

With the B-52G, Boeing had audaciously determined to cut empty operating weight by 15,000 pounds, and the methods by which they decided to do it promised to achieve a 30% increase in range and a decrease of 25% in maintenance man hours.

The design called for an entirely new "wet wing," one with machined alloy wing skins and integral stiffeners. The long skins reduced the probability of fuel leaks and fatigues, although another factor was to intervene in this equation.

The reduction of the height of the vertical fin from 48 feet to 40, coupled with the elimination of the aileron system, saved another 12,000 pounds. New equipment, including an improved fire control system, was designed to make the B-52G a missile platform as well as a gravity bomber. The supersonic GAM-77 Hound Dog was produced for use with the G, a true cruise missile long before the name became controversial.

The wing structure was not only lighter, but had to be stronger, as gross weight was increased to 488,000 pounds. The problem proved to be that, in addition to being strong and extraordinarily flexible, it had to be leak proof under conditions of repeated flexing, hard landings, gusty air and the poundings encountered in aerial refueling. Aerial refueling, no matter how routine SAC likes to make it seem, is a grueling extension of the capability of both men and machines, fatiguing and dangerous every time.

It was found that with the shorter fin and the lack of ailerons, which had been replaced by spoilers, the aircraft had an increased tendency to Dutch Roll, an inbred characteristic of all swept wing aircraft. The existing yaw dampener was not adequate, and aerial refueling was hampered because the deployment of the spoilers for lateral control during aerial refueling induced pitch-up. This combination of desired and unexpected responses to a control input was very fatiguing and frustrating to the pilot and was a subject of a later modification.

There were numerous other, less visible changes in the G model, including cockpit layout, repositioning of the gunner to the forward compartment, new engine driven hydraulic pumps in place of the pneumatic packs, and so on. SAC demonstrated the G's range capability on December 13, 1967, when Colonel T.R. Grissom flew his 5th Bombardment wing B-52 for 10,000 miles, without refueling, in 19 hours and 47 minutes.

Wichita was now the sole source for B-52s, and delivered 193 G models between November 1, 1958, and February 7, 1961, and at the same time geared up for the last and the finest of the series, the B-52H.

The B-52H received Pratt & Whitney's revolutionary new TF33 turbofan (fan jet) engine. The turbofan was one of the very few instances in engineering when one seems to obtain a great advantage without sacrificing elsewhere. By adding a large diameter fan element (in effect, a propeller pushing masses of cold air), the total thrust was substantially increased, while specific fuel consumption was substantially reduced. (The incorporation of turbocharging on today's cars is not too dissimilar.)

The TF33 was flat rated at 17,000 pounds of thrust, a 30% increase over the G model using water injection. However, the very quickness of throttle response and the immense power delivered posed an insidious problem to drivers of the H model. Too rapid movement of the throttle could cause the aircraft to pitch up at a rate beyond the pilot's ability to control with available elevator authority. To prevent this a mechanical gate was placed on the throttle quadrant and the harnessing of the TF33's extra power was assured.

Time for Changes

Long before the last of a total of 744 B-52s was delivered in the form of the 102nd B-52H on October 26, 1962, it was apparent that new mission requirements and totally unanticipated fatigue problems would require massive modifications if the fleet was to be kept in being.

It was an unprecedented situation, in which more money would be spent on modifications than had pre-

There were big friends and little friends in World War II—B-17s and P-51s, for example—and there were big friends and little friends in Southeast Asia as well. There, because of the stupid way the war was run from Washington, the strategic B-52s were used against tactical targets, while the tactical McDonnell F-4s were used against strategic targets.

viously been spent on a new production bomber's development. It was possible only because Congress was more amenable to appropriations to modify an existing aircraft than to making the decision to commit to a new one, and because Boeing had demonstrated an amazing ability to plan modifications that kept the B-52 competitive.

The structural modifications were required in part by the extraordinary longevity of the B-52. Previous bombers, up to and including the B-47, had enjoyed relatively short service lives, with average lifetime flight hours ranging from 1,500 to 4,000. The B-52 was being required to serve on after logging 5,000 hours, and was envisaged to have an unheard of prospective life of 10,000 to 17,500 flight hours. Compounding the problem was the change from the relatively stress free, high altitude mission to bone jarring, rivet shaking, skin crinkling, low level work. A flight in a B-52 at 35,000 feet can be a serene pleasure. The aircraft responds to the controls smoothly, and except for occasional wind shear, it is virtually bump free. A flight in a B-52 at 300 feet on a hot day over mountainous terrain is a murderous, slam bang, head knocking, vicious experience that can make 10,000 hour veterans air sick, and induce stresses that cannot be fathomed.

Boeing thus had a double problem. On the one hand it had to convince the Air Force that it could design equipment which would permit the B-52s to penetrate Soviet airspace, including the necessary terrain avoidance equipment, electronic countermeasures, and so on, and at the same time modify the aging B-52s so that they could stand the totally new stresses involved.

The full story of these extraordinary modifications is too long and too complex to tell here; suffice to say that Boeing succeeded well enough to have the B-52 survive the competition of the B-58, the XB-70 and, for many years, the B-1. The future may well reveal that it will survive not only the revived and modified B-1, but also its sneaky follow-on, the Stealth bomber. If that is so, the day may well come when the B-52 has been flown by grandfather, father and son combinations.

A Boeing B-52G approaches for landing, wheels down, flaps down, the underside showing the wear and tear of years of use. The B-52 was changed from a high-altitude to a low-altitude aircraft because of the increased efficiency of Soviet surface-to-air missiles. The new flight regime, flying at 300 feet at 300 mph or better, really battered and shook the airframe—and the crew.

Flying the Buff

Flying the B-52 is hard work. It is especially demanding during low level flight and in-flight refueling, for different reasons. During low level flight the aircraft is

One of the greatest teams in the history of aviation, the Boeing KC-135 and the B-52. Refueling could be downright pleasant, despite the implicit danger of two 500 mph aircraft loaded with fuel coming this close to each other. It could also be terrifying, especially when you had to refuel at night, in bad weather, or under radio silence. Yet it was done hundreds of thousands of times, almost always without incident.

assisted by a new and sensitive autopilot, but the nervous strain on the crew is extraordinary. Inflight refueling is done manually, and exacts both a nervous and a physical strain. At the end of a routine refueling, the pilot is left sweaty and drained; refueling during adverse conditions of weather and turbulence, often the case, invariably results in almost complete enervation.

A routine flight profile for which the aircraft was designed, i.e. takeoff, climb to altitude, cruise, descent and landing, is uneventful and as pleasurable as heaving large iron around can be. Unfortunately for the crews, such idyllic conditions rarely prevail, and a standard training mission involves a continuous series of training efforts that turn an eighteen hour day into an endless nightmare of mental and physical demands.

Fortunately for the U.S. taxpayer, the Air Force and the Strategic Air Command have devised an inexpensive way to overcome these difficulties. They simply take it out of the crew's hides by demanding utmost performance at all times, regardless of the expenditure of time and effort involved.

The only thing that compensates from the unfair labor practices which routinely call for week long separation from the family, 80 hour work weeks, low pay (compared to civilian equivalents) and danger is the loyalty and comradeship which the SAC crew concept engenders. Each aircrew works, lives, trains and often socializes together; it is a unit that the pressure of hard work, danger and propinquity molds into a mini-society. The value of the concept was proved in Viet Nam, where SAC crew members were subjected to the most boring, fatiguing, demanding and dangerous missions in history. Day after day, month after month, the big bombers would lumber into the air from their Pacific bases, drone endless hours over the ocean, to drop iron bombs on seemingly identical plots of jungle. Yet, when the call came in 1972 to carry the war to North Vietnam, where the heaviest concentration of anti-aircraft guns and missiles ever seen were located, the B-52 crews responded with diligence and skill. It had been feared that the B-52s, encumbered with bombs, slow, and unable to maneuver, would not be able to survive the SAM studded skies of Hanoi. Yet in 11 brutal days, from December 18 to 28, 1972, the B-52 not only

The Strategic Air Command was a proud outfit, and the pride was reflected in the way the enlisted ground crews took care of their airplanes, showering them with attention, and somehow, despite every difficulty, getting them ready for mission after mission.

B-52s were naturally pressed into service as test vehicles, conducting all sorts of experiments ranging from dropping the North American X-15 to testing huge new engines.

reduced the military targets selected in Hanoi and Haiphong to shambles, it presented the North Vietnamese negotiators in Paris with a message they could understand, and the shattered peace talks were resumed. The B-52 had prevailed, because its crews had used its capabilities to the utmost.[1]

Now, almost 30 years after its first flight, almost a decade after Viet Nam, the B-52 is still the strong third leg of the strategic triad. Armed with SRAM (Short Range Attack Missile) and ALCM (Air Launched Cruise Missile), the B-52 shows the flag in areas as diverse as the Arctic, Egypt and the Indian Ocean. It still resembles externally those first sketches made in the Dayton hotel room; internally it is a very different machine. The one common denominator which has kept it in the forefront of aviation and politics for this period has been its human crew members, who have been able to stretch its capability beyond the designers' rosiest dreams, and keep it a viable weapon. When (if?) the B-52 is ultimately retired, it will always be a testimonial to the adaptability and courage of the men who flew and serviced them.

B-52s also carried what later became known as "cruise missiles." They would also have carried the joint American-British Skybolt missile had not it been cancelled for political reasons. The Skybolt installation is shown here. Ironically, it had its first successful flight on the day it was cancelled.

[1] Fifteen B-52s were lost.

This balsawood model of the Boeing B-52—carved overnight in a Dayton hotel room and presented at a briefing the next day—secured approval for Boeing to proceed with the eight-jet bomber. The model still exists in Boeing's archives.

27 The Fabulous Phantom

McDonnell F-4 Phantom II

Wings December, 1985

The story was told at the old McDonnell plant in St. Louis about a great contest that was held to come up with a name for the company's new Navy fighter. When the time came, however, old Mr. Mac rejected all the submissions and picked the name himself: Phantom II. It had only been a little over a decade from the time of the first Phantom, but that was the first successful McDonnell aircraft, and he had a soft spot in his heart for it.

I was pretty proud of my book Phantom in Combat *(Jane's Publishing Co.) when it was first published in 1985, for I'd been able to spend a lot of time at the plant and talked with all the principals, including Bob Little and Don Malvern; I also interviewed George Spangenburg of the Navy and Gerhard Neumann of G.E. But I have to confess that in the next 15 years there came a lot of good Phantom books, none better than* McDonnell F-4 Phantom, Spirit in the Skies, *edited by Jon Lake. Thanks to a talented group of writers, including Bob Dorr and Bill Gunston, the book is filled with details. (Aerospace, 1992)*

The initial plan by McDonnell was to build a single-seat fighter, designated the F3H-G, with twin engines powered by General Electric J79 engines. The head of the design team told the author that this would have been only "a pretty mediocre fighter." Changes came swiftly.

The Navy issued a letter of intent to purchase two prototype attack aircraft from McDonnell. The mission was to fly out 250 miles from the fleet, patrol for up to two hours, engage in combat, and return to the carrier. It would carry missiles, but there would be no guns. McDonnell revised the F3H-G to become the AH-1 with two seats. The first prototype was redesignated XF4H-1, and it is shown here with willing hands moving it across the factory floor.

Work got under way quickly in the fabulous McDonnell plant, which was one of the most modern in the world. Rugged construction of the Phantom is revealed here. A rigid but relatively light titanium structure forms the keel between the engines. Large forgings and billets were machined down to make up the incredibly strong 27-foot-wide wing center section. The torque box of the wing was sealed to provide two tanks with a capacity of 315 gallons each.

The very name Phantom carries with it images of early record breaking, yeoman service in Vietnam, overwhelming firepower in Israel's wars with the Arabs, and now, sadly, the aimless conflict between Iraq and Iran. It is a marvelous airplane, conceived speculatively, bred in combat, matured over time, and possessing potential well into the twenty-first century. Despite its incredible achievements for Israel, despite its soldiering on with limited spares and ill-trained pilots for Iran, the F-4 will forever be remembered for its role in Vietnam, where against all odds, under the worst conditions, it permitted U.S. forces once again to dominate the MiG threat.

Curiously, the tremendous difficulties of the time, the self-inflicted wounds imposed by a series of stumbling U.S. administrations, have been forgotten, and to the extent they have, they diminish the Phantom's reputation, and mask lessons we *must* remember. Before going into the design and structure of the Phantom, it might be well to take a brief philosophical look at its Vietnamese employment, where men like Robin Olds, Steve Ritchie, Chuck De Bellevue, Fred Olmsted, Randy Cunningham, Willy Driscoll and others labored to triumph over politics, weather, and the enemy.

In addition to its armament, the Phantom carried with it the seeds of controversy. It was bigger, heavier and uglier than fighter planes of the past, as it was twin engined, had a two-man crew, and eschewed gun armament for missiles. Of these characteristics, the idea of a two-pilot fighter was most radical and, of course, anathema to fighter pilots, who are forced by their personalities and their profession to proclaim a banty-rooster sense of superiority, and whose ego must be constantly assuaged with self-administered doses of personal superiority. Yet the systems of the Phantom were so complex, and the radar so demanding, that two crew members were essential. As a result, a tremendous psychological problem was induced;

As part of his effort to establish greater uniformity among the armed services, Secretary of Defense Robert McNamara called for a new system of aircraft nomenclature. As a result, the Phantom was redesignated the F-4. Hardworking ground crews never get sufficient credit for their efforts in keeping aircraft in commission.

In the Phantom's first major rebuild program, Project Bee Line, 178 older F-4Bs, some of which had already seen 10 years' service, were revamped into F-4Ns. The Marines were delighted with them.

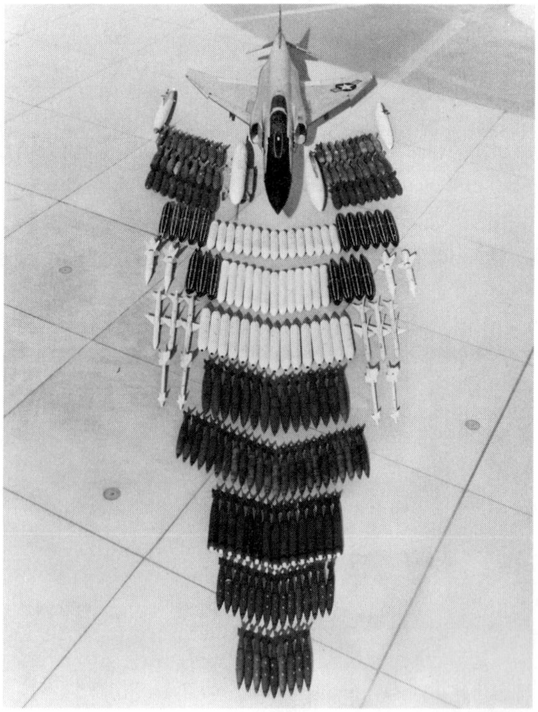
The Phantom was incredibly versatile, and could carry an amazing variety as well as an amazing amount of weaponry. The weapons in the photo were not all carried at the same time, of course, but they could be mounted in many different lethal combinations. These include a variety of iron bombs; Sidewinder, Sparrow, and Bullpup missiles; miniguns; and more.

front seaters—always pilots—but not always born and bred fighter pilots—resented the GIBS—"guy in the back seat"—whether they were fellow pilots, Flight Officers (Navy) or retread navigator Weapons Systems Officers (Air Force). Because of the prudent North Vietnamese tactics, air to air combat was not easy to find; victories were few, and sharing these victories was anathema. But that was the policy; a single MiG shot down by an F-4 resulted in a victory for the pilot *and* the guy in the back seat. As a result a condition could—and did—result where a back-seater, not a pilot ("not even a pilot" the front seaters would say) became the leading ace of the war by the simple process of gaining victories with more than one pilot. This rattled fighter pilot cages forever, to the point that the Fighter Aces Association does not admit other than pilots to its membership. If this offends anyone, remember that I am a bomber pilot, and like all bomber pilots have suffered the slings and arrows of fighter pilot razzing through the years. It's nice to take a crack back.

The determination to not have a gun and use only missiles was more critical. Despite the press reports, missiles had never developed to the point that they were certain to be useful in dogfighting. Intended originally for the bomber-intercept role, the missiles had to be successively improved for the high g turn environment of combat. In fact, the improvements were never achieved to the desired level, and the Vietnamese war might be characterized as "good fighters, bad missiles" on both sides, with the percentage of kill (Pk) remaining at the 15% level or less.

There are two other significant factors in dealing with the F-4's achievements in the Vietnamese war. The first is the political factor. Never in any war in history, did a country do so much to limit the effectiveness of its weapons by concocting extraordinary rules of engagement which gave away every ordinarily sought military advantage. Fortunately the political climate has changed, and it is doubtful if Jane Fonda (who visited the abominably treated prisoners of war while the conflict was going on, giving aid to the enemy, and then denounced them as liars upon their return) and her ilk would have much effect with this administration.

The second factor was fundamentally more important, and has been vigorously rectified. It developed that the F-4 provided so much capability that the type of air combat training previously given (which had a glaring defect in being conducted with similar types of aircraft) was simply inadequate for the new conditions of war and the airplane's enormous potential. The result of this was the establishment of the Top Gun school for the Navy, and Red Flag for the Air Force, where "dissimilar types," representative of—or, in some cases, actual—MiG and Sukhoi fighters, are used to provide realistic training. There was also a penetrating look at the degree of rigor required in training, resulting in a much more demanding syllabus. Consequently, today's fighter pilot generation, beneficiaries of the new philosophy and training, are an order of magnitude better than those of the Vietnamese war, and have to be, given the complexity of the new equipment and the dangers of the potential battle environment.

Let's take a look at a few of the political considerations mentioned as the first factor in inhibiting employment of the Phantom. First, the F-4s were hampered by rules which forbade the engagement of the enemy until there was a positive visual identification, even in situations where there could be no doubt, from radar tracking, size of formation, tactics, etc., that the aircraft actually were Vietnamese. This had a number of effects. It lost all elements of surprise (hard enough to obtain in the excellent ground controlled environment of North Vietnam, and compounded by the fact that the F-4s smoked excessively and could be picked up visually by the MiGs long before the latter were sighted). Worse, it gave away most of the capability of missiles, which were designed for long range launch, and which could, at a distance, have a better chance to lock in on an

Flying the Phantom off a carrier was a demanding job; returning to land after a combat sortie in bad weather at night made the task even more difficult. The superb training of the Navy pilots can never be fully appreciated by anyone who has not attempted their job. The same may be said of the talented enlisted people who get the aircraft off the deck, one after the other, day after day.

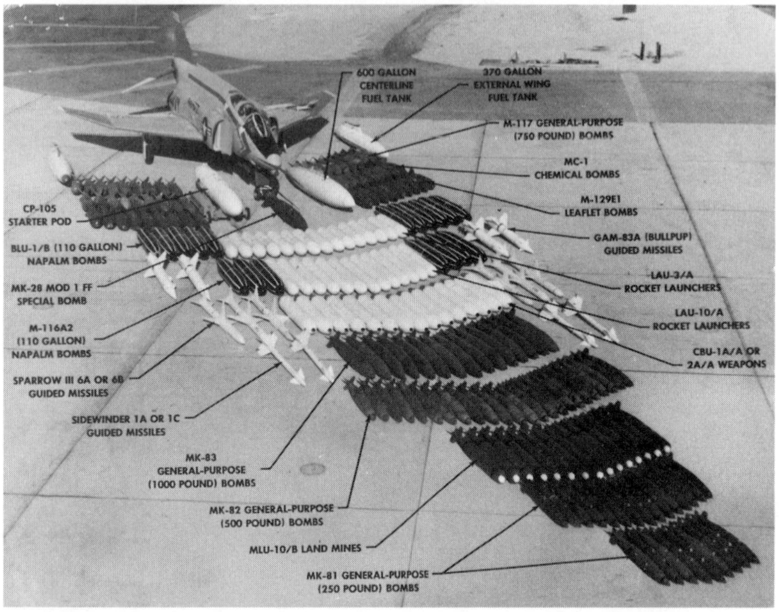

Another publicity shot, with the ordnance labeled. What a load!

enemy, accelerate, and home in. The F-4 pilots were often forced to withhold fire against a known enemy until absolute visual identification was acquired (tough with the small MiGs). Then, when combat was engaged, the MiGs would naturally go into evasive tactics that made it difficult for the F-4 crew to keep within the very definite G and angle limitations of their missiles.

Second, and perhaps even more important, for almost unknowable political reasons, enormous areas of North Vietnam were out of bounds, not only for ingress and egress routes, but as targets. It was in keeping with the ordinary conventions of war that schools and hospitals should be out of bounds, but the safe area coverage was extended to dikes, industrial plants, utilities and any industrial target closely impinged upon by residences. The North Vietnamese, tough, shrewd customers, immediately sited their flak and missiles and stockpiled their ammunition along the target routes, but inside these sanctuaries. I've often wondered how the North Vietnamese leaders must have gathered about the bar—or wherever they gathered—and laughed about American sensibilities that allowed them to operate with such relative impunity.

Perhaps the worst example of restraint was the fact that the very airfields from which the MiGs flew were off-limits for attack during most of the war. When, as happened on occasion, the limitations were removed, the F-4s and F-105s would go in and clear out the airfields with a series of precision raids. Yet this rule of war, so obvious from the days of Bill Bishop until Doolittle turned the fighters loose in Europe, was denied by politicos in Washington.

Although the Phantom could never be stealthy, the Navy attempted to minimize its visibility, and the great aviation artist Keith Ferris was asked for his ideas on how to make the aircraft less visible at a distance.

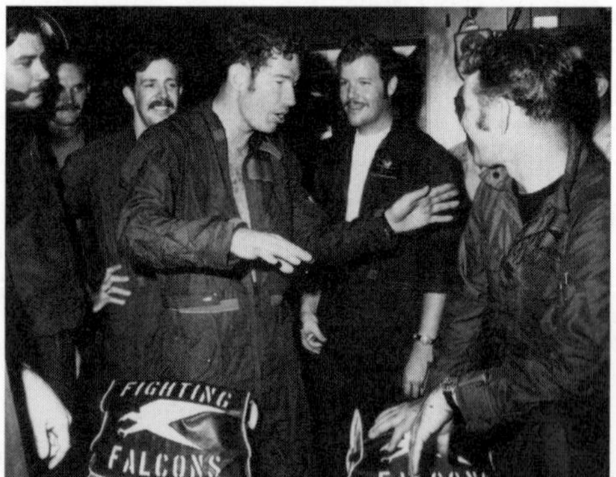

Top scoring Navy ace Lieutenant Randy Cunningham (now Congressman Cunningham from California) shows how he knocked down three MiGs on May 10, 1972. Then he and his back seater, Lieutenant Willy Driscoll, were hit by a SAM-2 and had to eject. They were rescued in 20 minutes by Marine helicopters. It was all in a day's work.

A third disadvantage, more applicable to the results of bombing than the air to air confrontation, was the fact that not only individual targets, but weapons loads, were often chosen from the White House at Tuesday lunches. This ultimate departure from the American tradition of having the commander in the field make tactical decisions, this highpoint in military-politico idiocy, was made possible by the fabulous communications networks, which permitted the President to play warlord on targets that had already been abandoned by the enemy. (If Hitler had had the same communication equipment, he could have lost the war in 1943.)

Even more ludicrous were restrictions which placed SAM sites off limits while they were being constructed, and allowed attacks only after they were operational. Instead of being able to destroy the missiles while they were still on the ships in the harbors—where it would have been most profitable and least costly, or while they were being assembled and readied for action, the attacks could only be made when the enemy could fire back. No country has ever been so stupid before, and one can only hope that we will not be so stupid again. Any war is an abomination and should be avoided, but if war it is, then it is criminal not to pursue it vigorously to win.

In the end, almost all of the difficulties were solved by the valor of the U.S. pilots and the awesome outpouring of dollars by the government. In one of the typical imponderable circumstances of the time, the same U.S. government which imposed impossible rules of war—preannounced strikes, standard tactics, sanctuaries for the enemy, etc.—also provided brilliant new equipment including TISEO, to identify the enemy at a distance, smart bombs to avoid overflight of the target, massive ECM efforts to jam the SAMs, plus every creature comfort from air conditioners to microwaves.

The net result was that airpower, not allowed to win the war, at least prevented the humiliation of having the Americans and South Vietnamese driven into the sea in 1972, and forced the North Vietnamese to negotiate in Paris, where they promptly won at the conference table what they could not in the field.

The methods used to achieve a victory against all odds is a tribute to the leadership and the flyers, both USAF and Navy. When forced to fight the big Phantoms against the nimble MiGs, they adopted the concepts of energy maneuverability, fighting in a vertical as well as horizontal plane to win. When the enemy refused to fight, they lured them up with flights of F-4s masquerading as F-105s. When the bombers were turned loose on the North in December 1972, they went in and took out the missile defenses. If the training was insufficient, they would conduct training on the way home from a combat strike. Morale was always high, and no matter what the odds, no matter how frustrating the conditions, no mission was ever turned back. Perhaps the greatest page in the military history of the war was the valorous conduct of the prisoners of war, who maintained their dignity and honor despite the most horrible conditions, unending torture, and worst of all, ultimate uncertainty of release.

The Era Begins

The big, ugly, angular McDonnell Douglas F-4 Phantom has been with us so long that it's hard to realize that it, like every other airplane, was the product not only of a long development process, but also

The Phantoms were assigned many missions, including reconnaissance. This is a Marine RF-4B of the 1st Marine Aircraft Wing at Iwakuni, Japan, in 1973. *Robert F. Dorr*

The USAF swallowed its pride and agreed to buy the Phantom in 1962, originally calling it the F-110A. The first F-110As, later F-4Cs, were Navy aircraft with their serial numbers changed. Of the 3,904 Phantoms built for U.S. service, 2,640 went to the Air Force.

Phantoms from Marine Air Group 31 at Beaufort, South Carolina, fly in company with a Douglas A-4 Skyhawk. A beautiful shot.

of strategic, tactical and political considerations long forgotten.

First flown on May 27, 1958, the Phantom was clearly the dominant fighter in the world for the first twenty years of its existence, until its descendant, the F-15, and its rival, the General Dynamics F-16, began to equal it in squadron strength. Its one-on-one domination of the Vietnamese era MiG opposition caused the birth of the copycat generation of Russian MiGs and Sukhois, those F-15 and F-16 look-alikes.

The F-4 still constitutes a significant portion of the free world's air arms, and there are endless variations of the airplane still on the drawing boards which might extend its lifespan indefinitely. A twenty year old Phantom can be given new engines, armament and electronics which make it a formidable competitor even with the newest fighters—at far less cost, and with enormous effect on the requirement for training, spares, and so on.

McDonnell took a gamble to build the F-4, opting to create an airplane for which there was no official requirement, counting on the considerable persuasive abilities of James McDonnell and project manager David S. Lewis (who would later head General Dynamics) to sell it to the Navy. The sales forecast for the airplane was as modest as the design was ambitious; initial order quantity was to be for eighty-three aircraft, with full production to reach perhaps two or three hundred. As the airplane—and the world's battle climate—developed, exactly 5,195 were built, including 138 manufactured in Japan.

To understand the degree of McDonnell's daring and achievement, it is instructive to look at the development of fighters over time. In the first World War, limitations of knowledge on airframes and engines resulted in fighters of very similar capability being developed on both sides. There was no significant difference in the range, speed or maneuverability of the Fokker D VII or the S.E.5a, perhaps the premier opponents of the time. The concept of flying from airfields fairly near the front, rising to patrol or intercept on almost a demand basis, was codified, and for the next twenty years, fighters did not depart from the formula. This natural, if not especially perceptive, development resulted in some serious problems for all the major powers.

The Messerschmitt 109 is a classic case. Designed to be the smallest possible airframe built around the largest available engine, it succeeded admirably as a short range, point defense fighter, and in situations where airfields could follow the advancing infantry in relatively close proximity. But the English Channel, as narrow as 30 miles at Dover, proved to be an insurmountable object. Messerschmitts could fly in such a limited arc over England that air superiority was out of the question; combat time was extremely limited, and there is no doubt that the pilot's combativeness was diminished by the

A pair of F-4Js from VF 101. The aircraft were first flown in June, 1965; deliveries began six months later. The last J was delivered in January, 1972. Over 900 pounds of titanium were used in the construction of the Phantom. The photo was taken by an old friend of the author's, the late, great Harry Gann.

In March, 1964, this Air Force F-4C was testing the Bullpup air-to-ground missiles at Edwards Air Force Base, California. The photo offers a good view of the undersurfaces, showing how the missiles were hung in place.

Camouflage styles changed over time, but the one thing that could not be camouflaged until very late in the Phantom's life was the black smoke it left behind. This made the aircraft very easy for the enemy to detect and follow. *Author's collection, courtesy Fred Dickey, Jr.*

thought of a flight back across the Channel with the red fuel warning lights blinking.

The 109's counterpart, the Spitfire, encountered exactly the same problem when its role had to change from point defense interceptor to a "rhubarb" mission fighter, seeking combat over the Continent.

Only the Japanese, with the Zero, had sought to solve the problem of long range while retaining combat maneuverability, and they did it at the expense of armor and armament.

In America, the impasse was finally broken with the North American P-51, which could fly long ranges, and when finally engaged in combat was superior to the enemy.

Yet apparently the lesson was forgotten in Korea, where F-86s and MiG-15s mixed it up with the same sort of short-legged limitations of Spits and 109s. In this case, however, it was not an oversight but a technical problem. The United States had seen the need for a long range penetration fighter, and a number were in development, including the Curtiss XF-87, McDonnell XF-88, and Lockheed XF-90. (See March *Airpower*, April *Wings*, 1981.)

Once again, however, the technology was not there. The essential combination of refined airframe and engine were not available, and Korean war aces were faced with the same range and time in combat considerations as their predecessors were in World War II.

The stand-off in Korea, and the spread of the potential for combat throughout the world brought into clear focus the necessity to have U.S. fighters take a leap forward in capability. It was obvious that war was going to have to be waged at long distances from U.S. bases; once again, as with the Mustangs of old, American pilots were going to have to fly long distances to engage an enemy who would be operating over his home turf in a very effective ground controlled environment. The enemy could afford to be shorter ranged, and hence smaller and more maneuverable.

In addition, the cost of weaponry was skyrocketing, and specialized types were virtually out of the question. The long range penetrator/dogfighter also had to have significant ground attack capability.

The question of range itself was solvable simply through an increase in size; if the airplane was designed to haul enough fuel, it could fly long enough to engage in combat. But size was an impediment, for the fighter eventually had to fight, and not act as a sitting duck for its maneuverable opponents. The true answer had to be found in a combination of advanced airframe designs and new engine technology, where a great increase in thrust was combined with a relative increase in fuel efficiency.

For a long period of time, the McDonnell Phantom was the premier fighter of the western world. This takeoff shot displays the angularity of the aircraft, with its anhedral tail plane, cranked wings, huge engine air intakes, and leading edge devices.

The outstanding characteristic of the Phantom was its versatility. It could do air superiority missions, reconnaissance, close air support, FAST FAC, level bombing—whatever was required, the Phantom managed to do. The two-man crew greatly increased its utility.

Then there were the political factors. Robert McNamara was Secretary of Defense, determined to bring to the services the same sort of financial soundness that he had provided the Ford Motor Company. He was an advocate of commonality, of aircraft being tailored to the joint use of the services, rather than to have individual types developed. His primary effort in this regard, the TFX—later the F and FB-111s—was not a total success. In the F-4, quite by accident, his philosophy would be proven to be correct, but in a way no one could have envisaged.

The McDonnell Background

Few men have been regarded with the respect and affection of his employees as James Smith McDonnell, and even fewer are regarded in the same way by their peers and competitors. McDonnell, "Mr. Mac" still to those who worked with him, systematically prepared himself for success. After earning a Bachelor of Science at Princeton in 1921, and a Masters of Science in Aeronautic Engineering from M.I.T. in 1923, he joined the Air Service and learned to fly at Kelly Field. Those were the days of short service contracts—the shorter the better from the Air Service point of view—and he went to work as an aircraft engineer in 1924 at a time when there were only about 200 genuine aeronautical engineers in the country. His first efforts were with Huff-Daland, and he was instrumental in causing that firm to drop its somewhat *ad hoc* design methods and adhere to the standards being promulgated by McCook Field handbooks. Like every other engineer worth his salt,

In a surprising display of flexibility, the Air Force elected not to prescribe too many changes for the Phantoms it procured, retaining the folding wing, for example. Both services would have been happier if an internally mounted gun had been included from the start.

A pair of Marine F-4Js from VMFA-251. Slotted stabilators—literally slotted leading edges—are fitted to forward portions of horizontal tail plane for better low-speed handling. The F-4J also featured a seventh fuel tank. The J79 engines provided 17,900 pounds of thrust each.

McDonnell wanted to be in business for himself, but like most others he had to make progress through the firms with contracts to learn his trade. He went to Consolidated in 1926, and Stout in 1927. For a brief period in 1928 and 1929 he had his own firm, and built the "Doodlebug" for the Guggenheim Safe Aircraft Competition. Bad luck dogged the aircraft, and he reluctantly returned to work for others, beginning with the Airtransport Engineering Company in 1929–30. He was with Great Lakes Aircraft briefly in 1931, then joined Glenn L. Martin in 1933. He stayed with Martin for five years, designing among others the Martin Maryland and Baltimore bombers.

By 1939 he had saved and borrowed $195,000—a considerable sum for the time—and went to St. Louis to found the McDonnell Aircraft Corporation.

McDonnell prospered during the war years, and established an excellent relationship with the U.S. Army Air Forces, building components or other people's designs, including the Fairchild AT-21 bomber trainer. The first original McDonnell fighter design was the lovely XP-67, which combined untried Continental XI-1430 engines with a sophisticated new airfoil, coordinated blended wing and body design. The engines were trouble prone and the

Yet another pattern of camouflage, obviously for use in the desert. The angle of the photograph makes it appear that the right-hand horizontal stabilizer is missing. Note how the slats are deployed on the wing leading edge, and the arrangement of the two-man crew. Most important, note the tubular protrusion from the left wing. This is TISEO, the optical device that was necessary because the ridiculous rules of engagement required that the enemy be identified visually before being fired upon.

At long last—an internally mounted gun. The F-4E carried an M61A1 20 mm rotary-barreled gun, often referred to as the "Gatling Gun." The Phantom actually looks best in a profile view like this. That's the gun sticking out under the nose.

Iran was a big customer for the F-4 in the days of the Shah. A total of 209 Phantom fighters and 16 RF-4Es were purchased by the Royal Iranian Air Force.

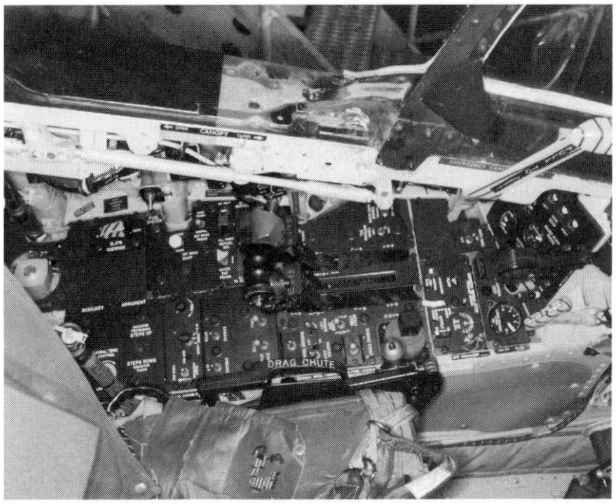

The F-4's cockpit was complex, and the ergonomics were far from the best. This is the left-hand side of the pilot's cockpit.

The cramped quarters of the cockpit were difficult to endure on long missions. One big complaint was that the often-needed maintenance on the radio system required the ejection seat to be pulled from the airplane. Standard round-dial analog instrumentation represented the end of an era that had begun with Doolittle's first blind flight.

aircraft never reached its design potential. (See *Wings* December, 1973, back issue.)

However, the foundation for future success was actually helped by the fact that McDonnell was not producing his own designs, but was available for development work, including experimentation with jet engines. This led to a contract in January 1943 which culminated in the development of the McDonnell XFD-1 Phantom carrier based fighter. This $4.4 million contract, under the guidance of Kendall Perkins and Robert J. Baldwin, established the principles of weight control, maintenance and production which are still in use at McDonnell today.

It really doesn't seem probable that a "sub-component" firm like McDonnell could have competed with the likes of Curtiss, Douglas, Boeing, Consolidated, Grumman and others in the first jet plane sweepstakes. Yet the confidence in the firm led the Navy to order the FD-1 into production on March 7, 1945. Woodward Burke made the first flight on January 26, 1946. For some reason a myth developed that Burke had flown with only one of the Westinghouse engines installed; both were in place, providing none too much power for the sleek, blue-black airplane.

The first Phantom was a real departure for the Navy, having not only jet engines but a tricycle undercarriage. All mental hazards were overcome on July 21, 1946, when Lt. Cmd. James J. Davidson made a series of takeoffs and landings on the USS *Franklin D. Roosevelt*—the first U.S. jet propelled plane to operate from a carrier.

The production order for 100 Phantoms was accompanied by a development contract for the XF2D-1 (later the XF2H-1) Banshee, the beloved "Banjo." The Phantom contract was subsequently reduced to 60, with orders for 895 Banshees following. (See *Airpower* Nov., 1979, back issue.)

The first XF2H-1 flew on January 11, 1947, with Bob Edholm at the controls, and it set a trend which would continue for the next four decades. The Banshee, originally conceived as an interceptor, served admirably in the roles of air superiority, fighter bomber, night fighter, reconnaissance aircraft and all weather fighter. It performed brilliantly in Korea, establishing a reputation for survivability and maintainability which would become a key factor in the Navy's regard for the firm.

Not all of McDonnell's efforts were successes. The little XF-85 Goblin parasite fighter did nothing to enhance the firm's reputation, except perhaps for daring, although the problem was more the requirement than the execution. (See *Airpower* Jan. 1985.) The XF-88 was more successful, but did not have the performance improvement warranted to enter production.

A long association with Constantine Zakhartchenko and acquisition of the Platt-LePage helicopter patents led to a series of vertical flight efforts, including the world's first twin engine, twin rotor helicopter, the XHJD-1 Whirlaway. This led in turn to the "Little Henry" and XV-1 convertiplanes, but none of the McDonnell rotary wing aircraft received production contracts.

As production of the Banshee began to run out, two other major developments were underway. The first was the unfortunate F3H Demon, which was handicapped by the Navy's insistence on the use of the Westinghouse XJ40 turbojet, an engine that ruined many designs. Production of the first 58 aircraft was halted after a series of accidents coincided with the certainty that the XJ40 was beyond help, and these Demons were barged down the Mississippi to be used for ground instruction at Naval Air Station, Memphis.

When the Westinghouse engine was replaced by the Allison J71-A2 engine, the Demon got a new lease on life, and subsequently became well liked in the Navy.

Almost simultaneously, the XF-88 design was being upgraded to become the XF-101 Voodoo for the Air Force. The Voodoo was extremely important to McDonnell, because it didn't wish to be identified, as Grumman and Vought were, as a "Navy only" producer—for that pie was becoming too small to be cut too many ways.

The XF-101 made its first flight at Edwards on September 29, 1954, with Bob Little in the cockpit. There were numerous stability problems reminiscent of the XF-88, but the speed and range potential were so satisfactory—1,134 mph and 1,930 miles in the F-101B—that a total of 809 were purchased. (See *Airpower* May, 1981, back issue.)

Besides establishing McDonnell as a tri-service producer, the F-101 helped the St. Louis firm establish a totally modern factory with a dedicated, highly trained work force. "Mr. Mac" was known for his frugality, but he never compromised on equipment for the plant, and as a result, the stage was set for the Phantom II.

Design Process

The almost uninterrupted prosperity of the McDonnell firm was threatened when the Chance Vought XF8U-1 Crusader was selected as the Navy's air superiority fighter in late 1953. Lead times were such that the expected production of the F-101s would be over before another competition was held, and it looked like the long established McDonnell production lines might grind to a halt.

To avoid this, Jim McDonnell and Dave Lewis decided to build a fighter so good that the Navy would have to buy it, even if there was no design specification for it. The problem was in determining what the Navy needed. As part of this determination process, a small team of engineers led by Herman Barkey and Dave Freeburg were assigned to an "advance design cage." The other engineers included Dave Lewis as Chief of Advanced Design, George Graff and Frank Laake as aerodynamicists, Mike Weeks for stress analysis and Gil Munroe for weight computation and control. Bill Blatz came on board later in time to design the crucial variable inlet.

McDonnell and Lewis made almost weekly trips to St. Louis to question senior naval authorities on requirements, and in an unusual gambit, they also took care to interview both pilots and their wives. For they found that while the pilots would always opt for a single engine airplane to their peers, they would confide to their wives the real need for twin-engine safety.

The first result of these efforts was a conventional appearing mock-up, the F3H-G (later the AH-1), powered by Curtiss Wright J65 engines and, in Barkey's words, certain to be "a pretty mediocre" fighter. But the concept of the bigger airplane, capable of flying out 250 miles in advance of the fleet to maintain a combat air patrol for two hours, intrigued the Navy, which added a further requirement: missiles only, no guns.

Expanding on these requirements, Barkey worked in close concert with Commander Francis X. Timmes at the Navy attack desk, and in fairly short order, the two came up with the essential elements which would dictate the final configuration of the F4HJ-1: two seats, J79 engines and the Sparrow III missile.

Over the next four months problems popped up and were solved. The new configuration no longer allowed room for a low set horizontal stabilizer, so it was raised and given 23 degrees of anhedral, providing stability while still avoiding the hot jet efflux. However, this solution to one problem led to severe stall recovery problems later.

In a similar way, wind tunnel tests showed that there was not enough dihedral in the wings. With the center section a single 27 foot span, immensely strong, the solution was to reengineer the outboard panels to have 12 degrees of dihedral for an "average" of 5 degrees across the span. It was a common sense approach, and gave the Phantom its characteristic bent wing appearance.

Chance Vought offered its superb XF8U-3 powered by a single Pratt & Whitney J75 engine in competition, and George Spangenburg's team in the Navy's Bureau of Aeronautics conducted a massive paper analysis of the two planes. In the end, the XF8U-3 was determined to be slightly faster, both on the deck and at altitude; it climbed faster, had better takeoff and landing characteristics, was more maneuverable, and cost 27% less in the first order quantity of 83 aircraft. (See *Airpower* July, 1977, in back issue.)

An F-4C tucks its gear up, powered by the thunder of its after-burning General Electric J79 engines. These were the brainchild of the famous Gerhard "Herman the German" Neumann of G.E.

Major Robert D. Russ and First Lieutenant Donald M. Nelson were forced to make a wheels-up landing in their damaged F-4 at Cam Ranh Bay Air Base, South Vietnam, in June, 1968. Russ went on to earn four stars and become the commander of the Tactical Air Command.

On the other hand, the margins of superiority were small, and the Phantom II had some performance advantages of its own. The deciding factor was the safety of having two engines and the two-man crew. It was felt that the extra man would make better use of the Westinghouse APQ-72 radar programmed for the aircraft, and thus in the long run give the Navy more for its money.

The so-called "fly-off" at Edwards Air Force Base between the two aircraft was not that at all, but instead a validation of Spangenburg's computations. The actual flights bore out the predictions with startling accuracy, but not without enormous effort on the part of airframe and engine teams to achieve the desired goals.

The first XF4H-1 (actually a misnomer; all the F4H-1s were built as production aircraft rather than as prototypes) was flown on May 27, 1958, again by veteran Bob Little. As might be expected of such an advanced design, there were many deficiencies, especially in the brakes and in the engine intake system. The success of General Electric's J79 (a product of "Herman the German," Gerhard Neumann) depended upon the air induction system. The Phantom had huge slab sided air intakes, held two inches out from the fuselage to avoid the slow moving boundary layer air next to the skin. (Slow air means low energy.) Each intake system had a variable inlet ramp, a bypass bellmouth, and auxiliary air doors. The ramp was supposed to control the incoming airflow by changing the inlet area and correctly positioning the supersonic shockwave in the duct. The amount of air admitted to the engine was controlled by the bypass bellmouth, which opened and closed to maintain the desired mass flow. The spilled excess air was used to cool the engine compartment, and then directed over the afterburner into the exhaust to increase thrust.

The problem was that it didn't work. Engine stalls were severe, and the whole fate of the program—and McDonnell—hinged on the solution. It took the combined efforts of Bill Blatz's team and a hacksaw to solve the problem. The team worked twenty hours a day, seven days a week; finally Blatz suspected that the curved lower section of the swept back inlet lip was causing air separation. He took a hacksaw and cut eight inches from the lip. He put in an aluminum plug, shaped it with a file—and it worked.

The big news came on December 17, 1958 (it's amazing the number of first flights and contract notices that are scheduled for December 17; perhaps they are timed to coincide with Christmas), with a limited production contract for 24 fleet all-weather fighters. The new airplane offered a significantly enhanced performance—1,459 mph and an unrefueled range of 1,750 miles. It was a big aircraft, with a span of 38 feet 4⅞ inches, a length of 58 feet 3¾ inches, and it weighed 28,000 pounds empty, 44,600 loaded. Despite the most stringent—and effective—weight control methods, the Phantom II would gain a pound a day for every day of the next 18 years, as mission requirements changed.

Barkey and his able team had brought together, almost unknown to themselves, a "next generation fighter." To make carrier operation possible, they had opted for broad, 530 square foot area wings, a happy choice that would make easier the later Air Force decision to buy the aircraft. The wings incorporated huge flaps and a boundary layer control system; later ailerons would be drooped and leading edge slats fitted to improve low speed handling. The construction methods were equally advanced, with a maximum use being made of large pressings and forgings, which, while expensive, were lighter and reduced the vulnerability to corrosion by reducing the number of fasteners. Titanium was employed in great quantities (more than 9% of total airframe weight in some aircraft), despite its expense, and chemical milling was used on a scale never before attempted.

The secret of the Phantom's longevity lies in part with the strength built into the design. Wherever possible, McDonnell used large forgings and billets machined down to size; this method of construction is costly to tool up for, but once a large production series is inaugurated, is less expensive.

Over its lifetime, the Phantom actually has flown with seven different wings. The first was flown on the first six prototypes; the second started with the seventh, when a boundary layer control system was added to the leading and trailing edge flaps to improve low speed handling. The boundary layer was supplemented with a greater flap deflection and ailerons which drooped 16.5 degrees. (The drooping ailerons caused their own stability problems, resulting in the stabilizer being fitted with slots.)

The third wing came when, as we'll see, the Air Force decided to buy Phantoms, and thicker tires were required for a softer footprint. The wing was bulged locally on the top and bottom surfaces by two or three inches to accommodate the tires, with a slight deterioration in top speed as a result.

The fourth wing had the leading edge slats, but with the boundary layer control deleted. The fifth wing (and perhaps stretching a point a little) was the canard surface used on the fly-by-wire test bed. (AF serial No. 67-17700). The sixth wing incorporated boundary layer control and leading edge slats, with the flaps now drooping to 60 degrees. The seventh revised the boundary layer control system to blow spanwise rather than chordwise.

There were literally thousands of modifications to the aircraft over time, from new canopies on the F4H-1s, through internal guns on the E, to the change of engines on the British Ks. The airplane has been fitted with every conceivable kind of fire control system, hundreds of varieties of missiles and bombs, set every kind of record and served in more than a dozen Air Forces. There is a possibility, god forbid, that it might even be found fighting itself if there were an Israeli/Egyptian clash. There is much more to tell of the Phantom, its development, modifications, and combat history, that space limitations preclude. But through the years, one thing stands out: McDonnell designed well and wisely beyond any concept that they or the Navy might have had, and the F-4 is clearly the dominant Western fighter of the last half of the twentieth century.

The beauty of the Phantom may not be immediately apparent, but it grows on you. It was really a remarkably successful aircraft. At the start, McDonnell had faint hopes of selling perhaps 200 of the aircraft; ultimately more than 5,000 were sold.

Cleaned up and without external stores, the Phantom was easier to fly. The unusual combination of wingtips with a lot of dihedral, and horizontal stabilizer with a lot of its opposite, anhedral, is obvious here.

Captain Steve Ritchie, 30, from Reidsville, North Carolina (right), and Captain Charles D. De Bellevue, 26, a weapons system operator from LaFayette, Louisiana, shot down two MiG-21s over North Vietnam on July 8, 1972. Ritchie went on to become the only USAF pilot ace, and the only pilot to shoot down five MiG-21s. De Bellevue wound up with six victory credits, one with a front seater other than Ritchie.

Index

page numbers in italics designate photographs

ML

4/02